2010 上海国际经济贸易发展报告

上海市商务委员会

上海科学技术文献出版社

图书在版编目（CIP）数据

2010上海国际经济贸易发展报告/上海市商务委员会.
—上海：上海科学技术文献出版社，2010.9

ISBN 978-7-5439-4482-4

I.①2…II. ①上…III. ①对外贸易-经济发展-研究报告-上海市-2010
IV. ①F752.851

中国版本图书馆CIP数据核字（2010）第157743号

责任编辑：忻静芬

2010上海国际经济贸易发展报告

上海市商务委员会

*

上海科学技术文献出版社出版发行

（上海市长乐路746号　邮政编码 200040）

全　国　新　华　书　店　经　销

上海市北印刷（集团）有限公司印刷

*

开本787×1092　1/16　　印张17.25　　字数320 900

2010年9月第1版　2010年9月第1次印刷

印数：1–2500

ISBN 978-7-5439-4482-4

定价：35.00元

http://www.sstlp.com

编审委员会

前 言

为全面反映2009年度上海市商务发展情况，加快推进政府职能转变和信息公开，上海市商务委员会组织编写了2010年上海商务发展系列报告。《2010上海国际经济贸易发展报告》作为系列报告之一，反映了2009年上海国际经济贸易发展情况、工作成效以及2010年展望和工作重点。

2009年，面对国际金融危机冲击和自身发展转型的双重考验，上海商务系统在市委、市政府的正确领导下，认真贯彻落实中央和本市一系列重大经济决策部署，深入贯彻落实科学发展观，借助国务院"两个中心"文件出台的东风，加快推进上海国际贸易中心建设，突出发展服务贸易，着力稳定对外经济贸易发展，优化发展环境。

2009年上海外经贸工作呈现规模持续扩大、质量不断提升、贡献日益突出等特点。对外贸易起稳向好，结构优化成效显著，进出口总额2777.3亿美元，在全国占比与2008年持平，实现保市场保份额的总体目标；服务贸易逆势增长，同比增幅10%以上，约占全国的四分之一；实到外资再创历史新高，达到105.38亿美元，同比增长4.5%，合同利用外资133.01亿美元。第三产业实到外资76.16亿美元，占全市总额的72.3%，同比增长11.4%。总部经济势头良好，吸引外资总部经济机构79家；对外投资总额15.36亿美元，同比增长 117%。新签对外工程承包和劳务合作合同额 124 亿美元，同比增长 12.2%。对外承包工程规模层次提高，合同金额过亿美元项目 14 个，新项目中 89.1% 分布在科技含量较高的制造及加工业、电力工业、交通运输建设、电子通讯等领域，改变了上海长期以来以土建工程为主的对外承包工程格局；会展业、跨境贸易人民币结算、贸易便利化工作以及公平贸易等得到进一步的重视，并取得不断进步。

从 2009 年下半年起，世界经济开始出现回暖迹象。在积极向好的全球经济大环境下，正逢世博会在上海举办，巨大的人流、物流、商流、信息流，将对商务发展带来全方位的影响和带动，造就一个新的机遇。上海将在 2010 年围绕国际贸易中心建设的主线，着眼形成新的建设框架；并进一步转变经济发展方式，突出服务经济的主导地位，加快经济结构调整。

编者

2010 年 6 月

Preface

With an aim to introduce the Shanghai's business development in 2009 and to accelerate the change of government functions, Shanghai Municipal Commission of Commerce hereby publishes this report collection on Shanghai's business development in 2010. This Report on Shanghai's Foreign Economy and Trade Development in 2010 reflects the city's economic achievements in 2009 and outlook for 2010.

In 2009, confronted with the global financial crisis and the city' s economic transition, Shanghai business community, under the correct leadership of Shanghai government, earnestly carried out major economic policies issued by both central and local governments, implemented the scientific outlook on development. In addition, thanks to the State Council's requirement on building international financial and shipping centers, Shanghai accelerated its development of international trade center, particularly its service sector, concentrated on the development of foreign trade and improvement of business environment.

In 2009,Shanghai's foreign economy related work continues to expand in terms of size, quality and economic returns. The city's foreign trade sector is performing well with the effect of economic restructuring gradually being materialized. The city's import and export volume amount to 2777.73 billion USD, same as last year in terms of share in the national trade volume. Despite adversities, the city's service trade increased 10%, a quarter of the national statistics. FDI inflow reaches 10.538 billion USD, an increase of 4.5%, contracted FDI reaches 13.301 billion USD. The city's service sector attracts 7.616 billion USD, an increase of 11.4%, or 72.3% of the city's entire FDI inflow. The Headquarters economy is also doing well with 79 headquarters of multinational corporations moved to the city. Overseas investment reaches 1.536 billion USD, an increase of 117%. Overseas engineering contract and labor cooperation reach 12.4 billion USD, an increase of 12.2%. Also such engineering projects have improved in quality, of which 14 projects exceed 100 million USD benchmark, 89.1% are advanced manufacturing, processing, electric powers, transportation, telecommunications sectors. Such a trend puts an end to the civil engineering projects being the vast majority in overseas engineering projects. Progress has been made in exhibition industry, RMB settlement in cross-border trade, trade facilitations and fair trade.

Starting from the second half of 2009, the global economy recovered. In a favorable global environment, the Shanghai Expo will creat a new opportunity for the city as it brings people, business, information and commodity. In 2010, Shanghai will focus on the development of international trade center in a new framework. The city will continue to change its mode of economic development, give priority to its service sector and accelerate economic restructuring.

The Author

June 2010.

目 录

Contents

Chapter Five Economic Topics in Shanghai

Chapter Six Districts and Counties

第一章 总 论

一、2009 年上海外经贸发展总体概况

（一）外经贸发展规模持续扩大

2009 年上海实到外资再创历史新高，达到 105.38 亿美元，同比增长 4.5%，高出全国 7.1 个百分点；合同利用外资 133.01 亿美元，仍处历史高位。对外投资总额 15.36 亿美元，同比增长 117%，新签对外工程承包和劳务合作合同额 124 亿美元，同比增长 12.2%，完成营业额 73.4 亿美元，同比增长 31.8%，规模和增幅均居全国前列。对外贸易起稳向好，上海市进出口总额 2777.3 亿美元，同比下降 13.8%，好于全国 0.1 个百分点，在全国占比与 2008 年持平，实现保市场保份额。

（二）外经贸发展质量不断提升

对外贸易结构优化，高新技术产品出口达到 636.16 亿美元，占全市总额的 44.83%，高于上年同期 2.7 个百分点。服务贸易逆势增长，进出口有望超过 800 亿美元，同比增幅 10% 以上，约占全国的四分之一。利用外资质量提高，第三产业实到外资 76.16 亿美元，占全市总额的 72.3%，同比增长 11.4%。总部经济势头良好，吸引外资总部经济机构 79 家，其中地区总部 36 家、投资性公司 13 家、研发中心 30 家。对外投资大项目增多，超过千万美元项目 20 个，占全市投资总额的 70%。对外承包工程规模层次提高，合同金额过亿美元项目 14 个，过 10 亿美元项目 3 个，新项目中 89.1% 分布在科技含量较高的制造及加工业、电力工业、交通运输建设、电子通讯等领域，改变了上海长期以来以土建工程为主的对外承包工程格局。

（三）外经贸发展贡献日益突出

外资企业销售收入保持增长，纳税总额同比增长 30% 以上，继续成为上海市经济的重要支柱。商务领域吸纳就业不断增加，商业从业人员已占全市就业人员总数的 22.5%。在 2009 年全市提供的 60 万个新增就业岗位中，商业占 50%以上；外资企业吸纳就业人员接近 300 万人；对外经济合作派出劳务人员 1.39 万人次；服务外包从业人

员超过10万，其中新增4万人，90%以上为大学以上学历，有效缓解了大学生就业压力。

二、2009年上海外经贸工作重点

（一）加快推进上海国际贸易中心建设

借助国务院“两个中心”文件出台的东风，按照上海市委、市政府“破题”要求，组织全委力量，协调全市资源，吸取全国智慧，开展国际贸易中心建设课题研究。在研究的关键环节和重要问题上，得到了上海市委、市政府主要领导的明确指示和商务部领导的大力支持。上海市政府与商务部重点围绕上海国际贸易中心建设，签署新的“部市合作”协议。上海市商务委员会也与长宁、闵行、卢湾、杨浦等区签订“委区合作”协议；与虹桥商务区管委会计划在虹桥商务区商务功能、引进外资、建设大型会展设施等方面加强合作；与市人大财经委共同开展的国际贸易中心立法调研，已取得初步成果。

（二）加强规划引导，突出发展服务贸易

根据国家有关服务业发展以及对上海“两个中心”建设的意见和要求，上海市政府发布《2009-2012年上海服务业发展规划》，明确了服务业发展的总体目标、重点领域、布局建设和推进措施，出台了《上海服务贸易发展中长期规划》等专项规划。上海市20个服务业集聚区已全面启动，部分已成为上海市服务业发展的标志性区域。新认定闸北服务外包示范区和3家专业园区以及44家服务外包重点企业。出台《促进上海服务贸易全面发展的实施意见》、《促进服务外包产业发展的实施意见》及技术先进型服务企业、服务外包示范园区认定管理办法。建立服务贸易和服务外包专项资金，形成“上海服务贸易统计和评估系统”内容框架。成功举办上海软件外包国际峰会，重点推进软件出口和软件外包、文化贸易、中医药、国际物流等行业发展。上海市服务外包企业承接离岸服务外包合同金额16.83亿美元，同比增长18.3%；承接离岸服务外包累计执行金额10.36亿美元，同比增长20.3%。

（三）着力稳定对外经济贸易发展

1．全力抓订单促成交，保市场保份额

积极抓展会促成交，成功举办了第19届华交会和华交会波兰展，华交会出口总成交22.4亿美元；跨采大会采购清单金额为180亿美元；工博会产品和技术成交17.44亿元，比2009年增加42.8%。大力开拓海外市场，重点开拓了北非、东盟、拉美等新

兴市场。首次采用部市合作方式举办阿尔及尔中国商品展，在突尼斯举办的投资贸易洽谈会，成为迄今我国在突尼斯规模最大的投资贸易活动。积极推进人民币跨境贸易结算试点，上海市 92 家企业获得试点资格，第一单落户上海。截至 2009 年底，试点企业实现交易额 21.35 亿元，其中进口 17.49 亿元，出口 2.19 亿元，服务贸易 1.67 亿元。扩大出口信用保险支持范围，2009 年短期出口信用保险规模已达 59 亿美元，完成国家安排规模的 103%。大型成套设备出口承保规模达到 11.2 亿美元，占全国的 17%。稳步推进国家科技兴贸创新基地（生物医药）和国家汽车零部件出口基地建设。认真做好经贸外事和进出口公平贸易工作。协助出口企业应对贸易摩擦案件 24 起，参与 12 个产业进口贸易救济调查，举办第六届中国产业国际竞争力论坛，合作开展了技术性贸易壁垒和知识产权应对工作。

2．优化利用外资结构，发展总部经济

开展针对性招商，组织多个团组赴美、欧等地拜访跨国公司，落实重大项目联系制度，推进大项目好项目落地，全年投资额千万美元以上的合同外资项目占到 81.1%。高度重视利用跨国公司地区总部的贸易整合功能，提高上海贸易营运与控制中心地位，出台了鼓励跨国公司地区总部发展专项资金使用和管理试行办法，进一步明确资助与奖励的申请程序、申请材料、拨付办法，取得了良好的促进效应。浦东新区、徐汇、嘉定、杨浦、虹口等引进外资总部机构成效明显。加强了对开发区的指导和服务，推进上海化工区升级为国家级开发区以及莘庄工业园区、漕河泾开发区、闵行开发区、上海化工区、青浦开发区、张江开发区创建生态工业园区等工作。

3．加快“走出去”步伐，拓展战略空间

抓住各国经济刺激计划带来的市场机遇，“走出去”成为上海商务发展的新亮点。积极引导企业对外投资，制定上海市《境外投资核准工作的实施细则（试行）》，简化项目核准手续，促进对外投资便利化，通过促进银企对接和政策培训，为解决企业融资难提供有效路径。发挥对外承包工程优势，制定上海市《对外承包工程资格管理实施细则（试行）》，加强对企业的管理和服务。依托上海市在电站设备、港口机械、地铁建设、大型场馆建设等领域的产业优势，推动对外承包工程，带动国内设备、材料、技术出口和劳务输出。妥善处理多起劳务纠纷，开展了清理整顿外派劳务市场秩序专项行动，建立健全外派劳务应急处置机制，解决各类外派劳务纠纷 30 起，涉及 493 名劳务人员，追讨各类拖欠劳务款 1661.9 万元。

4．加强内外贸企业对接，拓展出口商品内销市场

搭建内外贸企业对接信息平台、订货平台和销售平台，举办外贸企业新产品、新材料、新包装内销订货会。组织商贸企业参加了 2009 年的两届广交会，开展了加工贸

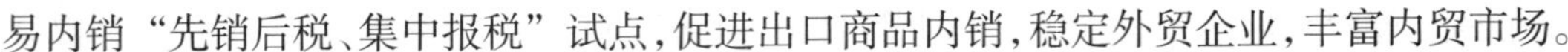

易内销“先销后税、集中报税”试点，促进出口商品内销，稳定外贸企业，丰富内贸市场。

（四）着力优化外经贸发展环境

1．积极推进贸易便利化

牵头成立上海市贸易便利化联席会议，出台了全国首创的《贸易便利化工作规程》和《上海市贸易便利化效率指标框架》，这个效率指标框架根据贸易开展前、中、后的时间顺序，设立服务管理、效率、成本等三大类指标。外高桥国际贸易示范区以及外高桥国际医疗器械展示交易中心、工程机械进出口交易中心相继挂牌，成为推进贸易便利化的重要平台。

2．稳步推进投资便利化

积极清理行政审批事项，取消10项，调整28项。完善“上海外资网上办事系统”，探索开展外商投资企业并联审批登记。外资网上办事系统已覆盖到全市16个区，项目平均审批时间是5.08天。外商投资总额1亿美元以下的鼓励类、允许类项目，以及外资并购领域和商业零售、人才中介、职业介绍、经营性租赁、会展等行业审批权全部下放到区县。

3．全力为企业排忧解难

适应应对危机的需要，积极协调解决企业遇到的共性问题，建立出口百强企业跟踪服务责任制，同时为重点企业提供个性化服务。先后与税务、银行等建立税贸、银贸合作机制。2009年帮助商贸企业解决融资贷款超过70亿元，信用销售超过275亿元。帮助国基电子（上海）有限公司、拜耳公司、上海普惠飞机发动机维修有限公司、英业达（上海）有限公司、巴斯夫（中国）有限公司上海分公司、上海金源、上海电器、锦江国际集团等多个企业解决了特殊困难。

三、2010年上海外经贸发展环境分析

（一）积极因素

1．世界经济和贸易积极向好

由于各国经济刺激政策的作用，从2009年下半年起，世界经济开始出现回暖迹象。据国际货币基金组织最新预测，2010年全球经济将逐步恢复并增长3.9%左右，其中发达经济体增长2%、新兴经济体增长6%；全球贸易额增长5.8%。世界经济和贸易恢复并转为正增长，特别是作为上海市主要出口市场的发达国家经济企稳回升，外贸出口的压力将会有所缓解。

2. 跨国直接投资流量缓慢回升

据联合国贸发会议调查，多数跨国公司预计其对外投资将于2010年逐步恢复，并于2011年重现增长势头。加之危机导致国际竞争加剧，跨国公司拿出先进技术的意愿加强，有利于利用外资质量的提高。同时，随着趋紧的外部环境有所缓解，企业“走出去”步伐有望加快，境外投资并购优质资产的机会增多，投资成本降低，交易条件改善。

3. 国内经济持续增长

2009年，我国率先实现经济形势总体回升向好，实现经济增长8.7%，2010年“保八望十”更有可能。上海在逆势中奋进、转型中发展，2009年实现8.2%的经济增长，2010年进入了平稳回升的轨道，落实国务院“两个中心”建设文件、加快推进国际贸易中心建设、建设虹桥商务区、高新技术产业化等将带来新的发展动力。

4. 世博会举办带来重大机遇

世博会巨大的人流、物流、商流、信息流，对商务发展的影响和带动作用将是全方位的。世博会不仅对扩大内需、促进消费、引进技术和项目产生极大的推动作用，其巨大的国际影响力，将提升上海在国际社会的形象和对全球商务人士的吸引力，有利于发展对外经济。

（二）不利因素

1. 世界经济复苏的基础尚不稳固

金融危机影响还在持续，主要经济体需求回升势头仍未明确，美国、欧盟、日本等市场的私人消费仍较疲软，发达国家金融体系中的问题还没有得到彻底解决，财政赤字和长期居高不下的失业率均创造了二战以后的最高记录，世界经济仍然十分脆弱，经济恶化的可能依然存在。

2. 贸易和投资保护主义愈演愈烈

危机爆发后，各国实施的各种贸易救济或其他措施是WTO成立以来最多的，中国成为首当其冲的受害者。2009年我国遭受各种贸易救济调查116起，涉案金额120多亿美元，其中涉及上海市68起，涉案金额6.67亿美元。同时，投资保护主义亦在抬头，各国的刺激经济方案成为投资保护主义的“温床”，国际引资竞争更加激烈。

3. 汇率稳定和国内通胀压力显现

随着我国经济率先复苏并保持高速增长，国际上要求人民币升值的压力不断加大，人民币面临较强的升值预期，企业对此普遍比较担心。同时，国际大宗商品期货价格加剧震荡，出于对通胀的预期和担忧，部分国家已实施加息的紧缩政策，部分国家酝酿经济刺激政策的退出。

4．体制、机制、政策的瓶颈制约尤为突出

上海的国际化和市场化程度高，新的业态和新的商业模式不断涌现，与相对稳定甚至滞后的管理体制、政策方面的矛盾比较突出。有的涉及多个部门，建立起多部门的合力推进机制难度较大，受制明显。

四、2010年上海外经贸发展的主要工作

2010年上海外经贸发展主要预期目标是：货物贸易总额增长8%左右，服务贸易总额增长15%左右；在优化结构的基础上，利用外资保持适度规模；对外直接投资增长10%左右。

（一）抓住世博会带来的重大机遇，助推外经贸发展

抓住世博会外商云集的机会，把商务外事与招商引资结合起来，建立市、区县和开发区联动招商机制，大力开展世博招商，着力吸引跨国公司地区总部、投资性公司、营运中心、研发中心和结算中心，引导外资投向现代服务业、高新技术产业和先进制造业，发展离岸服务外包。引进世博会应用及推广的技术项目，促成有影响的投资签约活动。继续推进部市服务贸易合作，以服务贸易《规划》、相关政策以及专项资金为抓手，在保持运输、旅游等传统服务贸易规模的同时，重点促进会展、物流、广告、文化、金融、保险、专业服务等新兴领域服务贸易发展。加强重点领域与区县的互动，建立服务贸易统计和综合评估体系，支持企业加大国际市场开发力度，力争全年服务贸易进出口突破千亿美元大关。

（二）围绕国际贸易中心建设主线，着眼形成建设框架

加快推进国际贸易中心建设，将是贯穿未来10年上海商务发展的主线。要在“破题”基础上，着力提高市场开放度和贸易便利化程度，加快建设市场体系和完善商贸环境。

1．推动建立工作保障机制

积极加强沟通协调，推动国际贸易中心建设文件尽快出台，推动相关政策突破，推动建立国际贸易中心建设组织领导和推进机制，推动举办虹桥贸易论坛，作为“部市合作”的新载体，制定国际贸易中心建设“十二五”专项规划。

2．提高贸易便利化水平

推动改革口岸通关模式，大力促推“一单两报”，提高无纸化通关水平和货物进出口通关效率。细化贸易便利化工作规程，完善贸易便利化工作机制，深化贸易便利化

效率指标体系，加强贸易便利化措施宣传，增加企业知晓度。深入推进长三角“涉外服务”专题合作，提高长三角贸易便利化水平。深化外高桥国际贸易示范区建设，建好国际医疗器械、工程机械两个交易中心，积极推进离岸贸易试点，大力发展离岸贸易。

3．推进虹桥商务区建设

加强市商务委与虹桥商务区管委会的合作，积极协助推进虹桥商务区建设。落实“部市合作”要求，打造上海作为国际贸易中心的标志性形态和中国会展之都的形象。抓紧形成标志性区域规划，着力集聚国内外重要的经济贸易性机构，建设具有国际先进水平的旗舰型展馆，适应高铁时代和轨道交通网带来的发展新机遇。

4．大力发展新型流通业态

加快发展电子商务，推出商务领域促进电子商务发展实施细则，发布上海电子商务发展白皮书，实施电子商务企业示范工程。高度关注电子商务新的业态，推进重点商务领域电子商务的应用，支持发展网上消费和网上出口贸易。加快发展现代物流，拓展洋山港物流综合服务功能，推动海陆空港物流市场联动发展，继续推进中国物流资源交易中心项目建设；深化城市物流配送体系，推进公共配送、医药、危险品、冷链、保税物流等专业配送。加快大宗商品市场建设，规范发展大宗商品中远期交易市场，加大服务功能拓展，提升市场的区域辐射力。支持和鼓励供应链企业的发展。

5．进一步实施品牌发展战略

以企业为主体、政策为导向，打造商品和服务的品牌代理、品牌培育和品牌创新集聚地。加大对自主品牌的政策支持力度，重视民营企业品牌的引进和培育，举办中华老字号博览会全国巡展，发布年度上海消费市场畅销品牌，开展“名品进名店”活动。争取上海市企业有效注册商标达到15万件，每百万人拥有注册商标数达到8000件，驰名商标数量达到100件。壮大一批具有核心竞争力、能与国际知名品牌媲美的本土产品和服务品牌。保护和提升老字号品牌，提升自主品牌的出口占出口总额的比重，吸引国内外知名品牌运营中心。

6．推进中国设计和贸易促进中心建设

搭建国际设计师与出口企业对接平台，拓展营销渠道，建立设计师与产品国际销售对接利益分享机制，提高我国贸易产品的国际竞争力。

（三）突出经济结构调整，加快形成服务经济为主的经济结构

率先转变经济发展方式是关系上海经济当前和长远发展的一项紧迫而重大的战略任务。商务部门要承担起推进服务业发展的重任，落实“在扩大开放中转变方式”的要求，在调整中发展，在创新中转型。

1．推进产业结构调整

以推进《2009-2012年上海服务业发展规划》落地为抓手，建立联席会议制度，明确部门责任分工，形成工作推进机制。重点抓好现代服务业集聚区建设，推动集聚区的整体宣传与招商，强化集聚区的功能完善和品质提升。着力推动会计、审计、法律、咨询等专业服务业加大对外开放力度，完善鼓励政策，降低准入门槛。进一步落实融资租赁支持政策，推进市场交易平台建设，扩大融资租赁企业试点，推动上海市融资租赁行业的发展壮大。

2．推进市场结构调整

按照外贸“保份额、调结构、促平衡”的要求，在巩固四大传统出口市场的同时，加大对开拓新兴市场政策支持力度，引导企业拓展非洲、中东、拉美及东南亚等新兴市场；加强市场调研和政策宣传，用足用好东盟等自由贸易区市场优惠政策，形成自贸区市场新的出口增长点。进一步完善对外承包工程资质管理办法，建立银企保联手推进大中型境外工程承包项目融资机制，积极推进第一轮“421专项”资金项目落地和新一轮申报工作，推动上海市企业联大联强，集成式参与国际工程市场竞争，拓展对外承包工程和对外援助的方式和领域。进一步规范外派劳务市场秩序，构筑安全保障体系。推进《内地与香港关于建立更紧密经贸关系的安排》（CEPA）协议的深化拓展，加强沪台经贸合作交流。进一步用好出口信用保险支持政策，扩大覆盖面，突出支持重点，发挥综合作用。

3．推进商品结构调整

充分利用出口退税、出口信贷、信用保险、援外贷款等手段，扶持拥有自主品牌和高附加值产品出口；用足用好进口鼓励政策，重点支持国家十大振兴产业、战略性新兴产业和上海九大高新技术产业，促进先进技术设备和关键部件进口。加强优质品牌和商品的集聚，推进外贸优质产品转内销。建设国内外农副产品物流信息和交易平台，建立农副产品双向通道，吸引国外优质农产品及先进加工技术入沪，同时推动国内的优质农副产品走向世界。

4．推进贸易结构调整

推动加工贸易转型升级，促进加工贸易企业加强产业配套，延伸产业链。推动建立国家级进口商品中心、设计中心、技术进出口交易中心、汽车及零部件交易中心。加强海外营销网络建设，建立上海海外营销服务中心。抓好上海国家科技兴贸创新基地（生物医药）建设。积极落实贸易融资政策，推动开展保单融资、出口退税账户托管贷款和优买优贷业务，用好中小外贸企业融资担保专项资金，加大对中小企业进出口信贷支持力度。抓好跨境贸易人民币结算试点。推动贸易与投资结合，“走出去”带

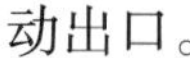

动出口。

5．推进投资结构调整

聚焦九大高新技术产业化政策，通过政策宣讲会、项目对接会等形式，推进外资参与九大高新技术产业发展。推动已设立的外资制造业企业加强技术改造、转型升级，推动外资企业境内上市，推动外资参与上海国有工业企业并购重组。在浦东新区试点中方自然人参与新设中外合资、中外合作企业。鼓励有条件的各种所有制企业“走出去”，着力推进内外资企业联手，通过海外并购获得市场、技术、品牌和营销网络，加大对重要资源产出国和发达国家投资，拓展新的战略发展空间。

6．推进主体结构调整

重点培育销售规模千亿元以上的跨区域、内外贸融合的国有控股大型商贸流通企业，支持有条件的企业发展和提升贸易流通功能，形成自主研发、自主品牌和自主市场网络，成为生产订单的策源地。抓住跨国公司业务整合的契机，继续发展总部经济。在重视引进外商总部机构的同时，向引进内资总部机构拓展，重点引进民营总部机构和央企功能性机构。加快培育本土跨国公司和国际知名品牌，支持中小商贸企业特别是民营企业做大做强。

7．推进展会结构调整

进一步做强工博会、跨采大会、华交会等国家级品牌展会，打造国际性会展之都。抓好英国品牌展、约旦展、越南展、印尼展，扩大展会的影响力。推动举办上海通航展，发展通航产业。鼓励企业参加广交会、东盟博览会等国内重要展会和自行参加境外各类专业性展览会。修订《上海市展览业管理条例》，加强对国际来展的管理，特别是世博会期间的展会管理，实行对国内展会临时性管理措施，进一步规范上海市展览业的市场秩序。

Executive Summary

Part One

Overall View of the development of Shanghai Foreign Economy and Trade in 2009

I. Shanghai Foreign Economy and Trade Continues to Expand

In 2009, Shanghai's attracted a new record of 10.538 billion USD, up 4.5% than same period of last year and 7.1 percentages higher than national average. Foreign investment in actual use hits 13.301 billion USD, a high level in history. Shanghai invested overseas 1.536 billion USD, up 117%. Overseas engineering and service contracts reached 12.4 billion USD, an increase of 12.2%, out of which 7.34 billion USD, or an increase of 31.8% worth of all business has been completed, ranking top nationwide in terms of both size and growth rate. The city managed to maintain its share in global trade as its foreign trade enterprises registered a moderate growth, total import-export volume reaching 277.73 billion USD. Although 13.8% lower than same period last year, it was 0.1% higher than the national figure, which is on par with the city's figure in 2008.

II. Enhancing the City's Foreign Economy and Trade

The city continues to optimize its trade mix. Its high-tech export increased 2.7% with a total volume of 63.616 USD, or 44.83% of its total foreign trade volume. Despite the grim trade situation, its service trade is likely to exceed 80 billion USD, an increase of 10% over same period of last year, which is one quarter of the nation's total. The city is making better use of foreign investment with its service sector attracting in all 7.616 billion USD, 72.3% of the city's total FDI, registering an increase of 11.4%. In 2009, 79 multinational corporations have moved their headquarters to the city, among with 36 are regional headquarters, 13 investment institutions and 30 research and development centers. The city also witnessed more large-scale projects, with 20 of them exceeding a total investment of 10 million USD

or 70% of total investment the city attracts. The city's enterprises are becoming more competitive in overseas engineering projects. In all, 14 such projects involve total contract volume of exceeding 100 million USD, 3 involve more than 1 billion USD benchmark. In addition, 89.1% of these projects in hi-tech sectors such as advanced manufacturing, power plant projects, transports and telecommunications. Traditionally, however, the city's overseas projects are mainly civil engineering.

III. More contribution to Shanghai Foreign Economy and Trade

Foreign-invested enterprises continue to achieve higher sales growth, as evidenced by 30% tax increase, a major source of municipal revenue. The city's commercial sector, which now employs 22.5% of the population, continues to create more job opportunities. In 2009, 50% of the newly increased job opportunities were generated by the business-related sectors. The foreign-invested enterprises employ 3 million residents. The city dispatched 13.9 thousand people. The service outsourcing sector now employs 100 thousand people, an increase of 40 thousand among which 90% earns a university degree, an effective way to alleviate employment pressure for college graduates.

Part Two
Focus of Shanghai Foreign Economy and Trade in 2009

I. Accelerating the Development of International Trade Center

As the State Council plans to turn Shanghai into an international center of finance and trade, the Shanghai Municipal Government has undertaken a comprehensive research project, mobilizing the city's best resources and tapping into the nation's best talents. In key areas, leadership from the municipal government and Ministry of Commerce offered their support. These suggestions have been submitted to Commerce of Department and waiting for approval from the State Council. To facilitate the city's lofty goal, the city government entered into collaboration with Ministry of Commerce. On city level, the Shanghai Municipal Commission of Commerce enters into cooperation with district-level government arms in Changning, Minhang, Luwan and Yangpu Districts. In future, for instance, the service functions of Hongqiao Business Zone and its FDI attraction and more conference facilities will be strengthened. In addition, the Financial and Economic Committee under Shanghai People's

Congress are working on legislative procedures. Some preliminary results have been achieved.

II. Better Guidance for Service Trade

In line with the State Council's requirements on Shanghai's development of its service Industry, international centers of trade and finance, the city government issued the 2009-2012 Outline of Shanghai Service Industry, in which it specifies goals, key areas, development mode, concrete measures and a Medium and Long-Range Plan on the Development of Shanghai's Service Industry. Shanghai has established 20 service industry gathering zones, some of which have become symbols of the city's service industry. Zhabei Service Outsourcing Zone and Specialist Industrial Zones have been established and in all 44 key enterprises have been awarded industrial leaders. The city also issued Suggestions on the All-dimensional Development of Service Trade in Shanghai, Suggestions on Promoting Service Industry in Shanghai as well as regulations on enterprises that specialize in advanced service technology and Service Industry Zones. A special fund has been approved to assist the growth of these enterprises under a newly designed framework named "Statistics and Evaluation System of Service Industry in Shanghai. The city has also successfully organized Shanghai Summit on Software Outsourcing with an aim to promote the export and outsourcing of software products, cultural trade, TCM and global logistics. Shanghai's efforts are paid off. The city's service enterprises have won off-shore service contracts amounting to 1.683 billion USD, an increase of 18.3%. So far, these enterprises have completed work of overseas contracts worth 1.036 billion USD, an increase of 20.3%.

III. Accelerating the Foreign Trade

1. Sparing no efforts to retain market share.

Trade Fairs are held to leverage trade. Shanghai successfully hosted 19th East China Trade Fair and Poland Fair, with the former sealed contracts worth 2.24 billion USD. The Sourcing Fair sold 18 billion USD of commodities. The Industrial Fair sold 1.744 USD of commodities and technologies, an increase of 42.8% compared with 2009. Efforts were made to explore overseas market with North Africa, ASEAN nations and Latin American countries as its key emerging markets. With cooperation with Ministry of Commerce, Shanghai organized China Commodity Fair in Algeria, investment fair in Tunis, which is so far the largest investment promotion activity that China has ever held in Tunis. Shanghai also initiated pilot programs of RMB international settlement in trade, 92 Shanghai enterprises were selected to join the program, one of them won the first order settled in Chinese currency. As of 2009, these 92 enterprises have transacted 2.135 billion USD, of which export contributes 1.749 billion USD, import 219 million USD and service trade 167 million USD. Another measure to assist service exporters is to expanded export credit insurance. In 2009, export credit insurance has reached 5.9 billion USD, 103% of what the central government requested. Insurance for large equipment export reached 1.12 billion USD, 17% of national count. Shanghai steadily promoted hi-tech export base for pharmaceuticals, bio-tech and auto parts companies, earnestly carry out work to promote fair trade. The city also assisted exporters to settle 24 trade disputes and 12 import safeguard investigation. The 6th International Forum on Chinese Industrial Competitiveness was held to countervail technological barriers in foreign trade and IP protection.

2. Optimizing FDI mix, promoting Headquarters Economy

Several trade delegations were sent to Europe and America to visit multinational corporations, establish liaison and follow up major investment projects. Of all the FDI projects the city attracted in 2009, 81.1% exceeds the 10 billion USD benchmark. The city attached great importance to the integration of trade function of these regional headquarters of multinational corporations, enhanced Shanghai's central role in running and controlling trade. With an aim to attract more multinational corporations to set up their regional headquarters in Shanghai, a pilot program, including a special fund and new regulations, was launched in to facilitate the application and the approval of the establishment of foreign companies' headquarters. In districts like Pudong, Xuhui, Jiading, Yangpu and Hongkou, their new FDI regulations seem to taking effect. Guidance and service to industrial development zones have been strengthened. Shanghai Chemical Industrial Zone was awarded state-level industrial zone status thanks to their good performance. In addition, remarkable improvements have been achieved in industrial zones of Xinzhuang, Caohejing, Minhang, Qingpu and Zhangjiang.

3. Accelerating Go-Global Initiative, Expanding Strategically

Shanghai enterprises seize the good opportunities brought by stimulus packages in various countries. Going-global has become a new highlight in the city's economic development. Vigorous efforts, such as the enactment of Regulations on Overseas Investment Approval, were made to guide capable enterprises to invest overseas and streamline their approval procedures. By strengthening the collaboration between enterprises and banking sector and offering training programs, Shanghai is seeking new methods to help enterprises raise fund. In order to make full use of Shanghai enterprises' advantage in overseas engineering projects, a detailed Qualification of Overseas Engineering Projects Contractors were issued to serve and regulate relevant enterprises. Relying on Shanghai's industrial competitive edge in power plant equipment, port machinery and equipment, public rail transit and coliseums, the city continues to push forward overseas engineering projects, which in turn drove the export of equipment, construction materials, labor service and technological transfer Labor disputes were properly handled, the labor service export market were rectified, a special mechanism were established to handle emergencies in labor service export. In all, the city handled 30 labor export disputes, involving 493 people and 16.619 million USD of payment in arrears.

4. Strengthening the Cooperation between International tradding firms and Domestic Trading firms, exploring domestic market

Shanghai has established a platform for domestic trading firms to exchange market information and trade online, organized trade fair for new products, new materials and new packaging techniques, organized two Canton Fairs in 2009, and carried out pilot programs for traders engaging in processing trade. These efforts have helped traders to explore the domestic market, which in turn help to enrich the commodity traded domestically.

IV Optimizing the Environment for Foreign Trade

1. Trade Facilitations

At the newly founded Shanghai Joint Meeting on Trade Facilitations, the country's first Procedures on Trade Facilitation Work and Shanghai Framework on Trade Effectiveness were launched. The latter evaluates the management, effectiveness and cost throughout the entire trade process. The International Trade Zone, International Medical Equipment Exhibition as well as Engineering Machinery Import-Export Trade Center in Waigaoqiao now serve as important platform to facilitate trade.

2. Gradually Pushing Forward Investment Facilitations

With an aim to streamline FDI investment approval procedures, 10 items were removed and another 28 modified. FDI Online Service, now covering 16 districts, has been improved. A new joint Application and Approval mechanism were trialed, shortening the waiting time to only 5.08 days on average. Now district- and county-level governments are allowed to approve FDI projects listed on the FDI-welcome category as well as M & A projects, headhunting, employment centers, commercial rentals and MICE (meetings, incentives, convention and exhibition) projects.

3. Alleviating Hardships for Enterprises

Shanghai government has actively coordinated the actions in solving the common problems that enterprises encounter. The city has also established follow-up and responsibility system in which taxation and banking authorities are required to join hands to provide customized service for enterprises. In 2009, the city helped to raise 7 billion USD and another 27.5billion USD in credit sales for enterprises such as Guoji electronics, Bayer, Hewlett-Packard, Inventec, BASF Shanghai, Shanghai Jinyuan, Shanghai Electric Appliances and Jinjiang Group.

Part Three
An Analysis of Foreign Economy and Trade Development in Shanghai, 2010

I. Favorable Factors

1. Global Economy and Trade is doing well

Thanks to the stimulus packages around the world, global economy is showing signs of recovery since the second half of 2009. The IMF forecast a 3.9% economic growth globally. The projected growth for developed economies is 2%, for emerging economies 6% and 5.8% growth for global trade. The recovery of global economy and trade, in particular the developed economies that target Shanghai as their main export market, has greatly relieved the burdens on trading firms.

2. FDI Gradual Recovery

A UN Conference on Trade and Development survey shows that, in 2010, most multinational corporations will begin investing elsewhere again, the trend will accelerate in 2011. The crisis, coupled with increasingly fierce competition, more multinational corporations are willing to transfer advanced technologies, offering a rare opportunity for Shanghai to make better use of FDI. In addition, as the international environment is improving, more opportunities to take over quality business assets in foreign countries, lower investment cost and better investment environment. As a result, more Chinese enterprises intend to invest overseas,

3. Sustained growth of Chinese Economy

In 2009, China was the first to tide over the financial crisis and achieved an 8.7% annual growth. It is more likely for China to achieve another 8% growth or even 10%. Likewise, Shanghai is negotiating all the impediments in its development while painstakingly transforming its development mode. In 2009, the city's economy grew 8.2% and moderate growth is expected for 2010. Building international shipping and financial centers, as requested by the State Council, building international trade center, the launch of Hongqiao Business District and industrialization of advanced technology will give impetus to the city's overall development.

4. The Expo Opportunity

The huge tourist brought business opportunities to logistic, retail and infotech industries, the expo's benefits is all-embracing as it helps to bolster domestic demand, introduce new technologies and creating new jobs, which in turn will promote Shanghai worldwide.

II. Uncertainties

1. Unsteady Economic Recovery

The impact of the economic crisis continues the revival of major economies face uncertainties down the road. Demands from US, Europe and Japan remain weak. Persistent fouls within the financial systems in development countries remain resolved, resulting in high government debts and jobless rate which hits record after WWII. Fragile as it is, global economy is likely to get worse.

2. Rampant Protectionism in Trade and Investment

In the wake of the ongoing economic crisis, all economies erected record number of safeguard/countervailing measures, of which China is the biggest victim. In 2009, in all 116 trade safeguard investigations, involving 12 billion USD, of which 68 cases totaled 667 million USD target at Shanghai-based enterprises, were against Shanghai enterprises, were filed against China by other WTO members. At the same time, investment protectionism is spreading among these countries whose stimulus packages became hotbed of such a wrong practice. Competition for foreign investment became more fierce.

3. Stability Currency Exchange Rate despite Inflation Pressure

With the revival of Chinese economy, more countries are demanding China to appreciate

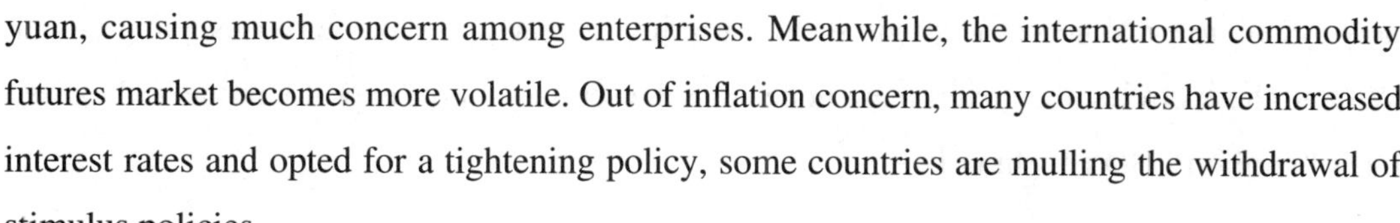

yuan, causing much concern among enterprises. Meanwhile, the international commodity futures market becomes more volatile. Out of inflation concern, many countries have increased interest rates and opted for a tightening policy, some countries are mulling the withdrawal of stimulus policies.

4. Mechanism, System and Policy Bottlenecks

With he rapid internationalization and marketization of Shanghai, new commercial and business related phenomena are emerging. Therefore, the disparity between the status quo and the obsolete systems and mechanisms becomes more salient. It requires coordinated actions among concerned government departments.

Part Four
Focus of Economic Work in 2010

Shanghai targets a 8% growth in commodity trade, 15% in service trade and 10% in FDI. The city will continues to optimize its economic structure and moderate use of foreign investment.

I. 2010 Shanghai Expo to Leverage City's Growth, Continues to Develop Foreign Economy and Trade

Making full use of abundant opportunities created by the 2010 Expo, Shanghai is to combine business activities and FDI attraction, establish a joint mechanism to attract more investment in suburban counties and districts. The focus will be regional headquarters of multinational corporations, investment-oriented companies, operation centers, R&D centers and settlement operations. FDI will be encouraged in sectors such as service, hi-tech, advance manufacturing as well as off-shore service outsourcing. New technologies displayed during the Expo will be introduced and promoted. The city will host major contract signing ceremonies. Cooperation between Shanghai and Ministry of Commerce with an aim to promote service trade will be further strengthened. Making full use of relevant policies, regulations and fund granted especially for service sector, the city will maintain its advantage in shipping and tourism sectors, promote the development of other sectors such as exhibition, logistics, advertising, culture, insurance, finance. In key sectors, the municipal government will strengthen its collaboration with district and county-level governments by establishing a new system to evaluate service trade sector, offering more support to enterprises going global. With all these efforts, the government hopes that the service import-export volume will exceed the 100 billion USD benchmark.

II. Establishing an Effective Framework for an International Trade Center

Promoting the development of international trade center will be the focus of Shanghai' s economic work in the next 10 years. The government aims to further open up the market, facilitate trade, accelerate the establishment of market system and improve business environment.

1. Promote Safety Measures

Shanghai will intensify its communication with central authorities with a view to accelerate the issuance of policies regarding the building of an international trade center. On the city-level, shanghai is working on new policy measures with an aim to establish a qualified leadership and relevant mechanism. The city will host Hongqiao Trade Forum, a new mechanism coordinating efforts of Shanghai and central government, during which the city's Twelfth Five-Year Plan focusing on the development of international trade center, will be formulated.

2. Facilitating Trade

Shanghai will reform Custom procedures by simplifying documentation and application practices, adopting paperless clearance. Other efforts such as detailed and better trade facilitation measures, a new evaluation system to measure customs effectiveness will be popularized among enterprises and other concerned parties. Also, these efforts will be put into use in Yangtze River Delta Region. Improvements will be made to Waigaoqiao International Trade zone, trade centers for international medical equipment and engineering machinery. Offshore trade will be put into trial with an aim to accelerate its development.

3. Developing Hongqiao Business District

Coordination between Municipal Commission of Commerce and Hongqiao Business Administration Committee will be strengthened with an aim to promote the District's development. Put into action the requirements of better cooperation between the Ministry of Commerce and Shanghai Municipal Government with an aim to build the core area for the exhibition industry. Efforts will also be made to establish major trade and economic institutions, build top-notch showrooms within the district served by high speed train and

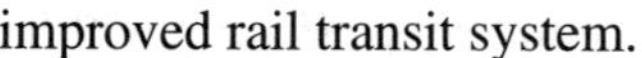

improved rail transit system.

4. Developing New Type of Logistic Industry

Shanghai will continue to expand e-business by issue new regulations and launching campaigns to promote its development. Also, the city will focus on the application of new e-business technologies, support online import-export and shopping. In addition, the city will promote modern logistic industry, expand the overall service function of Yangshan Port, promote the all-dimensional logistic by sea, air and ground and promote the development of resource and logistic trading center. Other efforts include developing a better delivery system for public goods, pharmaceuticals, hazardous objects, frozen goods and for the bonded zone. The city will accelerate the development of commodity market, regulate commodity futures market, expand service, increase the market's influence and encourage supply chains.

5. Brand Power Strategy

Under new policies, Shanghai is to foster a cluster of modern service industry, ranging from qualified agents to establishing a base for such creative service industry. Efforts include offering more support to self-own brands, bring in and foster more brands of private enterprises; organize tour for time-honored brand names, popularize famous brands of Shanghai and help more brand products to set up shops. The city aims to register 150,000 new brands this year, out of which 8000 registered brands and 100 famous brand names for every million residents. In addition, more world-beating local brands and time-honored brands with core competitiveness will be given more support with an aim to increase the share of brand products in export mix and attract more foreign businesses to establish brand operation center.

6.Promoting "Designed in China" and the development of international trade center

With an aim to promote the competitiveness of Chinese products worldwide, Shanghai will establish a platform where international designers can work with trading companies expend their marketing channel, ang share the profit.

III. Prioritize Service Sector in Economic Restructuring.

To change the mode of economic development is a pressing and formidable task for Shanghai's short and long-range development, in which the city's business sector should take the leading role in this process by strengthening renovation.

1. Promoting Industrial Restructuring

As requested in the Development Plan of Shanghai's Service Industry 2009-2012,

Shanghai will establish a joint committee to better define departmental roles. Efforts will be concentrated on the development of a cluster of modern service industries, its promotion and the attraction of more businesses; also, its service function will be improved and expanded. Service businesses such as accounting, auditing, legal counseling and consulting will further be further expanded with more incentives and lowered entry requirements. More policy support will be furnished to financial rental businesses with an expanded trading platform and a trial program aiming.

2. Accelerating Market Restructuring

In accordance with the central government's call, Shanghai is trying to retain its market share, restructure its economic mix for a balanced development. Efforts include, while consolidating its leading status in four traditional sectors, Shanghai will furnish more policy support to local enterprises to tap into the potentials of emerging markets in Africa, Middle East, Latin America and Southeastern Asian countries, carry out more market researches and popularize policies, make full use of preferential policies in ASEAN countries, create new growth sectors in free trade zone, improve regulations on the qualification requirements of overseas engineering projects, establish a fund-raising mechanism between banking and insurance institutions for large-scale overseas engineering projects, follow up the "Project 421" for fund-raising and initiate new round of application, rationalize Shanghai enterprises, form consortiums to compete for more overseas engineering projects, expand new fields and adopt new methods for engineering projects in foreign countries, rectify the labor service export, establish security system, promote CEPA, strengthen Shanghai's cooperation with Taiwan, make better use of support policies regarding export credit insurance by expanding the coverage of insurance, giving priority to key sectors and making use of comprehensive function.

3. Restructuring Product Mix

Making use of policies such as export tax rebate, export credit, credit insurance and foreign-aid loans, Shanghai will support the export of its own brand names and high value-added products, reinvigorate 10 national industries, new industries of strategic importance and 9 hi-tech industries of Shanghai by making full use of import incentives aim to promote the import of advanced technologies and equipment and their spare parts, foster the development of local brand products and promote the domestic marketing of these products. As for the city' s agricultural sector, Shanghai will establish an information and trade platform for domestic

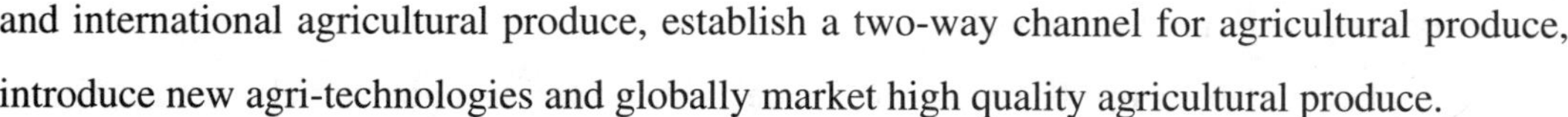

and international agricultural produce, establish a two-way channel for agricultural produce, introduce new agri-technologies and globally market high quality agricultural produce.

4. Restructuring Trade Mix

Shanghai is working hard to upgrade its processing trade and the development of their auxiliary industries, expand industrial chains and establish a national-level for the trading of national-level import commodity, design, technology import-export and automobile/auto parts. The city's overseas marketing network will be strengthened and special center will be established. Other efforts include establishing a national-level incubator for hi-tech, in particular the bio-science and pharmaceutical businesses, follow up trade fund-raising policies, promote insurance fund-raising, make good use of trade tax rebate, offering more support to small and medium sized enterprises by furnishing more import-export credit. Future works also include the off-shore settlement of RMB trade, combine trade and investment and promote more enterprises to go-global.

5. Restructuring Investment

Shanghai will promote industrialization policies of 9 hi-tech industries and encourage foreign investment in these nine sectors. To promote technological upgrade in foreign-funded enterprises, promote the domestic listing of foreign-invested enterprises, encourage foreign investment in the rationalizing of state-owned enterprises. In a pilot program, individual investment will be allowed in foreign-funded enterprises in Pudong. The city will continue to encourage more capable enterprises of various ownerships to invest overseas and obtain overseas market, technology, brand and sales network through mergers and acquisitions. For resource sector, enterprises are encouraged to invest strategically in resource-exporting countries and developed countries in a bid to expand market shares globally.

6. Promoting the Structural Reform

Shanghai will give priority to the development of large, state-holding, traders and businesses with sales exceeding 100 million USD in both domestic and international markets. Measures include support the upgrade of such enterprises' trade flow function; develop their own technology, brand and sales network so that they can generate more orders. The city will attract more multinational corporations, private enterprises as well as state-level enterprises to set their headquarters in Shanghai. The city will also foster more home-grown multinational corporations and their brands, assist small and medium sized traders and businesses, in particular in the private sector, to grow stronger.

7. Promoting Exhibition Industry

Shanghai will beef up its Industrial Trade Fair, Sourcing Fair as well as East China Trade Fair, promote other fairs such for brand products for UK, Jordan, Vietnam, Indonesia, promote Shanghai Shipping Fair. Enterprises will be encouraged to participate Canton Fair, ASEAN Fair; The city will revamp Regulations on Exhibition Industry to regulate the market especially during the Expo. Expedient measures will be adopted to regulate domestic fairs with an aim to rectify the exhibition market in the city.

第二章 对外贸易

第一节 2009年上海外贸运行形势及2010年展望

一、2009年外贸进出口运行情况及特点

2009年是上海外贸发展特别困难的一年，面对金融危机带来的严峻挑战，全市外经贸企业积极应对，迎难而上，经受住了严峻的考验。2009年本市外贸进出口累计为2777.3亿美元，下降13.8%；其中出口1419.1亿美元，下降16.2%，进口1358.2亿美元，下降11.1%。外贸进出口、进口分别好于全国平均水平0.1个百分点；出口与全国平均水平基本持平，高于江苏0.1个百分点。2009年，本市外贸出口、进口占全国的比重分别为11.8%和13.5%，与2008年持平，实现了保市场、保份额的目标。

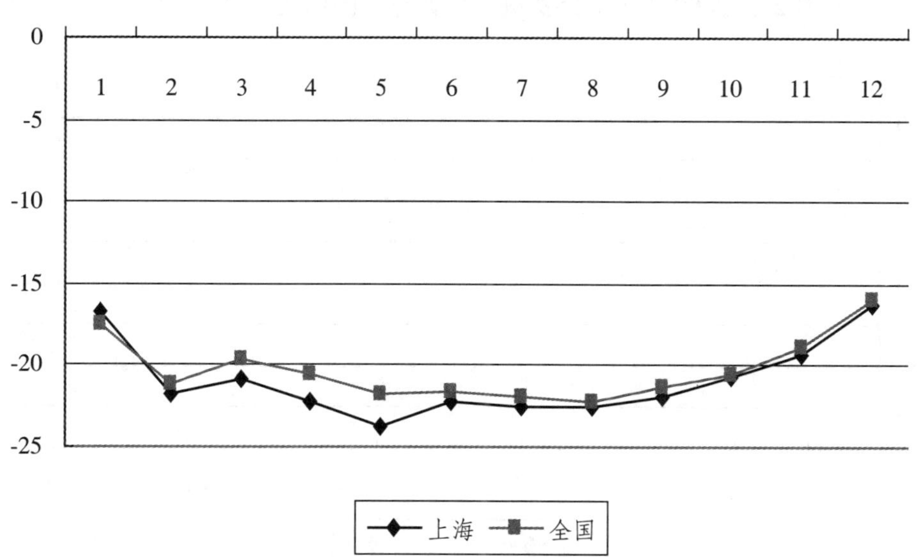

图2-1 2009年上海外贸出口增幅与全国比较（单位：%）

2009年上海外贸运行主要有以下特点：

1. 外贸进出口变动趋势

2009年，受金融危机的影响，呈现“前低后高”态势，进出口规模逐月扩大，累

计降幅逐月收窄，外贸形势趋于好转。1月、2月进出口分别仅为181.34亿美元和167.18亿美元，同比分别下降29.6%和26.5%。从3月份起进出口呈波浪形起伏，回升步履维艰，直至8月份后进出口才进入稳步上升态势，其中出口逐月扩大，12月份同比增长23.5%；而进口降幅也在逐月收窄，继11月首次同比增长26.7%之后，12月份同比增长49.5%。综观全年走势，呈现出明显的“前低后高”特点。

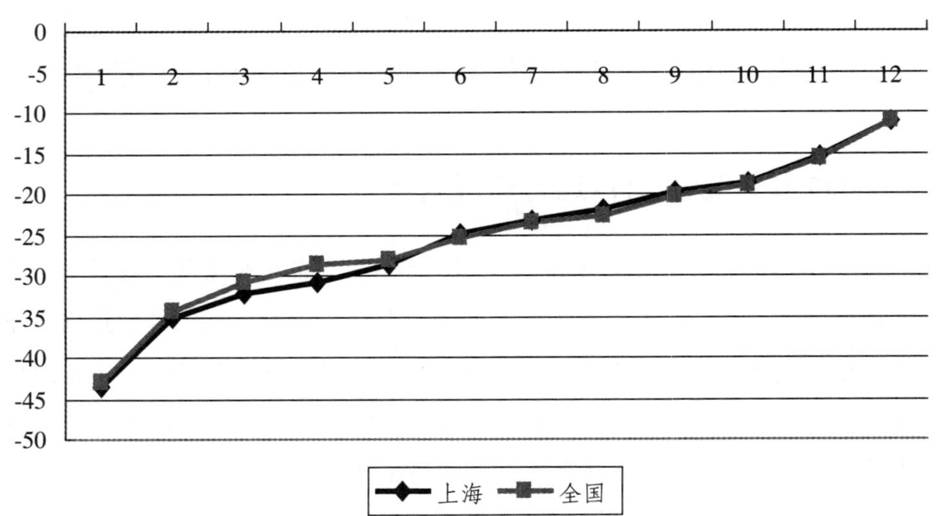

图 2-2 2009年上海外贸进口增幅与全国比较（单位：%）

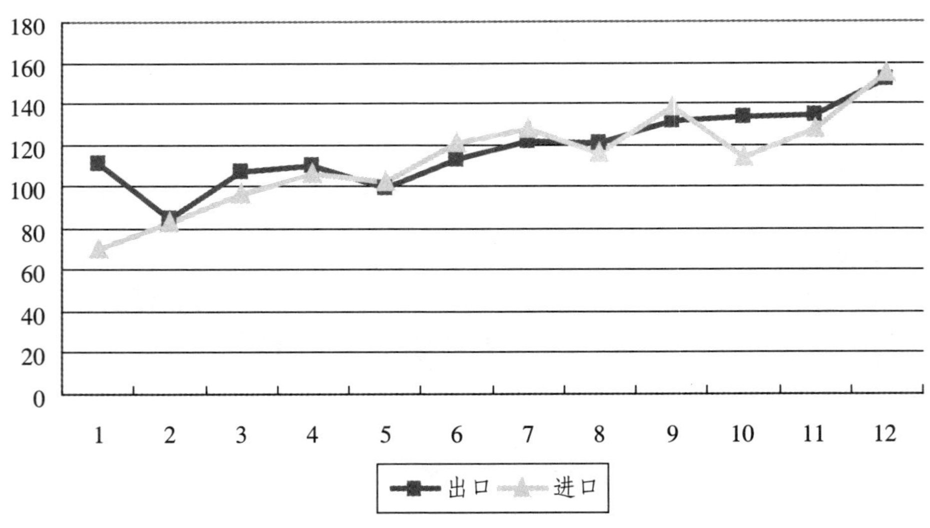

图 2-3 2009年上海进出口规模变化情况（单位：亿美元）

2．企业结构变动趋势

外商投资企业在全市出口占比进一步提高，国有企业和民营企业进口的占比有所提高，而出口占比则出现下降，民营企业进口出现正增长。2009年，外商投资企业出

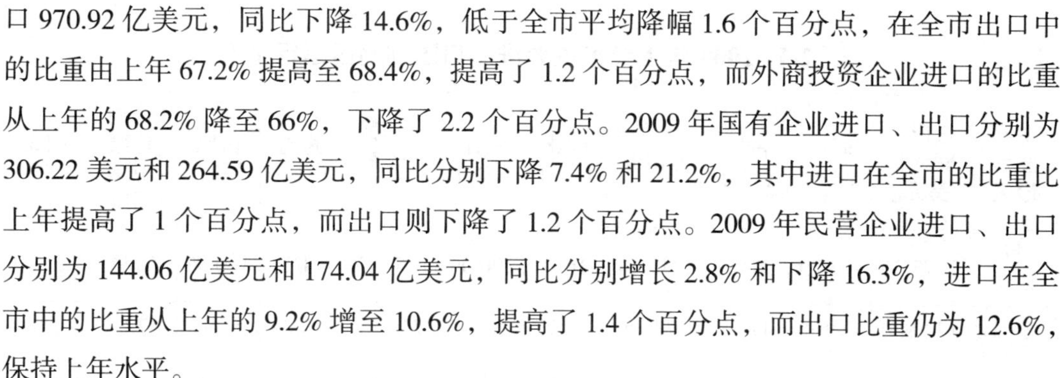

口 970.92 亿美元，同比下降 14.6%，低于全市平均降幅 1.6 个百分点，在全市出口中的比重由上年 67.2% 提高至 68.4%，提高了 1.2 个百分点，而外商投资企业进口的比重从上年的 68.2% 降至 66%，下降了 2.2 个百分点。2009 年国有企业进口、出口分别为 306.22 美元和 264.59 亿美元，同比分别下降 7.4% 和 21.2%，其中进口在全市的比重比上年提高了 1 个百分点，而出口则下降了 1.2 个百分点。2009 年民营企业进口、出口分别为 144.06 亿美元和 174.04 亿美元，同比分别增长 2.8% 和下降 16.3%，进口在全市中的比重从上年的 9.2% 增至 10.6%，提高了 1.4 个百分点，而出口比重仍为 12.6%，保持上年水平。

3．贸易方式变动趋势

一般贸易进口实现小幅增长，占上海市的比重进一步提高，而出口则出现大幅下降，比重也有所下降；加工贸易出口好于全市平均水平，进口降幅大大高于出口降幅。2009 年上海市一般贸易进口 611.16 亿美元，同比增长 2.1%，占全市进口比重由上年的 38.9% 提高至 45%，提高了 6.1 个百分点。一般贸易出口 488.62 亿美元，同比下降 23.9%，高于全市平均出口降幅 7.7 个百分点，比重由上年的 37.9% 减至 34.4%，减少 3.5 百分点。上海市加工贸易进、出口分别达 303.8 亿美元和 814.63 亿美元，同比分别下降 23.9% 和 11.3%，进、出口降幅分别落后本市水平 12.8 和好于 4.9 个百分点。其中，出口在全市的比重由上年的 54.2% 提高为 57.4%，提高了 3.2 个百分点，而进口比重则下降了 3.7 个百分点。由此可见，金融危机对一般贸易出口的影响要大于进口，而对加工贸易的影响则是进口大于出口。

4．贸易市场结构变动趋势

主要传统市场中，出口减量最大是美国，其次分别为欧盟和日本；进口减量最大的是日本，其次分别为欧盟和美国。欧盟仍是本市第一大出口贸易市场。2009 年上海与欧盟市场的进、出口分别为 251.4 亿美元和 349.55 亿美元，同比分别下降 11.3% 和 19.8%，出口占全市出口的比重降低了 1.1 个百分点。

上海与美国市场进、出口分别为 150.91 亿美元和 320.94 亿美元，同比分别下降 7% 和 13.8%，降幅在三大市场中是最低的。进、出口分别减少 11.4 亿美元和 51.16 亿美元，分别占全市进、出口减量的 6.7% 和 18.6%。在全市进、出口中的份额，进口扩大了 0.5 个百分点，出口缩小了 1.1 个百分点。

上海与日本市场 2009 年进、出口分别为 225.96 亿美元和 160.84 亿美元，同比分别下降 13.8% 和 19.7%，进、出口分别减少 36.26 亿美元和 39.55 亿美元，分别占全市进、出口减量的 21.4% 和 14.4%。在全市进、出口中的份额，进口缩减了 0.6 个百分点，出口减少了 0.5 个百分点。

表 2-1 2009 年上海市主要进出口国别地区运行情况

主要国别地区	进出口额（亿美元）	同比（%）	占比（%）	出口额	同比（%）	占比（%）	进口额（亿美元）	同比（%）	占比（%）	顺（逆）差额（亿美元）	同比（%）
国别地区	2777.31	-13.79	100.00	1419.14	-16.20	100.00	1358.17	-11.11	100.00	60.96	-63.19
亚洲	1320.50	-14.66	47.55	573.95	-14.17	40.44	746.55	-15.04	54.97	-172.59	-17.81
中国香港地区	119.78	-13.14	4.31	109.86	-12.61	7.74	9.91	-18.59	0.73	99.95	-11.97
日本	386.80	-16.39	13.93	160.84	-19.74	11.33	225.96	-13.83	16.64	-65.12	5.32
韩国	139.42	-25.20	5.02	46.90	-21.42	3.30	92.52	-26.99	6.81	-45.63	-31.94
中国台湾地区	151.92	-12.33	5.47	40.69	-7.38	2.87	111.23	-14.01	8.19	-70.54	-17.43
东盟	286.97	-18.01	10.33	127.94	-10.23	9.02	159.03	-23.35	11.71	-31.09	-52.13
印度尼西亚	24.68	-16.48	0.89	12.24	-21.65	0.86	12.45	-10.69	0.92	-0.21	
马来西亚	78.24	-3.90	2.82	30.04	6.51	2.12	48.20	-9.41	3.55	-18.15	-27.37
新加坡	75.17	-5.72	2.71	48.43	-5.16	3.41	26.75	-6.72	1.97	21.68	-3.17
泰国	57.93	-10.73	2.09	14.51	-17.48	1.02	43.42	8.22	3.20	-28.92	-2.75
中东	69.42	-6.51	2.50	49.41	-12.30	3.48	20.01	11.70	1.47	29.41	-23.48
非洲	47.34	-2.34	1.70	32.18	-3.53	2.27	15.16	0.30	1.12	17.02	-6.71
欧洲	668.52	-15.04	24.07	370.76	-20.77	26.13	297.77	-6.64	21.92	72.99	-51.01
欧盟	600.99	-16.44	21.64	349.55	-19.79	24.63	251.44	-11.29	18.51	98.11	-35.60
比利时	31.16	0.92	1.12	13.67	-24.98	0.96	17.49	38.21	1.29	-3.82	
英国	51.62	-24.57	1.86	35.17	-22.18	2.48	16.45	-29.23	1.21	18.72	-14.71
德国	168.02	-17.83	6.05	71.32	-23.26	5.03	96.70	-13.31	7.12	-25.38	36.40
法国	86.68	-10.34	3.12	50.39	-7.24	3.55	36.29	-14.31	2.67	14.09	17.80
意大利	47.50	-18.40	1.71	23.56	-24.56	1.66	23.93	-11.28	1.76	-0.37	
荷兰	59.04	-17.22	2.13	51.16	-17.67	3.60	7.89	-14.17	0.58	43.27	-18.28
瑞士	24.80	-0.49	0.89	2.91	-18.33	0.21	21.89	2.49	1.61	-18.98	6.66
俄罗斯	25.33	-6.81	0.91	10.34	-42.76	0.73	14.89	64.41	1.10	-4.65	
拉丁美洲	147.02	-10.59	5.29	58.64	-21.35	4.13	88.37	-1.66	6.51	-29.73	94.31
巴西	46.86	-8.35	1.69	14.92	-13.46	1.05	31.94	-5.74	2.35	-17.02	2.25

（续 表）

主要国别地区	进出口额（亿美元）	同比（%）	占比（%）	出口额	同比（%）	占比（%）	进口额（亿美元）	同比（%）	占比（%）	顺（逆）差额（亿美元）	同比（%）
智利	35.26	2.70	1.27	4.05	-25.18	0.29	31.21	7.91	2.30	-27.16	15.53
北美洲	510.62	-12.51	18.39	343.68	-14.66	24.22	166.94	-7.75	12.29	176.75	-20.29
加拿大	38.66	-20.64	1.39	22.74	-24.59	1.60	15.92	-14.23	1.17	6.82	-41.17
美国	471.85	-11.71	16.99	320.94	-13.75	22.62	150.91	-7.02	11.11	170.03	-18.95
大洋洲	83.28	-7.94	3.00	39.92	-13.73	2.81	43.37	-1.87	3.19	-3.45	
澳大利亚	71.14	-10.12	2.56	34.15	-14.64	2.41	36.99	-5.49	2.72	-2.83	

5. 贸易产品结构变动趋势

机电产品出口降幅小于全市出口平均降幅，出口占比进一步提高。矿产资源类产品进口、电子电器类产品出口、材料设备及民用类产品的进、出口比重比上年均有所提高。

2009 年，机电产品出口 1025.96 亿美元，同比下降 13.6%，好于全市平均水平 2.6 个百分点，在全市出口中的比重由上年的 70% 提高至 72.3%，提高了 2.3 个百分点。出口减量最大的机电产品主要是自动数据处理设备、汽车及零部件、半导体器件和液晶显示板，分别减少出口 41.81 亿美元、8 亿美元、4.49 亿美元和 3.53 亿美元。

表 2-2　2009 年机电产品进出口情况

商品	累计出口额（亿美元）	同比（%）	累计进口额（亿美元）	同比（%）	累计进出口额（亿美元）	同比（%）
机电产品	1025.96	-13.57	788.11	-15.00	1814.06	-14.20
金属制品	50.16	-26.12	22.51	-14.76	72.68	-22.94
机械设备	546.52	-11.41	225.77	-19.55	772.29	-13.95
电器及电子产品	284.14	-15.77	396.86	-13.01	681	-14.18
运输工具	87.48	-6.71	52.24	-5.04	139.72	-6.09
仪器仪表	40.37	-16.45	80	-17.55	120.36	-17.18
其他	17.29	-24.36	10.72	-10.27	28.01	-19.52

电子电器类产品 2009 年累计出口 547.57 亿美元，同比下降 9.7%，在全市出口中

的占比由上年的35.8%扩大至38.6%。矿产资源类产品出口63.54亿美元，同比下降46.8%，在全市出口中的占比由上年的7.4%缩减至4.5%。出口减少的商品主要有钢材、成品油、铝材、铜材、水泥等，同比分别下降59.3%、49%、51.3%、33%和46.3%。材料设备类产品出口163.72亿美元，同比下降13.3%，在全市出口中的占比由上年的11.2%上升至11.5%，出口增长的商品主要是船舶，同比增长57.5%。民用消费类产品出口273.39亿美元，同比下降11.1%，占比由上年的18.2%扩大至19.3%。出口增长的商品主要有电视摄像机、医药品和录放像机，同比分别增长10.1%、14.6%和43%；出口下降的商品主要有体育用品设备、家具、箱包、玩具和服装纺织品，同比分别下降23.9%、18.4%、15.2%、14.9%和8.8%。

表2-3 2009年高新技术产品进出口情况

商品	累计出口额（亿美元）	同比（%）	累计进口额（亿美元）	同比（%）	累计进出口额（亿美元）	同比（%）
高新技术产品	636.16	-10.79	508.73	-16.51	1144.89	-13.43
生物技术	0.39	-16.91	1.41	9.90	1.8	2.73
生命科学技术	14.25	-23.97	28.87	19.53	43.12	0.52
光电技术	14.66	-20.83	26.05	-41.54	40.71	-35.46
计算机与通讯技术	485.48	-10.15	132.46	-16.39	617.94	-11.57
电子技术	108.86	-5.82	267.52	-13.55	376.94	-11.45
计算机集成制造技术	8	-33.14	24.45	-33.51	32.44	-33.42
材料技术	2.19	-11.68	4.98	-23.90	7.18	-20.54
航空航天技术	2.11	-55.47	22.23	-19.65	24.35	-24.89
其他技术	0.22	-8.74	0.74	57.56	0.96	34.89

矿产资源类产品进口186.17亿美元，同比下降8.5%，在全市进口中的占比由上年的13.3%扩大至13.7%，进口增长的商品主要有液化石油气、铜材、铝材等，同比分别增长94.5%、34.9%和172%。材料设备类产品进口157.23亿美元，同比下降9.7%，占比由上年的11.4%升至11.6%，进口增长的商品主要是汽车整车及零部件，同比增长12.4%。民用消费类产品进口151.82亿美元，同比下降2.1%，占比由上年的10.1%升至11.2%，进口增长的商品主要有医疗器械、医药品、箱包和钻石，同比分别增长29.8%、21.4%、17.7%和14%。

二、2010 年上海外贸发展展望

2010 年是经历金融危机严重影响后的第一年，外贸进出口形势不确定因素依然较多。2010 年上海外贸进出口预计为 2900 亿美元左右，比 2009 年增长 8% ~10%，其中出口预计 1500 亿美元左右，增长 8%左右，进口预计 1400 亿美元，增长 8%左右。与 2008 年的外贸规模相比，外贸进出口、出口、进口分别下降 10%、12% 和 6%。对于 2010 年外贸发展形势的预测主要基于以下几个因素：

1．2009 年秋季广交会成交成果

企业反映到会客商、出口价格、签单等方面均比春交会有所好转，对主要出口市场欧盟、美国、东盟和日本市场的成交均有所增长，但对我国香港市场出口仍大幅下降。上海成交额比春交会增长 2.72%，但比秋交会下降 16.87%。从参展企业调研显示，三分之二的企业认为成交比上届持平和增加，三分之一的企业认为有下降。

2．企业对 2010 年外贸形势的预测

近期对 68 家重点企业调研，52.9%的企业认为 2010 上半年外贸形势会好转，比对四季度的预测提高 4.3 个百分点，但仍有超过 10%的企业认为形势很差。此外，被调研企业认为轻工、纺织等劳动密集型产品出口回升较为缓慢。

3．外贸发展仍面临许多不确定因素

世界经济形势好转的基础仍不牢固，贸易保护主义抬头，人民币汇率不稳定因素仍然存在。同时，原材料等国际市场价格波动频繁。因此，2010 年外贸发展总体上仍有一个缓慢回升的过程，要实现全面回升仍需要付出艰苦的努力。

三、2009 年上海外贸政策变化情况

2009 年，上海外贸面临了十分严峻的挑战。为积极应对挑战，上海市商务委按照国家有关文件精神，牵头起草了保持上海外贸稳定增长的政策，提出了八个方面共 21 条措施，这对 2009 年上海市外贸推进“一稳两保”工作起到了重要的作用。

（一）增强了为企业服务的意识

1．加强领导，深入开展调查研究

针对今年严峻的外贸形势，上海市商务委员会深入开展调查研究，为企业排忧解难。如建立了月度分析制度，密切跟踪外贸进出口企业动态。上海市商务委员会先后

于2009年初、6月份、10月份和12月份四次大规模开展调研，及时了解企业进出口情况。同时，利用广交会、华交会等重要展会，了解企业成交情况，预测未来趋势，先后在广交会、华交会上下发调研表近3000份，回收率达到95%以上。2009年6月份，上海市商务委由委领导带队，开展了百强企业调研，形成了调研报告，为下半年政策出台提供了依据。

2．建立了面向企业的公共外贸平台

上海市商务委员会建立了百强企业、区县外贸工作、机电和高新技术百强企业等联络员制度，每月对企业出口、订单、开工率等进行调研，了解动态信息，并于每月中旬召开月度外贸运行情况分析会，加强外贸运行分析和外贸形势研判工作。

3．加大对企业参展成交的支持力度

积极鼓励企业参展成交，3月份华交会上，上海交易团累计成交1.5亿美元；4月份春季广交会上，上海交易团累计成交11.89亿美元，10月份秋季广交会上累计成交12.2亿美元；5月份完成韩国企业上海采购会，共有来自韩国的38家企业和上海200家企业参加了展会。同时，搭建了内外贸企业对接的信息平台、订货平台和销售平台，举办外贸企业新产品、新材料、新包装内销订货会，实现成交1亿多美元。顺利完成了中国跨国采购大会，采购金额180亿美元。成功举办了工博会，产品和技术成交17.44亿元，比去年增加42.8%。

4．帮助企业积极应对技术性贸易壁垒

上海市商务委积极参与建立本市技术性贸易壁垒应对信息平台的有关工作；积极参与商务部贸易摩擦信息数据库的建设；加强技术性贸易壁垒培训工作；将全市应对技术性贸易壁垒的落实意见写入全市“关于促进与贸易有关知识产权工作的若干意见”中。

（二）大力推进加工贸易转型升级

1．做好加工贸易产品目录调整

2009年3月底，上海市商务委已初步完成了加工贸易目录调整，同时启动实施加工贸易内销集中报税可行性和操作方案研究。目前，该项工作已进入实施阶段，首批100家联网企业被列入试点，贸易企业的内销成本大大降低，效率进一步提高。

2．加快推进特殊监管区域功能拓展

上海市商务委积极推进外高桥国际贸易示范区有关工作，举行了示范区揭牌仪式并建立了示范区推进工作机制。积极协调各部门，优化示范区贸易便利化工作，并大力构建国际贸易商品交易平台，重点推进“国际医疗器械展示交易中心”和“工程机械进出口交易中心”的筹建工作，并争取进一步将功能拓展扩大到各海关特殊监管区。

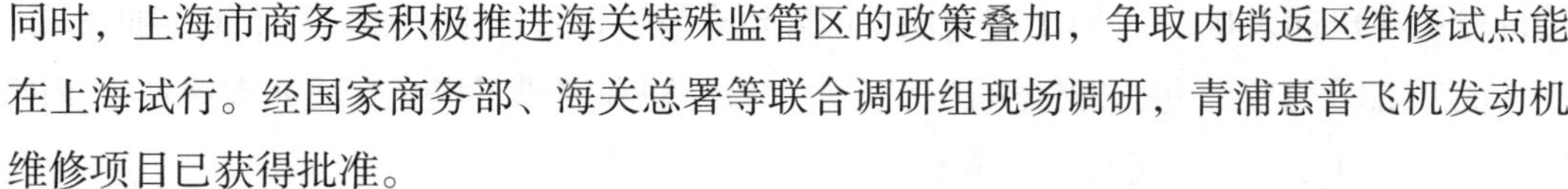

同时，上海市商务委积极推进海关特殊监管区的政策叠加，争取内销返区维修试点能在上海试行。经国家商务部、海关总署等联合调研组现场调研，青浦惠普飞机发动机维修项目已获得批准。

3．推进医药和汽车出口基地等有关工作

2009 年 7 月，上海市领导为张江、周康等 6 个生物医药产业基地进行了授牌，确立了三个基地共建的格局。另外，完成了“以发展上海国际贸易中心为契机打造上海国际汽车零部件交易中心方案”的论证工作。

（三）加大金融扶持力度

1．加大对外贸企业的信贷支持

2009 年 4 月 30 日，上海市商务委与工商银行上海分行签署了《关于全面支持上海商务事业合作备忘录》，积极为企业信贷寻求支持，缓解企业融资难问题。

2．建立了出口信用保险保障机制

一方面上海市商务委会同中信保公司、外贸企业协会、外资企业协会、外贸会计协会和上海市工商联等单位，在全市范围内宣传、推介出口信用保险有关政策，组织了几十场各类企业参加的推介会、研讨会和政策说明会。另一方面积极与市财政局协调、研究，出台了有关扶持政策，对企业投保出口信用保险给予财政资金支持。

3．推动跨境贸易人民币结算试点

截止 2009 年年底上海有 92 家企业获得跨境贸易人民币结算试点资格，跨境贸易人民币结算的首单也花落上海。

（四）支持企业开拓新兴市场

2009 年上海列出了 29 个重点支持的海外展会，其中由政府重点支持的展会 6 个。为此，市商务委会同市财政局专门制定了支持本市企业“走出去”开拓海外市场的鼓励政策，同时也支持企业自行赴境外参展，鼓励企业千方百计抓订单、促出口。

2009 年 6 月举办的阿尔及利亚国际博览会上，上海共有 34 家企业参加，占中国馆展位的三分之一，累计实现成交 2243 万美元，其中现场成交 363 万美元，意向成交 1880 万美元，现场接待客户 2830 余人。此外，上海企业还与当地企业达成了 6 个合作项目意向。11 月 15 日举办的第六届中国（约旦）商品展上，上海共 250 多家企业参加，共 350 个展位，累计成交 4239 万美元，其中现场成交 765 万美元，意向成交 3474 万美元，共接待客户 5934 人。第八届印尼中国技术设备和商品展上，参展企业近 60 家，105 个展位，累计成交 2695 万美元，其中现场成交 955 万美元，意向成交 1740 万美元，共接待专业客户近5000人。第十四届埃及国际汽车及零部件展上，上海有21家企业参展，现场成交23万美元，意向成交410万美元。另外顺利完成了华交会波兹南展览、越南展等展会，推动了一大批订单的成交。

（五）鼓励企业扩大进口

1．顺利完成进口贴息资金申报工作

上海市商务委会同市财政局按要求在全市开展进口贴息项目申报工作，按时完成初审并上报商务部和财政部。

2．抓紧制定地方鼓励进口政策

加强与市经信委的联系，密切关注“上海市重点技术改造专项资金”政策中有关鼓励本市企业引进先进技术和设备的内容。

（六）积极推进贸易便利化工作

为贯彻落实国务院关于外贸保稳定增长的文件精神，市政府于2009年3月10日召开了贸易便利化工作专题会议，研究讨论上海如何推进落实贸易便利化工作。专题会议以后，市政府成立了由上海市商务委员会牵头，市发展改革委、市国税局等9部门组成的上海市贸易便利化联席会议，联席会议下设工作小组，并先后召开三次联席会议和10余次专题协调会议，各成员单位之间建立了各种紧密合作关系，形成了各部门共同推动上海贸易便利化工作的良好氛围。目前，已先后为企业解决和向上反映了17个问题，涉及通关、检验检疫、外汇管理、退税等各个方面，得到了企业的肯定。由市商务委牵头，起草了《上海市贸易便利化工作规程》、《上海市贸易便利化联席会议各成员单位职责》和《上海市贸易便利化效率指标框架》，经市政府同意已一同向社会公布。同时，贸易便利化工作开展以来，各成员单位按照贸易便利化联席会议的要求，结合自身职能，纷纷出台了许多促进贸易便利、降低企业成本的措施。

（七）大力促进投资与出口的互动

1．进一步提高利用外资水平

（1）注重吸引外资结构的调整。在保持吸引外资适度规模的基础上，努力提高外资的质量和水平，在吸引外资工作中坚持优先发展先进制造业、优先发展现代服务业的基本方针，特别注重在商业、外资功能性项目、物流、金融配套服务业、服务外包、房地产、基础设施等行业的利用外资，使本市的吸引外资工作始终走在全国前列。（2）提高审批效率，改善投资环境。通过逐步向区县下放审批权限、推进外资网上审批系

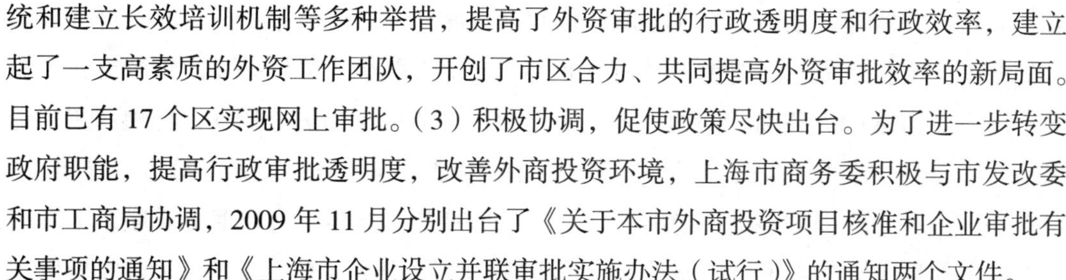

统和建立长效培训机制等多种举措，提高了外资审批的行政透明度和行政效率，建立起了一支高素质的外资工作团队，开创了市区合力、共同提高外资审批效率的新局面。目前已有17个区实现网上审批。（3）积极协调，促使政策尽快出台。为了进一步转变政府职能，提高行政审批透明度，改善外商投资环境，上海市商务委积极与市发改委和市工商局协调，2009年11月分别出台了《关于本市外商投资项目核准和企业审批有关事项的通知》和《上海市企业设立并联审批实施办法（试行）》的通知两个文件。

2．建立重点外商投资出口企业联系制度

（1）加大调研力度。2009年以来，由于受金融危机的影响，企业普遍面临较大困难。为了帮助企业解决发展中面临的困难和问题，及时沟通信息，加大了调研力度，尤其是2009年7、8两月，先后走访了几十家重点出口企业，了解企业现状和面临的困难，宣传最新政策，取得一定效果。（2）加快大项目落户。专门制订《大项目情况表》，根据行业分工，派专人负责跟踪协调，力促其落户上海。

3．大力发展国际服务外包

建立了服务外包工作网络，编制发展规划，加大政策支持力度，整合人才培训资源，打造精品园区、重点企业，扎扎实实地推动上海服务外包发展。概括起来，主要有“五个一”：一是建立服务外包工作机制，形成一个工作网络；二是制定一个服务外包发展规划，力争到2015年，服务外包收入超过1300亿元人民币，其中离岸外包收入达45亿美元；三是出台一揽子政策，包括：《关于促进服务外包产业发展的实施意见》（沪府办发［2009］16号），制订了本市《促进服务外包产业发展专项资金使用和管理试行办法》，制定《上海市技术先进型服务企业认定管理试行办法》（沪科合［2009］031号），另外还出台了本市《服务外包示范区认定管理暂行办法》，知识产权局也会同相关部门拟定了《关于加强本市服务外包产业知识产权工作的若干意见》；四是共建一个培训中心；五是打造一系列精品：在园区建设上，坚持走专业化道路，在重点企业培育上，引进与培育相结合，帮助企业做大做强，支持服务外包企业创建品牌，打造一系列公共服务平台，先后构建了信息、技术、培训、研究、知识产权保护等五大公共服务平台。

4．鼓励企业“走出去”对外投资

（1）积极推动企业以境外资源开发、跨国并购等方式开展对外投资。上海市商务委针对金融危机后跨国并购机会增多的背景，把鼓励跨国并购作为年度重点工作，加大了对跨境并购重点企业和项目的跟踪、协调和服务工作。（2）鼓励企业参与境外合作区建设。在鼓励企业参与境外经贸合作区建设方面，目前民营企业设立的境外经贸合作区中，由上海达之路国际贸易有限公司和达亨控股集团有限公司共同投资设立的“达之路博茨瓦纳经济贸易合作区”项目发展前景良好。（3）发挥政府资金的引导作用，妥善安排专项资金。在帮助企业争取扶持政策方面，上海市商务委员会通过进一步建立健全财政支持政策，坚持为各种所有制的“走出去”企业提供必要的财政支持，积极帮助企业争取中央和商务部的“走出去”专项支持基金和优惠贷款，合理利用“走出去”专项资金，从而减少企业在资金方面的困难。(4）研究设立上海市“走出去”信息平台，为企业提供各类“走出去”信息。2009年上半年上海市商务委联合上海市对外投资促进中心出版了《境外投资简明联络手册》，下半年针对新的《境外投资管理办法》，出版了《境外投资实务手册》，为企业办理对外投资业务提供了全面细致的政策说明和操作办法。

（八）加大财税支持力度

1．落实出口退税政策

上海市商务委员会与市国税局签署了税贸合作协议，双方已多次联合召开专题会议，商讨出口退税中存在的问题，并帮助企业协调解决。同时，做好出口退税专用账户质押贷款。

2．适当扩大外经贸专项资金规模，调整使用结构

资金支持重点是鼓励企业开拓新兴市场、建立海外营销网络、鼓励引进先进技术和设备、扩大使用出口信用保险、培育自主品牌、支持汽车及零部件出口基地和国家科技兴贸基地建设、应对技术性贸易壁垒和摩擦等方面。

案例：打造自主品牌实现可持续发展

——上海丝绸集团股份有限公司

一、公司及品牌概况

上海丝绸集团股份有限公司（以下简称上海丝绸公司）是一家以纺织服装产品出口为主，集设计、开发、采购、生产、销售于一体的大型外贸企业。多年来一直是中国最大的服装出口企业，年出口额6亿美元。上海丝绸公司的前身是成立于1949年的中国蚕丝公司，至今已有60年的历史。作为一家上海最早的、最传统的国有专业外贸公司，长期以来，贴牌加工占据了企业出口主导地位。随着市场竞争日益激烈和企业自身持续发展的需要，公司自2000年起开始着手实施品牌创新战略，希望通过打造自

主品牌提升企业核心竞争力，从根本上转变公司的贸易发展方式。

LILY 是上海丝绸公司拥有的一个具有 40 多年历史的老品牌，但作为女装成衣品牌运营始于 2000 年。为此，上海丝绸公司专门成立了一家子公司——上海丝绸集团品牌发展有限公司，专业从事 LILY 品牌的运营。LILY 把 23 岁至 32 岁的都市女性作为目标客户群，同时把产品定位为帅气而又不失女人味的时尚日装，准确的定位使 LILY 这个老品牌焕发出新的生机。2006 年 9 月，LILY 被意大利“米兰时装周”组委会选中，作为两个中国品牌之一受邀与全球最佳 100 个服装品牌在“米兰时装周”同台展演。

二、2009 年品牌发展概况

经过 10 年的培育和发展，目前 LILY 品牌已进入快速发展阶段，建立起融企划、设计、研发、制版、打样、测试、采购、物流、销售、服务于一体的品牌链，品牌价值和品牌影响力不断提升。至 2009 年底，LILY 在全国范围内的直营店及代理商数量达到了 260 余家，实现营业总额 3 亿元，年增长幅度超过 50%。除了国内市场的快速扩张，LILY 从 2005 年开始进入沙特、科威特、阿联酋、叙利亚、印尼、希腊、挪威、俄罗斯等十几个国家和地区，开设了近 30 家零售店铺，呈现出了内外贸联动的良好局面。

三、品牌建设过程

品牌建设是一个艰巨复杂的系统工程。LILY 的快速发展得益于上海丝绸公司在人才队伍、产品开发、渠道拓展、终端建设等方面的不断投入和持续完善。

1．募人才

对一家传统的专业外贸公司来说，开展自主品牌运营业务是一项巨大的挑战。首当其冲的就是需要组建一支专业的人才队伍。为此，早在 1996 年，上海丝绸公司就开始着手引入和培养服装设计人才，为今后自主品牌建设打下人才基础。2002 年上海丝绸公司专门组建品牌发展有限公司开展品牌运营业务后，上海丝绸公司更加注重队伍建设。一方面积极整合内部人力资源，优化人才结构，另一方面从社会上广罗人才，建立起一支涵盖了企划、设计、生产、物流、销售等各环节的专业队伍，以适应品牌业务运营的需要。

2．出产品

开发产品是品牌建设的核心内容。准确定位则是开发产品的关键。自萌生了打造自主品牌的想法，经过反复研究，上海丝绸公司提出了针对都市女性的产品定位，并确立了“时尚平民化”的品牌理念。为了打造一个高业绩的大众流行成衣品牌，LILY坚持以顾客为关注点，以市场为依托，不断优化整合开发和生产环节，缩短设计开发周期，加快市场周转和运作。2009年，公司在不断提升产品品质、明确产品优势、强化产品气质的基础上，将已往每年2季的设计开发变为一年4季的设计开发，大大促进了店铺销售的快速周转，LILY的品牌影响力和产品美誉度也与日俱增。

3．拓渠道

LILY自2000年上市以来，就制定了立足国内市场、开拓国际市场的原则。根据这一原则，上海丝绸公司首先集中精力开发国内市场，通过开设直营店和发展代理商，拓展营销渠道。如今LILY在国内已建立起较完善的销售网络。截至2009年底，LILY品牌已在上海、北京、深圳、广州4个城市开设了60余家直营店铺，并在全国30个省市发展了100多个代理商，门店数合计超过200家。随着LILY的快速发展，合理规划市场通路和营销网络对品牌的市场扩张显得更加重要和紧迫。为此，上海丝绸公司一方面继续加强在核心城市优化直营店铺管理，提升品牌影响力，树立高业绩店铺榜样，为店铺拓展提供强力支撑；另一方面积极吸纳培养大型优质代理客户，不断淘汰替换不良客户，改善通路质量，为LILY未来市场网络打下坚实基础。

除了国内市场的迅猛发展，从2005年起，LILY开始进军国际市场。发展国外代理商开设专卖店是上海丝绸公司目前开拓国际市场的主要方式，这种方式既能快速进入国外市场，又不需要上海丝绸公司太多的市场投入，适合上海丝绸公司当前品牌运营的发展需求。

2005年7月，LILY首次通过独家经销的方式，登陆世界时装之都——法国巴黎，随后又进入印度尼西亚、俄罗斯、希腊、沙特、阿联酋、科威特、叙利亚、挪威、美国关岛等海外市场。目前LILY已在海外10多个国家开设专卖店铺近30家。国际化进程取得了积极进展。

4．建终端

销售终端建设是上海丝绸公司品牌建设过程中的一项重要工作。销售终端作为营销网络的基石，对树立品牌形象、传播品牌内涵、建立品牌忠诚度等都有不可替代的作用。为此，本着“服务在终端”的工作精神和宗旨，上海丝绸公司一是改善终端形象。通过对门店的标准化、个性化装修及整改；提高终端店铺的陈列水平，加强终端管理和终端呈现，营造良好的店铺氛围，以此提升消费者对LILY品牌的认识。二是提升销售人员服务能力。通过加强对销售人员在配装、美学、服装及零售等方面专业技能的培训，提高对产品的理解力和客户服务能力。另外，在终端建设不断完善的过程中，上海丝绸公司也积极利用终端信息资源，收集市场信息，掌握市场动态，更好的把握

市场真实需求，为产品的策划、研发提供丰富的信息资源。

四、未来发展

品牌建设任重道远。然而，作为上海丝绸公司转变贸易发展方式的根本方式，自主品牌对实现公司的可持续发展有着不可替代的作用，也将是上海丝绸公司发展的最终方向。

随着LILY进入快速发展期，未来三年品牌的市场销售规模和营业效益预计每年将保持50%以上的增长速度。为此，上海丝绸公司将始终围绕提升单店业绩这个价值链的关键节点，重点强化产品研发，积极拓展销售网络，使规模与质量协调，业绩与管理并重，进一步打造基于高业绩特征的大众流行成衣的品牌内核，为LILY未来的跨越式发展奠定良好的基础，使LILY真正成为具有高知名度、专业化的大众流行成衣品牌。

第二节 加工贸易

一、2009年上海加工贸易基本运行情况

据海关统计，2009年，上海市加工贸易进出口额1118.43亿美元，同比下降15.1%，约占上海市进出口总额的40.27%，约占全国加工贸易进出口总额的12.3%。其中，出口814.62亿美元，同比下降11.26%，占上海市出口总额57.4%，约占全国加工贸易出口的13.88%。进口303.8亿美元，同比下降23.94%，占上海市进口总额22.37%，约占全国加工贸易进口额的9.42%。

2009年，上海加工贸易累计出口降幅低于上海市外贸出口降幅近5个百分点，低于一般贸易出口降幅近13个百分点，低于全国加工贸易出口降幅近2个百分点。主要表现以下特点：

1．出口开始恢复

2009年第三季度，出口开始恢复，第四季度出口强劲，12月单月出口同比增长42.23%。从2009年整体趋势来看，上海加工贸易出口自6月份以来连续7个月环比保持正增长，同比下降幅度持续收窄。其中，12月当月出口额89亿美元，创年度出口新高，出口同比从1月份的下降20.11%变为增长42.23%。

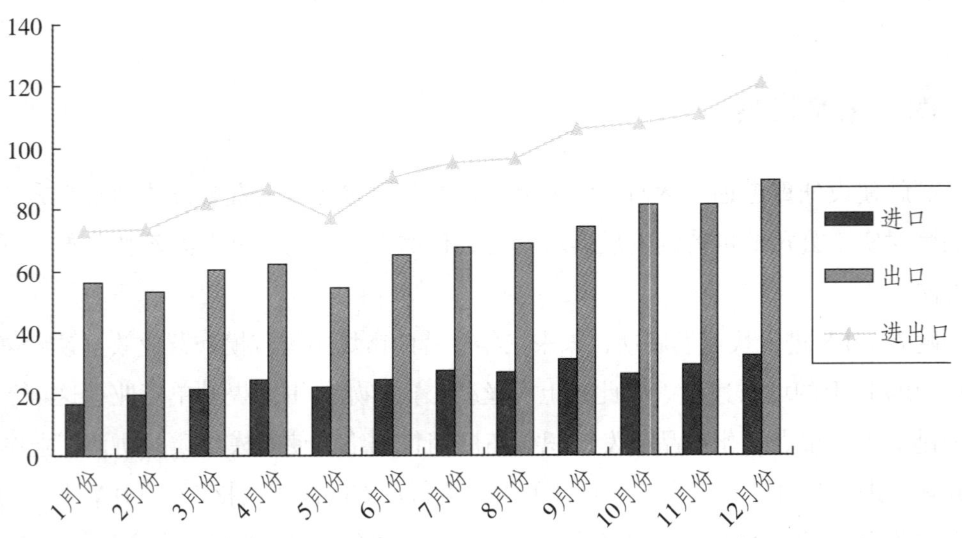

图 2-4 2009 年上海加工贸易进出口月度变化情况（单位：亿美元）

2．进出口降幅呈逐月收窄趋势

进料加工是上海加工贸易的主要贸易方式。2009 年，上海市进料加工贸易进出口总额 1008.56 亿美元，同比下降 11.12%，其中出口 742.51 亿美元，同比下降 8.2%，进口 266.05 亿美元，同比下降 18.37%。来料加工贸易进出口总额 109.87 亿美元，同比下降 39.84%，其中出口 72.12 亿美元，同比下降 33.91%，进口 37.75 亿美元，同比下降 48.65%。进料加工贸易占加工贸易的主体，进出口金额占整个加工贸易进出口金额的 90.18 %，来料加工贸易进出口金额占 9.82%。

3．外商投资企业仍是加工贸易的主要贡献力量，出口降幅逐月回升

外商投资企业加工贸易进出口 1016.79 亿美元，同比下降 16.83%，占上海市加工贸易总额的 90.9%；其中出口 732.8 亿美元，同比下降 13.68%，占上海市加工贸易出口的 89.96%。国有企业加工贸易企业进出口 80.23 亿美元，同比增长 13.38%，占上海市加工贸易进出口金额的 7.17%，其中出口 66.8 亿美元，同比增长 25.96%。民营企业加工贸易企业进出口 18 亿美元，同比下降 10.81 %，占上海市加工贸易进出口金额的 1.61%。其中出口 13 亿美元，同比下降 3.13%。

4．前 4 位主要商品出口情况稳定

加工贸易年度出口金额占上海市加工贸易出口金额 90% 以上的前 4 位主要商品出口情况稳定，机电、音像设备及零部件产品仍旧是上海加工贸易的主要产品。

2009 年，按照贸易额和出口额位列前 4 位的主要出口商品进出口额达 1000 亿美

元以上，出口 748.33 亿美元。依次是：机电、音像设备及零部件产品加工贸易进出口额达 860.75 亿美元，同比减少 13.53%，占上海市加工贸易进出口金额的 77%；车辆、航空器、船舶等加工贸易进出口额达 66.8 亿美元，同比增长 9.72%，占上海市加工贸易进出口金额的 5.97%；光学、医疗器械加工贸易进出口 37.77 亿美元，同比下降 28.33%，占上海市加工贸易进出口金额的 3.38%；纺织品加工贸易进出口 34.73 亿美元，同比下降 18 %，占上海市加工贸易进出口金额的 3.11%。

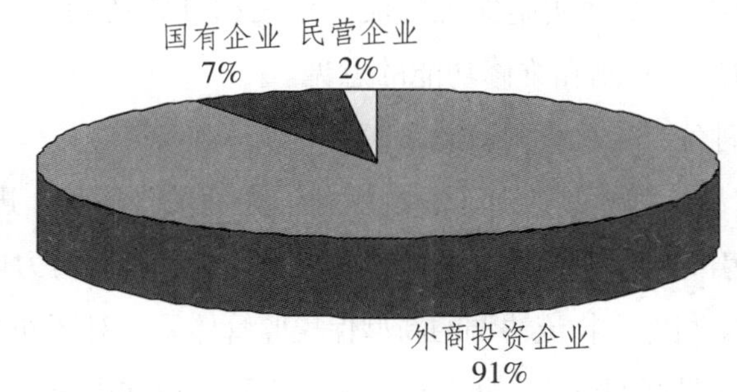

图 2-5　2009 年上海加工贸易企业结构

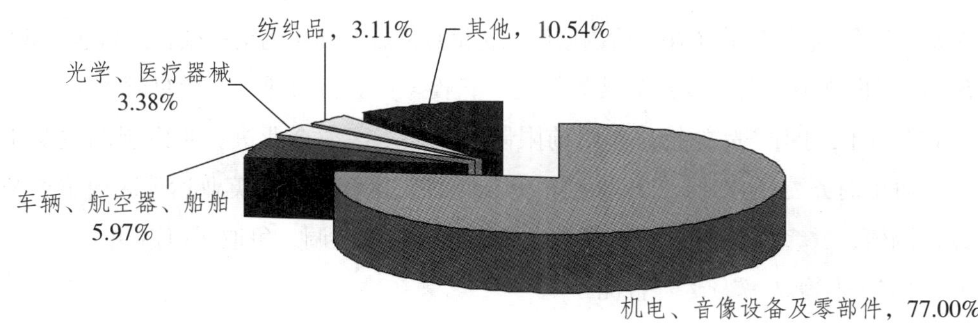

图 2-6　2009 年上海加工贸易产品结构

二、2009 年上海加工贸易发展的主要推进工作

1．推进“上海外高桥国际贸易示范区”建设

2009 年市商务委批复并在浦东外高桥保税区建设“上海外高桥国际贸易示范区”，组建示范区工作推进小组。

2．积极帮助加工贸易企业解决运行中的实际困难

深入调研、联系企业。先后帮助拜尔（中国）有限公司、巴斯夫上海等多家大型加工贸易企业的产品从禁止类限制类目录中剔除，避免了这些企业的倒闭、撤离和几亿美元的进出口损失及近千名员工的失业。帮助青浦出口加工区内普惠发动机维修公

司获取开展飞机发动机维修业务的批文，并帮助其解决7台飞机发动机紧急入区维修的问题。帮助中航光电子在最短时间内获得加工贸易生产能力许可。帮助国基电子获得高新技术企业资格。

3．推动完善海关特殊监管区功能

推动完善海关特殊监管区功能，使之在推动上海加工贸易发展中发挥更大作用。积极争取出口加工区功能拓展和政策叠加试点工作的深化和全面推开。2009年4月，国家批准所有出口加工区全面实施保税物流、检测和维修功能，上海研究制订出口加工区全面推进保税物流、检测和维修功能的意见。

4．推进贸易便利化、优化投资贸易环境

继续推进加工贸易管理体制改革工作，深化“大通关”工程，进一步优化上海投资贸易环境。以促进和引导加工贸易及配套产业转型升级为目标，努力创建严密监管与高效运作相统一，保税加工与保税物流协调的新型保税监管体系。对区外企业进一步推广电子联网监管模式，研究简易联网模式，将联网范围由大型企业向中小型企业扩展。上海市商务委员会与上海海关协商，制订了加工贸易内销“先销后税、集中报税”的试点措施，对140多家加工贸易联网监管企业实行内销便利化试点措施，简化内销手续，提高通关效率。

5．调研出口加工区内销产品维修情况，积极与商务部沟通争取予以解决

出口加工区内销产品的维修是目前限制出口加工区内企业进一步发展的主要瓶颈之一。上海市商务委员会对松江、漕河泾等出口加工区和达丰、英业达等区内重点企业进行深入调研，并多次赴商务部、海关总署等部门积极协调，争取予以解决。

6．研究分析加工贸易运行情况

上海加工贸易占到上海市外贸总额的一半以上。上海市商务委员会通过对上海加工贸易运行分析和趋势研究，为上海市和全国的综合运行分析提供素材。

7．参与人民币结算试点工作和“离岸贸易”研究

上海市商务委员会积极参与推进人民币结算试点有关工作，参与推进太船国际贸易公司参与试点的工作，为太船国际开展加工贸易中的人民币结算设计方案和便利化措施。积极调研，参与研究以外高桥国际贸易示范区为试点区域开展“离岸贸易”的方案。

三、2010年上海加工贸易发展的主要措施

按照中央经济工作会议和全国商务工作会议精神，根据上海加工贸易发展现状，探索研究上海加工贸易转型升级的方向、模式与路径，在保证上海加工贸易2010年出口增长15%左右的基础上，稳步推动转型升级，努力实现“保份额、调结构、促平衡”

目标。主要措施有：

一是结合国家发展低碳经济的大方向，培育、提升、淘汰并举，促进上海加工贸易转型。在加工贸易企业资质认定方面结合科技创新、节能减排等方面，设立一定的准入退出制度。

二是积极发展与先进制造业相适应的现代服务业，加强服务业的深度合作，为加工贸易转型升级提供基础性服务。大力发展生产性服务业，加大进出口报关、商品检测、物流、金融、法律、会计、信息、咨询等领域服务业招商引资力度。进一步完善和发挥保税物流园区和出口加工区保税物流方面功能，加快空港综合保税区建设，不仅为上海制造业服务，同时辐射长三角地区。

三是加快总部经济发展，打造多个交易平台。充分发挥现有优势，积极引进国外大型企业设立总部或区域总部，及物流、采购、研发、中介、培训、旅游和会展等服务中心。优化总部区域布局，逐步形成若干现代服务业总部相对集中、高新技术产业总部与保税区、出口加工区等相互依托的总部聚集区。成立专业交易平台，吸引国内外企业入驻中心，做大贸易规模，并行推进新旧产品展示交易。

四是鼓励内资企业尤其是民营企业通过加工贸易方式参与国际分工，融入跨国公司产业链，消化吸收国外先进生产技术和管理经验，提高自身生产制造水平，增强研发与市场控制能力，逐步向科技型、自主研发型企业转变。

五是推动加工贸易企业同时开拓国内外市场。组织和促进加工贸易企业与国内流通企业及内需企业的对接和交流。与海关等部门合作，进一步简化审批手续，提高审批效率。

案例：国内外飞机发动机维修业务得以开展

——普惠发动机维修有限公司

位于青浦出口加工区内的上海普惠飞机发动机维修有限公司（简称惠普公司）是由东航股份公司和美国普惠公司共同投资设立的，总投资规模达 9900 万美元，注册资本为 3950 万美元。其中东航控股 51%，普惠拥有合资公司 49%的股份。是国内第一家与发动机生产厂商合资的发动机维修企业，也是普惠公司唯一在亚太地区的发动机维修中心。2006 年 11 月中国东方航空股份有限公司和美国联合技术国际公司共同签署了组建 CFM56 发动机大修合资企业的协议，在上海设立 CFM56 系列发动机大修合资公司，这也是普惠公司惟一在亚太地区 CFM56 系列发动机的大修企业。

该维修中心拥有大修 CFM56-3、-5B、-7 型发动机和全部零部件维修能力，全面投产后，将拥有专业维修技师 800 人。预计未来三年内，该维修中心年大修 CFM56 发动机能力达到 300 台，年销售额近 30 亿元人民币。但是，由于政策等种种原因，企业不能正常开展国内外飞机发动机的售后维修业务，已签订的七台发动机入区维修合同不能正常实施，企业为此承担的仓储费用每月就高达 50 万美元。上海市商务委在了解到以上情况后，积极汇报、协调。在上海市商务委员会指导下，上海普惠积极与商务部和地方海关等协商，争取到商务部牵头，组成六部委联合考察组莅沪调研，最终特事特办，准予其开展相关业务，开创国内同类业务的试点先例。上海普惠该项业务的开展，有利于提高国内航空发动机维修水平、制造水平；有利于拓展亚太航空发动机维修市场；有利于拉动地方经济的发展，并大量节省国家资金；有利于为我国民航培养大量专业人才。

第三节　服务贸易

一、上海服务贸易发展现状

（一）2009 年上海服务贸易发展概况

1．上海服务贸易各领域利用外资势头良好

2009 年，上海服务贸易各领域实际利用外资呈现良好的发展势头，境内商业存在的规模进一步扩大。据统计，2009 年上海服务业合同利用外资 107.24 亿美元，占上海合同利用外资的 80.6%，比例首次超过 80%；服务业实际利用外资 76.16 亿美元，同比增长 11.4%，占上海实际利用外资的 72.3%。其中，批发零售业和商务服务业都保持了强劲的发展势头，实际利用外资金额同比增幅均超过 30%，科研和技术服务（主要是研发中心）大幅增长 72.1%，商务服务（主要是投资性公司）和商业稳步增长，合同利用外资分别增长 7.7% 和 5.9%。受到世博会的影响，宾馆和餐饮业合同利用外资增长 29.9%。

此外，在沪外国服务业机构发展迅猛。2009 年上海非金融类服务业外国附属机构境内服务营业收入达 345.96 亿美元，同比增长 58.6%。其中，非金融类服务业外国附属机构 8629 家，从业人员 40 万人。

2．上海服务业对外投资比重加大

2009 年，上海服务业对外直接投资 8.08 亿美元，占当年上海对外直接投资总额的 52.6%。其中，商务服务业对外直接投资 3.41 亿美元，占当年对外直接投资比重的 22%，批发和零售业对外直接投资 1.28 亿美元，占比 8%，交通运输仓储业对外直接投

资 1.23 亿美元，占比 8%，房地产业对外直接投资 1.05 亿美元，占比 7%。

3．上海服务贸易自然人移动

2009 年，因受全球金融危机影响，上海市对外经济合作企业派出劳务人员（含境外就业）13926 人次，同比降低 13.7%，期末在外人数（含境外就业）26250 人，同比降低 4.3%。人员结构层次有一定提高，海员、空乘人员、厨师等具有专有技术的人员比例提高了 2 个百分比。

（二）上海服务贸易进出口规模与结构

1．服务贸易进出口增速较快

2000~2008 年，上海服务贸易进出口额由 79.1 亿美元增加到 735.7 亿美元，年均增长 32.1%，高于同期上海货物贸易进出口增长率，高于同期上海国内生产总值（GDP）及第三产业增加值增长率，也高于同期全国服务贸易进出口增长率。服务贸易进出口额占上海国际贸易进出口总额的比重由 2000 年的 12.6% 上升到 2008 年的 18.6%。

表 2-4 上海服务贸易进出口增长情况

年 份	上海服务贸易进出口		上海货物贸易进出口增长率（%）	上海 GDP 增长率（%）	上海第三产业增长率（%）	全国服务贸易进出口增长率（%）
	总额（亿美元）	增长率（%）				
2000	79.1					
2001	95.0	20.0	11.3	10.5	9.7	8.9
2002	115.7	21.9	19.3	11.3	11.4	18.9
2003	160.5	38.7	54.7	12.3	12.0	18.5
2004	244.8	52.5	42.4	14.2	20.4	32.0
2005	324.9	32.7	16.5	11.1	12.8	17.5
2006	403.4	24.2	22.1	12.0	12.7	22.0
2007	559.1	38.6	24.4	14.3	19.6	30.9
2008	735.7	31.6	13.8	9.7	18.1	15.2

资料来源：上海服务贸易、货物贸易进出口增长率根据上海市商务委员会数据计算；上海 GDP 增长率、第三产业增长率根据历年《上海市国民经济和社会发展统计公报》；全国服务贸易进出口增长率根据商务部数据计算。

上海服务贸易进出口额占我国服务贸易进出口总额的比重从 2000 年的 11.2% 上升到 2008 年的 24.2%，是内地服务贸易进出口规模最大的省市。

上海服务贸易进出口规模与香港特区、新加坡等亚太服务贸易中心城市的差距不断缩小。2000 年香港特区服务贸易进出口额是上海的 8.2 倍，新加坡是上海的 7.2 倍；2008 年香港特区服务贸易进出口额是上海的 2.3 倍，新加坡是上海的 1.9 倍。

表 2-5 上海服务贸易占全国服务贸易的比重

年 份	上海服务贸易进出口额占全国服务贸易进出口总额（%）	上海服务贸易出口额占全国服务贸易出口总额（%）	上海服务贸易进口额占全国服务贸易进口总额（%）
2000 年	12.0	12.0	12.0
2001 年	13.2	14.0	12.5
2002 年	13.5	14.5	12.7
2003 年	15.8	16.7	15.1
2004 年	18.3	19.5	17.2
2005 年	20.6	21.8	19.6
2006 年	21.0	21.1	21.0
2007 年	22.3	20.6	23.8
2008 年	24.2	22.1	26.1

资料说明：计算中采用的全国数据来自商务部

表 2-6 上海、香港特区、新加坡服务贸易进出口规模比较

年 份	上海服务贸易进出口总额（亿美元）	香港特区服务贸易进出口规模		新加坡服务贸易进出口规模	
		总额（亿美元）	是上海服务贸易进出口总额的倍数	总额（亿美元）	是上海服务贸易进出口总额的倍数
2000	79.1	649.5	8.2	569.52	7.2
2001	95.0	658.5	8.2	587.2	6.2
2002	115.7	703.8	6.9	624.77	5.4
2003	160.5	724.9	6.1	759.9	4.7
2004	244.8	860.9	4.5	966.1	3.9
2005	324.8	975.4	3.5	1075.3	3.3
2006	403.4	1095.8	3.0	1207.0	3.0
2007	559.1	1237.6	2.7	1374.4	2.5
2008	735.7	1790.1	2.3	1480.1	1.9

资料说明：中国香港特区、新加坡数据根据 WTO 国际贸易数据库数据计算

2．服务贸易结构持续优化

运输、旅游这两项传统服务贸易一直是上海最主要的服务贸易项目，但比重持续下降。2008 年这两项服务出口合计占上海服务贸易出口总额的比重达 54.0%，比 2000 年下降了 7.6 个百分点。

表 2-7　服务贸易出口中各部门所占比重　（单位：%）

部门	全球		我国		上海	
	2000 年	2008 年	2000 年	2008 年	2000 年	2008 年
运输	23.4	23.46	12.2	26.2	41.7	41.4
旅游	32.0	25.34	53.8	27.9	19.9	12.6
其他	44.5	51.21	34.0	45.9	38.4	46.0
合计	100.0	100.0	100.0	100.0	100.0	100.0

资料来源：全球 2000 年数据来自 WTO 数据库，2008 年数据来自 WTO2009 年 3 月 24 日报告《2008 年全球贸易情况和 2009 年展望》（WORLDTRADE2008，PROSPECTSFOR2009）；中国数据来自商务部；上海数据来自上海市商务委员会。

近年来，上海计算机和信息服务、金融、电影音像等新兴服务贸易项目的出口增长迅速，大大高于运输、旅游等传统服务贸易部门的增长速度。

二、上海服务贸易重点领域发展趋势

（一）运输服务贸易

运输是上海服务贸易的传统优势项目，目前约占上海服务贸易进出口总额的 40% 左右，2008 年上海港货物吞吐量完成 5.82 亿吨，已连续四年位居全球首位；国际标准集装箱吞吐量达 2800.6 万标准箱，连续两年位列全球第二。上海运输服务贸易在全国服务贸易中占重要地位，其中出口占全国运输服务贸易出口 40% 上下，进口占全国运输服务贸易进口 30% 上下。

至 2005 年底，中国在货运代理、快递服务、仓储服务、公路服务等运输方面的市场限制都已基本放开。与航运服务市场的开放相对应，航运业务辅助服务单位也日益增多，不少行业呈现出良好的发展势头。特别是上海的国际货代行业服务水平、管理理念进步显著，与国外先进物流（货代）企业的差距逐步缩小，国有、外资、民营企业同台竞争、互相促进，已成为运输服务贸易的重要主体。

但由于种种原因，目前我国的航运业与西方发达国家相比总体竞争能力较弱，航运公司尚无法提供高效、准确、及时、遍布全球的航运服务，因此在国际贸易中，出口使用 FOB 条款，进口使用 CIF 条款的合同较多，由此造成国际贸易运输由外方负责运输环节的情况较多，这也是我国运输服务贸易长期处于逆差状态的主要原因之一。同时，政府各部门多头管理、政出多门，造成运输服务存在地区、部门之间管理比较复杂的局面，不利于发挥综合优势。

国务院《关于推进上海加快发展现代服务业和先进制造业、建设国际金融中心和国际航运中心的意见》提出到 2020 年，将上海基本建成具有全球航运资源配置能力的国际航运中心，上海运输服务贸易发展潜力巨大。

（二）旅游服务贸易

旅游是上海服务贸易中优势明显、基础较好、创汇能力较强的领域，目前约占上海服务贸易进出口总额的 20% 左右。上海旅游服务贸易进出口占全国旅游服务贸易进出口比例呈上升趋势。2008 年，上海接待国际旅游入境人数 640.37 万人次。2004 年以来，银联卡境外受理业务快速发展，由于其计算中心放在上海，使上海旅游服务贸易进口额持续增长。近年来，上海旅游服务贸易呈现旅游需求个性化、旅游产品多元化、经营组织国际化、旅游装备高科技化等趋势。

（三）金融、保险服务贸易

近年来，上海市金融服务贸易的增速强劲。2000 年至 2008 年，上海金融服务贸易进、出口额在 9 年内分别增长了 20.85 倍、23.33 倍。在上海服务贸易的分行业中，上海金融服务贸易占据重要地位：除个别年份外，上海金融服务贸易进、出口额占上海服务贸易进、出口额的比例，均高于同期中国金融服务贸易进、出口额占中国服务贸易进、出口额的比例。

与此同时，与香港特区、新加坡等服务贸易发达的国际大都市相比，上海金融服务贸易的发展水平还显得相当滞后。2007 年，香港特区和新加坡金融服务贸易出口总额占其服务贸易出口总额的比例分别是 12% 和 5.2%，而上海仅为 0.96%。

在近年来发展较快的新兴服务贸易行业中，保险服务贸易属于绝对值较高而相对增长率较低的行业。上海保险服务贸易的增速低于同期全市服务贸易平均增速。2000 年至 2008 年，上海保险服务贸易进、出口额在 9 年内分别增长了 5.62 倍、3.44 倍，而同期上海服务贸易进、出口额分别增长了 8.56 倍、7.98 倍。在全国范围看，上海保险服务贸易出口具有重要地位：上海保险服务贸易出口额占上海服务贸易出口额的比例，远高于同期中国保险服务贸易出口额占中国服务贸易出口额的比例。

（四）计算机和信息服务贸易

计算机和信息服务贸易虽然在上海服务贸易中占比较小，但从 2000 年至 2008 年间，进、出口额分别增长了 7.52 倍和 22.95 倍。近年来出口增长尤其快速，在全国计算机和信息服务出口金额中占比较大,发展日趋平稳。计算机和信息服务出口飞速发展，顺差规模进一步扩大。

表 2-8 上海计算机和信息服务贸易出口增长情况

年 份	2000	2001	2002	2003	2004	2005	2006	2007	2008
出口额（亿美元）	1.06	1.34	3.73	5.08	7.17	7.36	10.5	16.6	25.39
出口增长率（%）		26.4	178.4	36.2	41.1	2.6	42.7	58.1	53.0

资料来源：根据上海市商务委员会、商务部《中国服务贸易发展报告 2008》有关数据计算。

（五）与货物贸易相关的商贸服务

“与货物贸易相关的商贸服务”借鉴了香港地区服务贸易“商贸服务及其他与贸易相关的服务”的概念，主要指与离岸贸易（即在香港经营业务的机构向“非居民”输出服务）有关的服务贸易,包括“商贸服务”及“与离岸交易有关的商品服务”。近年来,“商贸服务及其他与贸易相关的服务”占香港地区服务贸易出口额的近 1/3，占香港地区服务贸易进口额的 7% 以上。

目前,我国外贸出口产品的分销渠道基本掌握在东道国企业手中。企业获得利润低，对国际化战略进行控制难度较大。因此，发展与货物贸易相关的商贸服务，不仅有利于增强我国服务贸易的竞争力，也有利于货物贸易的发展，对提高我国出口的附加值、转变我国外贸增长方式等，起到至关重要的作用。

从香港特区的发展经验看，附加值较低的大宗产品主要通过离岸贸易处理，附加值较高的产品如珠宝和钟表等则主要通过香港转口，这是因为高附加值商品的差异化大，存在质量分级，而在香港的中间人由于具备商品质量分级的专业技术，可以在提供信息服务、降低交易成本和提高交易效率方面发挥重要作用。

目前，上海汇集了约 3.5 万家外贸企业和约 4.5 万家有外贸经营权的企业，许多跨国公司在上海设立的地区总部和办事处业务均涉及商贸服务，本土跨国采购企业也逐渐发展起来。2002 年，经上海市政府批准，上海跨国采购中心有限公司正式成立，其承办的每年一届的“中国（上海）国际跨国采购大会”是目前中国最大规模的跨国逆向采购盛会。

但是，上海的商贸服务也存在着一些问题，诸如外贸企业国际竞争力总体偏弱、离岸贸易比例较小、在国外的分销渠道滞后、地域特征强（主要服务于长三角和长江流域）等。此外，在中低档次的商品领域，由于信息技术的发展和贸易扁平化趋势的深入，商贸服务持续发展的空间越来越小；而在相对附加值较高、差异化较大的商品领域，又缺乏相应的技术和专业人才。

（六）工程承包与建筑服务贸易

上海在对外工程承包和建筑服务贸易方面始终走在全国前列，每年对外工程承包合同金额、实际营业额、年末在外人员均呈上升趋势。近年来上海对外工程承包大项目日益增多，如上海电气与印度签订的一揽子框架协议，总合同额高达68亿美元，创上海市项目合同额新高。上海海外企业已在全球96个国家和地区设立了投资企业或办事机构，非贸易海外企业（包括工程承包与建筑企业等）主要集中在非洲、拉丁美洲和亚洲等地区的新兴市场。但上海对外工程承包和建筑服务进出口总额分别占上海服务贸易进出口总额以及全国建筑服务进出口总额的比例均呈下降趋势。

表 2-9　上海对外承包工程情况

年份 / 指标	1990	2000	2004	2005	2006	2007
签订合同项目（个）	12	143	180	277	2724	821
签订合同金额（万美元）	3929	76058	183831	225308	508953	734747
实际营业额（万美元）	4083	61906	129664	117214	429336	449076
年末在外人员（人）	121	1327	2356	2694	3531	6374

资料来源：《上海统计年鉴2007》，中国统计出版社；上海市商务委员会

上海工程承包和建筑服务贸易历来受到政府高度重视。近年来，一批高科技与民营企业积极参与境外投资，一些企业海外投资项目的规模逐步扩大、层次逐步提高，企业联合、购并、重组趋势增强，涌现了一批有较强国际竞争力的企业。对外工程承包和建筑服务参与方式日益丰富，EPC（Engineering、Procurement、Construction，设计、采购、施工总承包）、PMC（Project Management Contract，项目管理承包）、PFI（Private Finance Initiative，私人主动融资）等总承包交钥匙工程模式所占的比重越来越大，BOT（Build–Operation–Transfer，建设–经营–移交）、BT（Build–Transfer，建设–移交）、PPP（Public–Privatepartnership，公私合伙关系）等带资承包方式也越来越普遍。

和全国其他地区一样，上海的对外工程承包与建筑服务市场大多集中在发展中国家。这些国家政治经济不稳定，各种不可预见的风险更为突出，亟须进一步完善风险

保障制度。对外工程承包与建筑服务企业在海外经营中存在恶性竞争行为，业务领域集中在房建、水利、电力、交通、石化等领域的建设施工方面，同质化倾向严重。

（七）专业服务贸易

专业服务贸易主要包括法律、会计、审计和咨询服务等，是上海服务贸易的重要内容，是知识、技术密集型行业，具有较高的附加值，也是近年来全球和中国未来发展潜力巨大贸易内容。上海的专业服务贸易增长较快，外资企业对上海专业服务贸易进出口总额的贡献较大，是实现上海专业服务贸易的主体。从商业存在的角度看，境外专业服务企业特别是大型的法律、会计、审计和咨询服务跨国公司在上海的商业存在较多，竞争激烈；而上海专业服务企业在境外的商业存在处于起步阶段。从自然人流动的角度看，上海专业服务贸易领域的自然人流动日益增多。

上海咨询服务贸易增长较快，从2000年至2008年，其进、出口额9年间分别增长了9.56倍、23.07倍，2008年上海咨询服务贸易占上海服务贸易进、出口比例分别达7.33%、22.28%，成为服务贸易的主要领域之一。上海咨询服务进、出口额在同期全国咨询服务进、出口额中占有非常重要的地位。虽然从数量上来看，外资或合资的咨询机构在上海整个咨询业中占比不是很大，但外资咨询机构国际竞争力和创收能力远高于中资咨询机构，外资企业咨询服务出口金额占上海咨询服务总出口额80%以上。

上海的会计、审计服务进出口也以外资企业为主体。其中，普华永道、安永、德勤、毕马威四大外资会计师事务所占上海所有外资会计、审计咨询服务出口一半以上。上海的法律服务贸易近年来随着上海国际化趋势的增强而呈上升趋势，外资法律服务企业纷纷入驻上海。

（八）专有权使用和特许经营服务贸易

2000年以来，上海专有权使用和特许经营服务贸易进口持续增长，9年间增长了6.9倍；而出口一直低位徘徊。但相对于全国来讲，上海专有权使用和特许经营服务贸易发展依然比较领先，在全国专有权使用和特许经营服务贸易中占比较高。2008年，上海专有权使用和特许费进出口总额为20.18亿美元，占同年服务贸易总额的2.75%，比2007年增长40.73%。其中，出口0.3亿美元，较2007年增长20%；进口为19.88亿美元，较2007年增长41.10%。贸易逆差进一步拉大，达19.58亿美元。

（九）文化服务贸易

文化贸易在服务贸易中的重要性呈上升趋势，美国文化产品出口已超过航空航天工业而成为第一大出口产业。目前，全球文化贸易极不平衡，70% 以上的贸易额集中在美、英、法、德、日 5 国之间，我国对美国等西方国家的文化贸易逆差巨大，其中版权贸易逆差更为严重。

上海作为全国文化产业较为发达的城市，文化服务贸易逆差正在逐步缩小。近年来，上海文化服务贸易呈现出一些新特点，集中体现为文化信息服务贸易、动漫服务贸易等新兴文化服务出口超过演艺服务贸易、影视服务贸易、图书出版服务贸易、印刷服务贸易等传统文化服务出口。

目前，上海文化服务贸易的主要问题是文化出口规模小、原创少、国际市场拓展力度有待加大、出口支持政策不够明晰等。

（十）教育服务贸易

教育服务贸易是国际服务贸易的重要组成部分，已成为世界公认的新兴产业和新的经济增长点。上世纪 80 年代以来，全球教育服务贸易额每年高达 300 亿美元以上。上海教育服务贸易虽然在全国居于前列，近年来有较快发展，但规模依然偏小，在上海服务贸易总额中占比在 2% 以下，与纽约、伦敦、东京等国际教育发达城市差距甚远。随着经济全球化的深入、上海国际化程度的增加和国际教育事业的发展，上海的教育服务贸易将迅速上升，中外合作办学机构 / 项目、在沪外籍人员子女学校、外国来华留学生和外籍专家、外籍教师、中国出国留学人员、国际学术会议和其他形式的国际教育交流活动将会增多。

（十一）医疗服务贸易

上海医疗服务贸易近年来有所发展，但在上海服务贸易中占比较低。服务贸易的四种模式在上海医疗服务贸易领域中都有发展，以援外医疗队、外派医疗劳务、外国人在沪就医为主，上海到国外投资建立医疗诊所数量少、规模小，主要为中医。涉外远程咨询会诊系统和涉外医疗保健服务开始发展。

上海对外中医医疗服务合作逐步增长。上海中医药大学国际教育学院、曙光医院分别入选国家中医药管理局国际交流合作基地。上海对外中医药教育保持全国领先地位，对外中医药科技合作取得初步成效，一批国际科技合作基地、重大合作项目已经建成或进入具体实施阶段。

（十二）体育服务贸易

体育服务贸易在上海服务贸易中占比很小，但近年来呈迅速增长势头，上海举办

的国际体育赛事逐年增多，知名度和影响力日益增加；体育活动的电视、网络跨国播映与转播、跨国体育训练和比赛、运动员与教练等自然人流动日益增多，体育机构的“引进来”与“走出去”也逐步发展。

三、上海服务贸易推进工作

(一) 2009 年上海服务贸易推进工作

1．上海服务贸易推进工作进一步开展

在部市合作协议的框架下，在上海市服务贸易发展联席会议的指导下，先后制订出台了《关于促进上海市服务贸易全面发展的实施意见》和《上海服务贸易中长期发展规划纲要》；设立了“上海市服务贸易发展专项资金”，主要用于软件、国际物流和文化等服务贸易重点领域，鼓励、支持和促进其扩大规模、提升能级。

2．上海服务贸易统计体系不断深化

在建立上海服务贸易统计和综合评估体系方面积极展开探索和研究，并形成了初步方案，逐步实现服务贸易数据实时查询、分析、预测和信息共享等功能。

3．上海服务贸易调研工作进一步开展

结合上海发展服务贸易的特点，联合本市相关部门，就教育、国际物流和文化等服务贸易企业的发展现状、瓶颈问题和政策需求进行了深入调研，并相继完成多份调研报告，为进一步研究出台服务贸易促进政策提供了信息和依据。

此外，各类服务贸易促进活动也相继举办。2009 上海软件外包国际峰会顺利举办；中医药“走出去”的推进工作全面启动，“沪港中医药服务贸易合作发展论坛”成功召开；本市服务贸易企业也积极参加商务部主办的“香港服务贸易洽谈会”、深圳“文博会”和大连“软交会”等展会，加强了与海内外服务贸易企业的联系和交流。

(二) 2010 年上海服务贸易工作思路

为切实有效推进上海服务贸易发展，2010 年将主要开展以下工作：

1．抓住世博会的创新契机，促进服务贸易的服务方式创新

利用世博会作为全球最大“体验经济”平台的契机，加强服务方式的创新；挖掘世博会的消费潜力，扩大服务贸易出口；加强货物贸易与服务贸易的有机结合，提升货物贸易发展的质量。

2．加强工作联动，做好上海服务贸易发展“十二五”规划

一是依靠“联席会议”，加强服务贸易工作的统筹协调，全面开展服务贸易“十二五”

规划的思路讨论和重点调研。二是加强与各区县的联动，结合各区县现代服务业集聚区的建设，研究确立各区县服务贸易发展的重点领域、重点区域和关键环节。三是加强服务贸易的“部市”合作联动,积极争取国家的服务贸易发展政策在上海的先试先行，以国家中长期规划全面指导上海“十二五”发展。

3．发挥政策效应，完善服务贸易促进体系

将“上海服务贸易指南网”建成服务贸易企业交流合作的平台；利用“上海软件外包国际峰会”等国内各类展会为服务贸易企业提供服务；用好用足“上海市服务贸易发展专项资金”，发挥专项资金“四两拨千斤”的作用，帮助企业千方百计开拓国际市场。

4．立足原有基础，扩大重点领域服务出口

利用上海举办世博会和建设国际贸易中心的契机，进一步加强国际货代行业管理，推动上海国际物流的发展；进一步发挥部门和区域联动，深入促进软件出口；进一步加强多方合作，合力推进文化服务出口再上新台阶；进一步加强政策调研，促进专业服务贸易发展。

5．保持领先水平，不断完善和深化服务贸易统计体系

在原有统计平台的基础上，依托联席会议协调机制，进一步加强服务贸易统计体系的时效性，进一步完善服务贸易统计体系的完整性，并加快建立上海市服务贸易统计评估系统。

6．发挥行业协会作用，鼓励企业培育自主品牌

发挥行会协会的指导和协调作用，鼓励创立服务贸易自主出口品牌，鼓励服务贸易企业参与国际竞争，鼓励重点领域的企业优势互补，加强协作，做大做强。

第四节　服务外包

一、上海服务外包发展趋势和特点

（一）2009年上海服务外包发展概况

2009年,上海服务外包快速发展。据商务部服务外包及软件出口信息管理系统显示，截至2009年12月底，全市服务外包企业登记数共606家，从业人员10万多人，通过各种认证数量351个；1-12月份服务外包合同金额为17.62亿美元，同比增长20.8%；其中离岸外贸金额为16.83亿美元，同比增长18.3%；1-12月份服务外包合同执行金额

11.02 亿美元，同比增长 24.41%。其中离岸金额为 10.36 亿美元，同比增长 20.3%。初步形成 1 个基地城市、5 个服务外包示范区、8 个服务外包专业园区、84 家服务外包重点企业共同发展的格局。

(二) 2009 年上海服务外包发展的主要特点

1. 信息技术外包（ITO）、业务流程外包（BPO）、知识流程外包（KPO）渐成规模

2009 年 1–11 月，上海市服务外包合同金额为 10.78 亿美元，其中 ITO 占 76.5%，BPO 占 5.1%，包括 KPO 在内的其他类占 15.8%。合同执行金额是 4.48 亿美元，其中 ITO 占 71.4%，BPO 占 5.7%，其他占 21.4%。

2. 企业规模不断扩大，平均实力有所增强

截至 2009 年 12 月底，上海市共有服务外包企业 606 家，通过各种认证共 351 个，从业人员 10 万多人，其中，千人以上企业 20 家，经过认定的重点企业 84 家。

凯捷总部、埃森哲、INFOSYS、UNISYS、ADP，以及 IBM、汇丰、花旗、摩根等一批世界 500 强企业纷纷在沪设立亚太或全球数据处理中心；文思创新等国内知名服务外包企业也把上海作为重要的战略部署地。根据中国国际投资促进会发布的报告，药明康德位列中国十大服务外包领军企业，睿智化学、开拓者化学、桑迪亚、微创、高知特、中和软件等 6 家企业位列 100 家成长型企业。

3. 就业带动效应明显

截至 2009 年 12 月底，上海市服务外包企业吸纳就业人员 103831 人，新增从业人数 29176 人，其中大学学历 9.29 万人，占全部从业人员的 89.5%；其他学历 1.1 万人，占全部从业人员比重为 10.5%。大学学历从业人员中，本科以上学历 5.9 万人，占全部从业人员比重为 56.5%。其中博士学历 0.2 万人，占全部从业人员的 1.5%。硕士学历 1.2 万人，占比为 11.9%。本科学历 4.5 万人，占比 43.1%；专科学历 3.4 万人，占全部从业人员的 33%。

4. 园区集聚度提高，结构调整带动作用显现

上海市 5 个服务外包示范区共有企业 293 家，占总企业数的 48.3%；从业人员 61544 人，占总人数的 59.3%。5 个示范区服务外包合同金额 13.68 亿美元，占上海市总额的 77.6%。

中心城区通过发展服务外包，“腾笼换鸟”，发展“楼宇经济”，出现了近百栋亿元楼宇，尤其是浦东、长宁、卢湾、漕河泾等示范园区的产业升级已经显现。远郊区及上海周边、长三角地区甚至中西部也因此有机会承接制造业的转移，有助于区域经济结构平衡调整。

二、2009年上海服务外包工作推进情况

2009年服务外包工作从基础工作抓起，建章立制，主要是建立工作网络，编制发展规划，加大政策支持力度，整合人才培训资源，打造精品园区、重点企业，扎扎实实地推动上海服务外包发展。概括起来，主要有“六个一”：

1．形成一个工作网络

从纵向看，在国家商务部的指导下，分管上海市领导牵头，上海市商务委员会具体负责，基本形成了一个市、区、企业联动的工作机制；从横向看，上海市商务委员会与上海市发展改革委员会、上海市经济和信息化委委员、上海市教育委员会、上海市科学技术委员会、上海市财政局、上海市人力资源社会保障局、上海市国家税务局、上海市地方税务局、上海市工商行政管理局、上海市统计局、上海市知识产权局、上海市人民政府台湾事务办公室、上海市人民政府侨务办公室、上海金融服务办公室、上海市社团管理局、上海市公安局出入境管理局、上海海关、央行上海总部、上海保监局、上海银监局、国家外汇管理局（上海分局）、上海出入境检验检疫局、上海市通信管理局、浦东新区政府等24个相关部门初步形成了一个服务外包联席会议工作机制。同时，注意发挥中间力量的作用。如在具体工作中，充分发挥市服务外包专业委员会、上海软件对外贸易联盟、上海质量认证中心、上海生物医药协会和上海多媒体协会等行业协会的作用。

2．制定一个发展规划

在中国服务外包研究中心协助下，根据上海的实际情况，组织拟定上海服务外包产业发展规划。明确发展目标：力争到2015年，服务外包收入超过1300亿元人民币，其中离岸外包收入达45亿美元；培养服务外包人才18万人，从业人员数量增至15万人。明确重点发展领域是：金融、生物医药研发、人力资源、应用软件开发、生产性服务、航运、文化与创意、专业服务外包等领域。

3．出台一揽子政策

（1）根据国办9号文的精神，制定了《关于促进服务外包产业发展的实施意见》（沪府办发［2009］16号），从财政支持、人才培训、人才引进、综合工时、金融、工商、外汇、通关检验检疫等方面，支持服务外包产业发展。

（2）为促进本市服务外包产业健康快速发展，设立服务外包产业发展专项资金，制订了上海市《促进服务外包产业发展专项资金使用和管理试行办法》。资金主要用于服务外包发展中的重点领域和关键环节，具体包括支持服务外包人才培训，引导服务

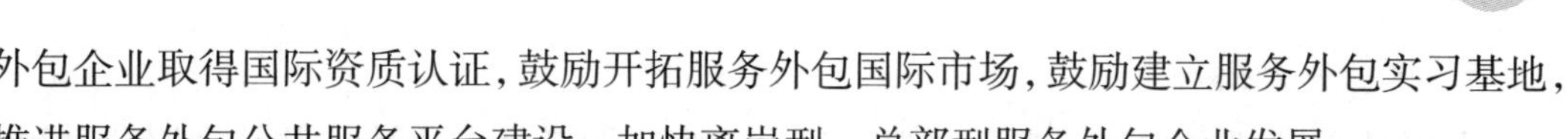

外包企业取得国际资质认证，鼓励开拓服务外包国际市场，鼓励建立服务外包实习基地，推进服务外包公共服务平台建设，加快离岸型、总部型服务外包企业发展。

（3）落实技术先进型服务企业政策。财税[2009]63号文发布后，上海市商务委员会、市财政局、科委等部门共同制定《上海市技术先进型服务企业认定管理试行办法》（沪科合［2009］031号），第一批认定65家技术先进型服务企业，第二批40家的认定工作已经结束，正在公示中。

（4）出台了上海市《服务外包示范区认定管理暂行办法》，据此认定了一批综合园区和专业园区。

（5）配合知识产权局及相关部门，拟定了《关于加强上海市服务外包产业知识产权工作的若干意见》，目前正在修改完善中。

4．争取一批支持资金

（1）2008年度国家专项资金足额拨付到位，并顺利通过商务部专项审计。2008年度，上海市共有110家服务外包企业，5家培训机构和1家认证企业通过商务部、财政部的联合审核，共获资助资金3279.10万元，已于2009年上半年全部拨付到位。

2009年8月16日至26日，受商务部委托，利安达会计师事务所进行了服务外包产业发展专项资金审计。这是商务部自2007年开展服务外包产业发展资金申报以来的首次审计，重点是2007、2008年度国际服务外包业务发展资金项目的申报、审核程序及专项资金拨付情况，同时抽取上海市23家企业（培训机构）进行重点现场审计。通过为期11天的审计，审计组对上海市2007、2008两个年度服务外包产业发展专项资金的申报及管理工作给予充分肯定。

（2）组织申报2009年度国家专项资金。2009年7–10月，积极组织申报国家支持资金。结合历年的申报经验和今年审计要求，重点加强了申报程序规范。截至2009年9月30日，根据44号文件所规定的申请条件和标准，经区县（区县商务委员会）初审、市商务委复审，上海市115家服务外包企业的5939名新录用员工，5家培训机构的1240培训人员，以及11家认证企业的11个国际认证符合申报条件，拟分别申请补贴费用2672.55万元、62.00万元和323.7万元，总计申请支持金额3058.25万元，申报材料已分别报商务部和财政部。经过争取，2009年获得国家专项支持资金2598.8万元。在金融危机的背景下，为企业争取到实际利益，帮助企业渡过难关。

（3）积极争取上海市配套资金。依据《促进服务外包产业发展专项资金使用和管理试行办法》，经过与市发改委、市财政局的磋商、协调，经审核158家服务外包企业（通过率68%）和6家服务外包培训机构（通过率100%）的相关项目符合规定，共申请服务外包专项资金2219.4285万元。

5．培训一大批人才

主要是通过部市共建、市区共建，建设上海市服务外包人才公共培训服务平台。上海市与商务部、教育部共建中国服务外包人才培训中心（上海），上海市商务委员会又与浦东新区共建上海服务外包人才培训中心。这两个中心实际上是一体的，作为全市服务外包人才培训的公共服务平台，主要负责整合全市的服务外包培训资源，制订培训计划和目标，指导全市服务外包人才培训工作，为企业与相关的培训机构开展多种形式的合作创造条件；并受上海市商务委员会委托认定全市服务外包人才培训基地、实训基地。目前，培训中心已正式运行，首批认定10家服务外包培训基地，聘请了首批10名专家；并出台上海市服务外包人才培训基地、实训基地两个认定管理办法，将据此对服务外包人才培训、实训基地进行认定和管理；同时，积极与国际知名外包企业合作，尝试开展领军人才培育项目。

与此同时，大力支持服务外包企业根据自身需求开展内训，积极鼓励相关高等院校，以及有条件的社会专业培训机构开展形式多样的短期培训、企业定制培训、项目培训、课程培训等。

6．打造一系列精品

（1）在园区建设上，本着“成熟一个、发展一个”的原则，继续推进新的示范区和专业园区的认定。其中闸北区服务外包发展态势良好，目前已经通过了有关委办局的评审，这将是继2006年以来的第5家服务外包示范区。浦东陆家嘴软件园、长宁多媒体产业园区、普陀天地软件园也已通过评审，将成为第三批服务外包专业园区。

（2）在重点企业培育上，依据《上海市服务外包重点企业认定管理暂行办法》，在去年底首批认定40家重点企业的基础上，今年新认定了第二批44家重点企业。

（3）继续加强信息、技术、培训、研究、知识产权保护等五大公共服务平台的建设。

（4）在投资促进、统计等方面也开展了一系列基础性工作。

三、2010年上海服务外包工作设想

1．加强宣传，统一认识，理顺体制

把认识统一到中央对上海实现“四个率先”要求的高度，要有发展的眼光；而且要把这种认识落实到具体的工作中，落实到操作层面；加强宣传，在调整结构的大格局下做好服务外包这篇文章；培育中间力量，充分发挥社会中间力量的作用。

2．因地制宜，明确重点，加强引导

从目前的以市场为主、企业自发性发展，增强导向性、引导性，逐渐走向全市合

理布局，错位竞争，最终实现共同发展；根据规划，结合上海特点，走差异化发展道路；同时加强对区县的分类指导，鼓励错位竞争，差异化发展。

3．落实政策

（1）贯彻落实国家和上海出台的一系列政策，用足用好，尽可能地让更多的企业享受更大的实惠。

（2）根据执行情况调整现行政策（专项资金标准过高问题），研究出台新支持政策（浦东部分地区探索个人所得税减免）。如：鼓励政府和企业通过购买服务等方式，将数据处理等不涉及秘密的业务外包给专业企业。提升和完善上海的城市综合功能，提高服务业的市场化程度，大力培育服务外包发展市场；争取对中小成长型企业支持；增加对在岸外包的支持力度。

（3）为国家政策调整及出台新政策作贡献，政策试验田（技术先进型服务企业认定标准）。

4．加强企业服务

服务贯穿于整个过程：在招商引资、审批管理、后续服务等各个环节，加强服务，特别是要根据服务外包产业对环境的独特需要，开展针对性服务，使企业“招得来，留得住，长得大”。

（1）“招得来”——坚持专业招商，加大投资促进力度。大力引进国际知名服务外包企业，抓项目落地，特别是要抓增量，实现服务外包的可持续发展。打造“上海服务外包”品牌形象，在全球范围内实施目标招商、产业链招商，有针对性地引进发包、接包企业及中介机构和第三方组织，完善产业链条。充分依托上海国际化城市背景，支持服务外包企业建立全球交付系统，加强国际合作，进行跨国并购，开拓国际市场，切实提高接发包能力。

（2）“留得住”、“长得大”——加强企业服务，帮助企业做大做强。要在已建立的重点企业联系制度基础上，密切关注企业运营情况；发挥现有的“市—区县及园区—企业”联动机制，了解企业需求，提高服务意识和水平。同时，想方设法支持服务外包企业创建品牌，鼓励企业走出去，通过并购做大做强。服务外包发展至今，已经具有了一批具有相当规模的外包企业。但要想短期内增强企业的综合竞争能力，帮助企业做大做强，则需要鼓励有条件的企业兼并、收购、重组、上市及引进风险投资，加强本土服务外包企业的竞争力和对国外市场的开拓力。

5．继续做好园区和公共服务平台建设（继续开展园区认定）

进一步加强服务外包软硬件环境建设，推进公共服务平台及园区建设。在园区建设上，将继续坚持走专业化道路，在发展综合性示范区的同时，重点发展信息、金融后台、人力资源、医药研发等专业园区。同时大力推动公共服务平台建设，为服务外包产业发展提供良好条件。明年将继续关注园区的发展，同时开展新的园区的认定，请各区县积极培育、发现好的种子。

案例：直面危机，把握机遇，勇于进取

——上海新致软件有限公司

上海新致软件有限公司（简称新致软件）成立于1994年，是一家由5个大学生自主创业，专业从事日本、欧美软件离岸外包及国内软件开发服务的高新技术企业。目前，新致软件人员规模超过1000人，软件出口超过千万美元。新致软件作为一家信息技术服务提供商，在多个地区、为多个行业提供基于金融、通信、政府公众、商业连锁、交通运输、医疗卫生、制造业和企业信息化咨询、设计、实施、测试、支持、培训等专业解决方案和服务。

新致软件在国家服务外包产业政策的激励下，一直保持着快速健康的发展。连续8年被商务部、发展改革委等四部委认定为“国家规划布局内重点软件企业”；获得科技部首批“中国软件欧美出口工程企业”认定；是“上海软件出口十强企业”和“上海市服务外包重点企业”；2007和2009年，新致和newtouch获得“上海名牌”称号；公司质量体系通过CMMI 5评估和ISO27001认证。公司在北京、大连、西安、杭州，日本东京和大阪，法国巴黎，美国费城等均设有分支机构，初步建立了软件外包国际化产业链。

自2008年末国际经济危机爆发以来，整个世界经济均处于变革和大调整之中。新致软件也未能独善其身,特别是日本和欧美离岸业务深受影响。但新致软件能直面危机，泰然应对，通过对国内外业务结构的调整，有效地化解了金融危机所带来的挑战，实现了2009年公司业绩稳中有升，确保了公司可持续发展，在不平凡的一年里做出了不平凡的业绩。

（一）坚守社会责任，认真履行“不裁员、不减薪”承诺

在受全球金融危机影响下，国内许多软件外包企业都采取了裁员、减薪和无薪休假等措施来降低企业成本和规避风险。而新致软件的海外业务尽管也受到了一定创伤，但是，新致软件高层能够“坚守社会责任，逆流而上”，积极响应市府号召，在艰难时

刻对全体员工做出“不裁员、不减薪”的承诺，新致软件的承诺不仅消除了全体员工的后顾之忧，还增强了企业的凝聚力。新致软件还与软件对外贸易联盟理事单位一起共同倡议开展“不裁员，共度危机”活动，为维护行业稳定和可持续发展作出了贡献。

（二）坚持国内外业务齐抓并进，增强企业抗风险能力

新致软件自成立以来，一直坚持国内和海外业务双向互补发展的经营策略。新致软件最初是靠开发国内金融行业软件和服务起家的，1998 年才正式开始进入对日软件外包领域。正因为有国内业务作为基础，才有后来新致软件对日和欧美离岸外包事业的大发展。新致软件的日本和欧美软件外包业务连续几年保持了高速增长，业务收入一度占到新致软件总收入的 70%以上。尽管新致软件海外业务一帆风顺，但新致软件始终没有放弃过国内业务的发展。2003 年，新致软件与许多出口企业一样，也经受了 SARS 危机的考验，当时因受 SARS 影响，国内很多单一对日外包的企业一筹莫展，而新致软件正因有国内金融和电子政务强大的市场需求支撑，新致软件整体收入状况才没有受到SARS的冲击。这几年由于受人民币汇率升值以及本次的国际金融海啸的影响，国内软件服务外包行业又再次经受了严峻的考验。新致软件好在已经做好了充分准备，建立了市场风险调节机制，当不少出口企业处在举步维艰的时刻，公司能够自我消化风险，保持业务收入相对稳定。

（三）抓住上海建设“两个中心”机遇，积极开拓国内新业务

金融危机不仅给企业带来了挑战，同时也给企业带来了新的发展机遇。在受国内需求拉动和上海“两个中心”建设的驱动下，国内相关行业 IT 建设需求旺盛，新致软件紧紧把握机遇，及时做好业务调整，积极利用在海外项目中学到的技术和经验，组织专业团队积极拓展国内业务。2009 年公司相继在北京、杭州和苏州成立了分公司。新致软件与国内交通银行、太平洋保险集团、建设银行、邮政储蓄等一大批客户建立了长期合作关系。2009 年公司金融 IT 相关服务收入增长迅速，与同期相比增幅超过 150%。除此之外，新致软件的软件服务还成功地进入了麦当劳和肯德基等著名商业连锁企业领域。新业务给新致软件带来了新的发展方向。

（四）与客户同舟共济，着眼未来

新致软件的海外核心业务主要是专注于日本和欧美客户的软件设计、开发及测试维护，海外客户大部分是 NEC、日立、TIS、IBM、阿尔卡特、标致雪铁龙公司（PSA）、CAI 等世界 500 强企业，新致软件与这些企业均建立有长期的合作伙伴关系。但随着金

融危机的爆发，这些海外大客户均受到重创，公司的海外业务也受到了一定影响，订单和报价与同期相比下降了30%，然而业务量的减少并未影响公司同客户长期合作关系，尽管公司无利可图，而公司以客户为中心、质量第一的方针始终没有改变。原来公司欧美业务受影响最大，如今却回升最快。2009年新致软件还成功地接到意大利和西班牙软件开发业务。

（五）勤练内功，蓄势待发

由于海外业务量的下降，昔日紧缺的技术人员也出现了冗余，为及时消化这些人员，新致软件根据国内业务需求及时对海外冗余人员进行转岗培训，通过培训，大部分技术人员找到了新的岗位，转岗培训不仅留住了人才，还提高了员工的工作技能。

为提升公司管理团队经营管理能力，新致软件专门为管理人员设计了微型EMBA学习课程：聘请了高校管理学院专家教授来公司培训，公司先后举办多期管理人员的培训班，通过对管理人员的充电，使管理人员知识得到了更新。

为培养合格人才，新致软件建立了完善的初、中和高级人才培养体系和培训规划，近几年，新致软件新招应届生超过300多人，培养各种软件专业技术中高级开发及管理人才达400多名，其中，通过美国PMP项目经理培训73人。人才培训获得了商务部和市商务委的资金支持，人才的培养和储备，大大缓解了公司发展所带来的人才需求压力，使公司保持了可持续发展。

为提升新致软件管理水平，实现管理与国际接轨，新致软件在通过CMMI5和ISO27001认证的基础上，自主研发了“软件服务外包技术管理平台”，该平台的应用，解决了公司与各分支机构协同工作技术瓶颈问题，为开拓海外市场，实现公司国际化、规模化发展，提升公司管理水平起到了技术支撑和保障作用。

新致软件还对软件外包的服务模式进行了创新，与NEC集团合作，在国内设立了首个“离岸软件外包研发中心”，该中心主要承接网络通信设备控制系统研发，具备需求分析和高端设计能力，对新致软件发展高端服务外包业务实现向高端转变具有示范作用。

金融危机不仅给企业带来了挑战，也给企业带来了新的发展机遇，随着国家产业结构调整的深入和上海“两个中心”建设的推进，新致软件对未来充满信心，新致软件将继续加强对新业务市场的开拓和投入，不断创新和优化软件外包业务结构。计划通过2~3年的努力，实现公司人员规模和服务收入翻番目标。

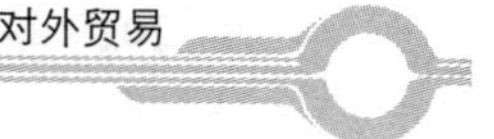

第五节 离岸贸易

一、关于离岸贸易的含义

1．离岸贸易的由来和发展

由于区域之间不同贸易体制的存在，在某些经济、金融发达地区出现了订单发出地与实际货物贸易执行地之间的分离，出现了新型的贸易方式。即：本地中间商分别与出口地出口商和进口地进口商订立买卖合同，货物实际并未在本地进出口，经由出口地直接运交进口地买方，但是单据经过本地中间商处理，本地作为资金流、货物流、订单流控制管理中心的一种贸易形式。

“离岸贸易”涵盖了转运贸易与直接付运两种形式。转运贸易是指以联运提单方式付运货物，其出货点与提货点均在本国（地）以外的地方；直接付运是指直接由生产地运到国外客户那里，无需经由本国（地）转运的一种贸易方式，是订单的发起者在一个中心城市，但真正的贸易进出口或者使用的港口设施可以在另外的地方，它只是发出指令，具体的贸易执行者可能是生产性企业，也可能是其他性质的企业，这类企业主要承担的功能是订单和资金结算，具体的贸易执行功能由其他企业承担，因而他们不需要大量港口等基础设施，最主要的是电信设施以及因为贸易额大而产生的税负需要合理规避。

由于上海周边长三角地区相对具有成本优势的生产加工资源、腹地的存在，以及巨大的消费市场的形成，使得传统意义上的“离岸贸易”有了更丰富的内涵，“离岸贸易”的定义为：就某一国家（地区）而言，该国家（地区）的某一中间商或多个中间商与不同国家（地区）或不同关税区的上下游企业之间进行的发生在该国关境以外的一系列贸易行为。

其本质特征是：① 贸易行为发生在关境外；② 体现全球贸易链中的订单中心功能和结算中心功能。

2．离岸贸易的特点

① 参与企业众多，对任何一笔离岸贸易业务而言，至少有三个或三个以上的企业参与其中；② 在离岸贸易业务中，资金流、订单流、货物流可以分离；③ 离岸贸易采用国际流通货币进行结算；④ 离岸贸易不是指单笔的交易，而是发生在众多企业之间的一个复杂的贸易链条。

3．离岸贸易发展的阶段

在离岸贸易发展的初始阶段，资金流、订单流、货物流基本一致，形成一定量的

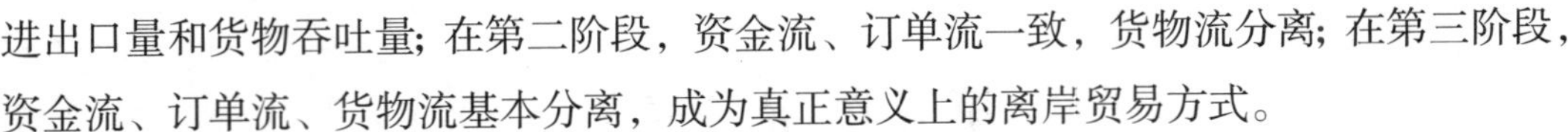

进出口量和货物吞吐量；在第二阶段，资金流、订单流一致，货物流分离；在第三阶段，资金流、订单流、货物流基本分离，成为真正意义上的离岸贸易方式。

二、外高桥保税区离岸贸易运作实务

1．外高桥保税区开展离岸贸易业务的基础

经过近20年发展，上海外高桥保税区紧紧抓住跨国公司的需求，率先与国际惯例接轨，创造了便利化贸易环境，为跨国公司的高密度、高质量聚集、国际贸易业务的发展壮大奠定了扎实基础。在保税区内集聚的5000多家贸易企业中，有140多家跨国公司在此成立了营运中心，成为其区域性资金调度、贸易结算、生产资料配置、物流运作的集中管理平台。2008年上海外高桥保税区完成商品销售额、物流企业营业收入、进出口贸易额和税务部门税收分别占到全国保税区的52%、65%、46%和53%。2009年上海外高桥保税区完成商品销售额5523亿元人民币、进出口贸易额551亿美元、税务部门税收234亿元，分别占到全国保税区总量的50%以上。

目前，保税区内已有一定数量的企业形成了一定规模的离岸贸易运作实务，具有进一步发展的基础，但与离岸贸易相匹配的贸易模式和监管方式尚待突破和完善。保税区内运作的5000多家贸易企业中有超过50%的企业都不同程度地参与到离岸贸易业务运作中，特别是许多跨国公司营运中心企业进行了一系列贸易行为的混合运作，较典型的企业包括：索尼、西门子、松下、英力士等。

据统计测算（如图2–7所示），2008年外高桥保税区内企业开展离岸贸易业务的销售额约为269亿美元，同比增长35%。2009年，受全球金融危机和全球贸易量骤降等因素的影响，开展离岸贸易业务的销售额下降23.5%，为206亿美元，约占区内商品销售总额的四分之一。

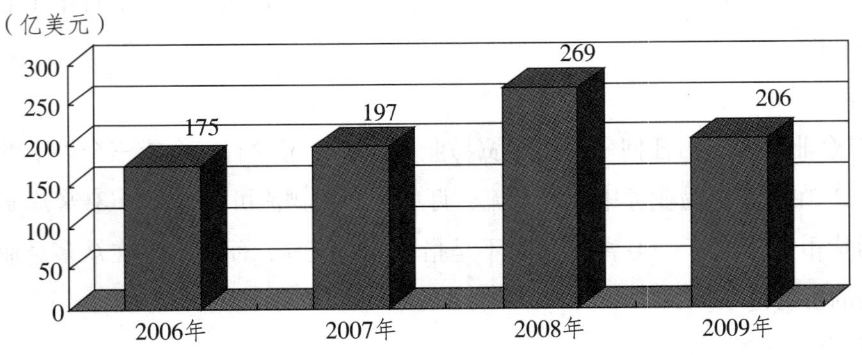

图2-7 外高桥保税区离岸贸易发展情况

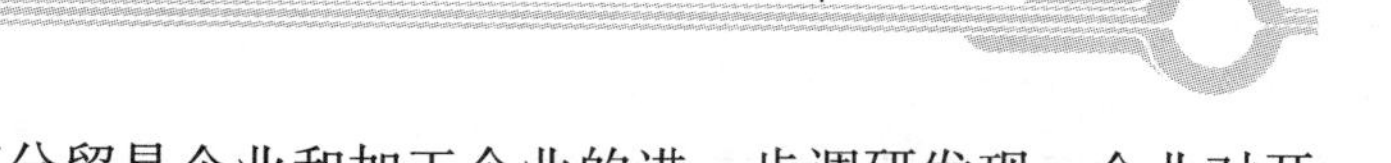

通过对保税区跨国公司、部分贸易企业和加工企业的进一步调研发现，企业对开展离岸贸易的需求正进一步扩大。

2．外高桥保税区离岸贸易运作模式

上海外高桥保税区目前在运作的离岸贸易业务主要可分为两大类，共 8 种模式，具体如下：

第一大类：“两头在外模式”。是指本国（地区）贸易中间商以外的其他贸易主体均位于本国（地区）以外，货物流在国境以外的贸易方式，包括以下 3 种模式：

第 1 种模式——“三国三地”模式（见图 2–8），是指上游企业（供货方）、下游企业（收货方）和保税区内中间商分属三个不同的国家，上游企业直接把货发给下游企业，而订单和资金通过保税区内中间商处理：

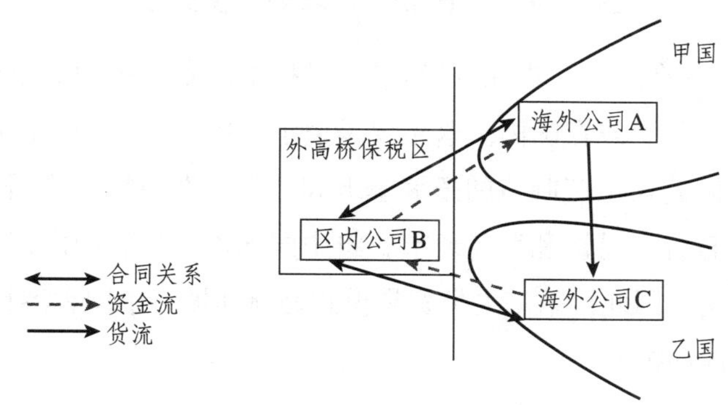

图 2-8 “三国三地”模式图

第 2 种模式——“两国三地”模式（见图 2–9），是指上游企业（供货方）和下游企业（收货方）在同一个国家的不同口岸，他们与保税区内中间商分属两个国家，上游企业直接把货发给下游企业，而订单和资金通过区内中间商处理：

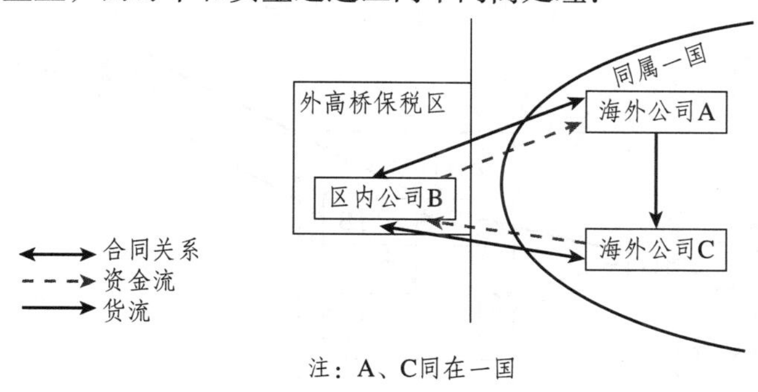

图 2-9 “两国三地”模式图

第 3 种模式——“跨国公司代表处”模式（见图 2–10），是指区内某一企业成为其境外总部的代表处，不具有法人地位。整个贸易过程中，货物流不经过该代表处，但是订单和资金全部由代表处操作：

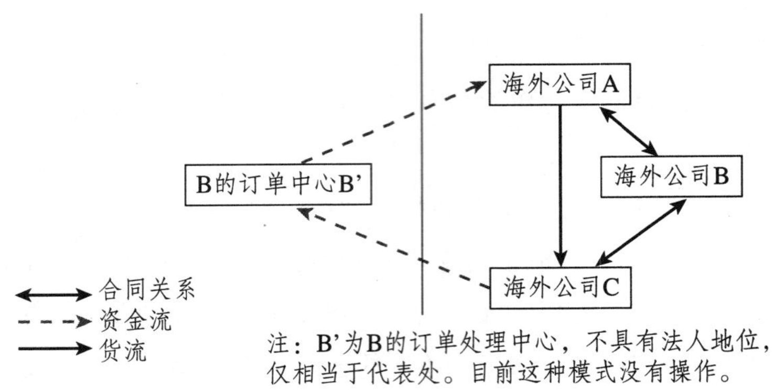

图 2-10 “跨国公司代表处”模式图

第二大类：“一头在外、一头在内模式”。是指本国贸易中间商以外的部分上游企业和下游企业或在境外、或在国内。这主要是由于中国有广大的生产腹地和巨大的国内市场需求作为跨国公司生产制造的拓展基地和产品消费市场，跨国企业需要利用其保税区内的子公司整合贸易链和贸易环节，将中国国内工厂和国内市场的资源加以有效整合、调配、利用。因此，第二大类贸易模式是新加坡、中国香港特区“两头在外”离岸贸易模式的延伸和扩展。

第二大类主要包括以下 5 种模式（第 4~8 种）：

第 4 种模式——“区内交易”模式（见图 2–11），它包含四个以上的贸易主体，其中一个在国外，一个在国内，另有两个及两个以上的贸易中间商是保税区内企业，即其主要订单关系和资金关系由两个及两个以上的保税区中间商之间完成。该模式大多见于区内保税交易：

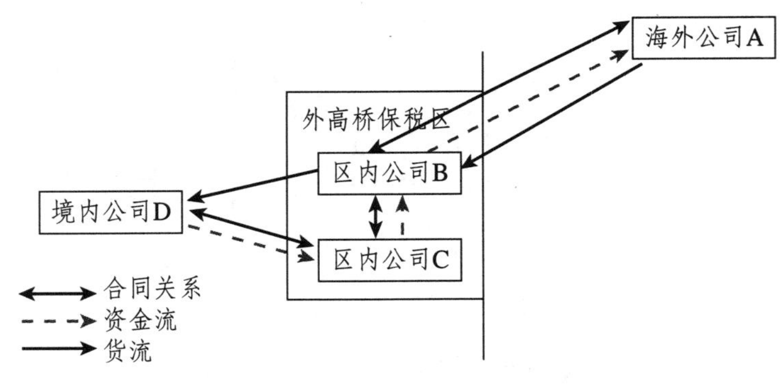

图 2-11 “区内交易”模式图

第 5 种模式——“区内交易延伸”模式（见图 2-12），是在上述第 4 种模式的基础上进一步发展为区内中间商不直接发生订单和资金关系，而是一个区内中间商与另一个区内中间商的国外母公司发生订单关系，而该国外母公司与其区内子公司（即另一区内中间商）之间再订立订单。该模式大多见于国外母公司具有区域总部职能的情况下：

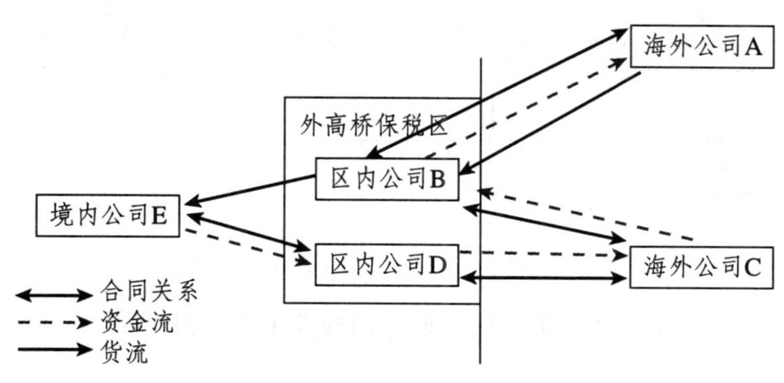

图 2-12 “区内交易延伸”模式图

第 6 种模式——“境内区外进出口报关”模式（见图 2-13），是指区内中间商从境外上游企业（供货方）进口的商品再卖给境内区外下游企业（收货方），但是货物由境内区外下游企业直接从其所属口岸报关，而订单和资金却通过区内中间商实现。该模式大多见于跨国公司在国内不同省市设立大量工厂的情况下：

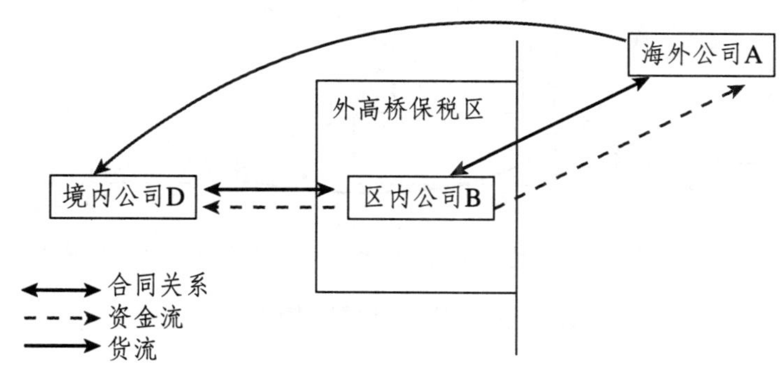

图 2-13 “境内区外进出口报关”模式图

目前，该模式的典型企业主要为区内的日本综合商社企业，如伊藤忠商事、三菱商事、住友商事等。

第 7 种模式——“境内区外进出口报关延伸”模式（见图 2-14），是在上述第 6 种模式的基础上进一步发展为境外的上游企业或下游企业是两个或两个以上。该模式大多见于货物在国际运输途中，其所有权已被多次转手的情况下：

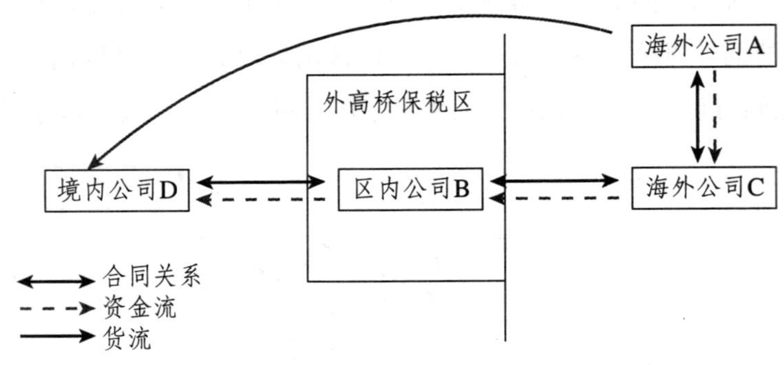

图 2-14 “境内区外进出口报关延伸”模式图

目前，该模式的典型企业亦为区内的日本综合商社企业，如伊藤忠商事、三菱商事、住友商事等。

第 8 种模式——“境外交易，原产地（或最终用户）在中国”模式（见图 2–15），是指国际贸易订单关系和资金关系在区内中间商和境外上下游企业之间发生，但撇开复杂的贸易关系，货物本身的原产地（或最终用户）是在中国：

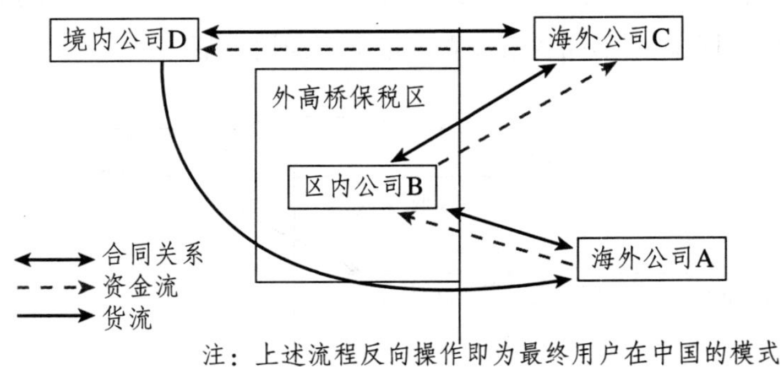

图 2-15 “境外交易”模式图

离岸服务正成为国际服务业的一种新的增长方式，与此相关的离岸贸易成为国际贸易的创新方式。贸易方式的创新使得传统国际贸易中心城市向现代国际贸易中心转变，并形成传统贸易和服务贸易、加工贸易和一般贸易、转口贸易和离岸贸易并驾齐驱的局面。但由于我国现行的外汇、税收政策制约，以及贸易便利化程度低等阻碍因素，上海主要仍以一般贸易和加工贸易为主，离岸贸易发展滞后。

为应对金融危机，跨国公司的全球布局发生了战略性变化，其地区总部、营运中心越来越多地发挥了生产资源调配、市场控制的作用，起到提高效率的服务性支撑功能。

但我国现有的外汇、税收政策及运作体制机制已经成为阻碍贸易转型、乃至上海国际贸易中心建设和城市竞争力的障碍和瓶颈。为了推动离岸贸易发展，需要发挥保税区境内关外的优势，先试先行，加大政策开放程度，接轨国际通行惯例。

第三章 外 资

第一节 2009年上海利用外资的趋势及特点

2009年是改革开放以来上海经济发展形势最复杂、困难最集中、挑战最严峻的一年，面对国际金融危机冲击和自身发展转型的双重考验，肩负筹办世博会紧迫繁重的任务。在党中央、国务院和上海市委市府领导下，上海市商务委员会坚决贯彻落实科学发展观，按照市委“四个确保”要求，积极、合理、有效地利用外资，坚持“立足当前，着眼长远，坚定信心，奋力推进”的方针，围绕“抓大项目，抓跨国公司总部经济，确保外资规模”的目标，重点在“政策、协调、服务、环境、招商和队伍建设”六个方面下工夫，努力克服国际金融危机造成的严重困难，促进了全市商务对外开放各项指标逐季回升，较好地完成了预期目标。

（一）总体走势是先抑后扬，逐月好转

从2009全年情况来看，一季度形势最为严峻，全市外资企业出现大面积亏损，这是多年来没有的；新批项目、合同利用外资项目全面下降，并有放大的可能。之后，采取政策措施的效应逐步显现，下半年各项指标逐月走好，四季度为全年最好，呈现实际利用外资单季同比增幅最大；新批项目数创单季度最高；合同利用外资连续6个月环比增长的良好势头。

（二）利用外资规模再创历史新高，明显好于全国平均水平

2009年上海实际利用外资连续第二年突破百亿美元，再创历史新高，达到105.38亿美元，同比增长4.5%，高出全国实际利用外资平均水平7.1个百分点，成为全国利用外资的新亮点：占全国当年总量900.3亿美元的11.7%。2009年合同利用外资连续第五年保持在130亿美元以上，达到133.01亿美元，同比有所下降，但降幅明显好于全国平均水平。全年新引进外资项目3090个，占全国23435个项目总数的13.2%，上海2009年利用外资取得新进展，得到了胡锦涛主席的肯定和赞扬。

截至2009年底，本市累计实际利用外资953.05亿美元。累计批准外商投资企业项

目 55591 个，吸收合同外资 1598.17 亿美元。

（三）现代服务业有序发展，服务经济为主的产业结构进一步优化

2009 年，上海市三、二、一产业实际利用外资占比分别超过 70%；合同利用外资占比超过 80%。以现代服务业为代表的第三产业实际利用外资继续保持增长，2009 年本市第三产业实际利用外资 76.16 亿美元，同比增长 11.4%，高出实际利用外资总体水平 6.9 个百分点，批发零售业和商务服务业都保持了强劲的发展势头，同比增幅均超过 30%。第三产业合同利用外资好于总体情况，全年合同利用外资 107.24 亿美元，同比下降 14.6%，扣除房地产业因素同比下降仅为 2.3%。以总部经济项目为主的科研、技术服务（主要是研发中心）、商务服务（主要是投资性公司）大幅增长，合同利用外资分别增长 72.1% 和 7.7%，批发零售业增长 5.9%，受世博的影响宾馆餐饮业合同利用外资增长 29.9%。制造业利用外资继续调整，全年实际利用外资 28.22 亿美元，合同利用外资 24.35 亿美元。

（四）外资项目质量和水平进一步提升

1．总部经济继续保持良好发展势头

2009 年度认定跨国公司地区总部 36 家，认定英特尔等 6 家投资性公司为国家级跨国公司地区总部，批准设立陶氏化学等投资性公司 13 家，研发中心 30 家。

截至 2009 年底，外商在沪累计设立地区总部 260 家，投资性公司 191 家，研发中心 304 家，在中国内地省市居首位。浦东新区 2009 年认定地区总部 17 家，占当年全市总量的 47.2%，地区总部历年累计 132 家，全市总量一半以上。与单一的制造业企业相比，外资总部经济机构功能更为完善，具有较强的服务贸易发展潜力。

2．服务外包示范区建设取得可喜进展

2009 年上海市商务委员会在闸北区市北高新技术服务园区举行授牌仪式，向新认定的闸北服务外包示范区、陆家嘴软件园、长宁多媒体产业园、天地软件园等 3 家专业园区以及 44 家服务外包重点企业授牌。2009 年上海服务外包快速发展。据商务部服务外包及软件出口信息管理系统显示，截至 2009 年底，上海全市服务外包企业登记数共 606 家，从业人员 10 万多人，通过各种认证数量 351 个，2009 年服务外包离岸合同金额 16.83 亿美元，同比增长 18.3%；离岸执行金额 10.36 亿美元，同比增长 20.3%。初步形成 1 个示范城市、5 个服务外包示范区、8 个服务外包专业园区、84 家服务外包重点企业共同发展的格局。

3．跨国公司投资大项目继续保持主导地位

2009 年全年新批 1000 万美元以上大项目 177 个，合同外资 107.92 亿美元，占全市合同外资的 81.1%，比去年提高了 1.7 个百分点。其中新批制造业 1000 万美元以上

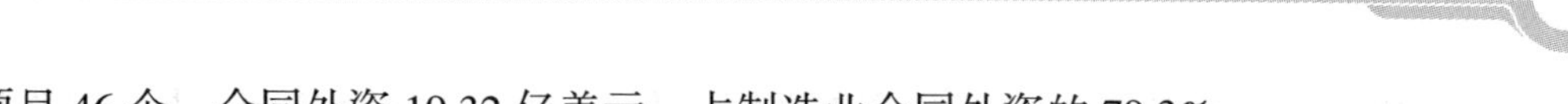

项目46个，合同外资19.32亿美元，占制造业合同外资的79.3%。

（五）利用外资领域进一步拓展

服务业领域利用外资亮点迭出：金融领域有高银保理（中国）发展有限公司和中银通支付商务有限公司。创投领域有星展资本创业投资企业、挚信创业投资企业、百仕通（中国）股权投资管理有限公司。物流领域有DHL空运服务（上海）有限公司、上海交运日红国际物流有限公司、上海远成实业有限公司、雅玛多（中国）运输有限公司。商业领域有摩根大通（中国）商贸有限公司、三菱汽车销售（中国）有限公司、上海高岛屋百货有限公司。研发领域有沙伯基础研发、阿海珐输配电技术等研发项目。其他服务业领域有上海波音航空飞行培训有限公司、东方明珠安舒茨文化体育发展（上海）有限公司、沪港机场管理（上海）有限公司和劳氏船级社、挪威船级社等船舶检验公司。

先进制造业新项目有日本三菱瓦斯投资的菱优工程塑料、上海电气阿海珐临港变压器、英国BP公司投资的上海碧科清洁能项目等。

（六）来自日本、欧盟等发达国家的投资者进一步看好上海

2009年日本来沪投资合同外资11.5亿美元，实到外资8.56亿美元，均列在沪投资各国地区前3位。欧盟国家来沪投资总体保持稳定，合同外资16.05亿美元，占比与2008年基本持平，其中荷兰合同外资4.52亿美元，同比增长72.9%；法国合同外资3.13亿美元，同比增长29.9%；这些项目尤其是制造业项目一般均为技术先进、设备先进、工艺先进，为提升上海外资总体质量水平发挥了引领作用。

（七）现有外资项目营运状况明显好于全国

根据刚刚公布的《2009上海外商投资环境白皮书》显示，上海的项目质量全国领先，企业运营率60.3%，高出全国平均水平约30个百分点。上海市外资企业的销售收入、纳税总额、盈利总额、人员就业比例等指标都明显好于全国平均水平。其中投资回报率超24%，高于全国2~3个百分点。上海财政收入总量7761亿元，其中地方财政投入2540.3亿元，同比增长7.7%以上；外资企业纳税占全年财政投入的1/3，同比增长30%以上；外资企业销售收入比上年仍保持一定增长势头。

（八）外资对社会的贡献进一步提高

根据统计快报数据显示，2009年外商投资企业的各项经济指标普遍回暖，对本市经济的贡献进一步提高。以可比口径计算，2009年外商投资企业实现销售（经营）收

入同比增长8%，就业增长1.6%，高出全市平均水平（0.5%）1个百分点，占全市就业的30%左右。2009年上海外商投资企业进出口总额1867.85亿美元，其中出口970.92亿美元，同比下降14.63%，降幅小于全市1.57个百分点，占全市68.42%，占比较去年提高了0.4个百分点；外商投资企业高新技术产品出口中，外商投资企业占94.2%，比去年提高了1个百分点。规模以上外商投资工业企业工业总产值14223.69亿元，同比增长4.2%（高出全市平均水平1个百分点），占全市的60%。外商投资企业完成固定资产投资617.9亿元，同比下降17.4%，占全市11.7%。外商投资企业消费品零售额503.44亿元，同比增长14.3%，占比为9.7%。

（九）外商投资出资方式以独资为主，所占比例进一步提高

2009年外商独资项目数2721个，占比88.1%，而中外合资、中外合作仅分别占比11.7%和0.2%。

从合同外资金额来分析，外商独资合同金额高达109.23亿美元，占比82.1%，而合资、合作分别仅占13.1%和2.8%。外商独资举办企业已成为当今外商投资的主要方式。

第二节 2009年上海外资主要工作

2009年全年的工作是以科学发展观为指导，按照上海市委“四个确保”要求，坚持“立足当前，着眼长远，坚定信心，奋力推进”的方针，围绕“抓大项目、保规模”的目标，重点在“政策、协调、服务、环境、招商和队伍建设”六个方面下工夫。

1．在政策方面

深入贯彻国家的有关经济政策，出台地方的服务外包、总部等政策，充分发挥吸收外资在产业结构升级、自主创新和区域协调发展等方面的积极作用。

深入贯彻国家的有关经济政策，做好政策的落实和见效，积极出台配套政策。利用多种途径积极推介政策，完成了2008年服务外包资金的申报。完成了鼓励跨国公司地区总部发展专项资金拨付的部分工作。推进审批改革，并进一步向区县下放审批权。将区县的外资鼓励类、允许类项目审批权扩大到投资总额1亿美元以下。

2．在协同合作方面

上海市商务委员会一直以与各相关部门协同合作，作为自身建设和工作的特点与重点。2009年进一步发挥外资工作领导办公室的作用，加强同相关单位的协同合作共同应对金融危机。如为方便外资企业衔接审批和登记手续，与上海市工商局一起制定

了《上海市企业登记注册并联审批实施办法（试行）》，并由上海市政府办公厅转发。召集上海市财政局、新闻出版局、安全生产监督管理局、食品药品监督管理局、交通港口管理局等有关部门，召开了各并联审批部门座谈会，对并联审批事项进行了梳理；配合审改办、政府公众信息网管理中心等有关部门进行“上海市网上行政审批平台”建设的前期调研。与上海市发展改革委就外商投资项目核准的分工进行了讨论与协商，共同下发了《关于本市外商投资项目核准和企业审批有关事项的通知》。

3．在服务方面

加大走访力度，服务前移，切实解决企业遇到的困难。建立长效的帮扶机制，进一步体现政府的“亲商、安商”。建立重点外商投资企业联系制度，由专人负责联系重点外商投资进出口企业、开展了“困难企业专题调研”，明确问题，帮助企业渡过难关。

4．在投资环境方面

进一步改善投资环境，提高投资便利化水平。进一步推进审批制度改革。较密集地下放了一批审批权，大力推动政府职能由重行政审批向重政策规划转变，进一步优化审批程序、减少审批事项。促进建立各部门齐抓共管外资新机制。上海市外资工作领导小组的运作也初步走上了轨道。同时，注重抓基础工作，练内功，用现代化的信息手段，提高便捷化。推出了市属项目的外资网上办事系统；推出了外资网上统计直报系统；推进联合年检工作。优化“上海外国投资促进平台”建设。加强开发区的建设，推进生态工业园区工作。

5．在外资队伍建设方面

招商人员和审批人员队伍建设并进，加强对区县人员的培训。

（1）举办外资工作人员培训班。外资工作领导小组办公室定期举办招商人员的培训班和招商引资报告会，分析上海招商引资形势，通报了在苏南、苏北、广东学习和了解的外资情况，邀请在上海招商引资工作突出的代表讲课，分享了各地的招商经验、沟通了相关信息，宣讲了影响投资人投资决定的知识和技巧，帮助招商人员开发本地区的投资促进规划，训练招商人员的潜在投资人服务观念，对潜在投资人的跟踪及衡量推广有效性。

（2）加强区县外资审批管理队伍建设。为了加强区县外资审批管理工作人员的队伍建设，外国投资管理处定期吸收区县外资审批管理工作人员短期挂职锻炼，进行在岗培训，通过工作实践提高业务水平和工作能力。

6．在招商方面

加强指导，促进招商。在2009年初发布了《目标外商目标企业》的系列招商手册，推进全市的针对性招商工作，推动招商由“坐商”向“行商”的转变。用好各类平台，拓展招商领域，招商形式。市区联动，开展特色招商。

第三节 总部经济

2009年全球经济体都深受国际金融危机的严峻考验，跨国公司也未能幸免，纷纷主动或被动地开始了新一轮的业务整合，谋划金融危机之后全球业务的布局和发展。上海市商务委员会抓住跨国公司业务整合的契机，积极开展工作，吸引跨国公司地区总部，保持了良好的发展势头。

一、2009年上海跨国公司地区总部发展基本情况

2009年上海共批准设立了陶氏化学（中国）投资有限公司、天合亚太有限公司、通用磨坊（中国）投资有限公司等13家投资性公司，认定36家跨国公司地区总部，其中特易购企业管理(上海)有限公司、可口可乐企业管理(上海)有限公司、圣戈班(中国)投资有限公司等7家为财富500强企业设立，还认定英特尔（中国）有限公司（简称英特尔）、百胜（中国）投资有限公司、统一企业（中国）投资有限公司等6家投资性公司为国家级跨国公司地区总部。截至2009年底，上海共批准设立了191家外资投资性公司，其中23家投资性公司被认定为国家级跨国公司地区总部；共认定了260家跨国公司地区总部，其中67家为财富500强企业设立。

从投资来源看，2009年认定的36家跨国公司地区总部中，主要以美国、欧洲企业为主，其中来自美国的15家，来自欧洲的13家，共占77%，其余分别为：日本3家中国香港特区2家、韩国1家、新加坡1家和巴西1家。

从区域分布看，仍以浦东新区为主，但有向其他区县加速扩散的趋势。浦东新区由于具有政策优势，一直是上海跨国公司地区总部最集中的区域，吸引跨国公司地区总部的数量历年均占到全市的50%以上，但随着《企业所得税法》、《上海市鼓励跨国公司设立地区总部的规定》等新政策法规的颁布实施，浦东新区的政策优势逐渐弱化，2009年认定的36家跨国公司地区总部中，有17家注册在浦东新区，占比仅为47%，首次跌入50%以内。其余19家分别注册在徐汇区(6家)、闵行区(4家)、嘉定区(4家)、黄浦区（2家）、静安区（1家）、闸北区（1家）和奉贤区（1家），区域分布呈现出加速向全市尤其是郊区扩散的趋势。

从功能提升看，跨国公司地区总部规模不断扩大、管理区域不断扩大。随着上海投资环境、运营环境的不断优化，在上海的跨国公司地区总部的发展也渐入佳境。一是跨国公司地区总部的规模不断扩大，截至2009年底，在上海注册的跨国公司地区总

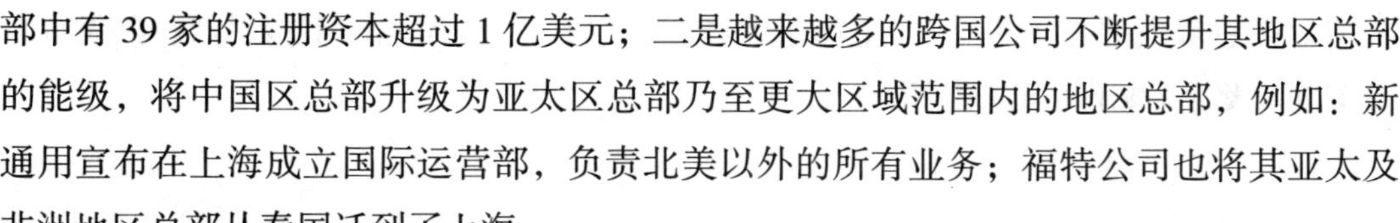

部中有 39 家的注册资本超过 1 亿美元；二是越来越多的跨国公司不断提升其地区总部的能级，将中国区总部升级为亚太区总部乃至更大区域范围内的地区总部，例如：新通用宣布在上海成立国际运营部，负责北美以外的所有业务；福特公司也将其亚太及非洲地区总部从泰国迁到了上海。

二、2009 年推进上海跨国公司地区总部工作的主要举措

1．加强服务

面对金融危机的影响，上海市商务委员会主动上门帮助跨国公司地区总部解决遇到的困难和问题。2009 年 2 月上海市商务委员会组团赴德国、法国和美国拜访了 15 家跨国公司总部（其中 12 家为 500 强企业），了解这些公司在国际金融危机的冲击下，对中国和上海投资战略的调整意图，受到了跨国公司的欢迎和赞赏。

上海市商务委员会还走访了多家在沪跨国公司地区总部，听取这些公司因金融危机影响而在经营中遇到的困难和问题，并主动协调相关部门帮助企业解决。例如，受金融危机影响和中国业务整合的需要，英特尔于 2009 年年初宣布关闭外高桥封装测试基地，将外高桥工厂的业务整合至成都工厂。为了将英特尔关闭外高桥工厂的影响降到最低，并帮助英特尔公司做好关闭工厂各项后续工作，上海市商务委员会一方面做好与英特尔的沟通工作，督促、协助英特尔公司做好上海外高桥工厂员工的安置工作，维护社会的稳定；另一方面赴美拜访英特尔总部，了解英特尔的善后计划，宣传上海帮助企业共渡难关的政策，坚定英特尔将其地区总部、研发中心等高端职能继续留在上海的信心和决心。

2．完善政策

2009 年一季度，上海市商务委员会与上海市财政局共同制定了《上海市鼓励跨国公司地区总部发展专项资金使用和管理试行办法》，对跨国公司地区总部给予资助与奖励的申请程序、申请材料、拨付办法等问题进行了明确规定。《上海市鼓励跨国公司地区总部发展专项资金使用和管理试行办法》的出台，标志着自 2008 年初开始的跨国公司地区总部政策的修订工作初步完成。

3．落实政策

为使上海市政府对跨国公司地区总部的优惠政策落到实处，上海市商务委员会加大跨国公司地区总部政策宣传力度，通过举办跨国公司地区总部颁证仪式、与外资企业协会共同举办跨国公司地区总部政策说明早餐会等多种形式宣传政策，效果显著。截至 2009 年底，上海市商务委员会已受理了 16 家跨国公司地区总部申请“鼓励跨国

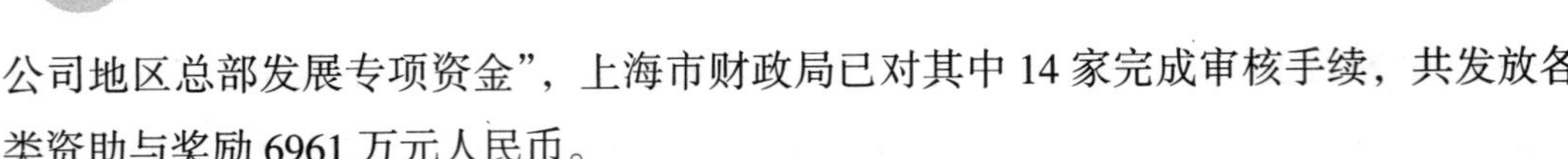

公司地区总部发展专项资金”，上海市财政局已对其中14家完成审核手续，共发放各类资助与奖励6961万元人民币。

三、2009年上海推进跨国公司地区总部发展面临的主要挑战

1．税务新政策使跨国公司业务整合面临挑战

2009年以来，财政部和税务总局出台了一系列税收新政策，如《关于企业重组业务企业所得税处理问题的通知》（财税[2009]59号）和《关于部分行业广告费和业务宣传费税前扣除政策的通知》（财税[2009]72号），使跨国公司利用地区总部平台进行业务整合面临新的挑战。

跨国公司在上海设立投资性公司地区总部后，往往会利用投资性公司的平台，通过股权转让的方式将其母公司在中国所投资的企业整合至投资性公司旗下，成为投资性公司的子公司，使跨国公司的中国业务在公司治理架构上得到优化。而根据《关于企业重组业务企业所得税处理问题的通知》（财税[2009]59号）的要求，只有税务局认定这种通过股权转让方式进行的企业内部重组业务符合文件规定的特殊重组的要求，该重组业务才能适用特殊性税务处理，否则企业就需要为这种以企业内部重组为目的的股权转让缴纳企业所得税，从而大大增加了跨国公司进行业务整合的成本。

2．上海吸引跨国公司地区总部面临着兄弟省市的竞争

2009年6月，北京市出台了《鼓励跨国公司在京设立地区总部的若干规定》及其《实施办法》，在上海政策的基础上“更上一层楼”。2009年北京市吸引地区总部势头非常好，批准设立了13家投资性公司，与上海持平。受北京市出台的地区总部政策激励，三菱重工空调系统（上海）有限公司、爱普生（中国）有限公司上海分公司还计划将上海的业务整合到北京的地区总部中去。同时，上海周边省市也加强了吸引跨国公司地区总部的工作力度，特别是江苏省。2009年5月，已在上海发展了6年之久的恩斯克投资有限公司从上海迁往了江苏昆山，归因于昆山为恩斯克提供一块价格比上海低得多的建造总部和研发大楼的土地。因此，如何营造更加适宜跨国公司地区总部发展的“生态”环境，创新上海发展总部经济独特的比较优势，形成与兄弟省市的错位竞争，将是上海市吸引跨国公司地区总部工作的新挑战。

四、2010年上海推进跨国公司地区总部的工作思路

2010年推进跨国公司地区总部工作既面临挑战，也面临着机遇。一是全球国际直

接投资流向变化带来的新机遇。国际金融危机改变了跨国公司对外直接投资的区域性格局，发展中经济体占全球外资流入量的比重大幅上升。联合国贸发组织最近发布的《2009-2011 年全球投资展望调查报告》将中国列于全球大型跨国公司未来对外投资最受青睐的 5 个国家之首。国际直接投资流向的变化为上海进一步吸引跨国公司设立地区总部带来了新机遇。二是跨国公司全球价值链重构和业务整合的新机遇。全球金融危机爆发后，跨国公司为应对金融危机开始了新一轮的价值链重构和业务整合，中国经济的表现和巨大的市场容量使跨国公司的重心不断向中国倾斜，这为上海进一步吸引跨国公司地区总部入驻创造了机会。三是上海“四个中心”建设带来的新机遇。“四个中心”建设的不断推进，必将进一步优化上海吸引跨国公司地区总部的投资环境，吸引更多跨国公司在上海设立地区总部。

上海市商务委员会将抓住新机遇，积极采取措施，进一步推进上海跨国公司总部经济的发展。一是鼓励跨国公司利用地区总部的平台进行业务整合。上海市商务委员会将加强与上海市政府相关部门和中央在沪单位的沟通与合作，为跨国公司地区总部的运营创造更宽松、更便利的环境，以促进跨国公司将其销售结算、研发、资金管理、共享服务、物流、投资经营决策等高端功能不断向上海集中。二是鼓励跨国公司地区总部的转型升级。随着跨国公司中国业务的不断发展和上海投资环境的不断完善，上海市商务委员会将鼓励、引导管理性公司地区总部转型为投资性公司地区总部，投资性公司升级为国家级跨国公司地区总部，中国区总部升级为亚太区总部。三是推动跨国公司的资本本地化。上海市商务委员会将积极探索跨国公司在华业务整体在 A 股市场上市，在跨国公司经营本地化、人才本地化的同时，推动跨国公司的资本本地化。四是积极向国家相关部委反映跨国公司地区总部运行中遇到的税收、外汇等方面的问题和困难，为跨国公司地区总部发展创造良好环境。

案例 1：以促转型为契机加快公司发展

——陶氏化学（中国）有限公司

自 2008 年下半年开始，席卷全球的金融危机给全球化学制造业带来了巨大的影响。随着汽车及建筑等市场需求的急速下滑，化学行业的产量和产值明显下降，化学品价格持续走低。这也是化学行业几十年从未遇到过的最为严峻的挑战，这一挑战不但在短期内严重地影响了化学行业的运行，也对行业的长期发展产生深远的影响。

作为全美最大以及全球最主要的化学品制造商，陶氏化学（中国）有限公司（陶氏化学公司）在2008–09年度也经历了历史上最为困难的时期之一。2008年第四季度，陶氏化学公司净亏损15.5亿美元，营业收入下滑23%，销售量也下滑了17%，几乎所有业务部门和各地区市场的需求均出现萎缩。针对困难局面，陶氏化学公司在2009年采取了更加严格的财务纪律，实施产品组合转型，大力拓展和提升包括中国在内的新兴市场的占有率，加快“转型战略”的实施，加速与美国罗门哈斯公司（简称罗门哈斯）整合的进度，从而使得陶氏化学公司在增加研发投资的同时，能够在整个2009年（尤其是第四季度）实现了连续的收入增长、销量和权益投资收益的增长和结构性成本的降低，同时也使得陶氏化学公司在经济复苏时占有先机，为构建“明日陶氏”迈出决定性的一步。

一、中国的成功进一步确立了大中华区的中心地位

新兴市场是陶氏化学公司在2009年第四季度取得优异成绩的主要原因之一，陶氏化学公司在这些地区的季度销量实现了非常令人瞩目的33%的增长。中国堪称亮点中的亮点，尽管2009年公司全球的销售额较上一年出现了一定幅度的下滑，但大中华区却实现了历史性突破，销售额取得了37亿美元的佳绩，比上一年度增长了近12%，大中华区已发展成为陶氏化学公司的全球第二大销售市场。随着陶氏化学公司与罗门哈斯的整合，包括中国在内的亚太区在陶氏化学公司全球业务版图上的重要意义愈发凸显。而在像中国这样的新兴市场取得不断的增长和成功，对于推动陶氏化学公司转型成为一家以特种化学品和高新材料为主导的利润增长型企业也变得十分的关键。

2009年，陶氏化学公司在中国不但取得了销售上的突破，更重要的是通过不断增加对大中华地区的投资，发展领先的创新能力，培养世界级本土人才，开发差异化产品组合，增强支持客户业务发展的能力等措施，进一步确立了中国在陶氏亚太区业务中的中心地位以及在全球业务中的战略性地位。

2009年，位于上海张江高科技园区的上海陶氏中心建成并投入使用。建成后的上海陶氏中心总建筑面积超过10万平米，中心包括一座世界级规模的全球研发中心、陶氏化学公司亚太区及大中华区总部及全球信息技术支持中心。上海陶氏中心内的研发中心是陶氏化学公司在美国领土以外的规模最大、技术水平最高的研发机构。中心拥有89间实验室和1间重型实验室，研发人员超过500名，中心承担陶氏化学公司全球前沿性的基础研发及应用开发工作，领域涵盖能源、建筑、汽车、健康和个人保健等多个与人类发展和进步密切相关的重要领域。上海陶氏中心也是一座充分体现创新科技和理念的绿色环保建筑。在上海陶氏中心项目建设过程中，上海市商务委员会、张

江集团等机构或部门给予陶氏化学公司以极大的支持和帮助。虽然陶氏化学公司遇到金融危机所带来的种种困难，但陶氏化学公司非但没有停止项目的建设，而且还增加了投资，以实际行动积极响应中国政府以及上海市政府“共对危机，共度时艰”的号召。

作为在上海乃至中国首屈一指的研发机构，上海陶氏中心的建成不但进一步增强了陶氏化学公司的全球创新能力，也大力地支持了陶氏化学公司在中国及亚太地区业务长期、持续和健康的发展。同时，上海陶氏中心的建成也推动和方便了陶氏化学和沪上企业及同济大学等高等学府在科研、产业升级、可持续发展等领域开展进一步的合作，对于完善张江园区及上海地区的科技基础设施和提高相关产业的创新能力起到了一定的作用。

上海陶氏中心的建成标志着陶氏化学公司在华发展新的里程碑，借此也正式确立了上海在陶氏亚太区业务中的中心地位。鉴于上海在陶氏业务中的战略地位以及其良好的商务和投资环境，陶氏化学公司也于同年将投资性公司的注册地迁至上海，并获得“跨国公司地区总部”的认定。

在其他投资方面，2009 年 6 月，一座新的环氧丙烷基醇醚生产厂在张家港投入运营；2009 年 3 月，陶氏化学公司在武汉建立了第一家环氧产品工厂，以满足市场对复合材料、风能和基础设施不断增长的需求。另外，陶氏化学公司与神华集团有限公司计划合作的在陕西省榆林市建设一个世界级规模的“一体化煤化工项目”进展也很顺利，目前双方正在积极准备该项目的各方面支持性文件，并计划在 2010 年提交国家有关部门进行审批。

2009 年，陶氏化学公司完成了对罗门哈斯的收购，这为陶氏化学公司战略转型奠定了坚实的基础。陶氏化学公司与罗门哈斯在本地的整合和重组进展顺利，这对于公司开发差异化产品组合，实施产品组合转型，增强支持本地客户业务发展的能力等方面起到了重要的作用。而通过将罗门哈斯研发中心出售给陶氏化学公司属下合资企业道康宁公司，也帮助上海引进了在硅行业领先的世界级企业。道康宁公司将在张江开展太阳能研发，这对提高上海在新能源方面的创新能力将起到很重要的推动作用。

二、积极参与社会建设，谋求共同发展

除了参与当地经济建设外，陶氏化学公司在 2009 年一如既往地继续关心和支持本地的社会建设。为支持 2010 上海世博会办成一届成功精彩难忘的世博会，陶氏化学公司为美国国家馆提供了赞助，并成为其化工和材料科学类别的独家赞助商，为美国政府顺利参展 2010 上海世博会提供了及时和有力的支持。与此同时，陶氏化学公司为世博会的多个场馆提供了可持续的创新解决方案，为低碳世博会作出了重要的贡献。作

为最早为上海世博会提供志愿者支持的外资企业，陶氏化学公司的世博志愿项目将持续至2010年10月，服务规模也将不断扩大。

2009年，全年陶氏化学公司近400个员工志愿者参与了社会公益事业，工时近4000个小时。特别值得一提的是，陶氏化学公司携手国际青年成就组织（Junior Achievement）推出“我们的城市”课程，将可持续发展的理念引入小学课堂。

凭借其以人为本的企业文化、履行企业社会责任等方面的突出表现，陶氏化学公司获得社会上广泛的认同，获得包括由国际企业研究基金会主办评选的“中国最佳雇主”奖，由《第一财经日报》发起评选的“中国企业社会责任榜杰出贡献奖”，新华网发起评选的“十佳节能减排标志企业”等诸多殊荣。

三、继续开拓，不断进取，开创2010新局面

2010年伊始，陶氏化学公司宣布了亚太及大中华区新的领导架构，以进一步推动陶氏在这一关键地区的业务发展。在新的一年里，公司将围绕“能力建设”这一战略重点，招募并培养大量本地人才，大力发展业务和团队，继续构建全球领先的研发实力，扩大和提升科研合作范围及水平；对下游高附加值产品组合进行大规模资产投资；继续推进业务的持续增长；积极参与大型合资项目，以促进战略和财务目标的有效实现。与此同时，陶氏化学公司将继续做好企业公民，为中国及上海的社会建设服务。

案例2：加大投入建设一流的药物研发总部

——诺华（中国）生物医学研究有限公司

诺华（中国）生物医学研究有限公司（简称诺华生物）在2009年取得了显著的成绩，时值诺华生物公司总部决定追加投资10亿美金之际，诺华生物公司将继续为成为中国最大的药物研发机构而努力，并以行动体现“承诺中华”的理念，支持中国经济发展、医疗卫生体制改革及其他国家重大方针政策的实施，致力于提高中国人民的健康水平和生活质量。

位于上海浦东新区张江高科技园区内的研发中心成立于2006年，它是诺华生物医学研中心全球10个研发中心之一。在短短的3年内，中心已有近200名员工，其中的70%以上是拥有硕士、博士和博士后学位的科研人员，他们中有约25%为海外学子。

中心致力于新药的研究与开发，着力于中国高发病率疾病如肝癌和胃癌等的研究。研究手段包括分析化学、药物化学、生物标记、活体药理学、蛋白表达等。

一、2009 年回顾

2009 年是诺华生物十分重要的一年，无论是在科研活动还是在投资方面，都有重大成果和增长，公司的员工人数与研发投入，较 2008 年分别增长了 73%与 63%；诺华生物继续与本土生物科技公司的合作；在癌症研究领域，与上海多家著名学院建立了合作关系。

科研领域的重要成果：与复旦大学和长海医院共同启动一项在癌症领域的合作项目；建立了肿瘤的研究新模型；在实验胚胎学领域，启动了一项研究课题；完成了对 SFDA 的 4 期培训；为 2 家中国大学附属医院提供关于临床试验规范化的培训。

其他领域的重要成绩：一是上海市政府与诺华生物在最近签署了关于在上海进一步加大研发投资的战略合作备忘录，在此备忘录的框架下，上海市政府将与诺华生物多边合作，努力提高生物医药领域的快速发展；诺华集团亦宣布追加投资 10 亿美元，旨在中国建立最大的研发中心。二是诺华生物研究中心已开始了对现有的实验室大楼的改建和翻新工程，实验室大楼自 2006 年公司成立，此次的改建工程，将进一步完善实验大楼的设施和环境，完成后，将可容纳约 160 名科研人员。此外，诺华生物在张江园区内的软件园，另租用了两层楼的办公区域，有约 100 位员工在此办公。公司将继续成长，随之而来的，是相应的人员增长，因此公司也已经着手对另外的办公区域的装修工程。三是为满足公司在中国长期发展的需要，研发中心的园区项目也正在加速进行中。该项目由一支富有经验的项目团队负责，而楼群和景观设计也正交由世界著名的建筑师团队负责。

二、2010 年的发展计划

诺华生物将继续通过投资来支持中国政府“保增长、保稳定、保民生”的发展战略。上海将在 2012 年前建成全国范围内生物医药领域中重要的研发中心，诺华生物非常荣幸地能为上海实现这一目标而尽一份力量。2010 年，诺华生物的目标将是：继续推动科学进步、新药研发，同时吸引更多的本地和国际人才。诺华生物在研发上的进一步投资，将促进对中国以及其他国家患者的创新治疗手段的开发，这也将得益于中国飞速发展的优异的科学技术。

对本地的贡献包括五个方面：

（1）追加投资将为本地带来更多的财政收入，同时将直接或间接地带动本地行业的成长。

（2）将继续在中国的大学中招募具有高学历的科研人员：诺华生物人员也将有同步增长。诺华生物将在 2010 年，与复旦大学和北京大学继续合作博士后和暑期实习生培训项目，在未来的五年内，预计将会有超过 50 名学生加入到这一项目中。

（3）将继续并扩大对中国临床试验从业人员的培训课程。

（4）继续并增加学术研讨会活动，为本地和国际学术社区提供更多的交流平台。

（5）继续引进多项先进科技，包括高流量筛选、生物标记物表达等，以此增进诺华与其他公司在国际先进技术应用和药物开发领域内的交流，带动本地相关领域力量。

第四章　对外经济合作

第一节　2009 年上海对外经济合作发展情况

一、对外投资总量、结构和行业特征

1．对外直接投资总额和中方投资额呈现双双快速增长态势

2009 年全年，上海市共核准对外直接投资项目 249 个，其中新设项目 144 个，增资项目 27 个，并购项目 22 个，股权划转、投资主体和经营范围变更等项目 28 个，撤销项目 3 个，新设代表处 25 家。2009 年 1–12 月，上海市企业对外直接投资总额为 153643.76 万美元，同比增长 117%；其中，中方投资额 148537.23 万美元，同比增长 143%。

截至 2009 年 12 月，上海累计核准新设对外投资项目 828 个，累计总投资 541190 万美元。其中，累计中方投资额 492606 万美元。对外投资的国家与地区达到 101 个。

2．非公企业继续保持对外直接投资生力军

投资主体方面，私营企业继续保持全市对外投资主体地位。私营企业为 139 家，占境内投资主体构成 56%；外资企业为 62 家，占比 25%；国有和集体企业为 44 家，占比 19%。

3．亚洲继续保持对外直接投资热点地区

2009 年全年，上海市企业对亚洲地区的投资总量为 73159 万美元，占对外投资总额的 48%；对开曼群岛等避税地投资总量为 47997 万美元，占比 31%；对北美洲的投资总量为 21727 万美元，占比 14%；其他地区为 10780 万美元，占比 7%（见图 4–1）。

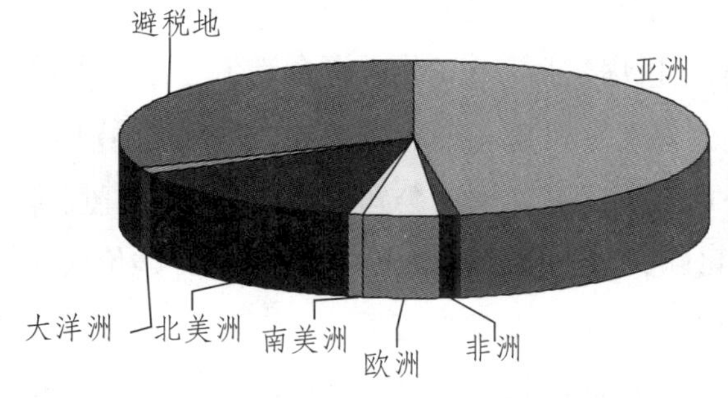

图 4-1　2009 年上海市对外直接投资地区结构

4．制造业和商务服务业对外投资发展迅猛

2009年全年，全市企业对外投资制造业60329万美元，占比39%；商务服务业34148万美元，占比22%；采矿业12472万美元，占比8%；批发和零售业12819万美元，占比8%；交通运输仓储业12285万美元，占比8%；房地产业10530万美元，占比7%；其他行业11061万美元，占比7%。

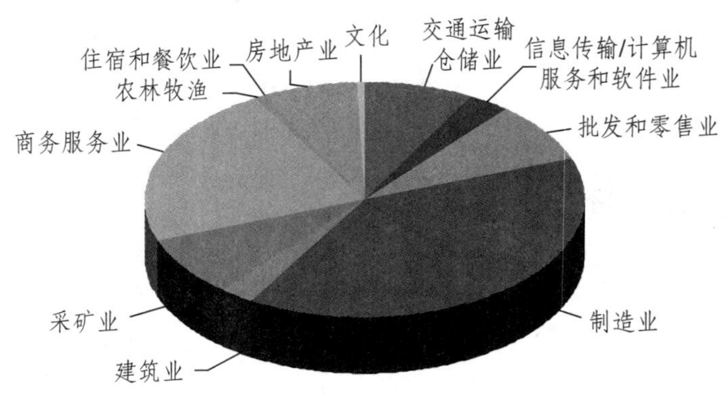

图4-2　2009年上海市对外投资行业结构

二、海外投资方式变动趋势

1．大项目不断增多，并购类项目一枝独秀

2009年全年，上海市对外直接投资超过1000万美元的重点项目共有20个，投资总额108187.5万美元，占上海市投资总额的70%。上海市企业参股及并购境外企业项目日益增加，已成为全市对外直接投资的主要方式，1–12月上海市对外直接投资并购类项目22个，投资总额为6.94亿美元，占全市投资总额的45%。

与此同时，随着国际金融危机影响的日益扩散，境外企业价值缩水，资金周转困难，为国内企业走出国门参与并购扩张，低成本地获得新的市场提供了最佳的机遇，如上海工字机械制造有限公司并购了其境外合作伙伴S/R Industries, Inc公司。最初外方报价1000万美元，金融危机爆发后，S/R公司资金断流、经营困难，现双方达成的收购价仅为140万美元，上海工字机械制造有限公司收购该公司100%的股权。2007年上海电气（集团）总公司与美国高斯国际公司初步洽谈并购事宜时，外方原报价为4亿美元，后因金融危机影响，最终该项目以1.6亿美元的并购价成交。

2．对外直接投资独资化趋势日益明显

一般来说，企业境外投资在起步阶段为降低经营风险，大多会采用与东道国企业合资经营的投资方式。近年来，随着对境外投资环境和当地市场的逐步熟悉，以及东

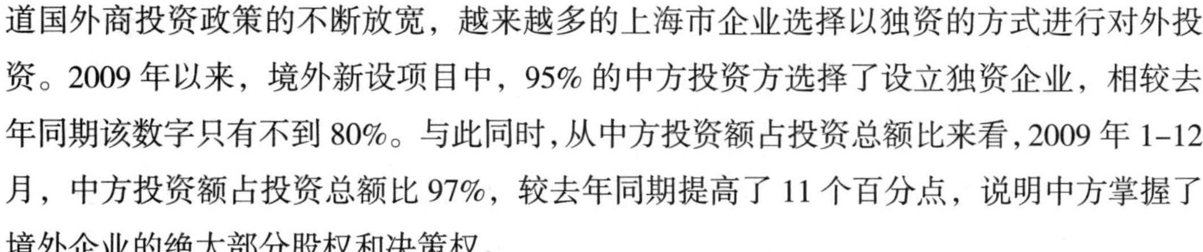

道国外商投资政策的不断放宽，越来越多的上海市企业选择以独资的方式进行对外投资。2009年以来，境外新设项目中，95%的中方投资方选择了设立独资企业，相较去年同期该数字只有不到80%。与此同时，从中方投资额占投资总额比来看，2009年1–12月，中方投资额占投资总额比97%，较去年同期提高了11个百分点，说明中方掌握了境外企业的绝大部分股权和决策权。

三、对外工程承包及劳务合作

1．新签合同额和完成营业额继续保持两位数的快速增长

2009年1–12月，新签对外承包工程和劳务合作项目合同额达到124亿美元，同比增长12.2%；完成营业额73.4亿美元，同比增长31.8%；其中，新签对外承包工程项目合同额为119.4亿美元，同比增长14.1%，完成营业额66.6亿美元，同比增长35.7%。

2．外派劳务人数下降，但结构层次有所提高

2009年全年，因受全球金融危机影响，境外雇主对劳务人员需求有所下降，上海与全国一样，劳务外派人数有所下降。全市对外经济合作企业派出劳务人员（含境外就业）13926人次，同比降低13.7%，期末在外人数（含境外就业）26250人，同比降低4.3%，但是人员结构层次有了一定的提高，在外派劳务人员中，海员、空乘人员、厨师等具有专门技术的人员比例提高了2个百分点。

3．对外承包工程项目规模不断扩大

1–12月，上海市新签对外承包工程合同金额在5000万美元以上的大中型项目36个，这些项目的新签合同额达98.5亿美元，占全市新签合同总额的82.5%，其中合同额在1亿至10亿美元的项目有11个，10亿至20亿美元的承包工程项目有2个，超20亿美元的境外承包工程项目有1个。

4．上海优势产业跨国承包呈现新亮点

上海对外承包工程项目89.1%分布在科技含量较高的制造及加工业、电力工业、交通运输建设、电子通信等优势产业领域。其中，电力工业项目合同额达45.4亿美元、制造及加工业项目合同额达39.18亿美元，分别占本市对外承包工程总量的38%和32.8%。值得一提的是，上海市交通运输建设领域和电子通信领域境外承包工程快速发展，电子通信企业新签对外承包工程项目10.6亿美元，同比增长152%；交通运输建设企业新签对外承包工程项目11.1亿美元，同比增长200%，电站、电子通信、地铁、隧道、高速公路、桥梁、港口建设和航道疏浚等领域已成为上海企业走出去的新亮点，充分反映了上海对外工程承包项目结构不断优化，以往土建工程为主的对外承包工程

结构在近几年中得到了根本性的改变。同时也表明上海有比较优势、产业优势的行业“走出去”的竞争实力大幅提升。

5．继续巩固国际工程的传统市场地位

2009年1–12月上海市企业继续巩固传统的对外工程承包市场亚洲和非洲的份额，在亚洲新签境外工程项目合同额达74.9亿美元，占业务总额的62.8%；在非洲地区新签境外工程项目合同额达29.1亿美元，占业务总额的24.4%；同时，积极拓展准入壁垒顽固的欧美发达国家市场和其他新兴市场，初战告捷，在欧洲地区新签境外工程项目合同额达5.7亿美元，占业务总额的4.8%；在美洲地区新签境外工程项目合同额达7.6亿美元，占业务总额的6.4%；在大洋洲地区新签境外工程项目合同额达1.8亿美元，占业务总额的1.6%。

四、对外援助工作取得新的进展

2009年上海市对外援助工作取得新的进展。1–12月，上海市共计完成对外援助物资项目32个，合同金额2.94亿元，同比增长3倍；完成援助成套项目13个，金额34.59亿元，其中，利用优贷项目8个，金额30.05亿元，占援外成套项目的86%，成为对外援助工作的新增长点；完成援外培训班9个，培训共计约331名官员和技术人员；此外，报经商务部备案认定的援外专家共有30人。

第二节　2009年上海对外经济合作重点工作

1．保增长抓关键，针对大中型项目和队伍建设主动作为

在投资方面，2009年以来，上海市商务委员会针对金融危机后跨国并购机会增多的背景，把鼓励跨国并购作为年度重点工作，提出“要实体经济，不沾虚拟经济；要营销网络，不染房产泡沫；要知名品牌，不搞假冒侵权”的指导思想，分别召开民营企业跨国并购座谈会和国有企业跨国并购座谈会，深入了解企业需求。针对企业的困惑和需求，举办并购专题交流会，邀请会计师事务所和律师事务所为企业提供辅导。同时，加大了对跨境并购重点企业和项目的跟踪、协调和服务工作。

在承包工程方面，上海市商务委员会组织了对外承包企业金融危机受影响情况的问卷调查，从企业境外项目是否受到影响、受影响项目数量、金额、原因、企业已采取的措施和希望政府给予的帮助等多个方面入手设计问卷，在掌握一手资料的情况下

写出了较高水准的调研报告，为帮助企业摆脱困境提供决策参考。针对企业在调查问卷和调研中反映的种种困难，上海市商务委员会根据“抓重点、攻难点、突破关键点”的工作思路，举办银企合作研讨会、“走出去”政策培训班、讲座、交流会共 8 次，积极主动为银企合作牵线搭桥，分别邀请口行、中国银行、中国工商银行、中国出口信用保险公司等相关金融机构与企业开展深入交流，帮助企业从中获得国家最新的金融支持政策信息，为解决危机下融资难的问题提供了路径。此外，为应对外需市场萎缩、外向型经济受到严重冲击的严峻形势，党中央、国务院果断决策，推出保持外经贸稳定增长的六条政策措施，其中一条是安排专项买方信贷和信保额度，支持中国企业承包境外项目。上海市商务委员会积极组织上海工程承包企业、银行、中国出口信用保险公司开展大中型境外项目专项信贷、信保政策规定和操作程序的宣讲和培训，及时撮合已签约或正在投议标的大中型工程承包项目与银企一一配对，落实专人指导和督促企业开展项目融资申报工作，多次赴京向商务部、中国进出口银行、中国出口信用保险公司汇报工作情况和澄清项目问题，争取上海市项目更多、更早地列入国家境外项目专项融资支持清单，并对申报遇到困难的企业提供帮助。上海申报工作取得良好效果，为确保 2009 年和 2010 年境外工程承包合同额和营业额的增长奠定了扎实的基础。

在援外方面，针对国家援外事业的发展趋势，上海市商务委员会重点加大援外政策的宣讲力度，分别联合外经协会和外贸协会，加强对外贸企业及对外承包工程和设计企业的政策宣讲力度，引导进入援外队伍，参与国家援外事业，推动上海市企业通过援外“走出去”开拓国际市场。截至 2009 年底，已有 9 家企业和单位在参加宣讲会后，新提出申请援外资质，其中 3 家已获批准，1 家事业单位已在商务部备案。

2．促改革找突破，扫清束缚企业“走出去”的政策障碍

在投资方面，自 5 月 1 日商务部新的《境外投资管理办法》颁布实施以来，上海市商务委员会在吃透文件精神的同时，多次与上海市企业和相关部门协调沟通，根据上海市的实际情况拟定了《关于境外投资核准工作的实施细则（试行）》。新的《实施细则》出台后，项目核准手续大大简化，在资料齐全情况下，3 个工作日即可完成核准，效率大大提高，政策效应得以体现，提高了企业对外直接投资的积极性。2009 年 5–12 月，共核准新设与并购项目 140 个，项目数与前年同期相比增长 130%，由此可见政策效应显著。

在承包工程方面，商务部《对外承包工程资格管理办法》于 11 月 1 日正式实施。为更好的贯彻并落实资格管理办法，更符合上海的实际情况，借助此次制度改革的良机，上海市商务委员会制定了《上海市对外承包工程资格管理实施细则（试行）》。在原有基础上积极寻求制度突破，从多个方面扫清了束缚企业“走出去”的障碍并从源头上

加强管理。

在对外劳务方面，针对商务部即将出台《对外劳务合作管理条例》，市商务委积极组织行业协会和相关企业认真研究和讨论《条例》草案，提出针对项目审查时间、对日研修生派遣、劳务人员依法维权等18条规定的具体修改意见，为国家政策法规发挥更大的规范指导作用，提出切实有效的建议。同时，商务部和国务院法制办还专门派调研组来上海听取意见和建议。另外，上海的2名劳务行业专家参与了《条例》集中修改6人小组的工作，为国务院出台《条例》作出了重要贡献。

3．争资金助发展，充分运用财政扶持政策帮助企业渡过难关

积极帮助企业申报国家各类“走出去”扶持政策。2009年以来，为进一步鼓励支持上海市企业实施“走出去”战略，上海市商务委员会主动积极帮助企业申报国家2008年度对外经济技术合作专项资金，经过上海市商务委员会多次召开政策宣讲会，反复帮助企业修改申报材料以确保符合相关要求，最后共计向商务部上报17家企业的37个项目。同时，商务部将纺织企业“走出去”专项资金的决定权下放给各省市后，上海市商务委员会针对上海市实际情况,制定了相关的申报和管理办法。经过多方努力，2009年有2家重点企业已获得纺织企业“走出去”专项资金补贴。此外，在获悉商务部将要出台境外营销网络扶持政策信息后，上海市商务委员会提前两个多月制订好了上海市有关的《实施办法》，并报商务部备案同意，这样在商务部正式文件一下达后，马上组织培训宣讲，由于工作做得早，企业准备时间充分，上海共有49家外经企业顺利通过项目评审。

4．保民生促和谐，清理整顿外派劳务市场秩序和构筑安全保障体系

2009年，为贯彻落实商务部等七部委联合开展清理整顿外派劳务市场秩序专项行动的要求，上海市成立了清理整顿专项行动领导小组，办公室设在上海市商务委员会外经处。为此，上海市商务委员会牵头在全市范围内开展清理整顿外派劳务市场秩序专项行动，累计排查各类外派劳务相关企业和机构2384家，依法查处无证无照经营企业12家，清理有经营资格外派企业2家，破获涉及外派劳务诈骗案件4起，对37家不够规范经营的企业提出限期整改意见。同时，借清理整顿的东风下大力气，解决各类外派劳务纠纷案件共30起，涉及493名劳务人员，追讨了上述劳工各类被拖欠劳务工资福利款1661.9万元，为落实中央制定的“保增长、保稳定、保民生”的大政方针作出了贡献。中国对外工程承包商会在全国信访上访文件通报中以“事事有回音，件件有着落”充分肯定了上海市处置解决对外劳务纠纷的工作成绩，成为通报表扬的唯一省市，维护了一方稳定。

此外，在全国清理整顿外派劳务市场秩序专项行动中，建立健全了由12个政府机

关部门和18个区县政府及商务主管部门、外派劳务救援中心、各外派劳务企业、涉及工程项下派出劳务人员企业为成员单位的外派劳务应急处置机制，进一步确保妥善处置各类外派劳务纠纷，切实维护劳务人员和外经企业的合法权益，为确保上海社会和谐、平安迎接世博作出了贡献。

5．维稳定化危机，为企业境外经营和生产营造安全环境

（1）及时全面布控上海在海外人员的甲流防控工作。2009年年初，在墨西哥等地发生甲型H1N1流感疫情并迅速蔓延后，上海市商务委员会第一时间采取行动，全面开展本市在境外的对外投资企业人员、外派劳务人员、在外工程项目中方人员、对外援助项目人员共3万多人的流感感染情况排查工作和现有海外人员防控教育措施的告知工作，检查措施落实情况，每天专报坚持达一个月之久，确保外派人员的生命安全。

（2）及时化解多起境外突发事件。2009年，由于金融危机的爆发，境外投资项目效益下滑，部分对外承包工程业主方由于资金紧缺而造成的合同推迟执行、工程款延期支付的风险因素加剧，导致境外突发事件时有发生，2009年全年上海市商务委员会先后成功化解多起境外纠纷和事件，有效维护了我方在外企业、人员的合法权利和人身安全，消除了隐患，把可能的损失减少到了最低程度。

案例1：努力扩大电气设备和工程服务在全球电力市场份额

——上海电气（集团）总公司

一、企业概况及发展历程

上海电气（集团）总公司是中国最大的综合性装备制造集团之一，其历史可追溯到中国最早的机器电气工业。上海电气（集团）总公司前身是上海市机电工业管理局，1995年改制为上海机电控股（集团）公司，1996年改制为上海电气（集团）总公司。

作为上海电气（集团）总公司的主体部分，上海电气集团股份有限公司（简称上海电气股份）2005年在香港联合证券交易所上市，2008年在上海证券交易所首次发行A股股票。2009年上海电气集团总资产1433亿元；净资产387亿元；主营业务收入725亿元；净利润23.3亿元；职工总数9万人。

上海电气集团拥有7家上市公司，其中，1家H+A股公司、1家H股公司，5家A+B的境内上市公司，分别是：上海电气股份、上海集优机械股份有限公司；上海机

电股份有限公司、上海海立集团股份有限公司、上海自动化仪表股份有限公司、上海二纺机股份有限公司、中国纺织机械股份有限公司。上市公司在上海电气集团中，总资产约占75.9%，净资产约占88.25%，主营业务收入约占90%以上，合计净利润超过100%。上市公司平均资产负债率62.7%；平均净资产收益率9.23%。

上海电气集团与西门子、ABB、阿尔斯通、三菱等跨国公司共同投资建立100家中外合资企业，主营业务涉及电站、输配电、电梯、交通运输设备、冷冻空调、制冷压缩机等产业。

上海电气集团拥有电站、重工、输配电、轨道交通设备、电梯、机床、环保、印刷机械、制冷压缩机、机械基础件、工业自动化等产业，具有设备总成套、工程总承包和提供现代装备综合服务的优势。

上海电气集团火力发电设备产量位居世界第一；核电核岛产品覆盖中国核电建设所有项目，核电常规岛产品批量进入国内外市场；单体企业电梯产量位居世界第一；印刷机械、冷冻空调、数控磨床、制冷压缩机等产品国内市场占有率第一。上世纪90年代以来，上海电气（集团）总公司销售收入始终位居全国机械工业第一名。上海电气品牌获2008年度中国十大行业领袖品牌，入选亚洲品牌500强、全球最大225家国际承包商。

上海电气集团致力于高效清洁能源、新能源和环保、工业装备、服务业等四大产业发展。大力发展大型火电设备，大型核电设备，陆上、海上风能设备，整体煤气化联合循环发电机组，工业废水再利用及海水淡化、脱硫脱硝设备，制冷压缩机、工业自动化等重点业务。通过持续不断的技术进步，上海电气（集团）总公司制造的发电成套设备已成为高效节能的标志；大型铸锻件、电梯、机床、电机、冷冻空调、制冷压缩机等产品广泛采用节能减排最新技术，深受各行各业用户欢迎。

上海电气（集团）总公司正在加快新一轮发展步伐，推进闵行、临港制造基地建设，增强技术创新能力，提高集约化程度、国际化程度，提升在大型先进装备制造业的领先地位，将上海电气打造成一个主业突出、优势明显、具有自主创新能力和可持续发展的国际化大型装备集团。

2009年全年，在金融危机的影响下，也是上海电气集团经受冲击、承受压力最大的一年，公司上下锐意进取，坚定信心，积极应对金融危机，及时调整经营策略，实现了集团业务的平稳较快发展，核心业务取得了持续增长的良好业绩。上海电气（集团）总公司抓销售、保增长、保现金，电力设备、重工设备、电梯等核心业务方面继续保持行业领先，主营业务收入均实现了同比增长。同时，不断探索转变增长方式，调整产业结构促经济增长取得初步成效。核电、风电等新能源产业，以及电站工程产业继

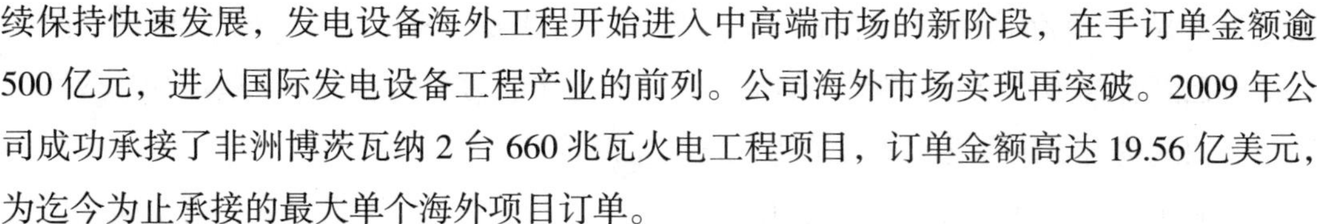

续保持快速发展，发电设备海外工程开始进入中高端市场的新阶段，在手订单金额逾500亿元，进入国际发电设备工程产业的前列。公司海外市场实现再突破。2009年公司成功承接了非洲博茨瓦纳2台660兆瓦火电工程项目，订单金额高达19.56亿美元，为迄今为止承接的最大单个海外项目订单。

二、对外投资合作概况

1．海外渠道初具规模

截至2009年底，上海电气（集团）总公司在美国、德国、俄罗斯、日本、印度、南非等全球12个国家/地区共设有22家海外机构，其中12家为公司，10家为办事处，涉及了电站、电梯、机床、印包、压缩机、焊材等业务，分别承担了研发制造、市场销售、服务维保、事务协调等职能。近年来随着加大力度开拓印度、中东等市场，相应地建立了若干家海外办事处。

2．电站EPC项目成为海外业务突破口

自1985年以来，上海电气（集团）总公司为海内外用户提供了多个电厂工程总承包、电站设备总成套和发电设备供应等优质工程项目。近年来瞄准国际市场，抓住东南亚、南美洲、非洲对电力需求日益增长的发展机遇，以国际市场为重点，实现资源调动和运作国际化，进一步加强与国际跨国公司的战略合作，在市场开拓、项目执行、风险控制、工程管理等方面都有了新的突破。

2002年以来，上海电气（集团）总公司的火力发电设备生产量、销售量以及订单数量保持世界前列，至2008年底，电站工程在海内外已签或已完成的EPC、EP（含BTG）等合同总量逾1600万千瓦。2009年被上海市商务委员会评为2006–2008年度上海市实施“走出去”战略先进企业，并带动了整个上海电气相关产业的发展，同时提高了国际化的运作能力。

目前电站工程中海外项目比重达80%以上，分布在印度、印尼、越南等国家和地区，特别在印度市场有较大的发展，已经生效的合同超过1000万千瓦，尽管经受大环境的严峻考验，但项目执行的工期、质量总体情况良好。在国际化程度上更是一马当先，海外销售的比例超过了国内销售，成为上海电气实施“走出去”战略的“龙头”产业。

3．对外投资合作的经验与启示

（1）海外投资的经验与启示

上海电气（集团）总公司海外机构的发展经历了两个阶段，前一阶段是在海外设立办事处，主要从事市场开拓和综合服务工作，后一阶段是逐步设立公司，主要从事进出口贸易、招商引资服务、协助项目并购等。这些海外机构经过一段时间的运作后，一部分已经在当地“立稳脚跟”，具备了一定的运作能力和影响力，一些成功的收购帮助企业快速提升了国际化水平并取得先进的生产技术。

上海电气（集团）总公司于2002年收购了“日本秋山国际”，单张纸双面胶印机技术能级得到迅速提升，带动了国内相关企业技术的联动发展。2004、2005年控股日本池贝、德国沃伦贝格，取得了14项大型数控机床的关键专利技术，构建了机床高端产品技术研发平台。

2009年上海电气（集团）总公司开始逐步完成收购美国GOSS的全部股权，GOSS是一家跨国公司，在英国、法国、荷兰、日本、澳大利亚、新加坡共有7家全资子公司，有约3000名员工，其轮转印刷机技术在国际上是最先进的，这将是上海电气（集团）总公司在国际化运作上迈出的重要一步。通过这次国际并购，将形成一个营业收入达百亿元的产业，使我国轮转胶印机产业达到国际先进水平，同时有利于提高整个电气集团的国际化程度。

跨国购并既是机会，也存在一定风险。上海电气（集团）有跨国购并的成功案例，有较强的经济实力，有市场和低成本优势。但是缺少收购中大型跨国公司的经验，没有在欧美企业分流安置员工的实践；缺少有效的管控模式，没有形成强有力的管理团队，海外资源的集团协同效应没有得到充分发挥；缺少具有跨文化管理能力的人才队伍，实行全球化经营，企业面临的是一个个与母国有着诸多差异的生产经营环境，包括经济环境、政治环境、法律环境、社会环境、文化环境等，其中文化环境对于企业的经营来说，其影响是全方位、全系统、全过程的，在不同文化背景下的企业经营中，最重要的就是要理解消费者观念、价值观和社会需求的差异。企业经营环境的跨文化差异是企业在全球化经营中所必然要遇到的一大难题，也是关系到企业全球化经营成败的关键所在。

（2）海外EPC工程承包的经验与启示

提升国际竞争力：EPC指承包商的工作范围包括设计（Engineering）工程材料和设备采购（Procurement）以及工程施工（Construction）直至最后竣工，并在交付业主时能够立即运行。目前上海电气（集团）总公司的电站EPC项目发展势头强劲，电站EPC项目将作为上海电气（集团）总公司实施国际化战略的突破口，通过发展电站EPC工程，集团拥有了具有国际影响力的工程公司，电气集团在2007年度ENR全球最大225强国际承包商中排名全球第148名，上海电气品牌获2008年度中国十大行业领袖品牌，位列亚洲品牌500强、全球最大225家国际承包商，2009年被上海市商务委员会评为2006~2008年度上海市实施“走出去”战略先进企业。

形成“走出去”的带动效应：海外工程项目的建设，不仅带动水泥、钢铁、建材等领域的需求，且对设计、制造、监理、调试、咨询、包装、运输、检验、海关、出口、金融等相关行业发展或产业升级具有强带动效应：一个 EPC 工程项目的分包合同可达 150~200 个，分包合同金额占总合同的 80%，其中：设备 40%~50%，施工 40%；其他：设计等 10 %；管理 10 %。工程总承包 1 元人民币可带动 0.4~0.5 元国内设备出口，从而形成海外承包带动产品出口的良性循环。

4．上海电气（集团）总公司的对外投资合作愿景

上海电气（集团）总公司 EPC 发展的目标是全球化经营，国际化运作，提高国际化资源配置能力，努力发展成为国际化、规范化、专业化、在行业内具有国际影响力的工程公司。并带动上海电气（集团）总公司相关产品走出去，争取每年有 200 亿元的 EPC 项目同时执行。

在国内电力市场需求结构变化的情况下，上海电气（集团）总公司利用主机设备制造优势，以电站工程为核心，积极拓展海外市场。

国际市场既是一体化的，又是多元化的。上海电气（集团）总公司国际化经营战略也应当是多层次的、多方位的。因此，在生产技术方面，企业应对不同的市场分别采取不同的技术以取得比较优势；在经营内容方面，企业不仅要扩大产品出口，而且还要积极开展技术输出、劳务输出、工程承包，有步骤地进行海外直接投资：从零散的并购到有质量、大手笔的行业整合并购；从被动思考到主动寻找并购目标，进行战略布局并实施大手笔并购。

案例 2：抓市场，降成本，不断拓展国际市场新领域

——上海振华重工（集团）股份有限公司

一、公司概况

1．企业发展历程及背景

上海振华重工（集团）股份有限公司（ZPMC）（简称上海振华重工）于 1992 年在沪注册成立。

在全球经济一体化、贸易大发展的年代，上海振华重工瞄准了港口机械市场。1992 年底，上海振华重工拿下了第一份海外订单，即加拿大温哥华港向上海振华重工采购 1 台岸桥，该项目成为了上海振华重工事业走向世界的起点。

进入本世纪，上海振华重工进入了高速增长期。为进一步做大做强企业，上海振华重工在大型钢结构市场、海上重工市场实现了高起点进入。在海工市场方面，公司成功建造了亚洲最大的“华天龙”号4000吨全回转浮吊，及世界第一的“蓝鲸”号7500吨自航全回转浮吊。在大型钢结构市场方面，上海振华重工承接了被世界造桥界视为难度最大的美国新海湾大桥全部钢结构项目，该项目为上海振华重工打开了世界钢桥市场的大门，另外还承接了世界最大的英国海上风力发电站桩体钢构项目。

2008年4月，为巩固又好又快发展，实现资源优化配置，上海振华重工合并重组了上海港机厂。

2009年5月，为使公司名副其实和有利发展，公司正式更名为上海振华重工（集团）股份有限公司（原上海振华港口机械（集团）股份有限公司）。

2．企业对外投资合作概况

作为一家外向型企业，上海振华重工成功将“ZPMC”品牌覆盖了世界76个国家和地区的120余个港口码头。截至目前，上海振华重工已生产岸桥1700余台，场桥3300余台及近300台散货装卸机械，其中80%的产品出口国外。

上海振华重工在对外合作的过程中，与世界各大知名企业建立了良好的合作关系，如马士基、迪拜世界、世界知名的工程承包商美国福陆公司等，上海振华重工能根据用户要求设计制作各类港机、海工产品等，做到保质保量按时交货，并提供完善的售后服务，为双方长期合作奠定了良好的伙伴关系。

目前，上海振华重工对外合作大项目有美国新海湾大桥钢结构、挪威HARDANGER大桥、韩国三星8000吨起重船、西班牙铺管船等等。

3．2009年发展概况

2009年，在全球金融危机的影响下，航运业和港口码头建设、特别是集装箱运输业大幅萎缩，造成对上海振华重工主要产品港口机械的需求大幅萎缩，市场疲软、订单少、价格下滑，上海振华重工传统产品经营订单额受到巨大影响，但上海振华重工管理层根据内外部经营情况发生的变化及时总结经验，迅速调整上海振华重工战略，大力开拓新经济增长点，全面部署生产、经营、财务、人事等各个方面工作，取得了一定的成效。2009年上海振华重工实现营业收入2756411.56万元，比上年同期增长0.44%。

面对种种不利局面，上海振华重工努力巩固世界港机市场中的龙头地位和市场份额，依然实现传统产品全球市场占有率连续第13年排名第一，进一步扩大了世界市场占有份额，远远领先于其他竞争对手，上海振华重工产品已经进入76个国家和地区；同时上海振华重工经营班子努力开拓市场，最终实现全年新签合同额39.15亿美元。

4. 对外投资合作对企业的影响

对外投资合作为上海振华重工成功打造了“ZPMC”国际知名品牌。在世界集装箱机械生产领域，“ZPMC”这个品牌已被全世界用户视为质量好、价格公道、最有竞争力、最能准时交货的优质品牌，世界上最大、最快、最先进的集装箱起重机都在振华重工制造。ZPMC品牌为上海振华重工营造了良好的国际美誉度，成为上海振华重工在商品市场的开路先锋。

长期以来，发达国家在技术方面形成了自己的优势，上海振华重工在“与强争锋”的过程中虚心学习先进技术，加快了对先进技术的理解与消化，并结合自主创新，形成了强大的科研技术能力。

5. 企业对外投资合作的经验与启示

企业在对外投资合作过程中，关键要抓住一个好的适合企业驰骋的市场。上海振华重工成立初期，正值外贸大发展促进了船舶大型化和港口航道等相应的大发展，港口为了缩短船舶在港时间，提出了对集装箱机械高效率、高可靠等一系列的新要求。世界装备制造强手均关注这个市场，“群雄逐鹿”非常热闹，上海振华重工瞄准港机市场应运而生。经过18年的奋斗，港机产品已进入全球76个国家和地区，占据本行业世界市场75%以上的份额。

近几年，因油价高昂，使困难重重的海上油气田开采提上世界各大油气公司的重要日程。全球已知的四个富油气海区（北海、中东海湾、墨西哥湾、中国南海）的油气开采方兴未艾。上海振华重工根据市场需求，将制造海上工程船列为主攻方向。目前，已成功建造了亚洲第一的“华天龙”号4000吨全回转浮吊，世界第一的“蓝鲸”号7500吨自航全回转浮吊等等。

钢结构桥梁市场也是群雄逐鹿之地。国外的重型制造厂（日本三菱、石川岛，韩国三星、现代、大宇等）均涉猎这个领域。上海振华重工的策略是“国内练兵、国外大举”，大型钢结构市场也是上海振华重工全力开拓的市场之一。目前，上海振华重工已成功完成了韩国仁川钢桥、美国加州卡昆兹公路桥、加拿大温哥华金穗桥、韩国釜山铁路桥等钢结构项目。

同时，成功对外投资合作的秘诀离不开技术创新。上海振华重工上下均将创新视为企业的灵魂。在激烈的市场竞争中，敢于与强争锋是上海振华重工不断技术创新的最好动力。上海振华重工重科学实验，首先要求各机电配套件生产厂必须设实验台，不断改进产品的质量和增加技术含量。上海振华重工在创新中奉行以实验开路的方针，不经实验证明其成功，决不贸然用于主产品，因而使新技术、新材料、新工艺得以迅速在公司开花结果，转化为生产力。上海振华重工利用全国和上海市强大的科研力量，实现产学研共同战斗，这些资源经常帮助公司分析化解科技难题。

二、事件案例

1．承接美国新海湾大桥钢结构项目的背景

原美国海湾大桥建造于1934年，多次地震对该桥造成严重破坏。从1997年起，美国加州交通部决定建造新海湾大桥，历经多次论证，2006年该工程终于开标授予美国桥梁公司（AB）和福陆（Fluor）组成承包。

2006年6月，上海振华重工凭借世界一流的设备和强大生产能力，获得了分包制造美国新海湾大桥全部钢构共4.5万吨工程。

美国新海湾大桥是业内公认的迄今为止世界上最昂贵、最美丽、能抗地震、技术含量最高、寿命最长（100年以上）的大桥。美国新海湾大桥坐落于美国旧金山湾，可与美国东岸标志性建筑自由女神媲美，将是今后进入美国西岸旧金山市的标志景观，是世界第一单塔自锚抗震悬索钢桥，跨度虽不大，为565米，但因要求抗地震，设计和制造难度均很大。

美国新海湾大桥主要由钢塔、钢梁和自行车道三部分组成。钢塔高度为148米，总重约13000吨,为世界抗震钢塔第一高度。塔身由4根五边形钢柱和连接“横梁”组成。最大板厚达到100毫米。其制作难点在于每段重量重，结构形式复杂，厚板焊接难度高，并对塔的垂直度的要求非常严。桥面的钢箱梁总长605米、总宽70米、高5.5米，为世界同类桥梁中第一大箱梁，钢梁由东西两线钢箱梁和联系梁组成，采用栓焊结构，总重量约30000吨。

美国新海湾大桥是美国加州的标志性建筑，多年来受到世界各著名桥梁制造厂商的瞩目，纷纷意欲获得此项目以树自己的名声，但又因为此桥难度大，质量要求高，罚款严，视为畏途。上海振华重工在强手林立的竞争中独占鳌头，一举拿下全部钢结构的制作合同，将这批质量要求极高的钢构全部交给中国制造商上海振华重工承造，而不是参与角逐的日本和韩国制造商，这是破天荒之举，在美国桥钢梁建造史上是第一次，这也为上海振华重工在世界钢桥市场上大显身手创造条件，为上海市和国家争光。

2．美国新海湾大桥钢结构项目的关键时间节点

在获得项目后的一年左右时间里，上海振华重工都在进行前期准备工作，为确保高标准、高质量、高效率地制作该项目打下基础。公司专门建造了重型码头和重型车间，2008年3月，重型车间完工，2008年7月重型码头完工。

根据合同要求，在正式生产之前必须完成两套共8个模型段的制作，其中每套为3个钢塔模型、1个桥面板模型，第一套需要通过总包方的审核，第二套需要通过业主加

州交通部的审核。2007 年 8 月，第一套模型全部完工，并顺利通过总包方的审核，标志着施工工艺得到总包方的认可。

2008 年 1 月 15 日，美国新海湾大桥钢塔部分开工制作，标志着该钢桥项目全面开工。

2008 年 10 月 14 日，随着钢塔第一吊装段东塔最后一块面板的顺利合拢，标志着该项目进入全面提速阶段。

2009 年 12 月 29 日，美国新海湾大桥第一船从公司长兴基地发运前往旧金山，包括 1 个钢塔吊装段和 4 个钢箱梁吊装段。该项目共分为 8 船发运，截至 2010 年年底全部交付。

3．美国新海湾大桥钢结构项目的结果

在制造期间，美方向上海振华重工生产基地派驻了庞大的督导队伍常驻现场，监督与指导该钢桥制造的现场作业，尽管在制造过程中涉及了数百次或大或小的变更，增加了制造难度，但上海振华重工上下奋力拼搏，创新生产管理流程，提高工艺标准，提升自主创新能力，与美方人员携手克服了种种困难，最终出色地按照节点完成了任务。该项目是上海振华重工在美国承接的最大钢结构项目之一，参建美国新海湾的桥是一项永载史册的事业，同时也是进军世界大型钢结构市场的重要标志。据市场调研，每年世界范围内将有数百亿美元以上的钢桥项目，美国新海湾大桥项目的制造为上海振华重工全面进入世界重型钢结构市场敲开了大门。

4．美国新海湾大桥钢结构项目的经验与启示

在美国新海湾大桥项目制造过程中，上海振华重工完成了材料的采购与验收、施工图纸的设计与改进、重型车间的建造与使用、先进设备的购置与投入、优秀人才的选拔与配置、严格的现场作业管理等环节的优化。同时也为上海振华重工进入钢结构市场奠定了坚实的基础，积累了宝贵的经验：在争取新领域的国际市场过程中，要树立市场和成本观念，抓市场，降成本，提高竞争优势；要树立客户和服务意识，以客户为中心，用心为客户服务；同时树立自信和必胜信心，用心培育新市场，全力支持新市场发展。

在与美国业主方及总包方的合作中，上海振华重工深切体会到管理是企业永恒的主题，也是经营结构调整战略取得胜利的保障。完善制度体系，梳理管理流程，调整组织机构，打造全新精干高效、责任明确、管理顺畅的经营管理系统；加快体制机制创新，调整生产基地产品布局，实施专业化和标准化管理。降低产品综合成本，确保品牌质量；发挥科技研发和自主创新的支撑作用，既要保证现有市场平稳发展，又要引领新市场的发展趋势；在企业做大做强的过程中实施人才强企战略，坚持自主培养和重点引进相结合，打造经营管理、专业技术和高技能人才三支队伍；提高质量安全管控能力，树立全过程精品意识，调整质量管理体系，实现产品卓越品质。完善安全监督责任体系，加大奖惩力度，提高全员安全意识，做到安全生产警钟长鸣。

第五章 专 题

第一节 展览业

一、2009 年上海展览会总体情况及 2010 年的展望

2009 年，全球金融风暴的袭击、H1N1 流感的蔓延，近年来保持稳步发展势头的上海会展业受到较大影响。在政府主管部门的支持和推动下，企业积极应对金融危机，克服重重困难，上海会展业实现了平稳发展。

（一）2009 年展览会情况及特点

1．总量基本持平，单体面积增加

2009 年在上海举办的各类展览会 526 个，比上年 544 个减少了 3.3%；总展出面积 723 万平方米，比上年增长了 2.3%：其中国际展览会 243 个，比上年减少了 17.3%，展出面积 560 万平方米，比上年减少了 6.2%；国内展览会 283 个，比上年增长了 13.2%，展出面积 163.2 万平方米，比上年增长了 48.4%。

2．国际展数量有所减少，国内展保持增速

2009 年，国际展数量有所回落，主要有三个方面原因：一是受金融危机影响，办展单位取消了 29 个项目，影响展出面积 34.6 万平方米；二是受主客观原因影响，多个项目转移到长三角地区、北京或广州等地，影响展出面积约 30 万平方米；三是为增强抗风险能力，近 30 个项目采取合作、合并。

国内展在国内各种拉动内需政策的影响下，实现了快速增长，项目数量增加了 33 个；展出面积增加了 53 万平方米。

3．展馆面积增加，部分展览规模得以扩大

至 2009 年底，上海已建和在建展览场馆 11 所（包括世博会的主题馆、新国际博览中心扩建的两个馆），可供总展出面积 36.7 万平方米。随着上海展览场馆建设的扩大，上海的国际展览会的规模也有所扩增，2009 年在上海举办的 243 个国际展览会项目平均展出面积达到了 2.3 万平方米，比上年扩大了 13.5%，其中展出面积在 5 万平方米以

上的项目已达 31 个，比上年减少了 3 个；总展出面积 322.96 万平方米，基本与上年持平。上海博华国际展览有限公司承办的国际家具展规模展出面积也逐步发展到40万平方米，已名列国际前茅。

（二）2010 年上海展览业发展展望

2010 年是上海世博会的举办年，也是实施“十一五”规划的最后一年，上海会展业认真做好十二五期间的上海会展业发展规划，进一步理顺会展业管理体制，重点实施“五个一”，即成立一个机构，修订一个法规，制定一个规划，出台一项鼓励政策，培育一批品牌展会。

1．建立一个统一的展览业管理机构

参照安徽、陕西、四川、宁波等地做法，成立展览业管理办公室，明确职责，加强对全市会展业的管理和协调，解决“多头管理”问题。

2．抓紧修订《上海市展览业管理办法》

启动展览业立法调研，对《办法》中有关管理部门、审批、档期、处罚等滞后条款进行修订，增加对内展市场管理的条款，规范内展市场秩序。

3．制定本市展览业发展五年规划

结合“十二五”规划研究，制定本市展览业发展第一个“五年规划”，为上海展览业发展提供指导意见。

4．制订鼓励会展业发展的财税支持政策

设立国际会展产业发展导向资金，重点支持本市重大国际会展活动宣传、推介，品牌展会的培育和扶持、会展行业研究、人员培训等。对会展企业给予营业税率优惠。

5．培育一批品牌展会

通过财税等政策，帮助一批条件成熟、知名度较高的品牌展会做大做强。同时，通过政策优惠大力吸引一批国际知名展会落户上海。

6．探索建立会展行业市场准入和退出机制

制定会展行业市场准入标准，对符合条件的会展企业允许从事会展业务，对有骗展、虚假办展等行为的企业建立“黄、红牌”警告制度，同时加强各有关职能部门信息沟通，建立黑名单制度，规范会展市场秩序。

7．进一步增强会展行业协会的功能

重视发挥会展行业在行业自律、诚信经营等方面的作用，赋予会展行业协会一定的职能职责，不断增强行业协会的权威性。

三、第19届中国华东进出口商品交易会

由上海市、江苏省、浙江省、安徽省、福建省、江西省、山东省、南京市、宁波市共同主办的第19届中国华东进出口商品交易会（简称华交会），于2009年3月1日至3月5日在上海新国际博览中心举行。

本届华交会是在国际金融危机、外贸出口形势相当严峻的情况下举办的中国外贸“开春第一展”。本届华交会在商务部的具体指导下，在9个主办省市、3个组团城市和全体参展企业的共同努力下，认真贯彻中央经济工作会议精神，树立信心，应对挑战，化危为机，寻找对策，转变贸易增长方式，提升国际化水平，取得了比预期要好的效果。

（一）本届华交会的基本情况

1．招商效果明显，到会客商踊跃

由于千方百计加大招商力度，尽管金融海啸迅速蔓延，境外客商到会仍然比较踊跃，达18229人，比上届略有减少，下降5.37%；到会境外客商来自140个国家和地区，比上届减少了5个。

一是亚洲到会客商高居首位，日本到会客商最多。本届华交会亚洲到会客商13306人，比上届增长7.37%，占客商总数的73%。其中，日本客商最多，达6878人，增长7.81%，占客商总数的37.7%；香港客商2331人，增长10%，占12.8%。进一步体现出华交会的国际影响力。

二是欧美客商下降幅度较大。经济发达地区是金融危机的重灾区，本届华交会欧美到会客商减少五分之一，欧洲到会客商2546人，下降28.38%；北美洲到会客商1495人，下降32.57%。

三是到会采购团组略有下降。本届华交会依然有许多国家组团或国际大买家到会采购。华交会5天内共接待来自21个国家的78个团组801人，国家和团组分别比上届减少2个和15个，组团人数同比减少14.42%。

2．金融海啸冲击，出口成交下降

本届华交会遇到了前所未有的困难，出口成交大幅度下降。出口总成交为22.4亿美元，比上届下降39.06%。出口成交的主要特点如下：

（1）成交全面下降

据统计，本届华交会纺织服装类成交12.45亿美元，比上届下降32.47%；轻工工艺类成交8.98亿美元，比上届下降43.67%；其他类商品成交9786万美元，比上届下降59.13%。

（2）市场格局仍以传统市场为主

本届华交会成交量最高的是日本，成交65689万美元，比上届下降27.53%；欧盟成交位居第二，成交52436万美元，比上届下降40.36%；美国成交位居第三，成交31057万美元，比上届下降46.70%；新兴市场中，东盟成交5451万美元，比上届下降47.06%；海湾六国成交4118万美元，比上届下降50.43%；中南美洲成交5334万美元，下降32.07%。

（3）生产企业成为华交会的成交主体

从企业性质看，本届华交会国有企业成交32871万美元，比上届下降54.76%；集体企业成交7710万美元，比上届下降27.07%；民营企业成交10331万美元，比上届下降35.94%；外商投资企业成交43901万美元，比上届下降46.87%。从社会属性看，生产企业成交124329万美元，比上届下降38.25%；流通企业成交99338美元，比上届下降40.26%。生产企业占总成交的比例由上届的38.65%上升到55.47%，超过半壁江山；民营企业成交继续增长，占总成交比例由上届的42.52%上升到46.09%。

3．双向功能强化，进口成交扩大

为进一步扩大进口，减少贸易顺差，本届华交会打破原有的展览格局，将国内参展企业与境外参展企业划分开来，单独设立境外参展企业专区，进一步强化华交会双向贸易功能，使境外参展企业既可将产品进口到中国，也可借助华交会这个国际化的平台从事转口贸易活动。本届华交会境外参展企业交易团有120家企业，分别来自美国、英国、意大利、日本、韩国等11个国家和地区。总成交435万美元，比上届增长3.72倍。

由于华交会的品牌效应和影响力不断扩大，加之招商工作措施到位，本届华交会到会客商数超出预期，仅比上届减少5%。与香港同期客商减少了36%相比，招商工作是本届华交会的亮点之一。但是，出口成交却出现大幅下降，据初步分析有以下几个原因：一是受金融危机影响，国际市场消费需求在衰退，本届华交会客商下单批次虽有所增加，但是小单多、短单多，不敢下大单，唯恐销售不当成为库存，造成成交金额大幅下降；二是由于近期中国政府和各地政府纷纷出台保增长、促发展的扶持政策，造成部分外商对未来政策还有很多预期，如出口退税等政策。因此他们仍在等待观望，落单比较谨慎；三是许多展商心态平和，对华交会的成交下降已有一定的心理准备。不少展商认为，他们到华交会是为了更多地了解信息，保持联系，展示形象，并不急于成交而降低定价标准。

（二）本届华交会的主要特点

1．迎难而上，企业参展热情不减

面对前所未有的困难，各地商务主管部门加大工作力度，动员企业参展，使大家

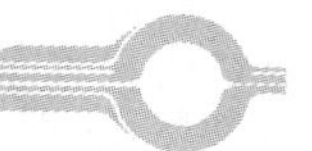

认识到，越是遇到困境，越要迎难而上，越要注重拓展，这样才能在危机中找到机遇。本届华交会企业参展热情不减，展览面积维持在前几届水平，参展企业为3351家，共有14个交易团。其中，国内参展企业3231家，共13个交易团；联合交易团参展企业来自19个省市自治区、8个城市及五菱分团。

2．调整结构，不断优化展览格局

本届华交会在保持原有的服装、家用纺织品、装饰礼品、日用消费品四个展区的前提下，针对产品范围较杂的日用消费品展区进行梳理，将原展区中较有规模的家居展品集中展示，形成日用消费品展区细分为家居用品、电子消费品和其他消费品三个专区的模式。

3．开发新品，品牌效应彰显魅力

华东地区是我国纺织品、服装、日用消费品、装饰礼品的重要生产地和集散地，也是品牌企业和品牌产品的集聚地。本届华交会继续实施品牌战略，各交易团高度重视参展企业和参展商品的质量，在展位分配上向品牌企业倾斜，在布展上突出品牌企业和品牌产品。本届华交会参展商品中，品牌产品占了较大比例。其中获商务部重点培育和支持的中国名牌出口商品有60多个，属省市出口名牌的企业、品牌商品有近700个，参展的商品中新产品、新款式和采取新技术、新工艺的商品2万多个。不少外商认为，这次华交会最大的亮点就是品牌较多，展品质量较好，是一次外贸出口精品、名品、新品的大检阅。

4．调查研究，共商应对危机良策

华交会是国际市场的“晴雨表”，是世界经济走势的“风向标”。本届华交会举办“积极应对金融危机，增强企业信心，保持外经贸稳定增长”高级研讨会，商务部领导和各省市领导同台研讨，共商对策。展会期间，还举办《当前我国外经贸形势及政策走向》专题报告会，邀请商务部专家李健作专题报告。各级领导和企业家，都试图把华交会作为化危为机的信息窗口，到会调查研究，探索应对困境的新招。在本届华交会上，各省市都用积极的心态应对危机：上海市出台了21条措施，保持外贸稳定增长；江苏省抓紧落实保外贸增长的促进政策，帮助出口企业开拓国内外两个市场；浙江省加大外贸资金扶持、开拓市场、强化服务三个力度，帮助企业渡过难关；安徽省优化外贸服务，优化市场结构，支持品牌建设，营造优越环境；福建省为企业创造商机保增长、加大扶持保增长、化解风险保增长、凝聚合力保增长，同时帮助企业转型升级，提升核心竞争力；江西省完善机制，优化外贸环境建设；山东省采取措施，帮助企业安全高效“走出去”，推动产业集聚；南京市把2009年作为“企业服务年”，千方百计帮助企业渡过难关；宁波市加强外贸形势跟踪分析，增强企业应对危机能力。

5．振奋精神，重塑保增长的信心

在经济危机时期，提振信心最为重要。本届华交会上上下下都形成一个共识："信心比成交更重要"。无论是商务部领导、省市领导，还是参展企业的负责人都表示，危机是危险和机遇并存，目前尽管外贸出口遭遇寒流，但是在逆境中也有不可多得的机遇，国家加大保增长的政策扶持力度、改善生存环境、劳动力成本降低、原材料降价等都是企业发展的机遇。大家认为，只要振奋精神、增强信心，就没有过不去的坎，就一定能战胜危机，夺取新的胜利。许多企业表示，朋友就是订单，信息就是财富。虽然本次交易会成交不太理想，但是结交了不少新的客户，为今后发展打下基础。有的企业通过本届华交会更深入地了解到国际市场的走势，从而明确了今后调整结构的方向。

6．精心布展，提升形象展示风采

越是遇到危机，越要注重形象，成为所有交易团和参展企业的共识。本届华交会展位总数5312个。其中，服装展区展位1578个，特装展位超过任何一届，布展形成"整体布展统一化、展区布展专业化、省市布展个性化、企业布展品牌化"的特色。各交易团精心设计，统一施工，突出地区形象、企业形象、品牌形象，体现了华交会的新形象和新水平。

四、2009中国国际工业博览会成果及经验

（一）基本概况

由国家发展改革委、商务部、工信部、科技部、教育部、中科院、中国工程院、中国贸促会和上海市政府共同主办的2009中国国际工业博览会（简称"中国工博会"）于2009年11月3日至11月7日在上海新国际博览中心隆重举行，并取得圆满成功。

本届"中国工博会"坚持以科学发展观为指导，在面临部分外国政府取消海外参展补贴、许多企业缩减市场推广费用等严峻局面的情况下，克服了金融危机的负面影响。在展览规模、专业化水平、国际化程度和服务全国等方面都取得了较好成绩。据上海会展协会对展览现场1245名参展商和1219名观众调查的数据分析：参展商总体评价为84.27分，高于上届的83.28分；观众评价分89.36分，接近上届的89.75分。有42%的企业表示明年再来参展。

（二）主要特点

1．展览规模、中外客商到会和现场成交均创新高

本届"中国工博会"展览面积12.65万平方米，参展展位5302个，比上届增长

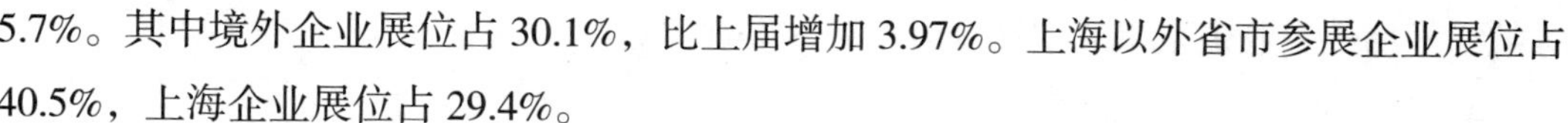

5.7%。其中境外企业展位占 30.1%，比上届增加 3.97%。上海以外省市参展企业展位占 40.5%，上海企业展位占 29.4%。

参展企业共 1869 家，比上届增长 2.92%。其中境外参展企业比上届增加 4.44%。上海以外省市参展企业比上届增加 1.73%。境外有 18 个国家和地区参展。境内有 30 个省市和计划单列市参展。共有 11.83 万观众前来参观、洽谈，比上届增长 1.37%。其中专业观众 9.82 万人，比上届增长 2.07%；境外观众来自 73 个国家和地区，包括澳大利亚参议长霍格、富士通株式会社董事高桥醇九等。本届“中国工博会”产品和技术成交 17.44 亿元，比上届增加 42.8%。

2．各专业展凸现装备制造业和高新技术领域的最新发展方向

本届“中国工博会”设置世博科技展、数控机床与金属加工展、工业自动化展、环保技术与设备展、信息与通信技术应用展、新能源与电力电工展、航空航天技术展、科技创新展等 8 个展区，每个展区都有一大批亮点项目。

在数控机床与金属加工展中，齐二机床、武重机床、上海机床、扬力集团、日本山崎马扎克、德国通快华嘉、瑞士百超精机等国内外知名企业带来代表国内外机床行业的最高水准的展品。在工业自动化展中，西门子、ABB、发那科、富士电机、菲尼克斯、威图、霍尼韦尔等自动化领域的知名企业带来最新研发的机器人技术等。在新能源与电力电工展中，河北省天威集团的 1000kV 特高压电力变压器处于当今世界前列。在环保技术与设备展中，有上汽集团最新研发的上海牌燃料电池车（plug-in3 代）、上海牌纯电动轿车、荣威混合动力轿车，上海雷博新能源纯电动巴士汽车自主研发的多款环保汽车新品，还有日本最新环保技术，如中水回收技术、环保汽车用活塞、再生纸甲醛吸收技术等。在信息与通信技术应用展中，有中国移动、中国电信带来的 3G 网络商用平台，国标 HD 系列地面数字电视解调芯片及解决方案，利锐、恩菲斯、奥的亮、三思等国内外著名厂商展示的新型 LED 节能灯具等。

3．世博科技展和航空航天展推动国家重大项目和新产业发展

世博科技展总面积 1.15 万平方米，围绕科技、城市、生活三要素，针对科技创新在建设、能源、环境、运营、展示及安全等领域的研发和应用成果，设置“总况”、“世博规划与工程建设”、“世博绿色能源与节能减排”、“世博园区环境改善与生态综合治理”、“世博信息服务”、“世博安全健康”和“未来城市发展”7 个分展区。世博科技展贴近资源节约、低碳排放、环境友好等国际热点，精选了 180 多个参展项目。据不完全统计，5 天共接待观众超过 6.5 万人次。观众对该展区好评率达 98%。航空航天技术展首次在“中国工博会”上亮相。中航商用飞机公司展出了 C919 干线飞机、ARJ21 支线飞机和涡扇喷气发动机等展品。俄罗斯客商展出了直升飞机。英、法、德、日、加

等航空零部件企业也来参展。观众对该展区好评率达97%。

4．科研成果参展、成交踊跃

全国高校分展区位于科技创新展，共有55所高校参展，全国综合科技实力排名前60位的高校有50%以上参展。其中包括上海以外地区的高校36所、上海高校17所和境外高校2所。香港理工大学和韩国汉阳大学两所境外高校首次参展。该分展区展出重大技术突破项目30项，重点推介的应用技术成果项目458项。其中上海大学“磷酸铁锂锂电池组控制管理系统及应用”在本届展会上成交额高达5000万元。高校参展面积虽然仅占本届展会的4%，但获奖数比例达到38.5%，进一步发挥了“中国工博会”科研成果产业化的平台作用。中国科学院高等研究院、上海微小卫星工程中心的“SZ-7飞船伴随卫星”和中国科学院上海药物所的“盐酸安妥沙星”等受到专家的高度关注。SAiNA超细纳米对撞机发放资料400多份，接待100多位客户，已与部分客户建立了长期联系。该机器具有自主知识产权，与美国生产的球磨机相比，其能耗为美国的1/10，填补了当今世界粉碎领域纳米超细机械粉碎的空白。

5．境外企业寻找金融危机期的商机

金融危机对境内外展会造成许多不利影响，但中国经济强劲的发展态势和蕴藏的巨大商机，对境外企业有很强的吸引力。由于“中国工博会”具有较大国际影响力等原因，境外企业纷纷前来寻求新的市场机会，进一步发挥了“中国工博会”引进国外先进技术设备的平台作用。如工业自动化展境外企业展位占55.6%，西门子、ABB、发那科、富士电机、菲尼克斯、威图、霍尼韦尔等自动化领域的知名企业都来参展。环保技术与设备展境外企业展位也高达44.4%。许多境外企业还利用展会在现场举行推介会。

6．国内企业展示建国60年来我国工业发展的巨大成就

2009年恰逢建国60周年，许多国内企业竞相推出一流设备和技术，让世界更好地了解中国，并进一步发挥了“中国工博会”服务全国的平台作用。如总部在北京的华锐风电科技股份有限公司展示具备国际先进水平的3兆瓦海上风力发电机组，已应用在国内第一个海上风电工程——上海东海大桥100兆瓦海上风电场上，实现了我国自有技术海上大功率风电机组零的突破。中航商用飞机公司的C919干线飞机、ARJ21支线飞机和涡扇喷气发动机，体现了我国航空工业的水平。其中江苏省的金方圆公司已连续4年参展，本届展会接到20台采购意向，包括MT200电伺服数控冲床、PR系列数控折弯机等。

7．获奖产品优惠政策有突破性进展，进一步提升了展会奖项的含金量

本届“中国工博会”继续设立产品类的金、银、铜奖和创新奖，不再评选技术交易最具潜力奖和产权交易最佳策划奖。共评出金奖4项、银奖9项、铜奖14项、创新奖12项。在中央有关部委和上海市各相关部门的大力支持下，给予“中国工博会”获

奖产品优惠政策的工作取得了零的突破。

国家发展改革委牵头，会同商务部、工业和信息化部、科技部办公厅已于2009年11月2日联合发文，对获得“中国工博会”金奖的产品给予国家重点产业振兴和技术改造专项列入、自主创新产品认定、机电产品结构调整等方面的重点扶持。上海市有关部门也于9月24日联合发文,对获得“中国工博会”奖项产品,给予认定专利新产品、自主创新产品、重点技术改造专项、高新技术产业化项目等方面的优先扶持。获奖单位来年再次参展，将给予特别优先优惠等支持。

8. 论坛选题贴近国内外经济发展热点，进一步扩大了展会的影响力

本届“中国工博会”论坛围绕当前经济发展的热点，坚持“少而精”的原则，共安排74项。其中发展论坛2项，包括商务部、工信部等组织的“第六届中国产业国际竞争力”论坛,上海世博(集团)有限公司等组织的“第二届中国国际节能环保论坛——金融危机催热低碳经济”; 科技论坛21项，包括主题是“金融危机下的上海城市竞争力”的院士圆桌会议，以及20个专题学术研讨会；行业与企业论坛51项，包括“2009上海国际设计创新高峰论坛”、第五届CIIF · MM · 新自动化论坛等。共有10000余人听取了来自国内外的专家、企业家的演讲，取得了较好效果。

9. 加强新闻宣传工作，境内外媒体高度关注本届“中国工博会”

新闻工作围绕“科技创新与装备制造业”的主题，组织国内外媒体进行了及时、深入和全面的宣传报道。共有120家中外媒体、220多名中外记者报名参加采访工作。其中中央媒体记者40名，境外媒体记者30名。截至11月6日，国内媒体(包括滚动播放、互相转载)累计发表文字新闻1620条、广播新闻80余条、网络新闻90300条(篇)、网络图片4370幅，海外媒体相关报道达16320余条(篇)。

10. 重视展会安全、保护国家机密和企业知识产权，展会秩序良好

本届“中国工博会”把提高管理与服务水平放在突出位置，在展区规划、现场管理、环境整治等方面充分体现合理、有效和人性化，为中外客商创造良好的环境和秩序。重点抓好安检、消防、治安和交通疏导、展览秩序等工作。坚持从源头上把好关，同时加强巡查，防微杜渐，把问题化解在苗头中。展会期间知识产权零投诉，没有发生安全、泄密事件，杜绝现场零售现象。观众对展览秩序的评价很高，得分达90.48分。

五、跨国采购发展态势

(一) 2009年上海跨国采购情况及特征

2009年，金融危机造成了欧美发达国家金融系统的剧烈震荡，金融资产贬值，银

行企业纷纷倒闭，失业率激增，内需锐减，这直接导致了我国许多依赖外需的制造型企业市场急剧萎缩，加之贸易保护主义抬头，“稳定国外市场”不再是一道轻松下咽的美食，而是现今攸关无数“中国制造”企业生死的严峻挑战。

然而，尽管往昔风光不再，外部忧患重重，“中国制造”产品依靠继续发挥多年形成的质量、技术和价格优势，同时全面调整企业战略，积极应对外部嬗变。

1. 2009年跨国采购概况

2009中国（上海）国际跨国采购大会（以下简称跨采大会）创历史新高。总面积2.3万平方米，参会总家数273家、供应商4800家，采购总金额达到200亿美元。具体体现为，主会场采购商211家，服务商20家。211家采购商来自32个国家和地区，55%直接来自海外，其中500强企业有21家。按采购清单统计，采购产品涉及13大类1200余种，合180亿美元。供应商4000家，来自中国东部地区的占84.15%，中部地区的占比为11.92%，西部地区的占比为3.93%，通过国际相关认证的企业占比为72%（ISO9000、ISO14000、TS16949、SA8000、ROHS等），比上一年增加3个百分点。汽配行业中，采购商42家，供应商800家，采购金额达20亿美元。

2. 企业自身注重增加竞争力

联合国采购项目已进入第四个年头，已成为国内同业中的领先者。经过几年的运作，上海跨国采购中心在联合国采购项目运作方面积累了一定的经验，包括独立开展多场联合国采购方面的培训，参加的供应商总计达到300多人次，为应标的联合国供应商提供咨询服务。累计指导了近千家国内供应商注册成为联合国指定供应商，占了全国指导服务总量的1/3。

与瑞典贸易委员会合作中瑞商业可持续发展项目，并组织了中瑞商业发展研讨会，该研讨会共邀请了100多家中瑞企业参加，会上中瑞企业就如何提升中国企业进入全球供应链体系作了交流；与瑞典贸易委员会和上海交通大学安泰经济管理学院组织中瑞商业可持续发展项目论坛，讨论中国企业在进入全球采购供应链体系后的社会责任问题。

与SMI（Supply Management Institute，欧洲供应链管理学院）合作高端供应商培训项目。该项目从2009年9月开始与SMI进行洽谈，目前已经形成初步合作框架，计划在2010年6月初进行第一个培训项目。

3. 更广范围、更深层次合作

跨采大会服务宗旨是为国际采购商构筑连接中国的桥梁，为中国供应商打开通向世界的大门，跨采平台就是连接国际国内两个扇形辐射面的枢纽，面对2009年的金融风暴和经济危机，上海跨国采购中心及时分析形势，确定对策，调整方向，弥补不足。

国际合作方面，与 BME（德国联邦采购物流协会）、NC（NC network）、PLMA（Private Label Manufacturers Association，美国自有品牌制造商协会）、SMI、ISM（Institute for Supply Management，供应链管理学院）、SSSBP（Sino-Swedish Sustainable Business Program，中国瑞典可持续发展的商业项目）等国际上重要的协会、机构建立合作互动，互利双赢的关系，引进荷中商会、中美总商会、日本大阪商会、美国大费城地区商会等带团参会。

国内合作方面，协办省市参与国际跨国采购大会程度进一步加强，浙江、江苏、山西、河北、北京、重庆、安徽、河南、广东、福建等 10 省市商务厅都切实组织了本地区供应商参加本届大会，浙江、山西、河北对本地区参会供应商实行普通洽谈门票的进行全额补贴。与地、县级政府部门直接对接开展推介，并以苏、浙两省经济发达地区为主，如湖州、平湖、太仓、张家港等。与有关协会的合作，如上海外商投资协会、宁波名牌产品产品促进会等，取得较好效果。

4．发挥经济集聚效应

在上海跨国采购中心旗下，两大实体平台架构已经确立，一是位于浦西长风生态区的“上海跨国采购中心基地”，以吸纳国际采购商总部、制造商总部入驻，其会展功能，将有条件成为每年一届跨采大会的主会场。另一是位于浦东新区的上海跨国采购中心五角世贸商城，其功能为进口产品与技术展贸中心。50 万平方米的航母式体量将吸引全球进口商入驻展销，成为一个 B2B 的进口中心平台，这将成为打造跨采体系的基础。

六、2010 年上海跨国采购主要工作举措

1．坚持逆向采购特色，做大做强跨采平台

2010 跨国采购大会定于 2010 年 9 月 16 日至 18 日在上海世贸商城举行，汽车零部件分会于 9 月 16 日 – 17 日举行。2010 大会的举办是在全球经济起稳回升的大背景下，在世博会后期作为上海建设国际贸易中心的一项重要功能和抓手，要在开拓创新和可持续发展上，坚持逆向采购特色，把跨采平台做大做强。预计 2010 年跨国采购大会主会场采购商达到 350 家，供应商达到 4000 到 4500 家。预计汽配分会采购商达到 40 家左右，供应商 800 到 1000 家。

2．大力发展电子商务，寻求国际化合作与开发

跨国采购电子商务平台不仅代表着跨采中心的网络品牌形象，同时也是开展网络营销的根据地，并实现将跨采中心的服务与合作对象聚集到平台内，为其提供相适应的电子商务服务方案。

3．组建跨国采购研究会，发布跨采指数，创办跨采期刊

组建跨国采购研究会是打造跨国采购体系的重要组成部分，巩固和强化与跨采中心客户群体的关系，跨国采购研究会的成员包括跨国公司、供应链企业、政府、高校、供应商。跨国采购研究会将有助于形成客户群体对跨采中心的向心力，同时对跨采中心的品牌度和影响力的建设起积极的推动作用。

为了巩固和强化跨国采购中心对跨国采购研究会的话语权，并考虑到研究会无形价值的建设，研究会将以下三个内容作为开展工作的核心抓手：一是跨国采购专家委员会，二是跨国采购指数，三是跨国采购期刊。

4．打造进口产品与技术展贸中心

跨采中心五角世贸商城的定位与主要功能是进口产品与技术展贸。经磋商在上海市政府支持下，协调浦东新区，外高桥保税区等相关机构，已确定组建“中国（上海）进口产品与技术展贸中心有限公司”，由跨国采购中心有限公司、五角世贸商城开发商麦格贸公司和外高桥保税区共同出资1000万注册成立，该公司将承担运营职责，结合商务部与上海市政府经济政策调整，打造进口产品与技术中心平台。

5．办好首届“全球零售自有品牌产品亚洲展·2010上海”

美国自有品牌制造商协会PLMA每年上半年在芝加哥，下半年在阿姆斯特丹分别召开美洲和欧洲的自有品牌制造商大会，2010年12月，跨采中心将与PLMA联合举办首届“全球零售自有品牌产品亚洲展·2010上海”，这是成功引进的又一个国际会展品牌。此次“全球零售自有品牌产品展”不仅是第一次在上海举办，而且也是第一次在亚洲举办，因此可以称之为“全球品牌，亚洲版块，上海亮点，跨采重点”，第一届的成功举办是这个展会在上海可能持续发展的前提。

第二节 跨境贸易人民币结算

一、背景

2009年4月，国务院常务会议决定在上海市、广州、深圳、珠海、东莞5城市开展跨境贸易人民币结算试点。2009年7月1日，中国人民银行、财政部、商务部、海关总署、国家税务总局和中国银行业监督管理委员会联合发布了由几大部委共同制定的《跨境贸易人民币结算试点管理办法》，这个办法的出台是一个里程碑，标志着人民币开始进入国际贸易结算领域，成为继美元、欧元和日元之后的第四种国际结算货币。

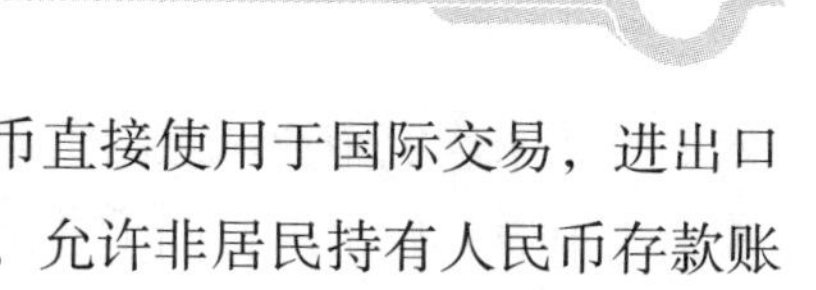

所谓人民币跨境贸易结算，规范地讲是指将人民币直接使用于国际交易，进出口均以人民币计价和结算，居民可向非居民支付人民币，允许非居民持有人民币存款账户。通俗地说就是在国际贸易结算中所使用的货币是人民币,进出口双方用人民币计价，出口方收到的货款是人民币，进口方付出的货款也是人民币。同时在本国居民与非本国居民之间的货币往来也可使用人民币。

二、2009年上海跨境贸易人民币结算的总体情况

2009年7月6日，跨境贸易人民币结算试点在上海率先启动。在上海市相关部门协同推进下，截至2009年年底，上海共有92家企业获得跨境贸易人民币结算试点资格。这92家上海市跨境贸易人民币结算超过21亿元，其中，上海企业通过人民币结算实现货物贸易进口约17.5亿元，出口2.19亿元；服务贸易实现交易额1.67亿元，居全国试点城市首位。

上海市推进跨境贸易人民币结算试点过程中，形成了以积极推进、上门推广、贴身服务等为特色的跨境贸易人民币结算试点工作推进方法：一方面，加强对试点企业的政策培训；另一方面，从2009年10月初起，相关政府部门到东航、大电气、宝钢、丝绸、五矿等大型国有企业现场办公，向企业当面介绍、征求意见，并针对企业提出的难题提出解决的办法。在推进过程中，企业开展跨境贸易人民币结算业务的积极性明显提高，促使上海市跨境贸易人民币结算业务在2009年第四季度呈井喷式增长，上海在这3个月中完成跨境贸易人民币结算业务约18亿元人民币，较为圆满地完成了2009年全年工作任务。

三、上海开展跨境贸易人民币结算工作尚存的一些问题

1．参与企业限制

根据《跨境贸易人民币结算试点管理办法》要求，试点地区的省级人民政府负责协调当地有关部门推荐跨境贸易人民币结算的试点企业，然后由人民银行会同财政部、商务部、海关总署、税务总局、银监会等有关部门进行审核，选择国际结算业务经验丰富，遵守财税、商务、海关和外汇管理各项规定，资信良好的企业参加试点，试点资质要求严格。目前，上海从事外贸的企业有4万多家，但能够被纳入试点的只有92家，加上已经报批准备试点的963家，也不过一千多家。

2．试点区域限制

目前试点政策把境外贸易对手限定在港澳地区和东盟国家的一些企业，采取行政准

入的方式来确定企业试点的资质，在一定程度上影响了跨境贸易人民币贸易结算的潜在需求。上海外贸进出口的主要市场在欧盟、美国和日本。2009年，上海进出口额2777.3亿美元，上海进出口欧盟601亿美元，占比21.6%；进出口美国471.85亿美元，占比17%；进出口日本386.8亿美元，占比14%；进出口香港地区119.78亿美元，占比4.3%。

3．贸易方式单一

跨境贸易人民币结算试点工作的重点是货物贸易，2009年，上海服务贸易进出口预计超过800亿美元，上海服务贸易开展跨境贸易人民币结算金额仅为1.67亿元，占服务贸易额的比重微乎其微

4．境外交易对手对人民币的接受程度有限

跨境贸易人民币结算业务开展后，进行贸易的境内企业可以直接使用人民币进行结算，在大幅降低贸易成本的同时规避了因美元贬值所带来的风险，因而受到广泛欢迎。然而这些企业的境外买家并不接受人民币作为结算货币，加上国内企业与境外交易对手相比普遍处于相对弱势地位，更加大了人民币跨境贸易结算业务开展的难度。在境外，人民币离岸市场功能不健全，海外人民币持有者难以找到保值增值的渠道。

另外，人民币的使用成本偏高。目前，人民币贷款年利率为5.31%，而美元等外币贷款年利率相应较低，也限制了企业跨境贸易人民币结算的积极性。

四、2010年上海推进跨境贸易人民币结算工作重点

在加快推进上海国际贸易中心建设，加快转变外贸发展方式、推进上海开放型经济发展的进程中，上海市商务委员会将把跨境贸易人民币结算作为重要抓手，重点推进以下三方面：

（1）扩大开展跨境贸易人民币结算试点企业和区域范围。一方面，在进一步加快推进上海国有大型企业开展跨境贸易人民币结算业务的同时，积极争取放开试点企业范围，允许合法经营、有进出口资质的上海企业开展跨境贸易人民币结算业务；另一方面，争取试点区域不受港澳、东盟限制，能够扩展到欧美等传统市场，并对境外使用人民币贷款产生的利率差给予适当补贴。

（2）发挥跨境贸易人民币结算在促进服务贸易均与货物贸易协调发展中的作用。上海服务贸易发展很快，2000~2008年，服务贸易进出口额从79亿美元增加到736亿美元，年均增幅超过30%。即使在去年货物贸易降幅较大的情况下，上海服务贸易仍然保持逆势增长，预计将超过800亿美元，约占全国的四分之一。随着上海世博会的举办和加快建设“四个中心”，上海服务贸易发展的优势将更加突出。2010年，上海将

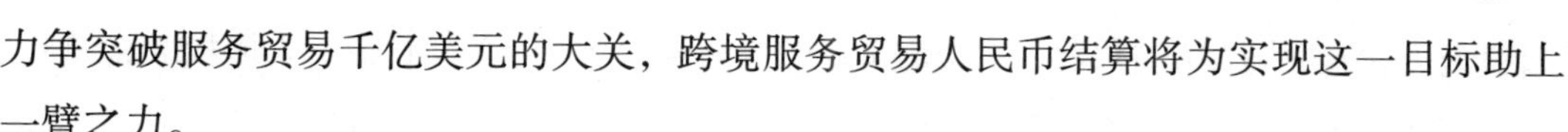

力争突破服务贸易千亿美元的大关，跨境服务贸易人民币结算将为实现这一目标助上一臂之力。

（3）发挥跨境贸易人民币结算在促进“走出去”与“引进来”协调发展中的作用。2009 年上海对外投资总金额 15.36 亿美元，同比增长 117%。新签对外工程承包和劳务合作合同额 124 亿美元，同比增长 12.2%；完成营业额 73.4 亿美元，同比增长 31.8%，规模和增幅均居全国前列。今年 1–2 月份，对外投资总金额 3.9 亿美元，同比增长更是高达 792%。新签对外承包工程和劳务合作合同额达到 18.98 亿美元，同比增长 10.9%；完成营业额 13 亿美元，同比增长 31%。从了解的情况看，上海外经企业，特别是对外工程承包企业，同样有人民币跨境结算的需求。目前，上海市商务委也在积极准备（草拟了《人民币对外直接投资管理办法》），希望通过对外投资、对外工程承包等“走出去”领域加快推进人民币结算，形成非贸易结算的增长点。

第三节 贸易便利化

2008 年下半年以来，我国外贸面临了严峻挑战，为实现“一稳两保”，国办下发了《关于保持对外贸易稳定增长的实施意见》，提出要推进贸易便利化。为贯彻落实国务院关于外贸保稳定增长的文件精神，市政府于 2009 年 3 月 10 日召开了贸易便利化工作专题会议，研究讨论上海如何推进落实贸易便利化工作。专题会议以后，上海市商务委员会按照市委、市政府“四个确保”的要求，认真落实专题会议精神，在各有关部门的大力支持和配合下，大力推进贸易便利化工作。

一、贸易便利化工作主要进展情况及取得的成果

为推进贸易便利化工作，2009 年在唐登杰副市长、沙海林副秘书长的直接领导下，上海市成立了由上海市商务委员会牵头，上海海关、上海检验检疫局、上海市发改委、市金融办、市口岸办、市国税局、外汇局上海分局等 10 个部门组成的贸易便利化联席会议，下设工作小组。分别于 3 月 10 日、5 月 28 日和 7 月 27 日召开了 3 次贸易便利化联席会议，研究推进上海市贸易便利化工作。唐登杰副市长、沙海林副秘书长亲自出席并讲话，各成员的分管领导和工作小组成员都参加。主要完成了以下工作：

1. 建立了贸易便利化工作机制

专题会议以后，上海市政府成立了由上海市商务委员会牵头，市发展改革委、市

国税局、市地税局、市口岸办、市金融办、市工商局、上海海关、上海出入境检验检疫局、外管局上海分局等部门组成的上海市贸易便利化联席会议，联席会议下设工作小组。上海市商务委根据专题会议的要求，会同各有关部门确定了联席会议的成员及联络员。工作机制的建立为上海市贸易便利化工作的顺利推进奠定了良好的基础。

2．形成了贸易便利化工作合力

2009年4月，上海市商务委员会与上海市国税局签署了《税贸协作备忘录》，双方联手主动服务企业，召开了出口退税座谈会、人民币跨境贸易座谈会等，就进出口企业关心的政策和遇到的问题进行解答。上海市商务委员会还与上海检验检疫局形成了贸检合作机制，双方联合组织工业产品出口企业检验工作规范便利推进会、农产品检验检疫培训等。上海检验检疫局与海关、港务和大型国有企业等加强了“关检协作”、“检港联动”和“检企合作”。市发改委牵头推动了市政府与国家质检总局、海关总署分别签订了《合作备忘录》。各成员单位之间建立了各种紧密合作关系，形成了各部门共同推动上海贸易便利化工作的良好氛围。

3．推动了贸易便利化工作的规范化

为做好贸易便利化工作，由上海市商务委员会牵头，先后召开了4次工作小组会和10余次专题协调会，并起草了《上海市贸易便利化工作规程》，对贸易便利化联席会议、工作小组的职责和工作流程、工作机制进行了规定，同时还制定了《上海市贸易便利化联席会议各成员单位职责》。经上海市政府同意，《上海市贸易便利化工作规程》及其附件《上海市贸易便利化联席会议各成员单位职责》已于2009年7月由市政府办公厅向社会发布。

4．完成了贸易便利化效率指标框架研究

根据3月10日专题会议要求，上海市商务委员会会同各成员单位起草了《上海市贸易便利化效率指标框架》。这是全国第一个衡量贸易便利化工作效率的指标体系。经贸易便利化第三次联席会议上通过后，报上海市政府同意，作为《上海市贸易便利化工作规程》的附件一同向社会公布。这套指标根据贸易开展的时间顺序，将贸易便利化指标分为贸易开展前、贸易开展中、贸易开展后，制定了13个指标，分为三类：服务管理指标（9个），效率指标（3个），成本指标（1个）。目前，该指标主要适用于进出口货物贸易，今后还将逐步扩展至服务贸易、国内贸易等方面。

5．推动解决了一批贸易便利化问题

贸易便利化工作开展以来，各成员单位结合自身职能，高度重视企业提出的贸易便利化问题，上海市商务委员会牵头先后召开10余次专题协调会议，研究解决企业的问题。如第一次联席会议以后，针对企业提出的10个问题，各成员单位认真研究，及时解决，对其中年底海关税款资金沉淀、暂缓执行新增法检目录、降低法检费用、增加出口退税申报次数、放宽申报时限、进一步完善收结汇政策措施等5个问题已答复解决，其余如完善海关分类管理办法、加强通关工作关联性、设立政策出台预告期、降低电子口岸收费以及解决企业出口退货等5个问题，由于涉及国家主管部门，也已分别上报相关主管部门。第二次联席会议上，各成员单位解决了企业提出的成套设备出口便利、特殊行业加工贸易手续延长、纺织品法检目录、企业出口收汇核查及扩大外汇网上核销试点等7个问题。目前，通过贸易便利化工作机制，已先后为企业解决和向上反映了17个问题，涉及通关、检验检疫、外汇管理、退税等各个方面，得到了企业的肯定。

此外，贸易便利化工作开展以来，各成员单位按照贸易便利化联席会议的要求，结合自身职能，纷纷出台了许多促进贸易便利、降低企业成本的措施。

二、2010年上海贸易便利化工作思路和措施

2010年，上海贸易便利化工作将面临新的形势，一方面上海市委、市政府对贸易便利化工作将更加重视，已将其作为建设国际贸易中心的重要内容之一；另一方面国内外经济复苏的基础仍不稳固，外贸保市场、保份额的任务依然很重。与此同时，目前贸易便利化工作所面临的问题都是多年来难以解决的难点和瓶颈问题，且多涉及国家有关部门，贸易便利化工作已进入攻坚阶段。因此，2010年推进贸易便利化工作的任务将十分繁重，协调的力度将要加大。

为此，贸易便利化工作的思路是：紧紧围绕上海建设“四个中心”的目标，实施“四个进一步”：即充分发挥联席会议的作用，进一步形成全市推进贸易便利化工作合力；围绕提高贸易便利程度，进一步推进贸易便利化工作创新；全力支持世博会举办，进一步落实贸易便利化各项措施；增强为企业服务的意识，进一步改善贸易环境，力争将上海建设成为“行政效率最高、行政透明度最高、行政收费最少”的城市之一。

1．深化贸易便利化工作，进一步完善工作机制

继续深化《上海市贸易便利化工作规程》，细化各部门工作流程，在认真落实现有贸易便利化工作机制的基础上，进一步建立贸易便利化快速反应机制。根据贸易便利化工作实际，适时增加贸易便利化联席会议成员单位，扩大贸易便利化工作覆盖范围，使更多的企业感受到贸易便利化程度。切实贯彻落实本市与商务部、海关总署、国家质检总局等部门的“部市合作协议”，推进贸易便利化各项政策措施落地。

2．围绕提高贸易便利程度，进一步推进业务创新

大力推进区域通关、通检合作，进一步提升上海口岸的集聚功能，通过扩大区域

合作范围，深化区域合作内容，提高为长三角、长江流域和内地货物在上海口岸进出的便捷程度。进一步优化口岸通关环境，在充分利用水水中转、一门式服务和邮轮通关便利等重点项目调研基础上，争取实质性取得突破。创新“水水中转”查验监管模式，继续深化完善“一门式”服务。加快建立综合信息共享平台的建设，尽快建成集中审单、电子派单的工作模式，推进上海“电子口岸”建设。加强部门协作，大力推进报关、报检实现“一单两报”。继续深化人民币跨境贸易试点工作，积极争取扩大试点范围和试点区域。进一步简化外汇管理内部审核流程，扎实推进依法行政，建立健全外汇业务处理的首问负责制，提升外汇管理部门的对外服务水平。推进贸易进出口收付汇核销制度改革，继续推进服务贸易外汇管理改革和特殊监管区的外汇管理工作，充分发挥上海特殊监管区种类多、业务量大的优势，积极探索新的业务监管模式。同时，积极稳妥推进境外直接投资便利化，支持境内企业开展境外直接投资。积极推进本市特殊监管区功能优化，继续协调推进“三区”、“三港”联动发展，积极争取洋山保税港区扩区，推动浦东机场综合保税区建设，协调落实封关验收工作。

3．全力支持世博会的举办，进一步落实各项便利化措施

积极支持世博会的筹备和举办工作，为世博货物进出口提供良好的服务。在检验检疫方面，在已建立的检验检疫工作机制基础上，进一步加强与世博会筹备相关单位的联络与沟通，认真落实世博会检验检疫通关的优惠政策和便捷措施，为世博会提供“一门式”服务。在通关方面，成立专门工作部门，落实专人负责，对世博货物进出口设立专门通道，为世博货物出入境提供优质服务。在外汇管理方面，认真落实世博会外汇支持政策，进一步给予境外参展机构外汇账户开立、使用以及场馆建设、世博局用汇等方面的便利和支持。

4．继续做好为企业的服务工作，进一步改善贸易环境

加大贸易便利化工作宣传力度。抓紧编制贸易便利化宣传手册，并通过行业协会、培训会议、调研等多种方式，向广大进出口企业进行宣传，扩大贸易便利化工作的影响。深化贸易便利化工作调研，学习主要国际贸易中心城市的先进经验和做法。针对进出口企业提出的各类贸易便利化问题，及时帮助企业解决问题。协调做好货物通关中收费问题，深入开展本市中转集装箱有关收费情况的调研，提出上海港有竞争力的收费管理体系和相关标准。继续做好2010年各类许可证管理工作，积极为企业申领提供便利，同时，积极向国家有关部门反映本市企业的诉求。

第四节 公平贸易

一、2009 年我国出口贸易摩擦形势特点

2009 年是贸易摩擦形势较为严峻的一年。受金融危机影响，国际贸易保护主义升温，中国出口产品面临的贸易摩擦也大幅上升。一年间，共有 18 个国家（地区）对我启动 119 起贸易救济调查，比 2008 年同期增加 11 起。其中，反倾销 76 起，同比减少 4 起；反补贴 13 起，同比增加 2 起；保障措施 23 起，同比增加 9 起；特别保障措施 7 起，同比增加 4 起。

（一）贸易摩擦立案创历史新高

在全球经济低迷背景下，2009 年我国出口增幅出现了一定程度的下滑。尽管如此，2009 年国外对我贸易摩擦立案数却是历史最高。在出口同比下降 15.9% 的情况下，贸易摩擦立案数同比上升 10%。对比 2002 年入世之初的 66 起，2009 年的发案增长率高达 80%。从下表中可看出我国入世以来的贸易量和受到的贸易摩擦案情况。

表 5-1 我国历年出口情况与贸易摩擦发案统计表

项目	2001	2002	2003	2004	2005	2006	2007	2008	2009
出口额（亿美元）	2662	3256	4384	5934	7620	9691	12180	14285	12017
出口增幅（%）	6.8	22.3	34.6	35.4	28.4	27.2	25.7	17.2	-15.9
外贸顺差（亿美元）		304	255	320	1019	1175	2622	2955	1961
贸易摩擦发案数（起）		66	56	65	78	84	74	108	119

（二）发展中国家反倾销立案数已超发达国家

以前对我国发起贸易摩擦的国家多集中在发达国家，2 年前已有迹象表明发展中国家对我国的发案在上升，2009 年这个上升的趋势已变成实际上的超越，即发展中国家对我国的立案数超过了发达国家的立案数。2009 年 18 个对我发起反倾销调查的国家中，4 个是发达国家，共启动 23 起反倾销调查; 发展中国家 14 个，共启动 53 起。其中，阿根廷居首位，发起 19 起，占 2009 年国外对我反倾销案件总数的 25%；其次是美国，发起 12 起，占比 15.8%；居第三位的是印度，发起 10 起，占比 13.2%。

（三）美国是反补贴调查的主要发起者

2004–2008 年，我国共遭遇 24 起反补贴调查，占同期全球反补贴调查总数（47 起）的 51.1%，居各成员之首，而且连续 3 年（2006、2007 和 2008 年）成为全球反补贴调查的最大受害者。2009 年，我国遭遇 13 起反补贴调查，创历年之最。其中，美国启动 10 起，高居榜首，占比高达 76.9 %；澳大利亚、加拿大和印度各启动 1 起。在国外对我启动的13起反补贴调查中，涉及冶金产品的案件数居首位，为7起，其中美国启动6起，加拿大 1 起；其次是化工，为 2 起，分别由印度和美国各启动 1 起；居第二位的是纺织、建材、造纸和有色金属，均为 1 起，其中，涉及纺织、建材和造纸的案件均由美国启动，涉及有色金属的由澳大利亚启动。

二、上海贸易摩擦涉案情况及相关工作

上海市产业转型相对较早，且出口企业以贸易公司居多，因此 2009 年贸易摩擦涉案数量与金额较 2008 年未出现大幅波动。119 起贸易摩擦案件中，涉及上海的有 68 起，涉案金额 6.67 亿美元。

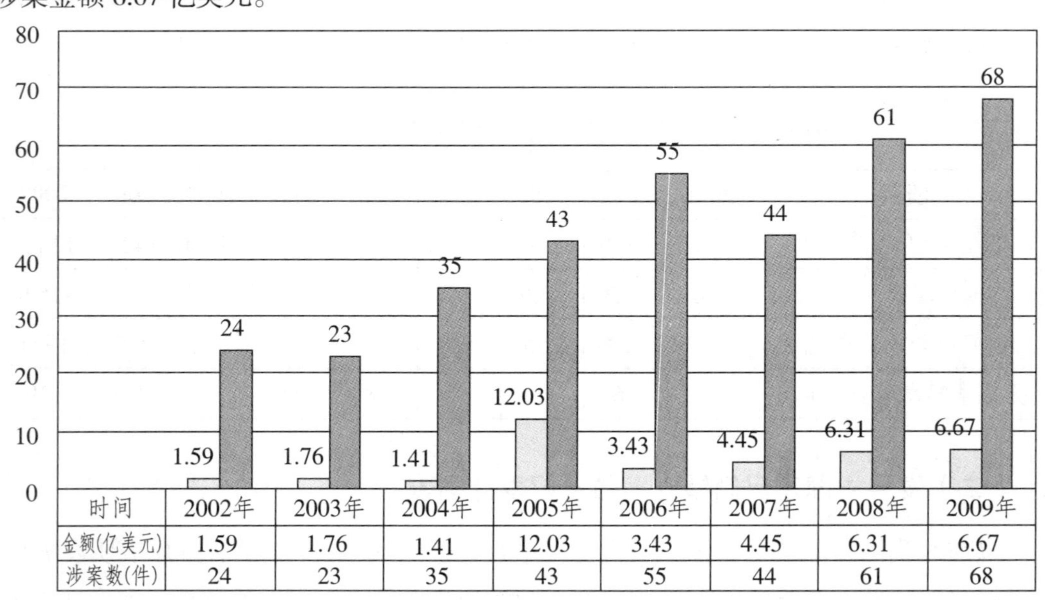

时间	2002年	2003年	2004年	2005年	2006年	2007年	2008年	2009年
金额(亿美元)	1.59	1.76	1.41	12.03	3.43	4.45	6.31	6.67
涉案数(件)	24	23	35	43	55	44	61	68

图 5-1　入世后各年度上海的涉案数和涉案金额

为有效应对贸易摩擦，确保经济平稳较快发展，上海市进出口公平贸易工作以行业协会为平台，强化了出口应对、技术性贸易壁垒及知识产权纠纷等方面的专业服务，并加大了司法维权、进口救济的协调力度。主要表现在五个方面：

1．深化出口贸易摩擦应对中的专业指导与协调

2009年以来，上海市商务委员会与上海市进出口商会、相关行业协会合作，以“培训指导、组织协调与重点跟踪”三头并进的方式协调了美国油井管、印度SDH光传输设备、澳大利亚铝挤压材、美国钢格板、欧盟铝合金轮毂等20余起反倾销、反补贴案件。在各方的共同努力下，上海企业在已裁决的美国的钢制螺杆反倾销、巴西的一次性注射器反倾销、加拿大的床垫用弹簧组件反倾销、欧盟的铝箔反倾销、印度的轮胎反倾销等多起案件中都赢得了低税率，保住了海外市场。

2．利用进口贸易救济保护国内产业

进口贸易救济调查是维护国家利益和产业利益的重要途径，也是金融危机形势下反击贸易保护主义的手段之一。自机构改革明确上海市商务委进口倾销与产业损害调查相关职能后，市商务委配合商务部开展了甲醇、苯酚、PVC、紧固件等相关进口反倾销案件的调研、协调，有效抑制了进口低价产品对国内产业的冲击。此外，上海市商务委还具体承办了由商务部、工业和信息化部、上海市人民政府联合主办的第六届中国产业国际竞争力论坛。国务院有关部委、省市相关主管部门负责人，进出口商会、行业协会、中外企业界和研究机构等350余名代表参加了论坛。论坛旨在为产业界提供一个充分交流经验、相互了解的平台，促进经济增长方式转变和产业结构优化。

3．重视技术性贸易壁垒应对的信息统计与资讯交流

技术性贸易壁垒应对是稳定外贸出口的重要一环。国际需求萎缩，贸易保护主义抬头形势下，上海市质监局、上海市商务委员会等相关部门合作开展了多项技术性贸易壁垒应对工作。

（1）开展“国外技术性贸易措施影响及应对情况调查”，通过对7大类行业、1288家企业发放调查问卷，基本摸清了上海市企业受技术性贸易措施影响的情况。

（2）创建“上海市技术性贸易措施信息服务平台”，以出口企业为主要服务对象，及时准确地提供贸易壁垒信息，建立技术性贸易措施信息沟通协调机制，加强政府和企业之间的信息双向沟通，实现技术性贸易措施信息发布、预警和服务，为政府决策提供支持。

（3）开展培训，提高企业、行业协会的技术性贸易措施应对水平。在2009年5月的企业公平贸易培训会上，将技术性贸易壁垒的应对作为重要内容融入培训。

（4）组建新的“上海市技术性贸易措施应对工作组”，对原有的“上海市技术性贸易措施应对工作领导小组”进行改组。

4．知识产权应对工作规范化

为落实市府《关于本市实施〈国家知识产权战略纲要〉若干意见》、《关于保持上

海对外贸易稳定增长的若干意见》等文件精神，推动上海外贸转型和升级，市商务委草拟了《关于促进本市与贸易相关的知识产权工作的若干意见》，并召开“技术性贸易壁垒与知识产权应对工作意见咨询会”，听取机关、协会、企业、院校各领域专家意见。

5．拓展工作平台，扩大服务内容

行业协会等中介机构是进出口公平贸易工作的中坚力量。从最初的9家到现在的20家，上海市进出口公平贸易行业工作站队伍不断壮大。除继续指导行业协会开展案件应对、预警调研、信息统计、标准制定、国际交流、培训宣传等工作外，2009年上海市商务委员会又指导相关协会开展了江浙沪进出口企业国际贸易现状调查、国际化妆品公司对中国化妆品市场的垄断和我产业损失情况调查、钢管行业补贴扶持政策统计、纺织出口市场协调、集成电路产业扶持政策统计、重点行业后危机时代产业竞争力调研等多项活动，将公平贸易工作充分融入行业发展、企业经营活动中去。

三、2010年上海公平贸易工作展望

1．进一步加大支持力度，推动发展中国家应诉

针对发展中国家立案多、案件应诉组织难问题，2010年，拟进一步巩固、健全发展中国家贸易摩擦应诉援助机制，联合行业协会组织符合一定标准的涉案企业集体应诉，开展对外协调，提供法律服务。

2．加强知识产权海外维权

推动出台《关于促进与对外贸易有关的知识产权工作的若干意见》，完善以对外贸易为导向的、跨部门的知识产权工作协调机制，加强与贸易发展相适应的知识产权法治建设，推进与知识产权有关的国际贸易争端应对工作，加强与知识产权相关的标准化工作，落实知识产权海外维权。

3．着力开展产业损害贸易救济相关工作

贸易救济工作是维护国家利益和产业利益的重要手段。近年来，面对国外低价进口产品的冲击，国内产业寻求贸易救济保护的呼声日渐高涨，救济诉求不断增多。2010年，拟在加强贸易救济培训和宣传的基础上加大贸易救济工作力度，密切产业联系，维护产业安全和合法权益。

第六章　区　县

第一节　浦东新区

一、2009年浦东新区外经贸发展情况

（一）外贸发展情况

1．外贸进出口总额下降，重点工业品优势明显

2009年，浦东新区进出口总额1389.89亿美元，同比下降12.9%，占全市的50%。其中，出口576.5亿美元，同比下降16.9%；进口813.39亿美元，同比下降9.8%。

（1）出口商品结构

重点工业品占总出口额的近60%，比2008年上升了0.5个百分点。其中，集成电路产品出口恢复较快，全年出口下降12.4%，占比8.7%，较去年上升0.5个百分点；船舶等成套设备产品由于订单周期长，此次受金融危机影响较小，全年出口增长率2.5%，占比20%，比去年上升4个百分点；汽车及零部件产品出口受金融危机影响较为严重，同比下降33.8%，占比1.8%，比去年下降0.4个百分点。受益于出口退税率提高、国内竞争优势明显等因素，纺织服装等劳动密集型产品出口下滑程度较轻，全年出口下降12.4%，占比15.1%，比去年上升0.9个百分点。

（2）出口市场结构

2009年，出口商品销往223个国家和地区，比上年增加1个。浦东新区的主要出口市场仍为亚洲、欧洲和北美洲，占比分别为47.3%、25.7%和17.4%。与2008年相比，亚洲和欧洲市场的份额进一步提高，北美则略有下降。

2．增长方式进一步转变，服务平台进一步完善

（1）转变外贸增长方式，完善外贸服务平台

与相关部门在质检十四条、海关改革、生物医药监管等方面推出监管新模式并试点推广。

（2）做好各类展会的管理与组织工作

组织浦东新区企业参加第105届、第106届广交会、第19届华交会、第六届中国－

东盟博览会等展会。

（3）推进“走出去”战略实施

积极组织企业参加中小企业国际博览会等有关展会。

（二）外资发展情况

1．外商投资以企业增资为主

2009年，浦东新区新设外资项目780个，引进合同外资55.29亿美元，同比增长0.3%，占全市总量约41.6%；实际到位资金39.08亿美元，同比增长0.9%，占全市总量的37.1%。

（1）企业增资占主要地位。2009年浦东新区共有846家企业增资，新增合同外资37.65亿美元，占当年合同外资总额的68.1%，分别比去年同期减少12.2%和10.1%，虽受国际FDI投资大幅收缩影响稍有下降，但企业增资依然是吸引外资的重中之重。2009年增资金额超过1000万美元的项目有106个，共增加合同外资28.75亿美元，占当年合同外资的52%。增资行业以三产为主，约占新区外资企业增资额的81.7%，主要集中在房地产经营、软件服务、仓储运输、商业、贸易、商务服务、专业咨询、企业管理机构、金融租赁等行业。

（2）跨国公司地区总部占全市半壁江山。2009年浦东新区共有获认定的跨国公司地区总部17家，占全市（36家）47.2%。至此，浦东新区历年累计获认定的跨国公司地区总部达到132家，占全市（共260家）50.8%。

（3）外资大项目仍起支撑作用。2009年浦东新区新批投资总额超过1000万美元以上的大项目有65个，占项目数的8.3%，同比减少8.5%，合同外资16.07亿美元，占当年合同外资的29.1%，同比增长43.5%。

（4）投资国别情况。截至2009年12月，来浦东新区投资的国家（地区）总数达到110个。投资前5位国家或地区（以合同外资为依据）依次为：中国香港地区、开曼群岛、英属维尔京群岛、美国、日本。

2．整体推进，注重协调

（1）做好招商引资整体推进工作。召开招商引资工作会议，组团参加“98厦洽会”并召开“浦东新区战略发展推介会”，外资企业早餐会、德国企业浦东日等活动。

（2）推进迪斯尼、大飞机、上海大唐产业园等一批重大项目落户浦东新区上海迪斯尼乐园项目已于2009年10月获国家有关部门正式核准。推进大飞机项目一总部、三个中心（研发设计中心、总装制造中心、客服中心）总体规划和建设。

（3）加强重点产业和重点项目的推进协调。推进威盛总部大楼、HENGSOFT、上

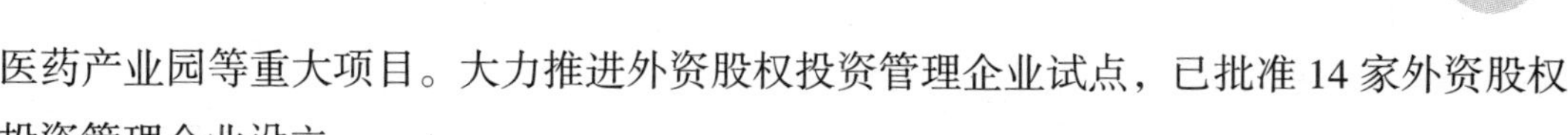

医药产业园等重大项目。大力推进外资股权投资管理企业试点，已批准 14 家外资股权投资管理企业设立。

（4）持续推动总部经济和服务外包发展。1–12 月新入驻 17 家总部机构。帮助 59 家企业、3 家培训机构服务外包企业申请商务部服务外包扶持资金。

（三）外经发展情况

2009 年，浦东新区共有对外投资项目 47 个，同比增长 198%，投资总额为 1.67 亿美元，同比增长 106%，投资的国别和地区分别为香港特区、美国、澳大利亚、韩国、法国、澳门特区、印度、安哥拉、土耳其等。

1．对外投资的规模逐步扩大

从 2000 年开始，随着上海市出台有关“走出去”战略的政策，浦东新区对外投资的项目从 2、3 个开始逐年增加。2004 年以后每年都有 10 个以上项目投资，增长的势头十分踊跃。2007 年全年项目已达到 33 个，2008 年受金融危机的影响回落到 23 个，自 2009 年境外投资项目进行网上申报核准，加上全球经济出现回暖，浦东新区境外投资的项目达到历史新高，全年项目数为 47 个。

2．对外投资的市场趋向国际化

浦东新区对外投资项目主要集中在亚洲，其次为北美、非洲和南美，最后是欧洲。按新区对外投资额前 10 位的国家和地区排位：泰国、墨西哥、开曼群岛、加拿大、中国香港特区、越南、美国、俄罗斯、尼日尔、巴西。由此可见，新区对外投资地域逐步扩大，已具有一定的国际化端倪，并且还在不断地向更多的国家和地区延伸。

3．对外投资的格局趋向多元化

到 2009 年为止，浦东新区对外投资项目中，生产加工类项目占 50%（以纺织、化工为主），贸易类项目占 20%，资源开发类项目占 14%（以矿产、木材为主），收购兼并类项目占 6%，高科技类项目占 10%。浦东新区对外投资的项目从原先单一以贸易和生产加工为主，逐步趋向高科技和各领域，多元化的投资使产业能级得到进一步的提升。虽然浦东新区的对外投资还未成规模，但与我国对外投资一般以贸易起步相比较，体现了起步晚、起点高的特点。

4．民营企业成为对外投资的主力军

目前民营企业的对外投资数已达 98 个，投资总额达 2.75 亿美元，占浦东新区对外投资的 30%。希望集团、华辰集团、美林康集团、上海丰佳投资管理有限公司、上海达之路集团有限公司等民营企业在境外都已连续投资了多个项目。

二、2010年浦东新区外经贸发展趋势

（一）全面落实保增长措施，推动外贸管理新思路

推动设立“浦东新区外经贸发展专项资金”。用好“中小企业国际市场开拓资金”、“广交会、华交会专项补贴”、“企业出口信用保险补贴”等专项补贴和财政配套资金。推动建立“中小外贸企业融资担保专项资金”。

设立并完善外经贸经济工作管理体系，构筑多层次的贸易促进体系。推动外经贸管理体制创新，促进贸易和投资便利化。积极引导有条件的企业实施“走出去”，培育一批有国际竞争力的浦东新区本地跨国经营企业。推动企业扩大重要能源、原材料和重要农业生产资料进口。鼓励支持企业以各种形式到境外办厂、开发矿山和境外收购等活动。进一步完善广交会、华交会等国内外展会的组织管理与服务工作机制，不断增强竞争力。

（二）协调推进大项目的落地

结合国际金融中心、航运中心、贸易中心建设，以及大飞机和重大旅游等项目，加强对中国移动视频基地、大唐电信产业园、民营企业总部园区、商业区、服务外包基地、旅游项目等基地项目，以及八大高新技术产业领域的重点招商。做好大项目储备、土地储备、资源库建设，研究制订纳税大户跟踪服务和责任落实机制。做好已落户项目的排摸、后期跟踪和协调推进等“安商稳商”工作。

（三）研究制定战略招商的机制，推进浦东新区整体招商

整合全区资源，研究制订战略招商、产业基地招商、功能招商计划。会同有关部门梳理原浦东和原南汇的招商政策，研究制订招商引资考核奖励办法，建立重点项目快速推进、投资项目信息共享和共赢机制。加强与国内新闻媒体、境内外贸易促进机构的合作，赴香港地区等地开展专题招商活动，加大浦东新区投资环境的宣传，提高浦东新区投资发展的国际形象。

案例：上海瑞柯恩国际贸易有限公司

上海瑞柯恩国际贸易有限公司（简称瑞柯恩公司）成立于1999年，是一家主营文

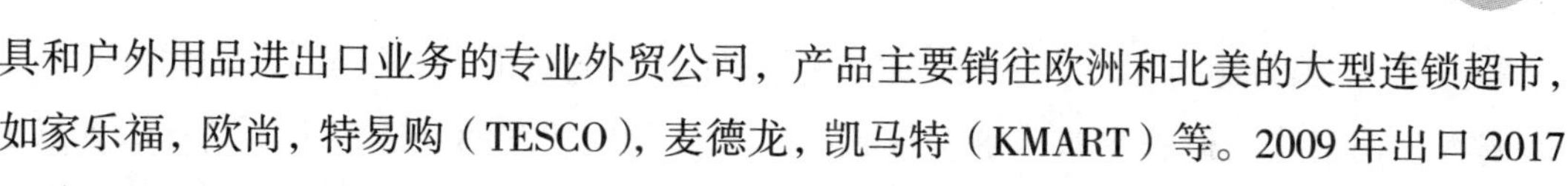

具和户外用品进出口业务的专业外贸公司，产品主要销往欧洲和北美的大型连锁超市，如家乐福，欧尚，特易购（TESCO），麦德龙，凯马特（KMART）等。2009 年出口 2017 万美元，同比增长 87%。该公司发展良好的经验主要有以下两点：

（一）重视品牌的建设

成立了品牌建设小组，努力创立自有品牌，并到国外打响自己的品牌。至今瑞柯恩公司的商标已在欧盟 25 个国家注册，印有瑞柯恩公司品牌的商品遍及这些国家的主流超市和卖场。瑞柯恩公司公司还积极参加国内外的各种展销会，如广交会、印度尼西亚中国商品展、英国伯明翰春季展等，通过这些交易平台，结识了国外新的客商，拓宽了交易渠道，销售额也突飞猛进。

（二）及时进行了战略转型

从原先的简单产品提供商转变为供应链解决方案的提供者，也就是"产品 + 服务"的提供者，为目标客人提供一揽子解决方案，提供增值服务。与生产厂家相比，瑞柯恩公司作为贸易商，优势不在价格，而在于增值服务，体现在如下几个方面：

1．一站式采购：ONE-STOP-BUY

文具和办公用品品类庞杂，大类有几十个品类，小类上千个品种。任何一家工厂最多提供两三个品类，没有办法提供所有的品种。瑞柯恩公司充分发挥贸易商的优势，为大型连锁超市提供一站式采购服务，极大地便利了零售商的供应链管理。

2．设计和研发

瑞柯恩公司每年初都会做预算，投入销售额的一定比例作为研发费用。瑞柯恩公司建有自己的研发团队，经常出国考察，做市场调研，对市场和产品的流行趋势有深刻的了解。同时，瑞柯恩公司每年做一次市场流行趋势发布会，提供采购建议给国外客商，引导瑞柯恩客人的采购行为。得益于创新和研发，瑞柯恩公司的产品总是能引领时尚潮流，总是能和竞争对手的大陆货产品区隔开来，从而能够取得定价的主动权，取得良好的经济效益，避开了恶性的价格竞争，开辟出一片新的蓝海。

3．向供应链下游延伸，做客人供应链管理的助手

瑞柯恩公司和国外一些大零售商建立了战略性的合作伙伴关系，按瑞柯恩公司的要求，零售商将全年的订单计划下给瑞柯恩公司，由瑞柯恩公司安排生产，然后产品库存在公司仓库里，这样买家随时要货，瑞柯恩公司就可以随时发货。这样做的双赢在于对国外零售商来说，他们不用囤积大量的库存在他们国外的仓库，大大降低了他们的库存水平，减少了资金占用；对瑞柯恩公司来说则拿到了全年的完整订单（而不是

零散订单），销售额有了很大增长。瑞柯恩公司还十分注重风险防范，与国内外大的资信调查公司合作，调查零售商的资信状况，并且做到动态的资信管理，只有信誉卓著的大公司，瑞柯恩公司才会提供这项增值服务。

第二节 黄浦区

一、2009 年黄浦区外经贸发展情况

（一）外贸发展情况及特点

据海关数据统计，2009 年黄浦区全年完成外贸进出口 215838 万美元，同比下降 4.3%，其中完成外贸出口 88147 万美元，同比下降 23%; 完成外贸进口 127691 万美元，同比增长 14.8%。

1．进出口规模扩大，降幅较小

黄浦区外贸进出口降幅较小。分季度看，一、二、三、四季度进出口总量分别为 41106 万美元、87910 万美元、143641 万美元和 215838 万美元，同比下降分别为 8.8%、9.4%、8.3% 和 4.3%。随着稳外需政策效应进一步显现，国际市场需求趋稳，全区出口连续数月超过 6500 万美元。即使在 12 月份的外贸“淡季”也达到月单 7400 万美元，创下 4 月份 7756 万美元以外的又一新高，同比降幅也由年中最高的 11.4% 收窄到年末的 4.3%，实际收窄幅度 7.1 个百分点。

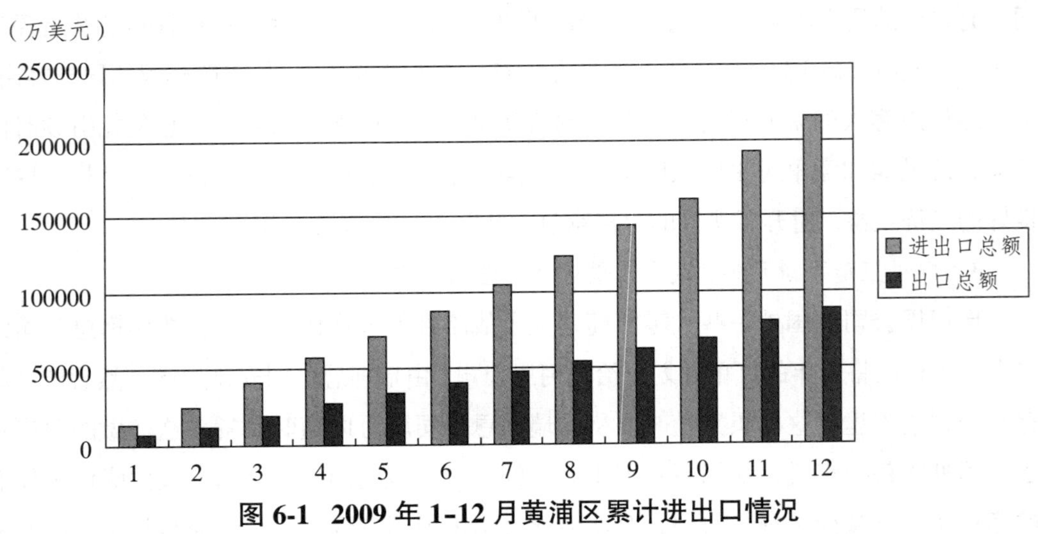

图 6-1 2009 年 1-12 月黄浦区累计进出口情况

2．大宗商品进口量增加，机电产品进口由降转升

2009 年大宗商品进口量保持较快增长，其中动物产品进口增长较快，达 153%；肉及实用杂碎产品增长 403%；初级塑料制品增长 62%。年初全区机电和高新技术产品进口大幅下降，经过二、三、四季度的调整已趋于好转，贸易量也由降幅转为增幅，截至 2009 年底，机电产品进口 57178 万美元，同比增长 12%。

表 6-1　2009 年黄浦区进口主要商品情况

商品名称	进口金额（万美元）	同比（%）	占比（%）
机电设备	57178	11.7	44.8
光学医疗等	11956	15.7	9.4
塑料及制品	8765	62	6.9
木浆纸浆等	6713	-6.8	5.3
化学工业及产品	6603	-13.1	5.2

3．劳动密集型产品出口下滑小，机电和高科技产品出口降幅大

因受益于国家提高出口退税政策，加上民生产品的需求，服装等劳动密集型产品出口，竞争优势依然明显，产品降幅明显低于出口总体降幅。2009 年服装类产品出口 8791 万美元，同比下降 4.9%；玩具类产品出口 1463 万美元，同比增长 0.6%。由于国际市场需求回稳迟缓，机电和高科技产品出口中，全年机电产品出口 18061 万美元，同比下降 35.7%，降幅较之总体降幅明显放大，且与年初的 20% 的降幅相比有扩大趋势。

表 6-2　2009 年黄浦区出口主要商品情况

商品名称	出口金额（万美元）	同比（%）	占比（%）
纺织原料及制品	24688	-13.5	28
机电设备	18061	-35.7	20.5
杂项制品	10828	-20.8	12.3
贱金属及制品	9120	-20.3	10.3
化学工业及产品	5969	-23.1	6.8

4．不同类型企业进出口情况不尽相同

黄浦区各类外贸企业在金融危机影响的困难形势下，积极用好政策，求稳保市场、节能促增长，取得了良好效果。三资企业完成进出口 103503 万美元，同比增长 13.4%，

占全区进出口量的48%。其中出口12213万美元，同比下降27%；进口91290万美元，同比增长22%。进口增幅保持稳定增长的企业有：NIKON仪器（上海）有限公司全年累计进口45853万美元，同比增长35%。

外贸公司及工贸公司完成进出口112334万美元，同比下降16.4%，占黄浦区进出口52%。其中出口75934万美元，同比下降22.4%；进口36400万美元，同比下降0.7%。外贸骨干企业出口贸易虽显降幅，但业绩仍然突出，如："上海豫园旅游商城股份有限公司"全年累计出口10052万美元，同比下降30%；"一百"全年累计出口6654万美元，同比下降22%。

5．日、美出口降幅缩小，新兴市场出口增多

2009年黄浦区出口前五大贸易伙伴国中，对日本市场的出口降幅持续低于出口总体降幅的5%。全年出口日本市场16165万美元，同比下降18.32%；出口美国市场13364万美元，同比下降26.7%；出口东盟7156万美元，同比降幅缩减为5.9%。而对部分新兴市场出口却有所增多，全年出口到南非、阿联酋市场分别为4788万美元和3017万美元，同比增长82.5%和91%。

表6-3 2009年黄浦区主要贸易国贸易情况

国家（地区）	出口		占比（%）
	金额（万美元）	同比（%）	
日本	16165	-18	18.3
美国	13364	-27	15.2
中国香港特区	11058	-32	12.5
南非	4788	82	0.5
阿联酋	3017	91	0.3
泰国	23638	44	18.5
日本	19438	33	15.2
德国	13931	-0.5	10.9
美国	10437	16	8.2
印度尼西亚	8799	24	6.9

6．新进外贸企业也有业绩表现

2009年新注册并已投入贸易运作的新贸易企业86家，其中商贸企业72家，三资企业14家。新注册企业全年累计进出口总额5223万美元，其中出口2101万美元，进

口 3122 万美元。

7. 进口产品大类变化不大

2009 年全区进口业绩良好，达到同比增长 14.8%，其中进口前 3 位的产品还是机电类产品，进口 57178 万美元，同比增长 12%；光学类产品进口 11956 万美元，同比增长 15.7%；塑料制品进口 8765 万美元，同比增长 62%。

（二）外经发展情况

2009 年由于受国际金融危机影响，国外中小企业人员紧缩，需求减少，故劳务业务受到影响。上海黄浦对外经济技术合作有限公司 2009 年外派劳务 15 人，15 人均为派往日本的服装制衣工，同比下降 37%。新签定合同金额 51 万美元，完成营业额 123 万美元，年末在外人数 134 人。

（三）2009 年外经贸工作重点

1. 积极宣传政策，为企业发展创造有利的环境

定期召开外贸工作例会。在例会上对每季度黄浦区外贸情况进行经济运行分析，使企业了解整个区外贸进出口概况。还安排了信保公司为企业讲解信用保险政策专题，帮助企业规避出口风险。另外还邀请农行、建行行长和企业交流、通过介绍“融税通”等金融产品帮助企业应对国际金融危机的冲击。

2. 积极用好政策，为企业发展提供有力支持

（1）根据上海市商务委员会要求做好保持外贸稳定增长专项资金的申报工作，主要对企业开拓新兴市场、建设境外营销网络、促进出口结构调整等业务上给予补助。

（2）做好“中小企业国际市场开拓资金”申报工作。在规定的时间结点内对全区 119 个项目完成了拨付工作。拨付金额为 186 万元，主要从企业网站建设、市场考察、产品认证等项目上有力地支持了中小企业的工作。

3. 做好服务外包工作

（1）积极组织企业申报上海市服务外包重点企业。截至去年年底黄浦区有 8 家企业（汇丰、爱吉、维音、菱通、电通、亿贝、爱德威、希世）被认定。这些企业主要服务领域是商业流程及软件系统的外包。

（2）积极组织企业参加第二届中国服务贸易大会。企业反映通过参加包括设计服务、数字动漫游戏洽谈专场、中国国际广告服务创新高峰论坛等专题活动，接触了客户，受益匪浅。

（3）积极组织企业申报 2008 年度上海市配套服务外包发展资金。根据市商务委统

一的工作部署，积极组织企业参加申报工作。共组织了9家企业301人进行服务外包人才录用资金申报和1家企业服务外包行业认证资金的申报。

（4）积极组织企业申报2009年商务部关于服务外包企业人才录用资金。共有9家企业126人申请。

（5）2家企业被认定为黄浦区第一批技术先进型服务企业（大专以上学历要占当年职工总数的50%以上、技术先进型服务业务收入综合占本企业当年总收入的70%以上、应获得包括开发能力和成熟度模型等有关国际认证、离岸收入不低于当年总收入的50%）。

4．组织企业参展，积极为企业开拓市场服务

（1）积极组织企业参加中国进出口商品交易会，今年春秋两季黄浦区共有17家企业参加，摊位173个。通过这个平台，企业充分展示自己的产品，签约意向合同金额4006万美元。

（2）积极组织企业参加第19届中国华东进出口商品交易会，共有9家企业参展，展位17个，主要分布在家具馆、饰品馆和纺织馆。

（3）组织爱姆意、豫园等4家企业作为采购商参加第六届东盟博览会，企业通过这一平台展示自己的产品，积极开拓东盟新兴市场。

5．做好加工贸易审批工作

审批加工贸易企业生产能力证明28份。实地考察新增加工贸易企业生产场地，主动上门指导其开展加工贸易，指出其管理不当之处。审批加工贸易合同115份，进出口总额4929万美元。其中：审批来料加工合同19份，进出口总额1174万美元；审批进料加工合同96份，进出口总额3755万美元。审批变更合同45份。其中来料合同4份，进料合同41份。

表6-4 2009年黄浦区一般贸易及加工贸易总量及比重（单位：亿美元）

项目	进口额	出口额	进出口总额
一般贸易	12.8	8.8	21.6
加工贸易	0.12	0.41	0.53
加工占比重	0.94%	4.66%	2.45%

6．关于“走出去”工作

组织企业参加由中智公司主办的跨国经营管理人员的培训。加强境外机构项目和人员安全保护工作，保障“走出去”战略顺利实施，确保落实各项安全防范措施。组织企业自查，落实各项措施。妥善解决黄浦外经公司派遣日本劳务人员事件。

二、2010 年黄浦区外经贸发展趋势

调整发展方式，逐步扩大高新技术、产品、装备制造产品和服务贸易的比重，大力发展离岸贸易，进一步提高贸易便利化程度，同时要在“走出去”和拓展国际新市场上实现新突破。

（一）千方百计扩大外贸进出口

继续培育区域外贸进出口持续发展后劲。着重抓好进出口大户企业的服务和促进工作，避免外贸进出口大起大落，不断增强区域进出口发展后劲。一是重点关注支持年进出口额在 500 万美元以上的重点外贸企业大户；二是支持具备条件的企业申报进出口经营权，引进和培养一批出口能力强的外贸企业；三是加强培训，使新增企业尽快开展进出口业务；四是定期召开外贸工作例会。借助召开外贸工作例会的平台，一方面传达国家关于外贸的最新政策精神，另一方面增进企业之间互相沟通了解，促进政府与企业、企业与企业之间的信息沟通。

（二）培育自主品牌，加大出口商品结构调整

不断提高外贸出口企业的市场竞争能力。做好做强黄浦区的出口品牌工作，不断提高外贸出口企业的市场竞争能力。继续组织企业参加韩国经贸洽谈会、美国亚洲商品采购大会、中国品牌出口商品欧洲展等。优先组织拥有自主品牌的企业参加国内外的展会。

（三）认真实施“走出去”战略

帮助有条件的企业开拓境外市场，争取在离岸贸易方面有所突破；经常“回头看”，加强对境外企业监控和管理；搭建平台，组织培训。邀请有关专家为企业培训有关业务知识，如企业要遵守所投资的东道国的法律法规、风俗习惯等专业知识，将企业“走出去”风险降低到最低限度。

（四）积极组织企业参会参展

参会参展是企业广交客户、拓展市场的最有效手段。2010 年黄浦区仍将积极组织企业参加中国进出口商品交易会、华交会、中国（上海）国际跨国采购大会、东盟博览会等有影响力的展会，使企业能充分展示自己的产品，有效拓展国际市场，争取更多的贸易机会。

（五）妥善应对贸易争端

随着国际金融危机带来的贸易保护主义抬头倾向，2009年包括印度等发展中国家也加入到针对我国出口产品的反倾销行列。通过对全区外贸企业的梳理排摸，制订和完善企业应对贸易摩擦联络机制，配合市商务委做好企业积极应对反倾销相关诉讼案件取证调查工作。组织召开外贸例会，请市商务委公平贸易处指导工作。不断增强企业应对“两反一保”（反倾销，反补贴、特殊保障措施）的能力。

（六）做好服务外包工作

服务外包产业是现代高端服务业的重要组成部分，它具有附加值高、环境污染少、吸纳就业（特别是大学生就业）能力强、国际化水平高等特点。一是组织企业登录商务部网站，使更多服务外包企业登录商务部的“千百十工程”。二是用好商务部的服务外包人才培训资金，使符合条件的企业都能享受政策。提高企业竞争力，把黄浦区服务外包企业做大做强。三是积极宣传（2009）49号文政策，组织企业学习《上海市促进服务外包产业发展专项资金使用和管理试行办法》。

（七）继续做好企业加工贸易的审核工作

要主动上门指导企业如何开展加工贸易,并对企业生产场地进行实地考察,杜绝“三无”企业从事加工贸易业务。

（八）关于服务贸易工作

为促进上海服务贸易全面发展，上海市政府已先后出台了《关于促进上海服务贸易全面发展实施意见》和《上海服务贸易中长期发展规划纲要》，上海市委、市政府高度重视服务贸易的发展，把服务贸易工作摆上了重要的位置。通过建立黄浦区服务贸易企业数据库、做好服务贸易统计指标体系工作、研究制定黄浦区服务贸易“十二五”发展规划、推选出50家重点服务贸易企业，进行重点跟踪走访，重点扶持，使其做大做强这几方面为工作抓手来做好这项工作。

案例：上海豫园旅游商城股份有限公司

上海豫园旅游商城股份有限公司（简称豫园股份）在汉堡投资的上海欧洲旅游中

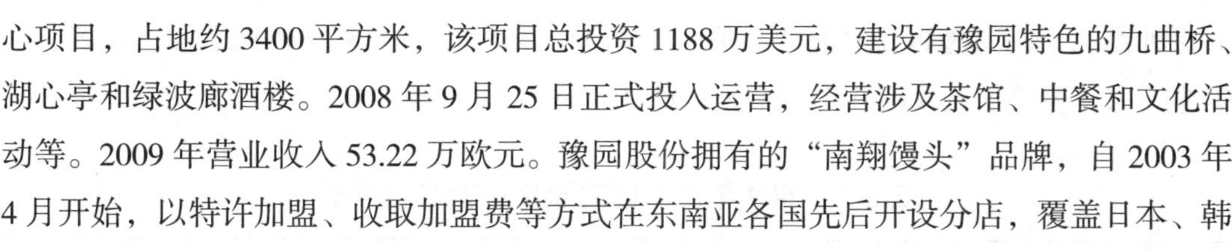

心项目，占地约 3400 平方米，该项目总投资 1188 万美元，建设有豫园特色的九曲桥、湖心亭和绿波廊酒楼。2008 年 9 月 25 日正式投入运营，经营涉及茶馆、中餐和文化活动等。2009 年营业收入 53.22 万欧元。豫园股份拥有的“南翔馒头”品牌，自 2003 年 4 月开始，以特许加盟、收取加盟费等方式在东南亚各国先后开设分店，覆盖日本、韩国、印尼、新加坡等地。目前分店总数已经达到 14 家，正在积极拓展开设澳大利亚的第一家分店。2009 年营业收入 10280 万元。

第三节 卢湾区

一、2009 年卢湾区外经贸发展情况

（一）外贸发展情况

2009 年，卢湾区加强外贸监管与服务，促进对外贸易持续、健康发展，外贸进出口受国际金融危机影响明显，全年实现外贸进出口总额 12.4 亿美元，比上年下降 11.9%，其中出口 3.6 亿美元，比上年下降 30.4%；进口 8.8 亿美元，比上年下降 1.2%。从进出口结构上看，进口贸易恢复较快，而出口贸易仍在低位运行。受国内经济企稳回升、居民消费强劲增长等积极因素影响，以及天万仓、劳力士等一批进口龙头企业的稳定表现，卢湾区全年进口额小幅下降，远小于全国同期 11.2% 和全市同期 11.1% 的降幅。

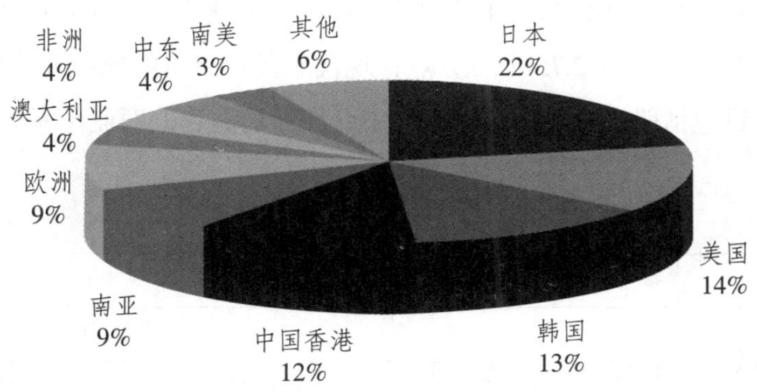

图 6-2 2009 年卢湾区出口商品市场结构图

纺织服装、贱金属及其制品、鞋帽、塑料及其制品、化工等继续在外贸进出口商品总额中排名前列。在全年外贸环境急剧恶化的大背景下，食品饮料进出口逆势大增，增幅达到了 144.19%，显示了此类商品良好的抗周期性。出口商品从传统的纺织品服装、玩具等拓展到纺织品服装、机电电子产品、建材化工、钢材和轻工产品等数十大类的

上百种商品，出口地区也从日本、欧洲、美洲及东南亚等国家发展到中东、非洲、南美等国家，覆盖了五大洲八十多个国家和地区。

表 6-5　2009 年卢湾区主要出口商品情况表

主要出口商品	出口额（万美元）	占出口总额（%）	同比（%）
合计	35892	100.00	72.34
化学工业及其相关工业的 制成品	7808	21.75	16.25
纺织原料及纺织制品	6734	18.76	6.6
机电及其零配件	5909	16.46	15.04
电子产品	5103	14.22	-
贱金属及其制品	4729	13.18	28.32
其他	5609	15.63	6.13

注：主要出口商品按照海关 HS 编码分类列出，与往年不同。

（二）外资发展情况

2009 年，受国际金融危机影响，卢湾区新批准外商投资项目 102 个，比上年下降 42%；增资项目 93 个；全年引进合同外资 6.53 亿美元，比上年下降 37.75%；实际利用外资 6.85 亿美元，比上年增长 4.9%。

2009 年引进的项目中，服务业项目占绝大多数，项目类型以外商独资为主。招大引强成效明显，新增 9 家世界 500 强及领袖级企业，引进的 500 万美元以上大项目共 9 家，大项目占比较去年上升 2.75 个百分点；现代服务业项目的能级和质量较往年有很大提高，引进项目包括船级社、广告、人才中介和知名品牌的商业零售等。

表 6-6　2009 年卢湾区外资项目分类情况表　（单位：万美元）

项目类型	投资总额	合同外资					
		合同外资总量	比上年（±%）	其中			
				新批项目		增资项目	
				项目数	合同外资	项目数	合同外资
合资	48995.36	21883.11	-46.98	7	93.18	11	21789.93
合作	500	266	-59.57	0	0	2	266
独资	68474.02	43840.18	-29.69	95	9270.04	80	34570.14
合计	117969.38	65989.29	-36.72	102	9363.22	93	56626.07

2009 年投资卢湾的国家和地区共 22 个，比 2008 年减少 5 个。其中香港地区、德国、日本是卢湾引进外资的主要来源地，新设投资项目合计 60 个，占项目总数的 58.82%；其在合同外资（包括新设、增资）中的占比达 87.72%。2009 年来自香港地区的新批、增资项目所引进的合同外资金额共计 38113 万美元，占比达 58.35%。

截至 2009 年底，卢湾区累计批准设立的三资企业总数为 1376 家，其中独资企业 912 家，合资企业 239 家，合作企业 225 家。累计总投资额 110.65 亿美元，合同外资 54.48 亿美元，实到外资 48.39 亿美元。

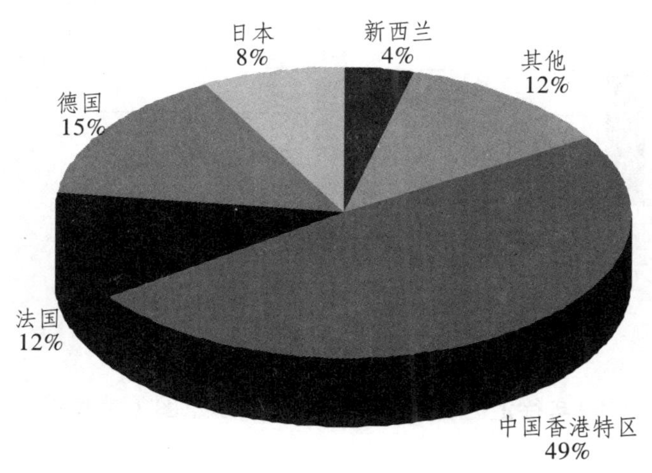

图 6-3　2009 年卢湾区外商投资国别地区情况（不含增资和转股项目）

（三）对外经济合作情况

卢湾区加强宣传，加大指导，改进服务，提高境外投资审批效率，切实帮助企业走出去，通过在境外投资创业来做大做强。2009 年受理 2 家企业在境外投资，上海卡固电器有限公司在韩国设立分公司，威士机械公司在日本设立分公司。这 2 家企业的投资额分别为 10 万美元。

第四节　徐汇区

一、2009 年徐汇区外经贸发展情况

（一）外贸发展情况

2009 年，徐汇区共完成外贸进出口总额 115869 万美元，同比增长 -16.13%。其中，进

口累计完成54489万美元,同比增长–4.85%;出口累计完成61380万美元,同比增长–24.12%。

由于受到国际金融危机的持续影响，国际需求疲软，2009年徐汇区外贸出口呈现明显下降，各类型的出口企业同比都出现20%以上的降幅，由于部分外资企业的海外订单锐减，三资企业降幅达到了30%以上。

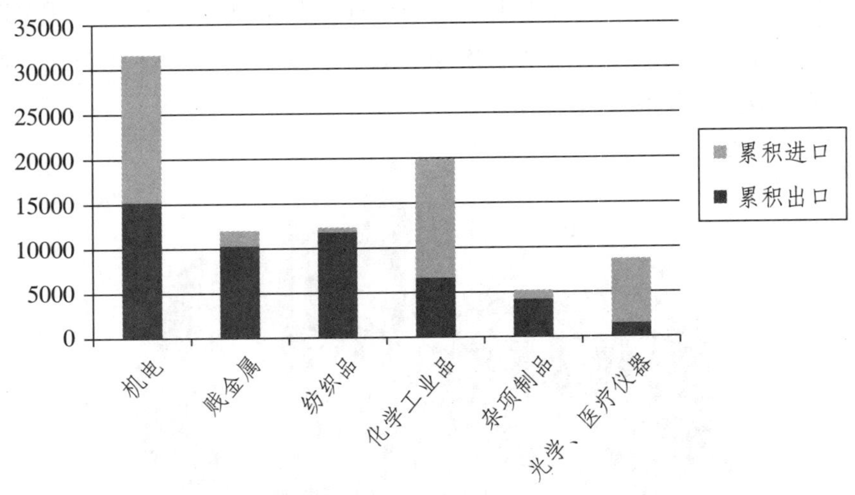

图6-4　2009年徐汇区各行业累积进出口示意图（单位：万美元）

1．加强协调服务，促进对外贸易平稳发展

通过走访出口企业调研，了解了企业所面临的困难，掌握企业的出口动态。加大中小企业开拓资金、出口信用保险等工作的宣传力度，帮助企业了解出口信用保险知识及相关政策，有助于企业降低风险、减轻成本，同时组织外贸企业参加广交会、中博会和东盟博览会等贸易活动，推动外贸企业走出去开拓国际市场。

2．继续推进服务外包工作

徐汇区已经集聚了一批发展较好的服务外包企业，2009年继续积极推进服务外包企业扩大承接离岸外包业务，通过专项政策支持，并和上海漕河泾新兴技术开发区一起构建企业服务平台以提高服务和扶持水平，为企业创造良好的发展环境。2009年离岸外包业务同比增加12%，取得进一步的发展。

（二）外资发展情况

2009年，金融危机使全市引进外资出现两位数负增长。徐汇区在零土地出让的情况下，全年徐汇区共引进合同外资8.6亿美元，同比增长11.2%左右，实际利用外资5.6亿美元，同比增长10.3%左右。

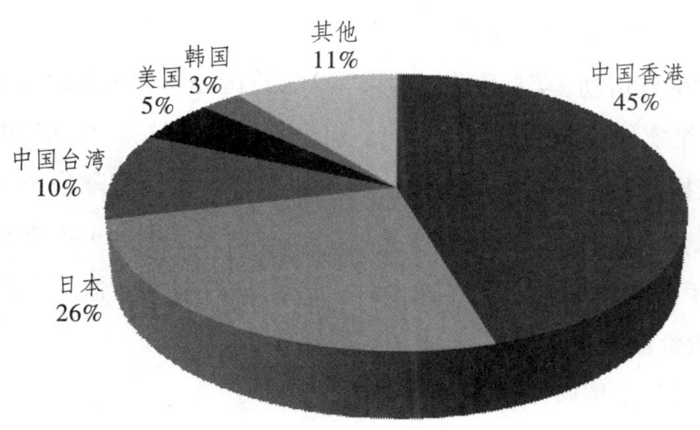

图 6-5 2009 年徐汇区外商投资主要来源地结构图

2009 年不仅保持引进外资月月增长的良好势态，而且外资招商创同期历史最高水平。

（三）外经发展情况

1．强化开放意识，拓宽对外经济合作渠道

切实帮助企业增强“走出去”意识，积极引导有条件、有实力的企业转变经营理念，帮助企业解决存在的困难和问题，促使企业在发展重点上从生产领域向服务贸易领域和技术产品的开发延伸。同时加大宣传有关鼓励对外投资的政策，并在办事程序上加以便捷化，做好有对外投资意向企业的服务工作。

2．推动出口品牌建设，引导企业改变增长方式

2009 年，继续鼓励有条件的企业申报出口品牌和名牌产品，并协同科委等部门研究政策扶持有高新科技的生产型出口企业，使企业更加重视自身技术升级和品牌建设。

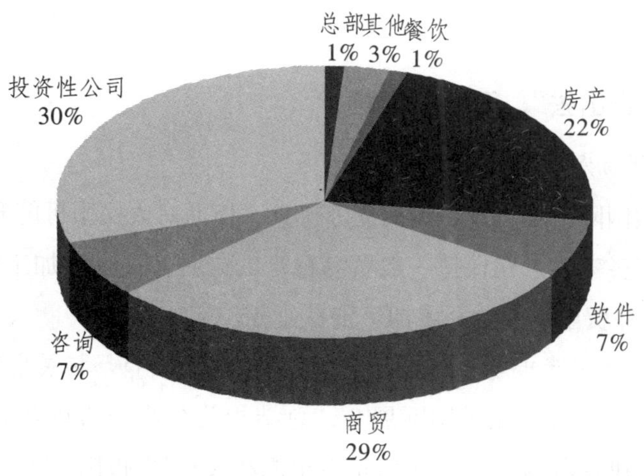

图 6-6 2009 年度徐汇区第三产业引进外资结构图

3．总部经济发展实现新的突破

2009年成功引进雷勃、美标亚太、达邦等3家跨国公司管理型地区总部；新设天合、陆逊梯卡、美德维实伟克3家投资性公司，引进美标（中国）、艾默生电气（中国）投资有限公司2家投资性公司，其中艾默生电气（中国）投资有限公司是一家国家级地区总部；另外原有的捷普投资（中国）有限公司、百胜（中国）投资有限公司2家投资性公司2009年被认定为国家级地区总部。截至2009年底，徐汇区共有跨国公司地区总部26家，投资性公司24家，其中国家级地区总部4家。

4．“引大引强”工作取得实效

2009年徐汇区共引进合同外资500万美元以上的项目19项，占引进外资总额的63.13%，在引资数量增加的同时，质量也有提升。2009年引进的世界500强投资企业，如艾默生、思科及安吉星（上汽与通用合资项目）等，每年产生税收都在亿元以上。

二、2010年徐汇区外经贸工作展望

徐汇是上海市较早涉及国际贸易中心建设相关内容的区，区内总部经济机构云集，商业高度繁荣繁华，具有良好的高端综合消费基础。至2012年，徐汇区将新建成各类园区和商务楼近80万平方米，到“十二五”期末有望再增加各类园区和商务楼近300万平方米，具备了参与国际贸易中心建设的基础条件。在此背景下，必须抓住本市建设国际贸易中心契机，在不具备发展口岸贸易要素支撑的前提下，充分发掘徐汇区现代服务业的整体功能和商贸商务方面的特色优势，聚焦发展与其相关的总部经济、商贸商务、金融和信息服务业，努力在上海国际贸易中心建设中有所作为。

（一）积极“走出去”，开拓新市场

1．稳步推进贸易发展

2010年，虽然国际市场出现一定的复苏迹象，但面对人民币可能升值等因素影响，外贸出口仍存在较多变数。在保持一般贸易稳定的同时，提高对加工贸易企业的服务水平，鼓励和引导外贸出口企业开展加工贸易业务。

2．进一步加大对国际市场开拓的引导力度，力促新兴市场拓展出现新成效

积极组织企业申报参加相关国际展会，总结相关企业开拓新兴市场的成功经验，大力开拓东盟、非洲等市场。2010年将重点组织相关培训和座谈会，使更多企业能了解政策、掌握政策，提高申报工作水平，有效提高企业扶持工作水平。

3．加强对出口名牌发展的引导力度，力推外贸增长方式得到有效转变

通过政府政策扶持、出口企业自主实践等方式积极引导出口企业拥有自主品牌。建立完善全方位的出口名牌培育机制，列出重点培育对象并加强动态管理。

4．以服务外包为抓手，推动服务贸易发展

提高对发展服务贸易对今后区域经济发展和建设国际贸易中心工作的重要性的认识，开展企业基础信息和数据的收集整理，并将具有良好发展前景的服务贸易企业作为重点关注对象，鼓励企业加大对外业务发展。研究推进服务贸易发展的相关政策，扶持企业做大做强。

5．做好“走出去”工作的安全防范工作

针对近年来企业走出去投资和劳务输出中所出现的各种突发事件，要未雨绸缪，根据国家和市有关部门的政策措施做好相关工作预案，并加强与相关企业的沟通联系，切实做到遇到突发情况能及时、有效应对，减少不安定因素。

（二）力促“请进来”，多角度引资

1．抓住现有线索，努力争取现有项目线索落地

经过长期跟踪和综合分析，徐汇区商务委员会掌握了一批较大规模项目的线索，要积极与相关职能部门和各招商分中心密切配合，采取人盯项目、分工负责的办法，努力使大部分项目顺利落地。

2．依托商务载体积极创造增量

紧紧依托区内计划出让的土地资源、计划开发的项目资源开展招商引资工作，提前介入，争取主动。发挥商务楼宇集聚作用，着重引进现代服务业“1+6”重点行业企业；加强产业园区招商工作，重点引进科技含量高、具有自主知识产权核心竞争力的电子信息、软件服务等企业。

3．主动出击对外开展招商活动

（1）有针对性地“走出去”促成项目落地，在招商洽谈的关键时刻，主动出击作用明显。

（2）有目标地去相关地区开展推介活动。外商投资企业准备来上海投资时，在众多条件相仿的中心城区中，首先考虑的一般都是相对了解的地区，因此有针对性地宣传徐汇显得尤为重要。

4．加大扶持力度，加快总部经济发展步伐

要积极贯彻落实上海市扶持总部经济相关政策。做好政策的细化和深化，尽可能用足用好政策，利用各种渠道进一步加大政策宣传力度，充分发挥政策的激励效应。

5．积极发挥社会中介力量招商作用

会计事务所、律师事务所等专业中介机构掌握着大量世界500强企业信息，通过积极与各种招商中介机构联系，今年以来，已掌握了数家500强企业有意设立地区总部的线索。今后将进一步扩大中介招商的范围，在区域招商引资和街镇企业服务过程中引进专业中介机构，尝试招商引资部分工作“服务外包”。同时注重发挥社会各界资源优势，努力畅通“以商招商、以外引外”的渠道。

6．引资与引税并重

注重企业对区域经济发展大局的贡献，对总部经济机构的税收情况综合分析，努力提高总部经济产出效益，实现总部经济从“量”的突破到“质”的飞跃。

7．积极服务企业

对在当前经济形势下企业可能会遇到的困难主动进行了解，从企业的需求出发制定切实有效的措施，将服务工作落到实处，做到细处。

第五节　长宁区

一、2009年长宁区外经贸发展情况

2009年长宁区商务委按照“拓展虹桥、提升功能、数字长宁、国际城区”的发展方针，以科学发展观为指导，着眼于总部集聚和服务外包发展，通过加强规划、完善政策、强化服务，促进产业结构调整优化，不断增强长宁区经济发展的竞争力和活力。

2009年，全区引进外资企业184家，引进合同外资5.30亿美元，比上年增长1.26%。外贸进出口总额34.74亿美元，比上年下降27.27%。其中进口额为21.15亿美元，比上年下降26.18%，出口额为13.59亿美元，比上年下降28.90%。

受全球金融危机的影响，西方发达国家消费需求大幅下降，对进出口造成了较大冲击，特别是上半年，进出口额大幅下降，部分企业生存困难，但从下半年开始，随着国家稳定外需各项措施逐步见效和国际市场趋稳，进出口开始回暖，降幅有所收窄。2009年长宁区进出口总额虽然依旧列上海市中心城区第一，但是进出口总额、进口额和出口额的降幅都高于上海市平均降幅。从企业来看，2009年进出口超过1000万美元的进出口企业一共30家，其中上海东方航空进出口有限公司依旧是长宁进出口的主力军，进出口额为12.82亿美元，占长宁的进出口总额的36.90%。从进出口商

品来看，除了航空器材进出口以外，商品主要以机电产品、纺织品、化学医学仪器、塑料制品和贱金属及其制品为主。从进出口国别来看，主要还是以美国、欧洲和日本市场为主。

表 6-7 2009 年长宁区主要进出口商品情况表

主要进出口商品	进出口总额（亿美元）	同比（%）
机电、音像设备及其零件	10.44	-15.76
纺织原料及纺织制品	5.64	-10.26
塑料及其制品；橡胶及其制品	2.31	21.87
化学医学仪器	2.30	-31.12
光学、医疗等仪器	1.39	5.74

表 6-8 2009 年长宁区主要进出口国家情况表

主要进出口国家	累计进出口额（亿美元）	同比（%）
美国	11.38	24.90
欧洲	9.54	-55.75
日本	4.98	7.5

2009 年长宁区一般贸易比重增长较大，从 2008 年的 48.48% 上升到 70.43%；加工贸易则略有增长，从 2008 年的 14.97% 上升到 2009 年的 15.16%。但是在绝对值上，总量和加工贸易都比 2008 年有所减少。加工贸易结构中，来料加工装配贸易占加工贸易的比重为 11.01%，比 2008 年的 16.22% 下降了 5 个百分点，而进料加工贸易占加工贸易的比重为 88.99%，比 2008 年的 83.7% 有所上升。

表 6-9 2009 年长宁区加工贸易与一般贸易总量及比重

贸易方式	2009 年进出口总额（亿美元）	2009 年各贸易方式占总量的比重（%）	2008 年进出口总额（亿美元）	2008 年各贸易方式占总量的比重（%）
总量:	34.74	100	47.76	100
一般贸易	24.47	70.43	23.16	48.48
加工贸易	5.27	15.16	7.15	14.97
其中：来料加工装配贸易	0.58	1.65	1.16	2.44
进料加工贸易	4.69	13.51	5.99	12.53

二、2010 年外经贸工作展望

2010 年是世博会举办之年，是“十二五”规划编制之年，长宁区商务委将认真贯彻落实区委、区府对全区外经工作的战略部署和总体要求，以科学发展观思想为统领，着眼于最大限度放大世博会带动效应，充分发挥世博会对区域经济的拉动作用，进一步优化产业结构，推动区域经济发展迈上新台阶。

2010 年，长宁区对外经济贸易工作目标为：实现合同外资 5 亿美元；实现外经贸进出口总额 26.8 亿美元。主要工作重点是：利用世博机遇，大力宣传长宁良好投资环境; 加强企业跟踪服务，增强服务企业实效性，帮助企业走出困境，扶持企业做大做强; 以发展总部经济为抓手，推动总部机构的功能整合，加大区域重点项目跟踪力度，促进地区总部集聚；深入推进服务外包工作，广泛宣传服务外包企业扶持政策，扩大政策的知晓面和惠及面，促进服务外包企业的引进和培育；以数字媒体服务外包专业园为载体，大力引进相关产业的企业，力争把长宁数字媒体服务外包做大做强。

第六节 静安区

一、2009 年静安区外经贸发展情况

（一）外资发展情况

1. 全面完成各项指标

2009 年，静安区共引进外商直接投资合同项目共 202 个；协议引进外资 111290.46 万美元。外商直接投资合同金额为 55799.75 万美元。其中，商贸流通业 23549.96 万美元，专业服务业 10168.42 万美元，房地产业 21854.99 万美元，宾馆旅游会展业 30 万美元，文化生活业 132.98 万美元。

外商直接投资实际到位金额为 58803 万美元，上年同期为 53446.7 万美元，同比增加 10.02%，超额完成年初制定的年度目标。

稳步推进外商投资性公司的引进、外资代表处的翻牌成立公司等有关工作。2009 年，成功引进多家地区总部，其中卡朋罗兰（中国）投资有限公司、雅马哈乐器音响（中国）投资有限公司为世界 500 强或投资性公司；引进上海高垣管理咨询有限公司、嫒碧知

商贸（上海）有限公司等10家知名品牌及企业；帮助斯丽贸易（上海）有限公司等5家外资代表处完成翻牌设立公司；协助常春藤大厦、静鼎楼2幢楼宇获得涉外资质。

2. 静安区利用外资的特点

2009年，静安区新审批设立的外资企业全部为现代服务类企业，且主要为商贸流通业企业和专业服务业企业。在国际金融危机的大环境下，静安区商贸流通业中的高端奢侈品、化妆品以及医药等行业呈现出抗冲击能力强、受影响程度小、恢复速度快的特点，使区域涉外经济未受到重大影响。同时，随着区域产业能级和集聚度逐年提升，吸引了一批高质量的新项目落户静安。

（1）商贸流通业集聚度不断增强

1–12月，外资商贸流通业引进项目104个，占比为51.49%，合同外资2.35亿美元，与去年相比，项目数虽然减少14.05%，但合同外资却增长了21.31%。在金融危机和全球消费萎缩的背景下，外资商贸流通业发展出现了逆势上扬的喜人局面，不少知名外资品牌来静安区投资，如美润贸易、完美珠宝、百郦嘉贸易等。静安区外资商贸流通业企业已逐渐形成涵盖世界著名品牌，知名跨国公司和高端企业，且具有较完整服务体系的产业链。

（2）世界500强企业和跨国公司总部经济增长快速

2009年，卡朋罗兰（中国）投资有限公司、雅马哈中国（投资）有限公司等2家跨国公司地区总部入驻静安。截至年底，静安区共有跨国公司地区总部、投资性公司16家。这些外资企业不断加大在华投资力度，申请上海或国家级地区总部认定，总部经济较去年同期呈现出快速发展的势头。

（3）外商投资来源地多样化

长期以来，中国香港特区、日本、美国一直是静安主要的外商投资来源国（地区）。近几年来，尽管来自中国香港特区、日本和美国的直接投资仍占很大的比重，但随着中国台湾地区、韩国、新加坡、其他欧美国家和离岸群岛投资的增加，静安区外资来源地已呈日趋多元化的趋势。

表6-10 2009年静安区外资来源地统计表

投资来源地	协议外资（万美元）	合同外资（万美元）
中国香港特区	57495.11	29600.02
英属维尔京群岛	13794.05	7030.04
日本	14576.93	5909.05

投资来源地	协议外资（万美元）	合同外资金额（万美元）
美国	11337.82	4522.77
法国	1547.75	1431.22
意大利	2675.25	1132.25
新西兰	1584.2	980.17
瑞士	1600.49	809.41
新加坡	1077.77	740.66
开曼群岛	1400	600
其他国家和地区	4201.1	3044.16
合计	111290.47	55799.75

2009年，在静安区设立外资企业数排名前5位的国家（地区）分别是：中国香港特区、日本、美国、新加坡、法国，合同外资额排名前5位的国家（地区）分别为：中国香港特区、日本、美国、法国、意大利。在设立外资企业数和引进的合同外资额排名中，中国香港特区均列首位，这固然得益于香港自身的高开放度和自由港地位，以及与内地的地缘关系，更主要还是在于近年来由于CEPA协议的签署，使香港企业投资内地的允许类领域更宽泛、方式更灵活、手续更简便。许多欧美公司也纷纷通过自己早期成立的香港分公司（或亚太地区总部）对大陆进行投资，从而直接增加了香港公司对静安区的投资额。

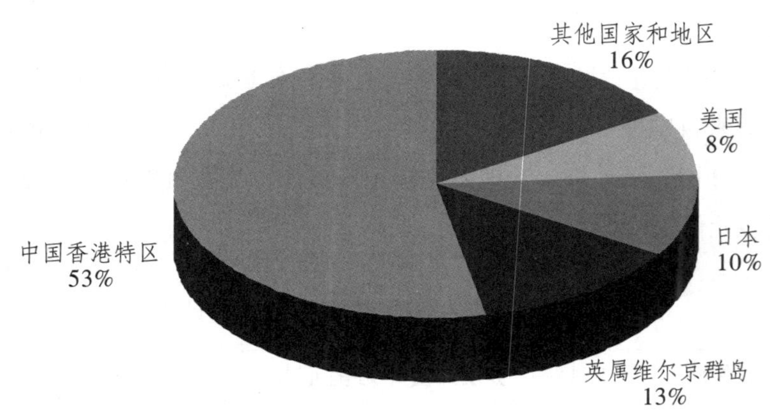

图6-7　2009年静安区外资来源地结构图

（4）商贸流通业和专业服务业两大支柱产业保持相对稳定态势

具体从行业分析，从事高端品牌销售企业、医药制造销售企业、化妆品销售企业、餐饮连锁经营的品牌企业受到本次金融危机的影响较小，抗衰退能力较强，企业在2009年取得了良好的业绩。如欧莱雅、路易威登、古驰、津味餐饮（85度C面包房）、辉瑞、惠氏等企业均取得了较大的发展，并进入静安纳税百强的行列。相对商贸流通业的繁荣，静安区专业服务业的外资企业在今年的发展略有不足，部分以承接海外公司业务为主的专业服务业企业受金融危机的影响较大，但部分世界知名的专业服务业机构在今年仍取得了一定的增长。

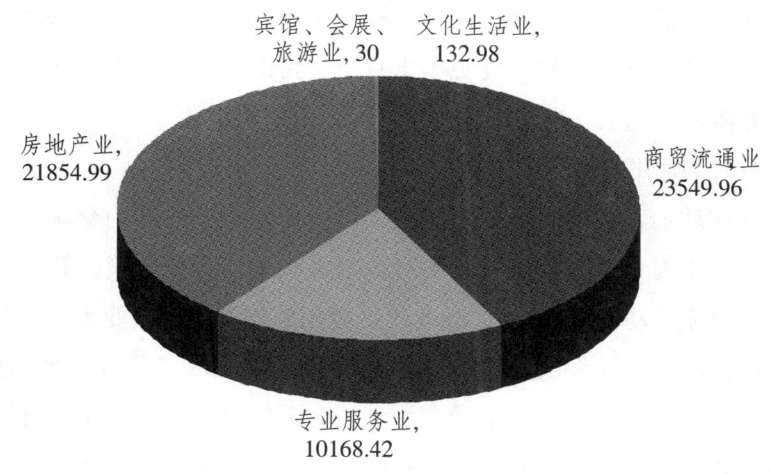

图 6-8　2009 年静安区外资投资行业结构图（单位：万美元）

（5）增资已逐步成为合同外资增长的主要力量

尽管国内外总体形势不断转好，但尚存在许多不确定因素，外资在国内设立新公司的步伐不断减缓，外商增资已逐步成为合同外资增长的主导力量。2009年，共有外商增资项目103个，合同外资36140.9万美元，占全部新增合同外资的64.77%。

3．2009年静安区外经贸工作发展重点

（1）招商与留商并重，以楼宇为基础和载体，积极开拓总部经济规模

静安以建设“高起点、外向型、国际化”的国际静安为目标，积极开拓楼宇经济；坚持招大引强，大力引进世界知名跨国公司地区总部、投资性公司或研发中心。根据静安自身的特点，积极引进商贸流通业、专业服务业、创意产业、服务外包产业等有关项目，以达到进一步提高利用外资的规模和水平的目的。通过外资招商引资，引导外资优势行业和优势企业的集聚。

（2）认真履行审批职能，结合审批权限下放，切实加强管理和引导职能

随着对外开放的程度进一步提高，商务部和上海市商务委员会逐步下放部分审批项目的权限，区域外资项目也呈现出愈加活跃的迹象。全年共审批新设、增资、变更等各类外资项目超过350个，较往年有所增加。通过认真研习有关政策法规，切实履

行好审批部门的有关职责，并为企业提供相关产业指导、设立程序、区域选址等方面的信息和建议，配合城区发展的最新产业动向，做好引导工作。

（3）管理与引导相结合，以服务促管理，成为企业发展过程中的好帮手

积极深入企业，了解在金融危机背景下的发展情况和遇到的困难。2009年，集中走访了永裕医药、辉瑞投资、久光百货等100多家区域重点关注企业，及时把握这些重点企业最新的发展动态，积极做好相应的配套服务，帮助企业共渡难关。全年坚持通过走访、来访、电话、活动、数据报表等多种形式，跟踪了解静安区外商投资企业，了解企业的发展动向和计划，对其变更等事宜给予帮助和指导，协助其解决在生产经营中所遇到的外籍员工用工、户外广告发布、人才引进等问题。

（4）搭建有效沟通平台，积极宣传最新政策和产业动向

为进一步加强政府部门与企业以及静安区内企业与企业之间的交流与互动，及时让企业了解国家、上海市以及静安区有关产业政策和最新扶持政策，静安区商务委员会积极组织相关交流活动，成功召开2008年度静安区外商投资企业表彰大会，举办了静安区商务工作会议、外商投资企业信息交流早餐会、静安区“奢侈品管理焦点论坛”、静安南京路　福布斯论坛、中秋联谊会等活动。为更好地发挥企业在建设国际静安中的作用，积极探索楼宇业主、品牌商家以及专业机构与政府之间的联动效应，推动静安南京路楼宇服务联盟的组建，共同营造静安南京路的良好商业商务环境。

二、2010年静安区外经贸工作展望

2009年，在国际金融危机和国际经济、金融环境不稳的情势下，静安区仍确保外商投资实到资金有所增长，主要得益于去年全区合同外资创新高所带来的注资惯性和国内市场相较于欧美日发达市场受到的冲击小且成长性好等因素，促使外国投资者的注册资本基本按期到位。2010年得益于国内良好的内需拉动和区内新载体，预计商贸流通业有望保持持续稳定增长，专业服务业有望摆脱低迷状况，实现复苏。

（一）调整结构，加快商业商务能级整体提升

以静安南京路为重点，承接上海国际贸易中心建设和静安“国际商务港”建设，积极吸引跨国公司地区总部、研发中心、销售结算中心和营运管理中心等新型贸易主体，加大静安南京路沿线高端品牌引进、更新力度。积极做好重点区域商业载体的改造和招商工作，不断优化商业布局。进一步完善静安商业商务综合配套服务功能，着力打造整体平衡、健康有序的静安南京路商业生态环境。继续加大力度培育本土自主创新

品牌。高度关注电子商务新的业态，推进重点商务领域电子商务应用。积极发展时尚创意等新兴产业，推进创意产业发展和园区建设。围绕重点商业商务楼宇，加大节能减排力度，推行合同能源管理，开展低碳经济试点。

（二）积极开拓，有效推进区域外向型经济发展

推进投资结构优化升级，继续强化引进商贸流通业、专业服务业外资项目。抓住跨国公司业务整合的契机，大力发展总部经济，推进投资主体结构调整。以重点楼宇为载体，加强项目跟踪、服务，做好外资项目增资工作，提高外资利用规模和水平。推进外贸市场结构调整，巩固传统市场，开拓新兴市场。加强外贸经济运行分析，提升对外贸易企业服务水平。用足用好鼓励政策，加大企业开拓国际市场和“走出去”专项资金扶持力度，鼓励企业参加各种展销会。探索发展服务外包，支持区域内服务外包企业开拓国际市场，承接境外服务外包业务，推动区域服务贸易发展。

第七节　普陀区

一、2009年普陀区外经贸发展情况

（一）外贸发展情况及特点

1. 受金融危机影响，出口额下降

2009年，普陀区外贸进出口总额为112965.2万美元，同比下降23.68%，降幅高于全市水平9.88个百分比。其中出口70138.2万美元，比去年同期下降了31.64%，降幅高于全市水平15.44个百分点；进口42827万美元，同比下降5.69%，降幅低于全市水平5.41个百分点。截至12月底，全区共有外贸进出口企业430家。其中，有出口业务的企业287家，有进口业务的企业265家。

全球范围的金融危机，对部分外贸依存度较高的企业产生很大的影响，特别是一些出口到欧美市场的电子机械类企业、出口到日本的服装类企业，2009年出口额大幅度下滑。

2009年，出口超1000万美元的企业有9家，累计出口额29226.3万美元，占出口总额的41.67%，与2008年相比，同比下降32.20%。出口在100万~1000万美元之间的企业有114家，累计出口36217.4万美元，同比下降26.81%，占出口总额的

51.64%。进口超1000万美元的企业有6家，累计进口总额22170.2万美元，占进口总额的51.77%，同比上升47.36%。

2．内资进出口企业同比降幅略低于外资企业

2009年，普陀区外资进出口企业达到183家，累计进出口总额达40162万美元，同比下降31.46%，占全区进出口总额的35.55%。其中出口25537.9万美元，同比下降39.38%；进口14624.1万美元，同比下降1.89%。

内资进出口企业有247家，累计进出口总额达72803.2万美元，同比下降18.58%，低于外资企业的降幅，占全区进出口总额的64.45%。其中出口44600.3万美元，同比下降26.24%；进口28202.9万美元，同比下降2.56%。

3．各类目商品进出口同比大多有所下降

目前,普陀区外贸企业涉及的进出口商品共22项大类,93项小类,784个具体产品。其中，机电产品出口31240.3万美元，同比下降40.13%，进口14419.8万美元，同比下降31.46%；纺织品出口13913.7万美元，同比下降13.22%，进口1466万美元，同比下降21.21%;贱金属产品出口6239.1万美元,同比下降58.42%,进口10028.2万美元,同比上升54.60%；高新技术产品出口5487.9万美元，同比下降36.44%，进口1645.7万美元，同比下降9.06%。

4．一般贸易进出口额远大于加工贸易进出口额

表6-11　2009年普陀区贸易方式分析

贸易方式	出口额（万美元）	同比（%）	进口额（万美元）	同比（%）
一般贸易	55457	-27.11	39796.5	25.41
加工贸易	7130	-57.81	2510.4	-60.10
来料加工装配贸易	2092.7	-21.39	1258.7	-25.48
进料加工贸易	5037.3	-64.62	1251.7	-72.80
其他贸易	7551.2	-21.43	520.1	-92.96
对外承包工程货物	7503.9	-21.73		

5．进出口市场呈多元化

2009年普陀区外贸企业进出口商品所涉及到的国家及地区共有147个。出口排名前5位的国家分别是：日本、美国、哈萨克斯坦、德国、印度，累计出口额35948.1万美元，占出口总额的51.25%。

表 6-12 2009 年普陀区出口商品涉及国家一览表

出口国别	出口额（万美元）	同比（%）
日本	14123.1	-5.62
美国	10195.2	-35.26
哈萨克斯坦	5334.8	1698.12
德国	3791.9	-38.25
印度	2503.1	-56.17

进口排名前 5 位的国家分别是：美国、德国、日本、法国、智利，累计进口额 20276.8 万美元，占进口总额的 47.35%。

表 6-13 2009 年普陀区进口商品涉及国家一览表

进口国别	进口额（万美元）	同比（%）
美国	5657.9	9.65
德国	5361.2	-0.79
日本	3993.1	-63.07
法国	2831.2	1.66
智利	2433.4	5.86

（二）外资发展情况及特点

2009 年，普陀区超额完成了全年引进外资 2 亿美元的目标，取得了较好的成绩。由于受全球金融危机影响，2009 年上半年吸收外资的形势比较严峻，合同外资的完成情况不尽如人意。部分项目因外商收拢资金而搁浅，原定的投资额被大幅度的削减，即将到位的注册资金被延期，有些外资项目准备迁至成本更低的区域等。面对严峻的形势，普陀区商务委及时把科学发展观落实到应对金融风暴的实践上来，及时把思想统一到区委、区政府对外资引进工作的判断上来，及时把行动拓展到调整工作思路、转变政府职能上来，及时把工作重心转移到重点区域、重点项目的推进上来。

2009 年普陀区共批准合同外资 30857.6028 万美元，同比增长 2.99%，完成全年指标 154.29%。其中新批外资项目 81 个，合同外资 16277.498 万美元，同比下降 3.26%；批准增资项目 40 个，合同外资 15226.4606 万美元，同比增长 12.57%；减资项目 6 个，合同外资 646.3558 万美元。

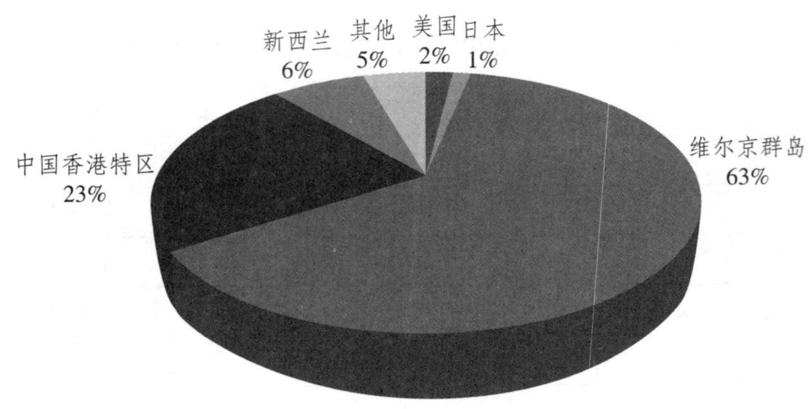

图 6-9　2009 年普陀区新设立外资企业国别比重结构图

2009 年普陀区共批准合同外资 30857.6028 万美元，同比增长 2.99%，完成全年指标 154.29%。其中新批外资项目 81 个，合同外资 16277.498 万美元，同比下降 3.26%；批准增资项目 40 个，合同外资 15226.4606 万美元，同比增长 12.57%；减资项目 6 个，合同外资 646.3558 万美元。

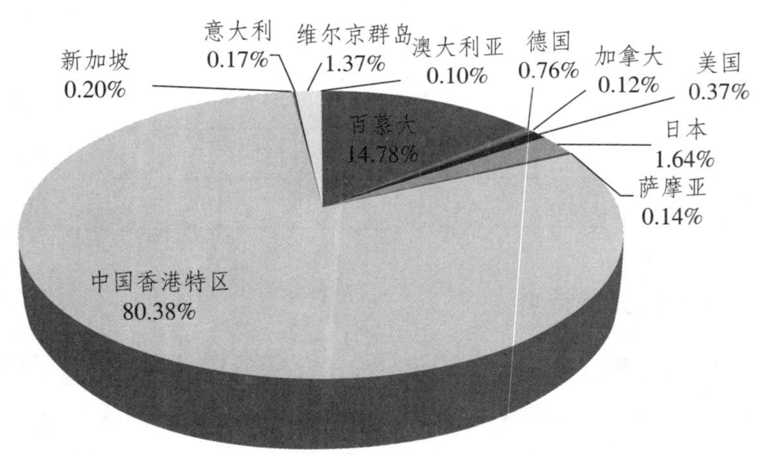

图 6-10　2009 年普陀区新增企业国别比重结构图

普陀区的外资引进工作之所以能逆势增长，归纳起来有以下几方面的原因：

1．学实活动为契机，各级领导高度重视外资引进

外资引进工作逆势增长的过程，也是普陀区商务委员会深入学习实践科学发展观的过程。结合学实活动的时间节点，对外资引进工作也经历了深入检查、分析问题、落实整改、体现实效的阶段。对检查、分析出的问题，都逐个进行了整改落实。

“特殊时期要有特殊精神，也要尽特殊努力。”普陀区区委、区政府主要领导多次对外资引进工作作出重要指示；区委常委会、区政府常务会议多次专题研究外资工作；

区府分管领导多次听取专题汇报、展开调研、协调各方工作。区委、区政府着眼于当前经济形势，及时地提出了“止跌、持平、回升、达标”四步走的目标，研究出台了一揽子“保增长”的政策措施。区商务委运用这些切实可行的政策措施使得外商重拾对普陀区经济的信心，为外资企业的发展创造了良好的氛围。6月25日，上海市商务委员会与普陀区签署关于共同推进普陀区加快“商贸物流”建设和商务工作全面发展的合作协议，在“区委合作”上先行一步。上海市商务委员会在一些重点项目上对普陀区的支持也是外资引进工作能取得成绩的重要保障。

2. 服务企业为方向，切实转变政府职能

企业是市场经济的主体，服务型政府是政府职能转变的方向。普陀区商务委员会牢固树立服务企业的意识，真正把“服务是普陀第一资源”理念贯彻落实到转变政府职能的实际行动中。普陀区商务委员会把与普陀区委、区政府所签的目标责任分解到各个科室，与各个科室分别签了目标责任书，做到层层落实、责任到人。为配合落实区委、区政府的“三联”制度、周四服务企业日等制度，普陀区商务委员会建立了领导班子外资企业走访制度。对年税收额在1000万美元以上的，由主要领导走访；对年税收额在500万美元以上1000万美元以下的企业由分管领导走访，做到对外资企业的情况了然于胸。在走访过程中，对于企业反映的水、电、基础设施配套等问题，普陀区商务委员会在自身职责范围内尽量予以解决；如果是超出自身职责范围的，立即转呈有关职能部门，会同有关部门协商解决。对于长风生态商务区、真如城市副中心、中环组团商贸群等重点区域，普陀区商务委也加大服务扶持的力度，多次组织、参加外资政策宣讲会；多次协助招商部门做好重点区域的招商工作；为外商了解、入驻重点区域作出了贡献。同时，普陀区商务委相关职能科室也努力把压力转变成“化危为机”的动力，优化外资审批工作流程，缩短审批时间，在企业服务中心专门安排了人员受理、解答外资事项，急企业之所急、想企业之所想，真正做到了让企业办事方便、快捷。

3. 以突出重点为抓手，加大对重点项目跟踪与服务的力度

普陀区委、区政府应对金融风暴，及时提出了在全区开展“迎国庆、战百天、保增长、作贡献”活动。其中“企业增效作贡献、引进企业扩大增量、确保通过服务使一批未落地企业落户普陀”，是这次活动的重中之重。同时，在项目引进前，做好投资环境的建设，完善服务体系；在项目引进过程中，加强业务指导，提高企业引进效率。在安商、扶商、富商的过程中，更是统一思想、真诚服务，处处为企业着想，特别是把握不同时期的相关重点，在帮助企业提升活力和价值过程中，提高普陀区为企业服务的力度。普陀区商务委员会响应区委、普陀区政府的号召，将这些重中之重落实到外资引进的工作当中，在“引进企业”、“扩大增量”等方面，成绩斐然。2009年较大的外资新设

项目有：颐泰（上海）置业有限公司汇丽大厦项目、上海远成实业有限公司外资并购项目、富鼎置业（上海）有限公司房地产开发项目等等。增资项目也丝毫不逊色：长江实业真如副中心地块项目、上海康鹏化学有限公司建设总部和研发中心等等。对这些重点项目，上海市商务委员会、普陀区委、区政府的领导十分关心，多次专门听取专题汇报，为某些项目亲自拜访外商，确保了项目落地。

4．着眼大局，加大落实招商引资工作

通过加强协作，整合资源，及时宣传普陀区最新的区情和政策，扩大影响力，变增长潜力为实力。在普陀区领导亲自主持和直接关心下，开展了外出招商、中介招商等形式多样的宣传推介活动。

（1）积极“走出去”招商，赴新加坡默沙东亚太总部宣传总部经济政策；赴日本参加软件外包、服务外包说明会；赴厦门参加经贸洽谈会；前往江苏兴化，浙江杭州、温州、台州等地进行生物医药等项目洽谈。

（2）积极参与全佳、基强联行、高力国际等中介机构组织的论坛、推介活动。加强了与香港工商业联合会、民营经济发展促进中心、温州商会、绍兴商会等机构的联系与协作。

（3）条块联动，加强项目合作，桃浦镇、长风街道、长寿街道召开保税物流中心宣传推介会，楼宇经济发展恳谈会、友力国际大厦推介会等。四是根据新的区域发展战略，编印新版普陀区招商宣传画册，汇编总部企业引进扶持政策，着手对投资普陀网站信息进行动态更新。

（三）外经发展情况及特点

由于受国际金融危机影响，普陀区2009年对外经济合作项目处于比较低迷的状态，全区没有一家企业申报对外投资或工程承包项目或设立办事机构；2010年普陀区对外经济合作项目随着全球经济形势的回暖而开始有所回升，目前已上报的项目有：上海欣达电梯工程有限公司境外投资项目（在卡塔尔设多哈建材批发中心，项目总投资950万美元，注册资本850万美元）；上海华之樱信息系统有限公司设立境外（日本）办事处。

二、2010年普陀区外经贸发展趋势

在金融危机有可能第二波袭来的大环境下，如何未雨绸缪，做好2010年的外资引进工作，普陀区总结了“盯、关、跟，抢、逼、围”的六字方针：

（一）“盯、关、跟”

“盯、关、跟”是指对已经在普陀区存在的外资企业和正在进行的外资项目，要“盯住”、“关心”、“跟牢”。真正把“服务是普陀第一资源”理念贯彻到对外资企业的服务当中去。要“沉”到外资企业里去，掌握其生产经营的第一手资料；对于外资企业碰到的困难，事无巨细，做到尽全力解决。营造良好的安商、爱商、亲商、富商的环境，努力做到外资企业不因政府服务的原因迁出或关闭。“外资网上审批系统”已在普陀区运行。该系统运行成熟以后，可以提高审批效率，缩短审批时间，为外资企业创造一个更加快捷高效的审批环境。

（二）“抢、逼、围”

为了让普陀区的外资引进更上一层楼，将采用“抢、逼、围”的方法尽量增加外资存量。“抢”是指对于有利于提升经济层级、改善经济结构的重点项目要尽量争取；“逼”是指对只有增资才能保证外资企业良好发展的项目，要尽量引导其增资；“围”是对其他区域成熟项目自身有迁出考虑的，要凭借普陀区的优势尽量的招纳。增加外资存量工作，把以往对项目的“等、靠、要”转变到更加积极主动争取的态度上来。

同时，要进一步提高招商引资的质量。一要切实提高引资企业的外向度，加大对外资先进制造业和现代服务业企业的引进度。二要注重“调结构”，坚持从招商源头加快转型，突出“择上选资”、“招商引智”理念，积极引进产业能级高、成长性好的优质企业。三要积极拓展产业链，加大对具有区域特色的汽车贸易、生物医药、金融服务、电子商务、LED、服饰等行业上下游配套企业的引进力度，促进企业集群式发展。四要加快引进总部型、行业龙头型企业，加大扶持力度，尽快形成区域发展新的增长点。

第八节 闸北区

一、2009 年闸北区外经贸发展情况

（一）外贸发展情况

2009 年闸北区进出口总额 6.61 亿美元，完成全年进出口指标 6.47 亿美元的 102.16%，其中出口 4 亿美元，同比下降 28.07%；进口 2.6 亿美元，同比下降 65.44%。

表 6-14　2009 年闸北区进出口情况数据表

项　目	2009 年（万美元）	2008 年（万美元）	同比（%）
出　口	40359	56111	-28.07
进　口	25704	74370	-65.44
进出口	66063	130481	-49.37

由于国际金融危机在全球范围内的影响没有消除，出口商品的海外需求尚没有恢复至危机前的水平，海外订单继续减少仍旧压抑外向型企业出口，进而继续影响闸北区进出口总额，2009 年和 2008 年相比，各项数据都明显下降。2009 年闸北区仅有上海益典船舶销售有限公司在香港特区投资设立了香港辉达船务有限公司，经营航运，投资总额 800 万美元，2008 年没有对外投资。

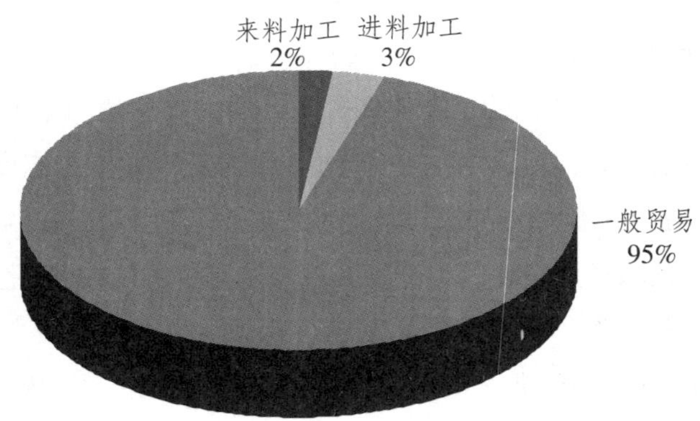

图 6-11　2009 年闸北区贸易方式出口情况结构图

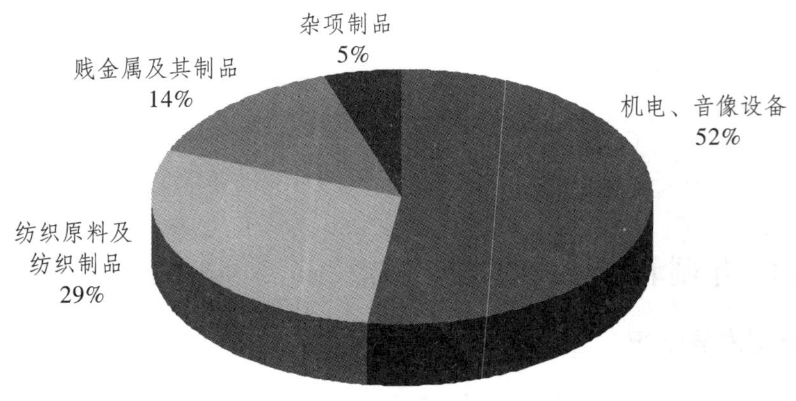

图 6-12　2009 年闸北区一般贸易出口产品结构图

（二）外资发展情况

1．区域外资发展仍实现稳步增长

尽管遭受了国际金融危机的冲击，在各方努力下，2008、2009 年区域外资发展仍然实现了稳步增长。从引资规模上看，2009 年闸北区共新批外资项目 131 个，共计引进合同外资 53112.888 万美元，同比增长 6.1%。从引资结构上看，2008 年房地产项目占引进合同外资比例高达 41.21%，出现了闸北区第一家创业投资管理类外资企业——安铂瑞创业投资管理（上海）有限公司、第一家从事融资租赁业务的外资企业——大洋国际租赁（上海）有限公司；2009 年房地产项目为零，外商投资领域主要涉及技术研发、质量检测、专业咨询、物流运输、商业贸易、服务外包等。从总部经济上看，2008 年引进了美国科勒公司的地区总部；2009 年引进了英国 TESCO、日本株式会社村田制作所与美国威世集团 3 家跨国公司地区总部。

表 6-15 2009 年外商投资行业（或产业）分布情况表

行业或产业	项目数		投资总额		合同外资	
	个数	同比（%）	金额（万美元）	同比（%）	金额（万美元）	同比（%）
合计	131	100	51139.4	100	35641.97	100
生产性项目	4	3.1	86.47	0.2	70.85	0.2
非生产性项目	127	96.9	51052.93	99.8	35571.12	99.8

注：以上数据不含增资项目

2009 年 1–11 月，闸北区共新批外资项目 131 个，涉及合同外资 35641.97 万美元；增资项目 34 个，涉及合同外资 17470.918 万美元，共计引进合同外资 53112.888 万美元，同比增长 6.1%，完成全年目标的 196.7%。

表 6-16 2009 年外商投资主要来源地情况表

国家（地区）	项目数（个）	投资总额（万美元）	合同外资（万美元）
日本	13	21475.62	13743.76
中国香港特区	40	9546.2	7634.21
新加坡	6	3544	3359.6
美国	10	3359.3	3288.3

（续 表）

国家（地区）	项目数（个）	投资总额（万美元）	合同外资（万美元）
英属维尔京	7	4694.42	2892.16
荷兰	3	4050	1635
加拿大	2	1020	1020
新西兰	3	619.92	546.68
毛里求斯	1	950	500
韩国	13	371.62	265.3
比利时	2	672.69	129

注：以上数据不含增资项目

2．引进外资工作中体现的三大特点

（1）跨国公司地区总部取得重大突破，引进跨国公司地区总部3家，全区跨国公司地区总部总数达到8家：由英国TESCO集团（500强排名56）投资设立的特易购企业管理（上海）有限公司，集中国区各商业网点的管理、经营和物流配送为一体；由全球第一的被动元器件制造商日本株式会社村田制作所投资设立的村田（中国）投资有限公司，注册资本1.2亿美元，主要从事新型被动元器件的研发、投资和管理；由全球知名半导体制造商美国威世集团投资设立的威世（中国）投资有限公司，注册资本3000万美元，主要从事该领域的研发、投资和管理。

（2）外商投资现代服务业领域趋于多元化，涉及技术研发、质量检测、专业咨询、物流运输、商业贸易、服务外包等众多新兴业态。包括由世界500强企业日本丸红株式会社和上海交运股份合资设立的上海交运日红国际物流有限公司，投资总额6亿元人民币，专业从事高端物流服务；全球食品检测领域领先的法国欧陆集团首次进入中国，在闸北区成立欧陆检测技术服务（上海）有限公司，专业从事食品领域的质量分析和技术检测。

（3）外商投资企业科技含量不断走高，出现能源科技、生物科技等高端技术研发项目。包括由上海电力集团与比利时比阳公司共同投资设立的比阳（上海）能源科技有限公司，投资总额4500万人民币，主要从事电站、能源设备、电力设备的研发和系统集成；由香港泛亚集团投资设立的泛亚环保（中国）有限公司，注册资本1亿港元，主要从事净化处理系统工程的技术服务。

3．以优质服务为抓手，创建更好的招商平台

（1）转变思路，以优质服务为抓手，做好招商、扶商、富商、留商各项工作。一

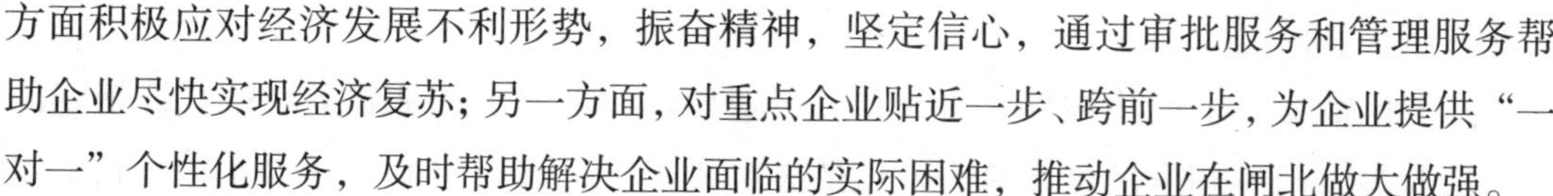

方面积极应对经济发展不利形势，振奋精神，坚定信心，通过审批服务和管理服务帮助企业尽快实现经济复苏；另一方面，对重点企业贴近一步、跨前一步，为企业提供“一对一”个性化服务，及时帮助解决企业面临的实际困难，推动企业在闸北做大做强。

（2）继续推进重点储备项目的引进和落实工作。进一步深化引大引强的对外投资促进战略，一手抓潜在重点项目信息和跟进，为下一年招商引资工作做好项目信息储备工作；另一手抓重点在谈项目的落实，确保完成今年引资目标。

（3）结合区内新建载体和园区开发，重点引进优质服务业态。根据区内产业结构调整升级的战略要求，围绕区内新建成的一批商务楼宇和园区载体，重点引进了数家现代服务业外资企业，包括专业服务、现代物流、服务外包等。

（4）加强中介联系，拓展项目信息渠道。继续加强与投资中介特别是五大行等知名中介机构的联系，通过上门走访和载体推介，吸引中介机构对闸北区载体建设的关注度和招商引资工作的支持力度。同时继续加强与市级外资审批和招商部门的联系，积极寻求对闸北区招商引进工作和经济发展的支持。

二、2010 年闸北区外经贸工作展望

（一）利用产业扶持政策，加大外资引进力度，推进区域经济结构调整

近两年，为应对国际经济衰退的不利局面，国家、上海市出台了一系列的经济刺激政策和具体措施，包括对服务外包、高科技产业、总部经济、服务贸易等方面的鼓励政策。2009 年年初，国务院又陆续紧密推出“九大产业调整振兴计划”，将钢铁、汽车、造船、石化、轻工、纺织、有色金属、装备制造、电子信息列为九大支柱产业，提出了 2009~2011 年九大重点产业的三年振兴规划。结合闸北区发展实际情况，2010 年将重点发展总部经济、服务外包、科技研发等现代服务业态，利用相关具体配套政策和实施细则，积极争取国家、上海市有关部门的专项扶持资金和鼓励政策，引导外资流向重点发展产业，进一步推动区域经济结构调整和能级提升。

（二）抓住外资审批权限下放的契机，进一步完善审批服务

根据上海市商务委员会有关政策精神，上海市商务委员会将依托全市统一的网上外资项目审批平台，逐步下放外资项目审批权限，具体包括所有投资总额在 1 亿美元以下的鼓励类和允许类外资项目。第一批九大现代服务业行业已明确下放，包括商业零售、外资并购、职业介绍所、人才中介、国际货代、经营型租赁、无船承运、会展公司、广告企业等，为闸北区发展现代服务业，特别是新兴的高端服务业态提供利好

条件。

闸北区商务委员会将在深入研究相关行业外资政策要求的基础上，做好政策宣传和审批服务，引导和推动更多符合资质的外商投资上述现代服务业新兴业态，利用优质外生资源发展区域现代服务业。

（三）结合区内新建载体和园区开发，引进优质外资项目

2010年闸北区一批新建高档商务载体将集中上市，对外招商。在吸引以往工作经验的基础上，闸北区商务委员会将加大对区内已建在建商务载体的排摸，及时掌握重点楼宇的详细信息，更好进行对外推介和招商指导；进一步加强与开发商和物业代理商的联系，积极探索各种方式有效介入商务载体的前期招商工作，提高入驻项目的属地率和商务载体的利用效益，配合相关部门开展楼宇属地化工作，提高新建载体对区域经济的贡献度；提升新建商务载体引资外资质量，重点引进数家高档外资服务业企业，包括高档餐饮、专业认证、会展服务、服务外包等。

（四）加强与各类投资中介的联系，不断拓展外资项目信息渠道

为进一步拓宽项目信息渠道，寻找新的储备项目，继续加强与投资中介特别是五大行等知名中介机构的联系，同时建立与主要商会、行业协会、招商代表处的联系，通过上门走访和载体推介，吸引中介机构对闸北区载体建设的关注度和招商引资工作的支持力度。继续加强与上海市商务委员会、投资促进中心等市级外资审批和招商部门的联系，积极寻求对闸北区招商引资工作和经济发展的支持。

第九节　虹口区

一、2009年虹口区外经贸发展情况

（一）外贸发展情况

1．基本情况

2009年虹口区海关进出口总额累计达到21.66亿美元，同比增长29.06%，完成年度任务13.8亿的156.96%。虹口区海关进出口总额在上海中心城区位居第二；2009年虹口区外贸进口总额10.18亿美元，同比增长61.93%；出口总额11.48亿美元，同比增

长 9.37%；2009 年一般贸易进出口总额 14.87 亿美元，同比增长 35.04%；加工贸易进出口总额 1.75 亿美元，同比增长 33.51%。

表 6-17 虹口区一般贸易及加工贸易总量及比重

项目	总量（万美元）	比重（%）
一般贸易	148696	68.65
加工贸易	17545	8.10

虹口区出口前三大产品中纺织类产品属于劳动密集型产品，受经济低迷影响较小，出口持续回稳。2009 年 1–12 月，纺织类产品合计出口 20319 万美元，同比增长 5.19%，占全区出口总额 17.70%。受 2009 年全球物流行业大幅萎缩影响，矿物燃料类产品市场交易平淡，矿物燃料类产品年进口和年出口均下降逾 20%。机电、音响设备类等中高端和大件类消耗型商品受美、欧经济影响较大，进出口形势依旧严峻，2009 年 1–12 月进出口总额 44396 万美元，进口、出口降幅均逾 10%。得益于“高保值、抗风险”产品不断被市场推高，珠宝、贵金属及制品类产品市场交易活跃，珠宝、贵金属及制品类产品进口获大幅增长，2009 年 1–12 月进口总额达 15114 万美元，同比 21.15%。

2009 年 1–12 月，对欧出口总额 20972 万美元，同比增长 48.89%，占出口总额 18.27%。日本市场保持稳步增长，年出口额 17220 万美元，同比增长 12.97%。美洲地区经济数据的不稳定性导致对美出口市场形势依旧严峻，仍处于下行走势，对美年出口总额 45980 万美元，同比下降 11.42%。

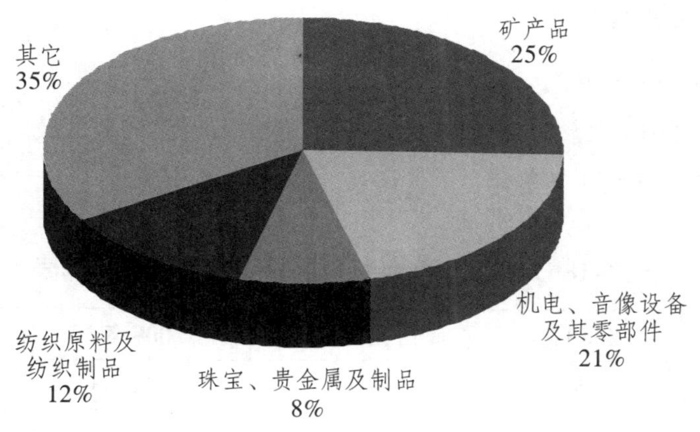

图 6-13 2009 年虹口区主要贸易产品累计进出口金额比重结构图

2．重点企业监测分析

根据对重点企业监测分析看，大部分企业同比下降幅度较大，但也有部分企业进出口额出现回升的迹象。

（1）出口

① 美钻石油钻采系统（上海）有限公司，年出口额达 2401 万美元，上半年同比上升达 211.25%，但年同比降至 50.80%。主要原因是 2008 年来自中东地区采油配套设备订单到 2009 年 5、6 月份才成交，导致 2009 年上半年业务量直线上升，但下半年受航运业等石油类相关产业低迷影响，石油钻采设备产品市场需求疲软，业务额呈现萎缩；② 上海申虹公司，年出口额达 2376 万美元，同比增长 59.62%，主要原因是自产的家居产品和婴儿用品不断寻求新市场，扩大了出口份额；③ 上海亚东盛进出口有限公司，年出口额达 9885 万美元，同比 14.89%，呈现触底回升的“V”字形走势，主要是出口代理产品类型多样，大客户交易较为稳定，注重市场拓展和新客户的开发。

（2）进口

① 中燃船舶燃料有限公司（简称中燃船舶），虽然业务带有行业垄断色彩，但同比下降的趋势并没有缓解，主要是 2008 年保税油和润滑油进出口创历史新高，2009 年受全球航运业下滑的影响，以及国内新增 2 家同类企业的竞争压力，进出口业务量下降幅度较大；② 上海中油能源控股有限公司，面临和中燃船舶同样的困难，受矿物燃油相关产业不振的波及，该公司进口同比由上半年 74.94% 降至年同比 54.13%；③ 上海市工艺品珠宝首饰进出口有限公司，主营珠宝、工艺品等产品进出口，由于 2009 年国内珠宝、工艺品类产品市场交易活跃，其进口业务额呈持续上扬走势，年进口额达 14996 万美元，同比增长 21.84%。

（二）外资发展情况

1．吸引外资情况良好

2009 年虹口区引进外资完成情况：合同外资 3.05 亿美元，完成区政府下达的目标数；2009 年实际利用外资 4.32 亿美元，同比增长 50.57%。

表 6-18　2008-2009 年虹口区外资投资行业结构表（单位：万美元）

	2008 年	占比（%）	2009 年	占比（%）
房地产业	38250.06	64	19586.53	64.14
知识服务业	2198.11	4	5182.266	16.97
现代商贸业	13313.73	22	4068.25	13.22
航运服务业	6198.57	10	1527.48	5

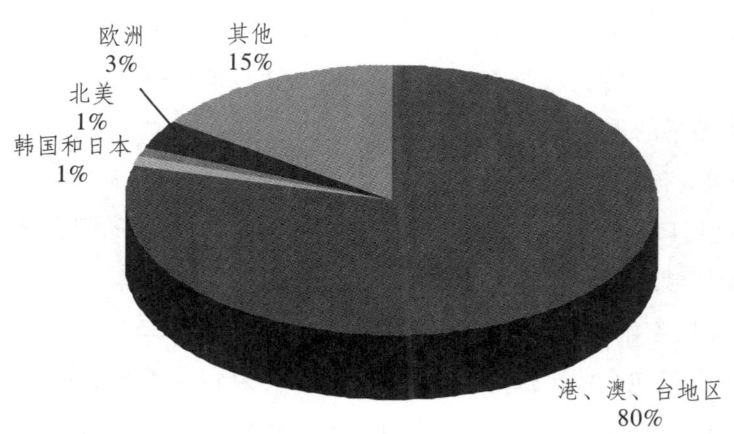

图 6-14 2009 年虹口区外资来源地结构图

2. 求合作、通渠道、重服务、与时俱进为外资工作加强服务

(1) 通力合作，参与外资项目的谈判和引进。2009 年以来，在虹口区商务委员会组建的基础上，增强内部资源整合，通过积极参与外资项目的谈判，引进多家知名企业，并就项目引进进行了大量的前期工作。

(2) 加强招商，通过多种渠道拓展招商范围。在与中介机构良好合作关系的基础上，定期联系，定向招商。与上海市外商投资企业协会共同接待了泰国房地产公司考察北外滩航运服务集聚区。积极筹备参加第十三届"中国国际投资贸易洽谈会"，制作展板，派员参加。在此次盛会上大力宣传、推介虹口新一轮的发展。

(3) 加强服务，为重点企业和外商投资企业解决困难。按照统一部署，将服务企业作为重要工作，不断完善软硬件环境，丰富服务手段，加强企业走访，切实解决企业经营过程中遇到的各项实际困难。

(4) 做好外资网上办事系统在虹口区的联网工作。为进一步改善上海外商投资环境，提高行政审批效率，上海市商务委员会于 2009 年正式开通了上海外资网上办事系统，并在年内向全市各区县推广。按上海市商务委员会统一部署，虹口区顺利完成系统对接，于 10 月 12 日在区内正式推广使用。

二、2010 年虹口区外经贸发展趋势

(一) 进一步加快外贸工作转型

1. 推进服务贸易工作

在巩固和提升货物贸易管理的基础上，加快启动对服务贸易的建设，共同推进外

贸发展。力争形成货物贸易与服务贸易互相发展、相互促进的良性循环模式。研究和探索贸易与航运联动发展，进一步集聚航运要素，逐步完善航运融资、保险、国际仲裁等贸易产业链上下游的关联业务，为贸易企业提供优质便捷的综合口岸服务，使北外滩成为国内外贸易的重要平台。

2．加强外贸类国际商业品牌引进

积极与市进出口商会等行业组织联系，重点引进国际商业品牌入驻主要商业街，提高外贸企业对区域经济的贡献度和影响力。

3．大力发展服务外包产业

积极引进服务外包企业，扶持一批从事国际服务外包业务的企业申请获批上海市重点服务外包企业，力争在未来2~3年内申请获得上海市服务贸易示范区认定。

4．加大服务重点企业

进一步转变服务方式，进一步发挥贸促会、国际商会、外资企业协会服务企业的优势，支持进出口企业境外参展，加强资源整合，扩大服务企业的覆盖面，增强服务企业的针对性和有效性。

（二）进一步提高利用外资的质量和水平

1．招商引资紧密结合虹口区重点产业

聚焦“一区一街一圈”的发展，招商引资工作以现代服务业为基础，对目前正在建设、正在洽谈以及潜在要争取的外商投资项目进行梳理，并进行筛选评估、优先引进等战略，引进大项目，并引导其在条件成熟的情况下在虹口区设立管理型总部，发展总部经济，争取吸引跨国公司全球总部、地区总部、投资性公司、营运中心等功能性项目，通过知名项目在国际上的影响和辐射作用，吸引更多的优质项目入驻，从而进一步深化虹口区重点产业的集聚效应。

2．跟踪大项目，做好服务工作，确保项目顺利落地

大力支持外资企业参与开发建设北外滩和四川北路等地区的开发建设。紧密跟踪如（新加坡）凯德龙之梦项目、德国alpha基金收购玫瑰广场项目等，积极争取政府有关方面的大力支持，确保项目早日建成投入使用，以提升重要区域功能和形象，为四川北路的新一轮改造增添亮点。

3．加强与国际知名邮轮公司联系，支持其在北外滩设立邮轮公司

力争与丽星邮轮、地中海邮轮、嘉年华旗下的歌诗达邮轮等世界知名邮轮公司保持经常的沟通，主动了解企业需求，传达北外滩在上海“两个中心”建设中的发展进程。与上海市商务委员会、市港口局和市旅游委共同调研，研究境外邮轮公司在上海注册

经营性机构和开展经批准的国际航线邮轮业务等工作。

4．密切关注区内储备地块推出进展，积极跟踪，加快项目进展

有计划推出若干地块公开招标。将积极向具有实力的外资房产企业进行前期信息沟通和地块推介，希望有实力有经验的外资房产企业最终能中标获得开发经营权，并为此设立外商投资企业，使之成为引进外资的重要组成部分。

利用外资将充分结合“宝矿”、“瑞丰”、“森林湾”等甲级高档商务楼宇，以及“1933老场坊”、“花园坊”、“智慧桥”、“绿地阳光园”、“空间188”等创意园区，大力发展楼宇、园区经济。如，提前介入开发商的招商进程，通过政策咨询、上门走访等各种形式引导开发商将注册地条款放入到谈判条件中去，从源头上把好企业属地化的第一关，使项目能够“进得来、留得下、长得大”，为企业税收稳定落地提供保障，保证入驻的外商投资企业为虹口区的建设添砖加瓦，真正做到楼宇、园区建设与产业形态改善和集聚相统筹。

（三）做好“市商务委下放外商投资审批管理权限”后虹口区的具体工作

为加快落实外资行政审批制度改革，进一步提高审批效率，转变政府职能，完善外商投资审批管理工作，上海市商务委从2009年8月1日起向各区县商务主管部门下放了部分外商投资审批管理权限。虹口区将认真学习相关法规，完善审批流程，规范审批行为，严格按照法律法规的要求，做好审批工作。同时，审批工作应紧密结合虹口区现代服务业项目特色，加快内部流转程序，缩短审批时限。通过电子政务平台，使项目单位清晰了解审批进程，使行政审批环节公开、透明，切实依法履行好外资审批管理职能。

案例：百丽鞋业（上海）有限公司

2010年新年伊始，香港百丽集团（简称百丽集团）入驻虹口区，成立港商独资百丽鞋业（上海）有限公司（简称百丽鞋业），投资总额为6000万美元，注册资本为3000万美元。

百丽集团旗下拥有Belle（百丽）、Staccato（思加图）、Teenmix（天美意）等多个知名品牌，同时也是著名运动品牌Nike、Adidas、Reebok的获权零售商。该集团主要在中国大陆、香港、澳门从事生产、分销及销售女装鞋品，以及分销及销售运动服装。据中国行业企业信息发布中心对全国重点商场及超市女皮鞋销售市场的监测统计，百

丽鞋业自2000年以来连续8年夺得中国真皮女鞋销量冠军。

百丽品牌自20世纪90年代进入大陆市场以来，已逐渐形成完善的销售渠道及强劲的影响力。百丽集团落户虹口区，将以百丽鞋业为总部，整合公司在大陆的各项业务资源，形成辐射全国、健康、迅速的发展态势。

第十节 杨浦区

一、2009年杨浦区外经贸发展情况

（一）外贸发展情况

1．基本情况

2009年，由于受国际金融危机、西方发达国家贸易保护主义抬头以及企业生产成本上涨、产品结构自身转型等多重负面因素影响，杨浦区外贸进出口下滑严重。全区外贸进出口总额为6.6亿美元，比上年度下降39.9%，其中：海关直接出口3.85亿美元，比上年度下降49.79%。由于受主要出口目标市场欧美等国家金融危机影响，消费疲软，导致出口减少。

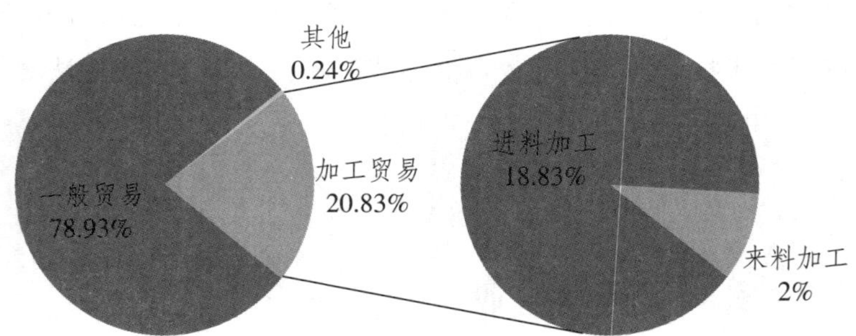

图6-15 2009年杨浦区贸易类型占海关进出口总额比重图

2009年全区纺织制品出口13842万美元，比上年下降35.13%，占出口总额比例35.98%；机电类产品出口20031万美元，比上年下降51.14%，占出口总额比例52.07%。

作为杨浦区主要出口市场的欧洲和北美洲，因受国际金融危机及贸易壁垒加剧等因素影响，2009年销往美国的商品占出口总额比例虽有所上升，由2008年的13.86%上升至17.84%，但出口总额仅为6863万美元，同比下降35.36%；销往欧洲的商品占比由2008年的34.29%下降至22.05%。相对而言，销往东盟和日本市场的出口量则有

所上升，出口总额占比上升 3.92 和 2.7 个百分点，分别为 11.7% 和 12.2%。

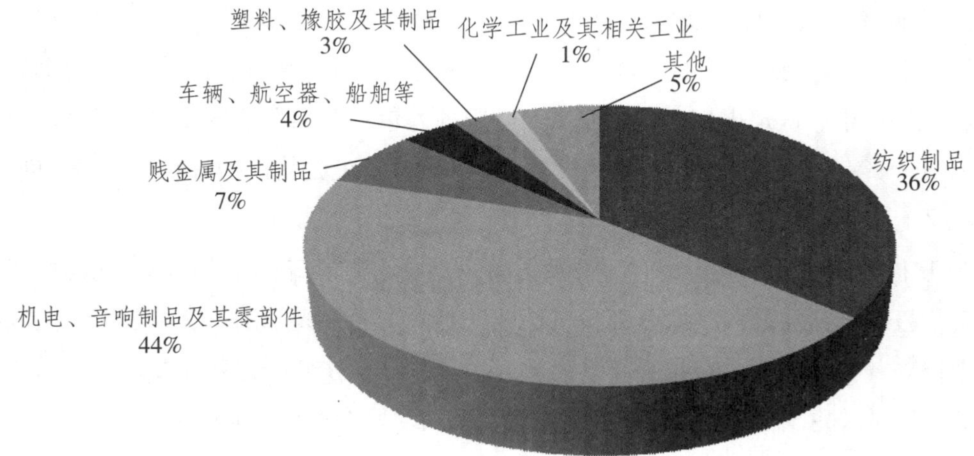

图 6-16　2009 年杨浦区主要出口商品结构图

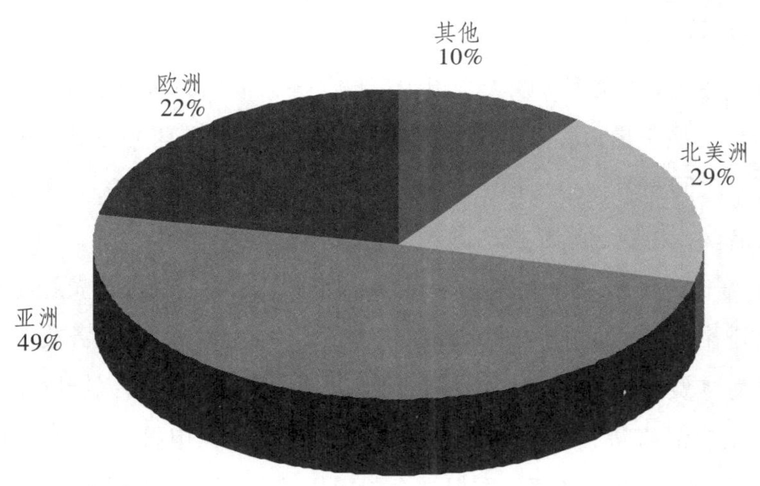

图 6-17　2009 年杨浦区出口商品主要输往地结构图

2．外贸工作重点

（1）开展相关调研

梳理排摸外贸企业相关信息，调查加工贸易禁、限类企业，进行服务外包现状调查。

（2）采取措施、应对危机

① 做好“中小企业国际市场开拓资金”申报审核。截至目前，共计受理并完成了全区 75 家企业申报的 386 个、合计 697 万元人民币的项目初审及上报工作。目前已经基本完成对第一批 41 家企业、149 个项目申报受理初审工作，涉及拨付资金额 182 万元。为使更多企业分享该项政策，在计划申报调整期及时通知已在“中小企业国际市场开拓资金”网上注册的 110 家区属企业。并受理项目 38 个，涉及开拓扶持资金 46 万元。

已完成所有受理项目初审并上报上海市商务委。

② 贯彻落实服务外包扶持政策。一是开展2008年度上海市服务外包专项扶持资金申报工作。二是受理、审核2009年国家服务外包专项资金申报工作。三是协助做好重点服务外包企业认定申报工作。四是鼓励服务外包企业网上信息注册。五是动员企业网上招聘。六是为软件出口企业积极咨询相关政策。七是协助做好软件出口（创新）园区申报工作。

③ 积极鼓励企业拓展市场。为鼓励杨浦区企业走出去拓展海外市场，杨浦区商务委员会积极帮助指导区内一家外商投资企业——上海光和光学制造有限公司，完成了在香港设立分公司的相关审批手续。另外，根据复旦科技园孵化基地要求，杨浦区商务委员会又对入驻该园区的一家软件公司计划到荷兰发展进行了前期指导。

④ 协助做好外贸内销订货会组织工作。为克服金融危机对企业带来的困难，开拓外贸企业内销市场的新路子，探索内外贸一体化的新模式。杨浦区有14家企业获得参展机会，企业反映良好。

⑤ 配合做好2009年跨国采购大会组织工作。为帮助杨浦区中小外贸企业，积极应对国际经济形势、稳定出口，寻找外贸新商机，根据上海市商务委员会要求，杨浦区商务委员会第一时间与各街道（镇）、经济、科技、创意等园区联系，动员广大内外贸企业积极参展洽谈，将自己产品推向国际市场。

⑥ 配合做好保外贸稳增长专项资金申报工作。为保持上海市外贸稳定增长，帮助企业缓解当前进出口所面临的困难。2009年10月10日，上海市商务委员会召开保持外贸稳定增长专项资金申报工作会议。此项专项资金涉及开拓新兴国际市场项目、境外营销网络（出口品牌等）项目、农轻纺贸易促进项目，申报截止日为10月31日。为做好此项申报工作，杨浦区商务委根据海关提供的相关企业数据名单，向全区60余家外贸出口情况较好的企业发出书面通知，由于此次专项资金申报与中小企业国际市场开拓资金不允许重复，通过对企业申报项目的主体资质认定，为3家企业递交书面上报材料并通过资质认定。

⑦ 协调解决企业对外贸易中的问题。注册杨浦区的上海水产集团下属华利船舶工程有限公司，2009年承接到一笔3000万美元的来料加工业务订单，按照海关通关规定，企业需要按合同比例支付一定数额的保证金。而该企业由于先前已为对方垫付了部分进料资金，如按照海关通关规定支付全额保证金企业感到困难。对此，在接到企业求助后，杨浦区商务委员会在区税务、区工商等部门协助下，对该企业经营及纳税等相关资信情况确认后，主动与海关协调并帮助企业解决了问题。上海腾龙国际贸易有限公司是杨浦区一家外贸公司，承接了三份进料加工业务，由于业务人员疏忽，对进口

料件称重发生错误，以至在核销时无法通过。为此，杨浦区商务委员会通过与海关积极协调并严格核对料件总量，使问题最终得到解决。

⑧ 组织申报国家级重点电子商务企业。为进一步推进杨浦区电子商务企业发展，按照市商务委关于申报国家级重点电子商务企业工作要求，主动联系相关园区、企业。目前上报东方希杰、易安信、联华电子商务三家企业的申请，并获得商务部认定。

3．做好日常审批、管理工作

（1）来料加工审批工作

2009 年，共审批来料加工合同 5 份，累计合同出口金额 90.48 万美元；审批进料加工合同 65 份，累计合同进口金额 532.38 万美元，累计合同出口金额 1194.76 万美元。

（2）加工贸易企业生产能力审批

2009 年，共计审批加工贸易企业生产能力证明 23 份。对新办企业坚持一一上门验厂，杜绝“三无”企业，对加工企业从严审核。

（3）“两类企业”年度考核和换证工作

2009 年，通过对申报的 6 家“产品出口企业”和 3 家“先进技术企业”进行年度考核并报请上海市商务委员会审核，除 1 家产品出口型企业因出口比例未达到标准而未通过审核，其他 8 家全部通过审核。

（4）清理整顿外派劳务市场秩序工作

根据国务院七部委召开的“全国清理整顿外派劳务市场秩序专项行动电视电话会议”及本市贯彻落实意见，作为牵头部门，杨浦区商务委员会根据领导指示，拟定了全区专项行动工作方案，并主动与区人力资源和社会保障局、区工商局、区公安局等专项行动主要职能部门会商，研究落实杨浦区清理整顿专项行动相关工作。通过近一个月的重点检查，未发现各类外派劳务违法违规行为，已按时间截点要求将阶段性工作情况汇报至市专项领导小组。

（二）外资发展情况

1．外资结构继续优化，增资结构良好

2009 年引进项目数 79 个，比 2008 年增长 2.59 %，合同利用外资金额 6.26 亿美元，比 2008 年下降 13.67 %。

2009 年 1–12 月，杨浦区累计引进外资项目 79 个，比 2008 年增长 2.59 %，其中，新批注册资金 500 万元人民币以上的项目 21 个，高新科技类和现代服务类项目为 75 个，占引进项目数的 95%，合同外资为 6.26 亿美元，外商直接投资主要来自美国、日本和中国香港地区，另外还有德国、法国、英国、荷兰、丹麦、卢森堡、澳大利亚、加拿大、新西兰、新加坡、伊朗、印度尼西亚、中国台湾等国家和地区的企业或个人在杨浦区投资。据税务部门统计,外资对区域经济的贡献不断提高,区外税占比约22%左右。2009年杨浦区外商直接投资生产性项目4个，合同外资267.2万美元；非生产性项目75个，合同外资62342.57万美元。项目中主要涉及：高新技术业、咨询服务业、房地产业、计算机软件业、环保科技业等。

2009年杨浦区利用外资的主要特点：一是外资结构继续优化，引进企业中现代服务类和科技类企业项目数占全年项目数的94.93%；二是企业增资势头良好，全年共有22家企业进行了增资扩股，增资额占全年引进合同外资的41.21%。

2．重点工作

（1）招大引强工作

1–12月，杨浦区先后引进了世界500强大陆集团投资的大陆汽车亚太管理（上海）有限公司、易保网络技术（上海）有限公司、易安信信息技术研发（上海）有限公司、全球最大的家居零售巨头丹麦JYSK集团投资的居事佳（上海）商贸有限公司、联合基因(上海)健康管理服务有限公司、上海沪风房地产开发有限公司、盛维创业投资管理(上海）有限公司、安莉芳（上海）贸易公司、上海仁恒杨浦房地产有限公司等重大项目。在招大引强同时，优化服务，提升效率，先后做好阿齐兰（中国）投资有限公司总部扶持基金申报、欧尚（中国）投资有限公司增资、上海波司登商贸发展有限公司股权转让等重大项目的服务及变更工作。

（2）积极推进重点涉外招商项目

会同区金融办等部门共同深化杨浦与联合国、湾区、硅谷银行的合作项目，协调推动北外滩世博水门招商项目，积极推动完美时空项目。

（3）积极推进外资审改工作

统一部署，稳步推进市区外资审改工作。根据上海市商务委员会的统一部署和安排，已正式开通杨浦外资网上办事系统，实现网上审批，市区联动，进一步提升了外资审批的效率。深入推进杨浦区外资并联审批工作。目前,随着杨浦区外资审改工作的深入推进，各外资审批部门的工作效率大幅提高，外资项目审批大幅提速，行政效率显著提升。

二、2010年杨浦区外经贸发展趋势

（一）把握外贸走势，加快杨浦区服务外包产业发展

1．加快发展软件和信息服务外包产业

根据杨浦区政府审核通过的电子信息三年行动计划，2010年以至今后相当一个时期，

重点推进软件和信息服务外包产业发展将是加快实现由货物贸易向服务贸易转变的重要外贸发展领域，也是建立以科教为特色、服务经济为核心的新型产业体系重中之重。

一是开展国家及上海市服务外包产业扶持政策评估工作；二是进一步贯彻落实好国家及本市服务外包产业扶持政策的宣传、受理、审核、上报工作；三是会同有关园区对上海市商务委员会授牌的两家软件出口（创新）园区，从产业集聚、资源整合、功能提升等方面做好相关指导、协调。并继续努力扶持和培育成长性好、具备国际竞争力的服务外包产业示范集聚平台和骨干企业，做好相关指导、服务工作；四是探索建立杨浦区软件及电子信息服务外包工作网络及重点园区企业例会制度。

2．加强跟踪分析，及时掌握外贸发展走势

在国际金融危机尚未真正企稳回升，对外贸易整体形势尚不确定的背景下，杨浦区将力争确保 2010 年全区一般贸易进出口额不出现大幅下降，基本与去年持平。一方面继续贯彻落实国家及上海市中小企业国际市场开拓专项扶持资金，积极鼓励、帮助外贸企业拓展新兴国际市场，并做好中小企业国际市场开拓资金的申报受理及网上审核等相关工作；另一方面将进一步完善对区域内重点外贸行业企业进出口情况的跟踪分析，确保及时准确掌握全区外贸走势，为领导正确决策提供依据。

3．继续做好宣传工作，鼓励、指导企业“走出去”

2010 年，将在上海市商务委开门会的指导下，进一步会同相关街道、园区，做好政策宣传、鼓励工作。引导更多企业“走出去”，开拓海外国际市场。

4．制订、完善应对贸易摩擦联络机制

随着全球后金融危机带来的贸易保护主义抬头倾向，2010 年杨浦区商务委员会将通过对全区外贸企业类型的梳理排摸，探索建立以街道（镇）、各园区为网络中枢的应对贸易摩擦工作联动网络，配合上海市商务委员会共同做好外贸企业应对反倾销相关诉讼案件取证的调查工作。

（二）促进结构调整转型，提高利用外资水平

2010 年是杨浦建设国家级创新型城区，进一步提升外向度和国际化水平的一年。外资工作要紧紧围绕杨浦区委、区政府的工作中心，根据区商务委员会总体工作部署，以工作机制和方法的创新为抓手，优质高效地完成外资审批、外资招商、重大外资项目协调和推进以及商务外事等工作，提升外资工作的影响力、整合力和凝聚力，为提升杨浦经济工作的外向度和国际化水平作出贡献。

1．2010 年外资发展的总体要求

（1）把握基调：促进结构调整和转型

（2）围绕核心：转方式、调结构、促转型

（3）聚焦目标：不断提高利用外资的质量和水平

（4）抓住三个发力点：① 更新引资理念；② 创新服务理念；③ 创新引资方式

（5）体现三方面成效：① 对杨浦产业结构调整的促进作用；② 在企业自主创新、产业升级等方面的推动作用；③ 对提升城区开放度和国际化水平的主导作用

2．2010 年外资发展的重点工作

（1）进一步做好外资项目招商工作

聚焦重点园区、重点楼宇，进一步加大外资招商工作力度。重点做好新江湾城国际社区、大连路总部研发集聚区北美广场、环同济经济产业带和北外滩项目地块的外资招商工作的信息跟踪、招商接轨、项目设立、企业落地的系列服务工作，进一步提高吸引外资的质量和水平。

（2）建立健全涉外招商工作绩效考核机制

为进一步提高杨浦区利用外资工作的质量和水平，提升杨浦区开放程度和国际化水平，拟联合相关职能部门建立政府体系内的涉外招商工作绩效考核和评估机制，明确责任部门，加快杨浦区外向型经济的规模和质量的提升。通过建立涉外招商工作绩效考核的方式，加大各相关经济职能部门对外资招商引资的积极性，形成合力，从而进一步做好外资招商引资工作。

（3）进一步推动外资招大引强工作

做好引进湾区杨浦联络机构、上海海锦房地产有限公司增资等重大项目的相关工作；做好大陆集团亚太总部的全面落地工作以及研发机构的引进工作。

（4）进一步深化重大外资项目建设

推动西门子中心、北美广场等项目按计划推进。

（5）进一步深化重点涉外商务与合作项目

会同区金融办等部门共同深化杨浦与联合国、湾区、硅谷银行的合作项目；继续协调推动北外滩世博水门招商项目。

（6）进一步深化外资审改工作

根据上海市商务委员会的统一部署和安排，做好市区联网审批以及审批权限下放的相关工作。继续深入推进杨浦区外资并联审批工作，并根据上海市商务委员会的要求，尽快做好市区并联审批接轨工作。

（7）进一步深化商务外事工作

正在探索建立外国投资工作海外联络处以及海外经济顾问的工作机制，立足杨浦实际，通过在北美、欧洲等重点区域设立“杨浦区外国投资工作海外联络处”并以聘

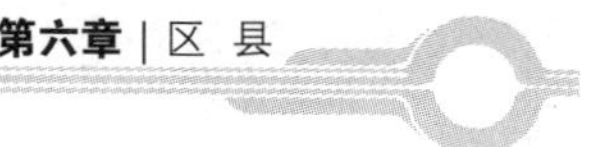

请海外经济顾问的方式，进一步探索推动外向型经济工作不断发展的有效机制，促进杨浦知识创新区的建设与发展。

案例：上海奥力福实业有限公司

上海奥力福实业有限公司成立于1995年，最初以羽绒制品为主，专业生产羽绒被、枕、垫等产品，如今扩展到床上用品、睡袋、野营帐篷等旅游用品。产品远销欧、美、加、英、日、澳及东南亚等地。企业在上海南翔有生产基地30000多平方米，拥有员工600余名。配套设备齐全，技术力量雄厚，年生产能力达800万条，年出口达3000万美元左右。上海奥力福实业有限公司连续6年列为上海市私企“百强”之一，连续7年荣获上海市“重合同、守信用”单位。是全国首批获得自营进出口权的私有企业之一，目前已在美国等多个国家和地区开设分公司。

第十一节　宝山区

一、2009年宝山区外经贸发展情况

（一）外贸发展情况

2009年度，宝山区外贸进出口总额18.2亿美元，同比下降48.33%。其中出口12.1亿美元，同比下降49.67%，进口6.1亿美元，同比下降45.47%。受国际金融危机影响，2009年度全年外贸出口降幅较大，按月份来看，全年出口走势呈U字形，1至3月份同比逐月下降；4、5两月跌至谷底，降幅达70%以上；6月份开始回升，降幅维持在50%左右；直至11月份降幅明显收窄，同比下降39.6%，而12月份同比仅下降21.5%。外贸进口情况基本与出口相仿，12月份当月进口额同比增长16.5%，全年首次出现正增长。2009年进出口具有以下特点：

1．加工贸易方式占出口总额逾五成

加工贸易是宝山区外贸出口的主要方式，2009年度以加工贸易方式出口额为6.4亿美元，同比下降59.05%，约占全区全年出口总额的52.61%。其中来料加工1.9亿美元，进料加工4.4亿美元。以一般贸易方式出口额为5.2亿美元，占出口总额的43.15%，同

比下降33.49%。其他贸易方式出口额0.5亿美元，同比下降20.90%。

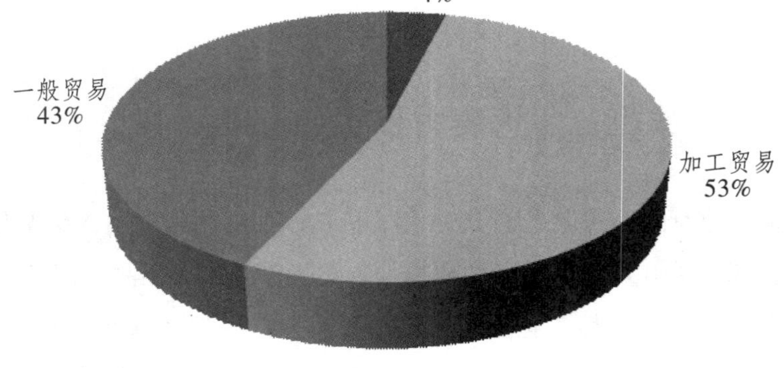

图6-18 2009年宝山区贸易方式占出口总额比重图

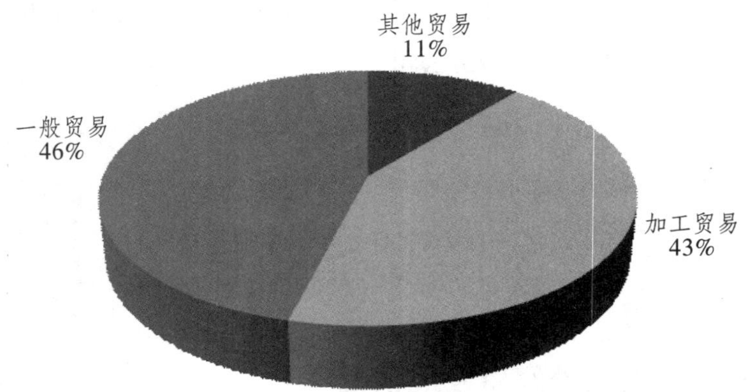

图6-19 2009年宝山区贸易方式占进口总额比重图

2．进出口产品结构调整升级

在2009年度出口商品中，集装箱、未锻造的铝及铝材、变压器、钢铁或铝制结构体及其部件、钢材、冷冻机和制冷设备的出口额居前，总额达7.26亿美元，占宝山区出口总值的六成。其中，受全球经济衰退、外需不足影响，集装箱和未锻造的铝及铝材出口额仅为3.3亿美元和1.7亿美元，同比降幅分别达65.64%和52.29%。变压器、医药品、印刷机械、半导体器件等技术含量、附加值较高的产品出口剧增，同比分别增长57.46%、17.73%、29.00%和90.53%。进口方面，区内企业积极利用国际市场资源，大幅度增加进口铝材、纸浆、铬矿砂、天然橡胶等资源类产品，增幅分别为4倍、0.5倍、4.1倍和3.6倍。

3．主要出口市场呈现多样化

2009年度，世界主要市场需求普遍低迷，宝山区对美国、欧盟、日本、东盟、中

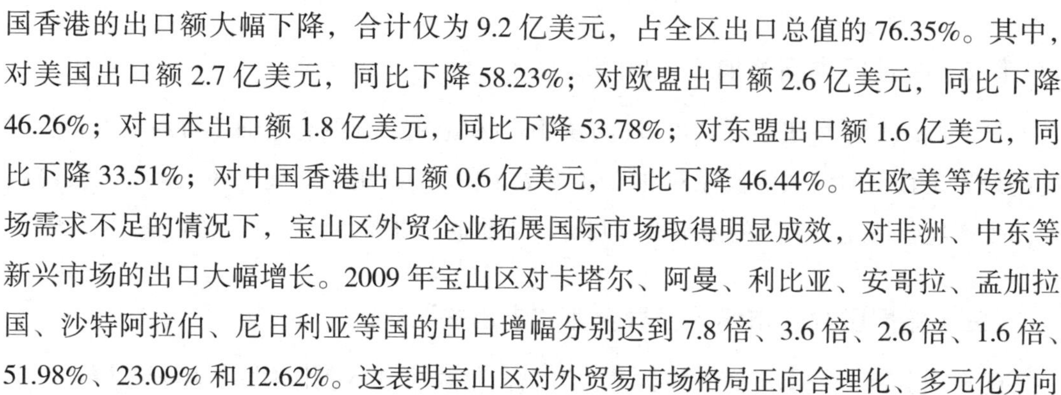

国香港的出口额大幅下降，合计仅为9.2亿美元，占全区出口总值的76.35%。其中，对美国出口额2.7亿美元，同比下降58.23%；对欧盟出口额2.6亿美元，同比下降46.26%；对日本出口额1.8亿美元，同比下降53.78%；对东盟出口额1.6亿美元，同比下降33.51%；对中国香港出口额0.6亿美元，同比下降46.44%。在欧美等传统市场需求不足的情况下，宝山区外贸企业拓展国际市场取得明显成效，对非洲、中东等新兴市场的出口大幅增长。2009年宝山区对卡塔尔、阿曼、利比亚、安哥拉、孟加拉国、沙特阿拉伯、尼日利亚等国的出口增幅分别达到7.8倍、3.6倍、2.6倍、1.6倍、51.98%、23.09%和12.62%。这表明宝山区对外贸易市场格局正向合理化、多元化方向转变。

4．外商投资企业完成出口近9.4亿美元

在年度出口中，外商投资企业的出口额为9.4亿美元，占出口总额的77.34%，同比下降52.57%。出口额在1000万美元以上的外资企业有12家，其中上海中集冷藏箱有限公司和上海新格有色金属有限公司的出口额过亿，分别为2.7亿美元和1.7亿美元。

5．内资企业完成出口2.7亿美元

2009年度内资企业出口2.7亿美元，占宝山区出口总值的22.66%。其中外贸流通企业出口0.8亿美元，同比下降23.17%，自营进出口企业出口1.9亿美元，同比下降40.54%。年出口额在1000万美元以上的企业有6家，分别为：上海东圣电子进出口有限公司5168万美元、上海月月潮国际贸易有限公司1903万美元、上海海泰钢铁国际贸易有限公司1637万美元、上海丹爱法企业发展有限公司1572万美元、上海前卫衬布厂1475万美元、上海昊群数码科技有限公司1301万美元。

（二）外经发展情况

2009年度，宝山区内有3家企业获准从事境外一般商品的进出口贸易。其中，上海业钢实业有限公司赴中国香港投资，投资额为20万美元；上海东方康桥房地产有限公司赴中国香港投资，投资额为50万港元；上海豪海国际贸易有限公司赴越南投资，投资额为50万美元。与2008年相比，项目数同比下降40%。

二、2010年宝山区外经贸发展趋势

（一）加强管理，协调关系

根据国家有关加工贸易政策的调整情况，加强审批与管理。协调与各部门的关系，积极营造良好的外贸发展和投资环境，切实为企业排忧解难。

（二）关注国内国外加工贸易情况

针对国际金融危机对外贸出口造成的压力和影响，开展有关加工贸易热点难点问题的调研工作。时时关注国家对加工贸易政策采取的措施，对宝山区从事加工贸易企业的生产经营情况、涉及的困难进行调研，帮助企业协调、解决急难愁问题。

（三）拓展国内外市场，引导企业“走出去”

配合商务部、上海市商务委员会，组织企业做好中小企业国际市场开拓资金、保持外贸稳定增长等各类扶持资金的宣传、申报，制定相关办法，更好地服务于为地方经济作出较大贡献的企业。积极为企业搭建平台，通过多种形式，帮助外贸企业拓展国际和国内两个市场，引导、扶持企业培育自主品牌，使企业具有更强的竞争力。

2010 年将进一步做好宝山区内企业“走出去”的审批管理和政策指导工作，举办各类“走出去”政策及实务宣传培训会，不断提升对“走出去”企业的服务水平，并进一步了解掌握企业在外的投资经营情况。

第十二节　闵行区

一、2009 年闵行区外经贸发展情况

（一）外贸发展情况

加快转变外贸发展方式，深入实施市场多元化战略，努力促进对外贸易的稳步回升。2009 年，闵行区进出口商品总额为 236.82 亿美元，比上年下降 5.6%。其中出口商品总额 175.65 亿美元，比上年下降 3.2%；进口商品总额 61.17 亿美元，比上年下降 11.8%。

2009 年，闵行区出口商品总额 175.6 亿美元，比上年下降 3.2%，虽然与上海市出口商品总额预计下降 16% 相比要好许多，但仍反映出闵行区外贸出口尚未止跌回稳。

从企业类型来看，三资企业出口 168.32 亿美元，比上年下降 2.4%；内资企业出口 7.33 亿美元，比上年下降 18.0%。从贸易方式来看，一般贸易出口 21.44 亿美元，比上年下降 24.2%；加工贸易出口 153.59 亿美元，比上年增长 0.5%。

外贸产品主要出口地为北美洲 63.55 亿美元，欧洲 53.62 亿美元，亚洲 45.36 亿美元，拉丁美洲 8.12 亿美元，大洋洲 3.67 亿美元，非洲 1.33 亿美元。主要出口产品为机电类

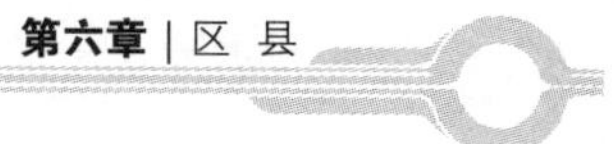

157.39 亿美元，比上年下降 0.9%；纺织品 6.36 亿美元，比上年下降 13.4%；光学、医学等仪器类 2.38 亿美元，比上年下降 62.1%。

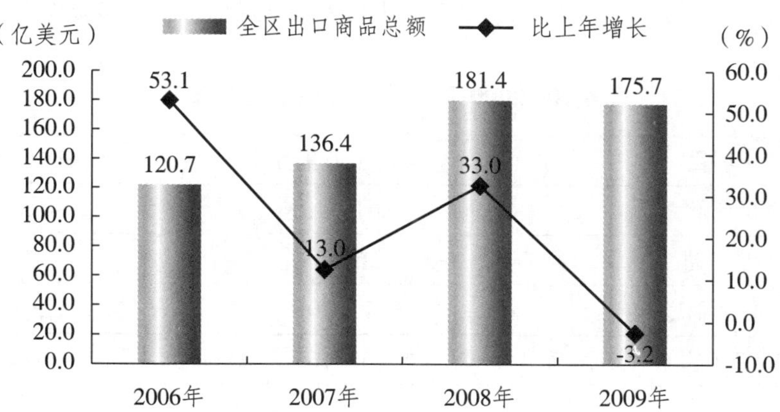

图 6-20 2006-2009 年闵行区出口商品总额与增长

表 6-19 2009 年闵行区外贸出口市场结构

类别	绝对值（亿美元）	比上年增长（%）
外贸出口商品总额	175.65	-3.2
北美洲	63.55	-7.0
欧洲	53.62	-0.1
亚洲	45.36	-2.2
拉丁美洲	8.12	15.8
大洋洲	3.67	-26.0
非洲	1.33	25.5

（二）外资发展情况

招商引资额在上海市名列前茅。2009 年，闵行区新批准三资企业 387 个，合同外资 12.02 亿美元，实际到位外资 11.26 亿美元，比上年增长 11.0%。新增内资注册资金 260.20 亿元，比上年增长 27.4%。全年新批及增资 1000 万美元以上的大项目 37 个，吸引合同外资 7.35 亿美元，占全区总数 61.1%。年末，全球 500 强企业已在区内投资了 93 个项目，其中 2009 年新增投资项目 1 个。

（三）受外需疲软影响，园区企业产品出口率有所下降

2009 年，经济园区完成出口交货值 1057.1 亿元，产品出口率达 54.1%，比上年同

期减少2个百分点，各大园区的出口率也均比上年同期有所减少。其中漕开发产品出口率为88.6%，比上年减少11.4个百分点；闵行经济技术开发区产品出口率为16.6%，比上年减少0.2个百分点；莘庄工业区产品出口率为25.2%，比上年减少1.8个百分点。

表6-20　2009年闵行区外贸进出口情况

项目	累计（万美元）	增长（%）
进口商品总额	611713	-11.77
外商投资项目（进口商品总额）	567268	-12.25
出口商品总额	1756505	-3.17
外商投资项目（出口商品总额）	1683167	-2.4

表6-21　2009年闵行区外商投资项目引进情况

项目	增长（%）	计量单位	累计
投产企业总数（上月）	31.9	个	3097
本年批准项目数	-15.32	个	387
合同吸收外资	-25.4	万美元	120169
实际到位外资（上月）	10.95	万美元	112595

表6-22　2009年市级以上工业园区产品出口情况

项目	工业总产值（亿元）	出口交货值（亿元）	产品出口率（%）
闵行经济技术开发区	364.06	60.60	16.6
漕河泾开发区	968.51	858.01	88.6
莘庄工业区	457.41	115.25	25.2
紫竹科学园区	96.5	7.87	8.2
闵北工业区	43.35	12.33	28.4
向阳工业区	24.89	3.04	12.2
合计	1954.72	1057.1	54.1

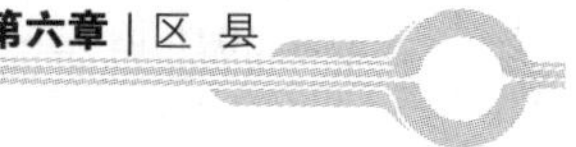

第十三节 嘉定区

一、2009 年嘉定区外经贸发展情况

（一）外贸发展情况

2009 年，嘉定区产生外贸进出口贸易额的企业共有 2300 多家，2009 年全区累计出口 62.7673 亿美元，同比下降 21.35%；全区进口 47.99 亿美元，同比下降 13.04%。

1．2009 年进出口同比略有下降

2009 年 1–12 月全区出口 62.77 亿美元，同比下降 21.35%，2009 年 1–12 月份全区进口 47.99 亿美元，同比下降 13.04%。2009 年，机电产品出口为 32.14 亿美元，汽车零部件产品出口为 6.8 亿美元，金属五金产品出口为 4.22 亿美元，纺织服装类产品出口为 3.48 亿美元。

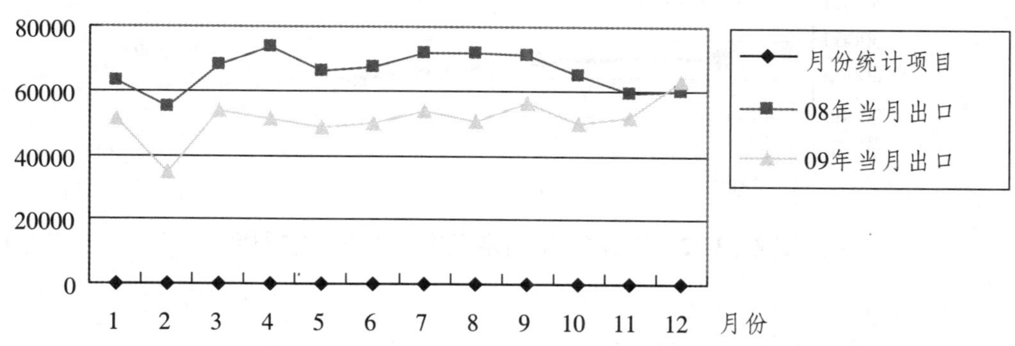

图 6-21 2009 年与 2008 年嘉定区外贸直接出口趋势比较图

表 6-23 2009 年与 2008 年嘉定区各类贸易方式比较表

贸易方式	2009 年累计出口	2008 年累计出口	2009 年与 2008 年同比
一般贸易	307942	363570	-15.3%
加工贸易	319452	434374	-26.46%
来料加工	38205	43204	-11.57%
进料加工	281247	391170	-28.1%

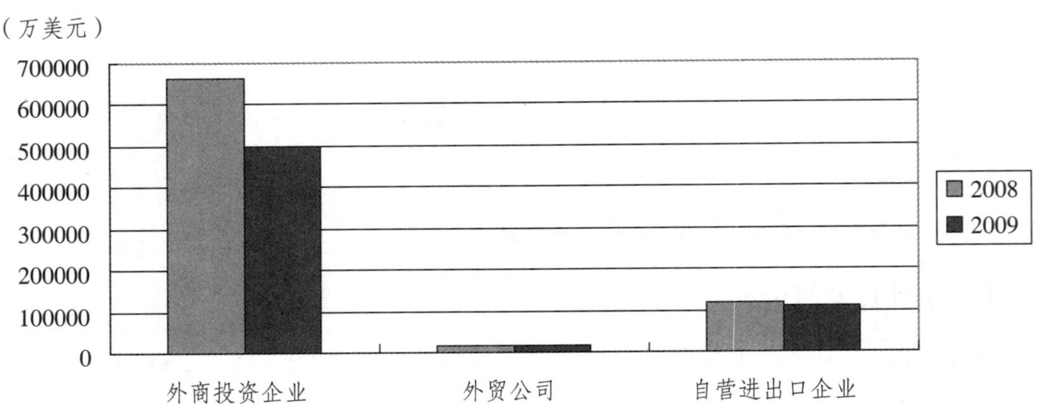

图 6-22 2009 年与 2008 年嘉定区各类企业比较图

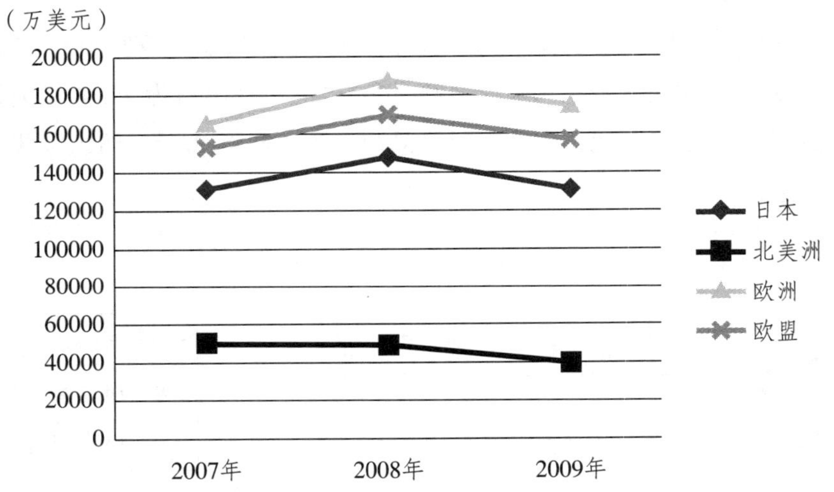

图 6-23 2007-2009 年嘉定区进口情况（按国别）

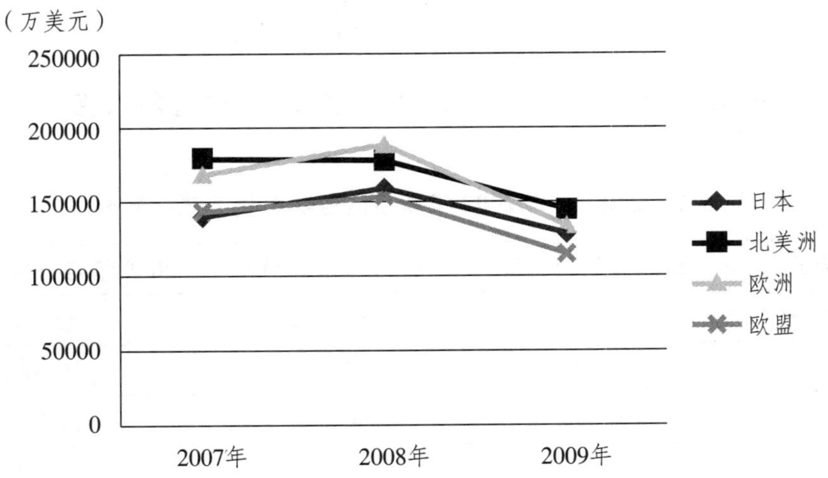

图 6-24 2007-2009 年嘉定区出口情况（按国别）

2．积极宣传扶持政策，搭建平台为企业服务

（1）切实为外贸企业服务

为进一步了解金融危机对嘉定区出口企业的影响，嘉定区商务委员会深入98家出口企业走访调研，了解企业所面临的困难，掌握企业的出口动态。2009年组织外贸进出口企业负责人及业务人员参加中小企业开拓资金、出口信用保险、海关分类管理政策等业务培训会共计6次，帮助企业了解出口信用保险知识及相关外贸政策，提升外贸人才队伍素质。2009年，全区新增海关AA类企业1家，A类企业33家。嘉定区商务委员会积极指导企业办理加工贸易生产能力证明528份，实地验厂98家。审批加工贸易批准证6288份，进口金额13.24亿美元，出口金额26.17亿美元。

（2）积极宣传外贸扶持政策，增强企业市场竞争力

中小企业国际市场开拓资金。完成了2009年中小企业国际市场开拓资金初审工作，共有132家企业，348个项目，总计人民币490万元左右。农轻纺产品贸易促进资金。该资金为了提高农轻纺出口企业的国际竞争力，2009年农产品申报了东锦饮品公司的质量可追溯体系项目，轻纺产品申报了荣威公司的自主创新研发项目，进口贴息申报了大昌铜业的进口铜粉项目，年自主品牌申报了飞利浦亚明的亚字牌项目等。中信保出口信用保险保费扶持资金。2009年，通过各种形式的宣传讲座，嘉定区共有16家企业参保，支持出口金额4593万美元，同比增长540%，已发放及待发放扶持资金累计139万元人民币。

（3）做好每月全区外贸情况汇报工作

每月统计全区出口、进口数据；按各类企业、贸易方式、所属区域、国别地区、行业类别以及全区重点企业进行数据统计与分析工作。

（4）搭建平台，鼓励企业参展

通过经委网络平台，发布各类境内外展会信息，鼓励区内企业参展，以获取更多的产品供求信息。

（二）外资发展情况

2009年嘉定区共新批外商投资企业143家，合同利用外资8.53亿美元，累计比去年减少25.5%，完成年度计划的100.4%。实际利用外资6.35亿美元，累计比去年减少3.3%，完成年度计划的141.2%。

全年利用外资与2008年比较呈现以下特点：

1．外资产业结构优化，“三、二”格局稳固

2009年，嘉定区服务业合同利用外资4.76亿美元，占总数的55.8%。主要来自于

房地产、总部经济和商贸业，分别引进合同外资2.64亿美元、1.52亿美元和0.53亿美元。以生产性和生活性为主的外资服务业进一步显现，三、二产业进一步优化，格局进一步稳固。

表6-24 2009年嘉定区外资企业经营状况数据

项目	数额（亿元）	同比（%）
工业总产值（全口径）	1309.5	1.10
工业总产值（规模以上企业）	1140	-8.70
利润	80.1	63.47
税收（制造业千万元税收大户）	33.69	19.60

2．服务业稳步发展，总部经济成效显著

2009年新批服务业项目100个，占总数的66.7%，扣除房地产因素，同比下降仅为6.7%，占比比去年增长了5.3个百分点。增长因素主要得益于嘉定区产业结构调整及时，招商观念转变到位，把总部经济、汽车研发、房地产等产业列为招商引资的重中之重，其中总部经济招商更是出现了前所未有的突破。在市、区两级扶持政策配套下，芬兰“美卓”、瑞士“吉博力”、中国香港特区“华宝”、中国台湾地区“震旦”等知名企业纷纷落户嘉定，全年共引进总部经济项目10个，占全市的13.8%，其中投资性公司1家，管理性公司4家，研发中心3家，销售中心2家，合同外资占总数的17.8%，招商成效显著。

3．项目规模提升，大项目主导地位明显

2009年新批、增资1000万美元以上项目共35个，合同利用外资7.28亿美元，占总数的85.2%，项目平均规模2696万美元，比去年增加了279万美元。主要来自于房地产、电子设备、食品、商贸等行业，合同外资分别为2.72亿美元、1.31亿美元、0.59亿美元、0.53亿美元。

4．亚洲地区投资势头踊跃，港资是最主要来源地

从引进合同外资国别地区排行看，中国香港特区、维尔京、日本列前三位，分别为4.55亿美元、0.67亿美元、0.53亿美元。其中亚洲地区合同外资6.03亿美元，占总数的70.6%。港资占了总数的53.3%，成为嘉定区引进外资最主要的来源地。

5．实际利用外资保持平稳，三产到位率接近一半

嘉定区2009年实际利用外资与去年基本持平，服务业到位资金2.91亿美元，占总数的45.8%，其中30%来自于房地产、批发业和商务服务业，外资到位分别为1.87亿美元、

0.47 亿美元、0.17 亿美元。

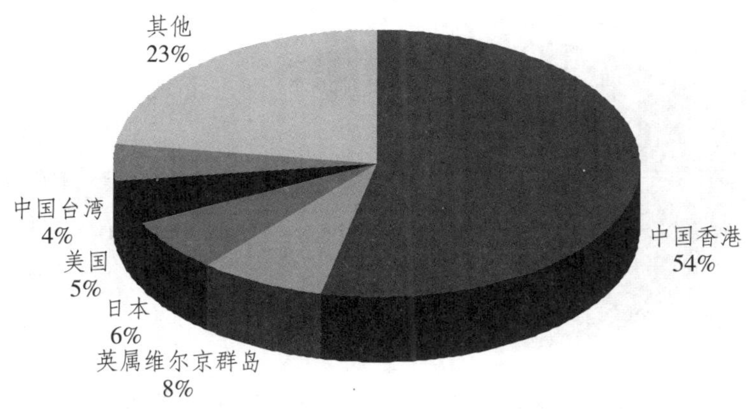

图 6-25 2009 年嘉定区外商投资国家（地区）分布图

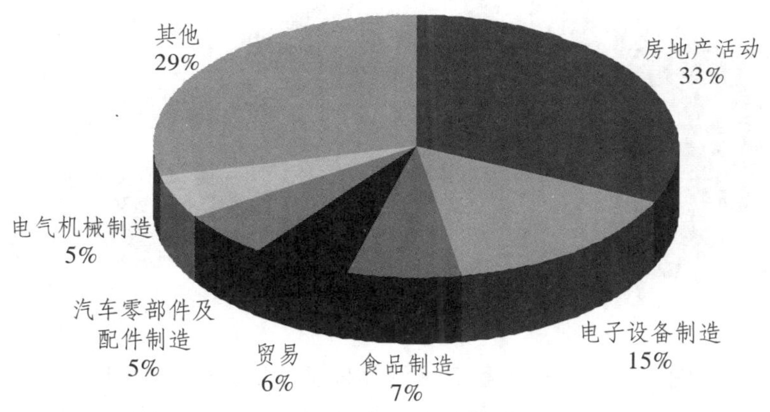

图 6-26 2009 年嘉定区外商投资行业分布图

（三）外经发展情况

2009 年完成境外投资项目 2 个，投资总额 31 万美元，2008 年完成境外投资总额 724.27 万美元。截至目前，嘉定区企业共设立海外企业 19 家，中方实际投资 1340 万美元。

从投资主体看，民营企业及外商投资企业分别占境外投资企业总数的 74% 及 26%；从地区分布看，主要集中于中国香港、日本、美国等地。

从境外企业所涉及的行业来看，除了经营进出口贸易外，非贸易性投资涉及到轻工、机械等生产性项目，还有互联网接入服务、数据中心、软件开发等。

从境外企业所涉及的行业来看，除了经营进出口贸易外，非贸易性投资涉及到轻工、机械等生产性项目，还有互联网接入服务、数据中心、软件开发等。

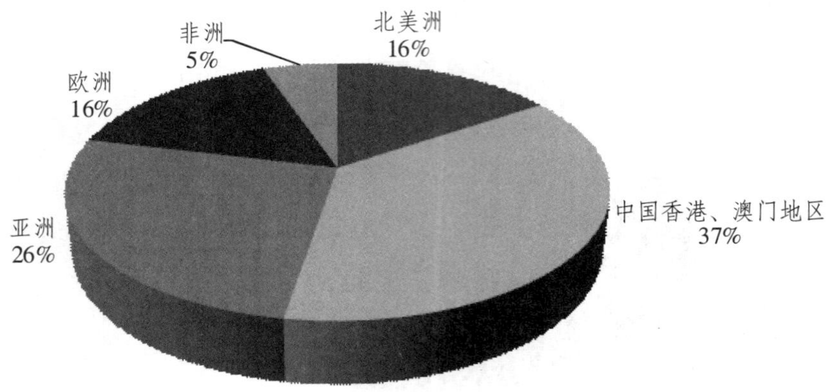

图 6-27　2009 年嘉定区海外投资地区分布图

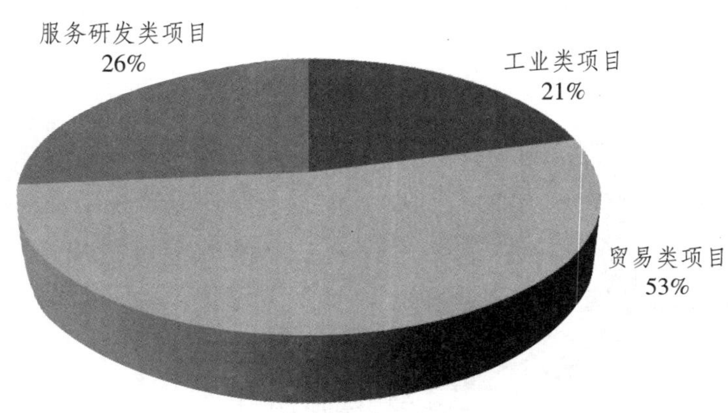

图 6-28　2009 年嘉定区海外投资项目比重结构图

二、2010 年嘉定区外经贸工作展望

（一）强化政策支持，优化贸易结构

向企业宣传国家支持外贸发展的有关政策，开展各类专项培训讲座，包括服务贸易、加工贸易、外汇管理、出口退税等方面内容；加强与外贸出口企业的联系，制定走访计划，定期调研重点企业，认真做好政策宣传，要在国际市场开拓、出口品牌建设等方面对企业给予支持，转变对外贸易方式，优化嘉定区的对外贸易结构。

（二）推动嘉定区服务贸易

2009 年，嘉定区大力推进总部经济、文化信息产业的发展，落实服务贸易相关政策。根据嘉定区发展现代服务业的规划，将在电子商务，现代物流、会展、旅游等服务贸

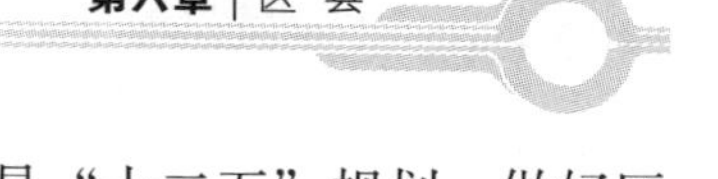

易领域有所突破。2010 年主要推进工作：制定区内服务贸易“十二五”规划；做好区县服务贸易统计工作；做好“市服务贸易专项资金信息沟通工作；做好《服务贸易工作简报》接收工作。

（三）做好各项扶持资金的推动和落实工作

具体工作要多与市商务主管部门请示、沟通，力争已批项目资金早日到位，待批项目尽快批准。继续搭建好企业与金融机构间的交流平台，为企业保驾护航，从而促进外贸出口平稳较快的发展。

（四）建立外贸情况数据库

根据企业出口产品行业类别、国别地区、贸易方式等几方面内容并参考区内统一的数据编码原则建立外贸情况数据库，以便平时工作中的统计与报送，同时将着力从原来的数据统计工作逐步转化和深入到分析领域，从而更清楚直观地了解到嘉定区的外贸发展情况。

（五）建立全区重点企业出口监测体系

以 2009 年度累计出口 1200 万美元为界线，建立起新的 2010 年全区重点出口企业名录，并完善重点出口企业数据月报系统。掌握重点企业产品出口形势和经营情况，如发现企业出口有异常波动的，及时联系企业相关负责人了解情况，以便更准确地分析嘉定区外贸发展情况。

（六）贯彻“走出去”战略

嘉定区外经工作尚属起步阶段，存在着项目投资规模总量小、综合实力不强、发展较为缓慢等问题。2010 年，嘉定区将进一步贯彻中央、上海市的“走出去”战略，顺应国际国内形势新变化。通过加大对区内企业境外投资的政策宣传工作，对有“走出去”意向的企业，重点跟踪和业务辅导，积极组织企业参加境外投资洽谈会等途径做好服务工作。积极引导企业激发境外投资的内在需求，坚持以市场为导向，鼓励企业利用境外资源，进行矿产、森林等资源开发型投资；开发技术合作项目、输出嘉定区已经成熟的先进技术；收购兼并带有品牌的国际项目，拓展海外销售、服务网络项目等多种形式开展境外投资，增加国际经济合作。同时，加强部门配合及自身队伍建设，提升对企业服务水平。

第十四节 金山区

一、2009年金山区外经贸发展情况

（一）外贸发展情况

1．各项指标多数呈下降态势

2009年，金山全区进出口商品总额累计为28.87亿美元，同比下降14.3%，其中：出口13.93亿美元，同比下降19.2%；进口14.94亿美元，同比下降9.1%。全区三资企业进出口商品总额为16.62亿美元，同比下降21.9%；其中：出口9.72亿美元，同比下降18.6%，占全区出口总额的69.8%；进口6.9亿美元，同比下降26.1%，占全区进口总额的46.2%。

1–12月份，一般贸易出口累计8.43亿美元，同比下降17.6%；加工贸易出口累计5.46亿美元，同比下降22.1%。一般贸易进口累计11.23亿美元，同比增长5.4%；加工贸易进口累计2.84亿美元，同比下降25.3%。

表6-25 2009年金山区一般贸易及加工贸易总量及比重（单位：万美元）

名称	累计出口	对比累计出口	增幅	累计进口	对比累计进口	增幅	累计进出口	对比累计进出口	增幅
加工贸易	54575	70039	-22.08%	28389	37993	-25.28%	82964	108032	-23.20%
一般贸易	84342	102387	-17.62%	112307	106532	5.42%	196649	208919	-5.87%
比重	累计出口			累计进口			累计进出口		
加工贸易	39.50%			24.80%			31.90%		
一般贸易	60.50%			75.20%			68.10%		

出口产品以纺织服装、塑料化工为主；出口市场以日本、欧美为主。

2．外资企业运行情况良好

金山区三资企业全年销售收入累计249.6亿元人民币，同比增长1.5%；三资企业利润总额累计19.6亿元人民币，同比增长106.7%；上缴税金累计13.49亿元人民币，同比增长3.3%。

表 6-26 2009 年金山区主要加工贸易企业行业分类表（单位：万美元）

年份 / 行业	2008 年	2009 年	2009 年同比增幅
纺织服装	19316	69886	261.80%
机械电子	4555	42702	837.50%
化工	5368	13845	157.90%
食品加工	0	25376	
其他	11414	88379	674.30%

3．外方到位资金略有下降

外方到位资金全年累计为 1.55 亿美元，同比下降 31.3%。

4．以主动服务企业为工作重点，在各方面为企业提供便利

（1）切实服务企业保增长。面对严峻的出口形势和复杂多变的国际市场环境，金山区经济委员会创新思路，主动服务企业。一方面加强政策宣传和指导，利用部门网站上的“外资外贸”专栏及时发布政策信息；通过走访重点企业、开展相关培训，加强对企业的政策辅导，帮助企业及时领会政策，用好政策。另一方面加强主动服务，帮助企业增强抗风险能力。通过商讨，与中信保上海分公司共建“上海市金山区出口企业出口信用风险承保金融服务平台”，为区内出口企业设计了行业集约投保模式与中小企业投保模式。

（2）优化加工企业生产能力证明审批程序。2009 年 1–12 月份，金山区加工企业生产能力证明累计审批 325 份，加工贸易合同累计审批 4000 份（包括变更）。在生产能力证明审批业务方面，与金山海关加工贸易科建立紧密的合作平台，在加工贸易业务的管理审批部门之间做到政策互通；同时，通过对加工贸易企业申请《加工贸易企业经营状况及生产能力证明》审批手续的分析，简化了审批程序，为企业提供了便利。

（3）规范有序开展出证认证业务。2009 年 1 至 12 月共签发一般原产地证 1837 份，同比下降 12.9%，网上签证率为 100%；认证各类外贸单据 178 份；代办领事认证及国际商事证明书 91 份，使用国别主要为：埃及、阿根廷、沙特、科威特、苏丹等。证明书为价格单、装箱单、发票、企业声明等。2009 年截至 12 月底发展新注册企业 10 家。2009 年 8 月 1 日开始签发优惠贸易协定项下原产地证书。

（二）外资发展情况

1．吸引外资有所下降

2009 年金山区新批准外资项目累计 79 个；投资总额累计（含增资）为 27592.6 万

美元，同比下降49.1%；合同外资累计（含增资）为12507.6万美元，同比下降58.7%。其中，增资项目累计25个，投资总额完成4072.8万美元，合同外资完成2613.2万美元，占全年合同外资完成额的20.9%，比较去年有所下降。

2．新批项目以第二产业为主导

79项新批项目中，第二产业项目39个，合同外资8407万美元，占新批项目合同外资总额的85%；第三产业项目39个，合同外资1337.4万美元，占新批项目合同外资总额的13.5%；第一产业项目1个，合同外资150万美元，占新批项目合同外资总额的1.5%。

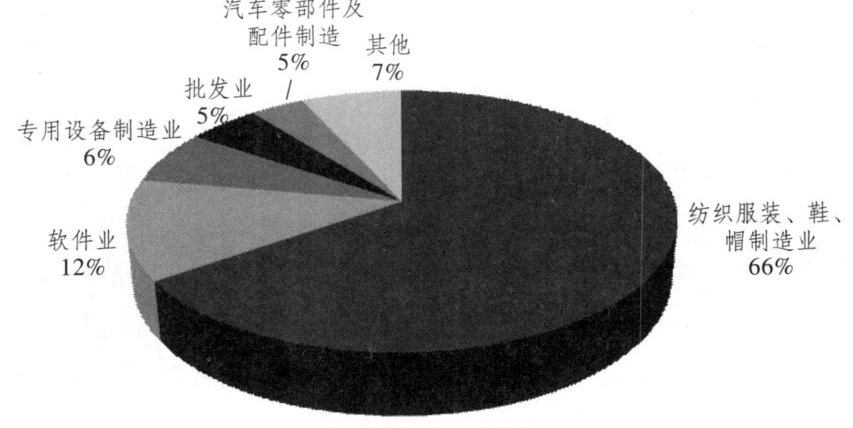

图6-29　2009年金山区投资行业结构图

3．抓好小项目，做大规模项目

从新批外资项目投资规模来看，虽然金山区新批项目数量比去年有所增长，但大部分为投资总额100万美元以下的小项目，外资总量不大。新批项目中，投资总额1000万美元以上的规模项目有8个，合同外资累计达6010.3万美元，占新批项目合同外资总额的60.7%。

表6-27　2008-2009年金山区外资经营状况　（单位：万美元）

年份	营业（销售）收入	实缴纳税总额	利润总额
2009年	2496158	134916	196515
2008年	2459504	130558	95077
2009年同比增幅	1.50%	3.30%	106.70%

4．重点工作

（1）2009年吸引外资主要来自台港澳地区。受全球金融危机影响，外资主要指标大幅下降。全球的金融危机对实体经济产生了巨大的负面作用，致使投资者投资意愿不强，消费者购买力下降，产能过剩。这些不利因素直接影响了外资的流入。制造业项目数逐年下降，服务业项目数上升的趋势在延续。2009 年第三产业外资项目数首次与二产外资项目数齐平，各占外资项目总数的 49.4%。中国台港澳仍然是金山区外资主要来源地之一。2009 年外商直接投资主要来自于中国台港澳、欧盟、美国、东南亚等 24 个国家和地区。其中，中国台港澳地区投资企业共 29 个，占项目总数的 36.7%；投资总额 10674.3 万美元，占 38.68%；合同外资 4416.2 万美元，占 35.3%。

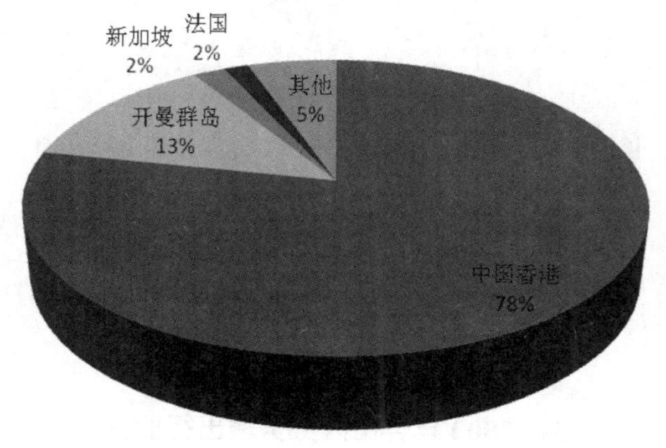

图 6-30　2009 年金山区外资来源地结构图

（2）积极帮助企业解决困难。金山区经济委员会不仅在项目设立前期为企业提供优质服务，在项目落地后仍主动关心企业的生产经营情况，对于在生产经营中所碰到的问题，积极给予帮助。今年以来帮助企业与区工商、税务、海关、出入境检验检疫局等政府职能部门进行沟通与协调，为企业解决实际困难的案例共达 20 余件。

（3）配合相关部门开展调研及其他相关活动。积极配合相关部门开展关于金山区外资情况的调研工作，提供相关外资数据及分析材料，包括外商历年在金山区投资、运行情况的详细资料；参加审批中心外资项目联席会议及预评估会议达 10 余次，协调外资项目落户相关问题；协助上海市商务委员会进行金融危机下外资企业运行状况、企业裁员的调研及外资企业“维稳”工作调研等。全程参与 2009“金山之秋”外商投资恳谈会。恳谈会的成功举行，对宣传金山、增强政策的支持力度、提高吸引外资的水平起到了积极作用，对重要外资项目的签约起到了实质性推动作用，也为今后的招商引资工作奠定了良好的基础。

（三）外经发展情况

1. 境外投资以批发业为主

2009 年金山区境外投资项目共 2 项，注册资本合计 360 万美元，投资国别和地区为美国、中国香港，行业均为批发业。

2．外派劳务主要输往日本等国

2009年金山区对外劳务（研修）人员148名，主要输往日本等国家，主要工种以缝纫、电子等为主。

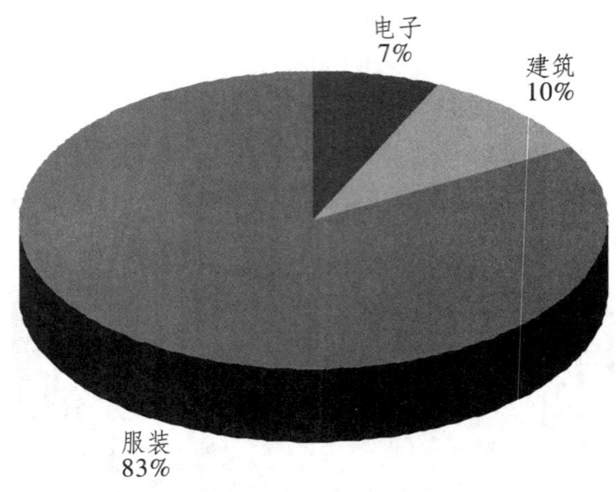

图6-31　2009年金山区劳务输出行业分布图

二、2010年金山区外经贸发展趋势

（一）加强对外贸工作的指导和服务

进一步坚定发展外向型经济的信心，着力在应对困难和挑战中抓重点、抓机遇，引导企业振奋精神，积极转变发展模式，兼顾海内外两个市场，寻找新的利润来源，化危为机渡难关。继续完善服务企业的长效机制，及时宣传各级政府扶持外贸发展的政策，指导企业用足用好政策，获得更多的资金支持；及时与区内进出口重点企业沟通，倾听企业呼声和建议，帮助企业解决实际困难。

（二）完善统计分析和调研工作

加强对外贸运行情况的统计、分析工作，深入各镇、工业区、重点企业就外贸运行中存在的问题和困难开展调研，多角度进行分析，及时掌握企业经营情况和外贸发展中的新情况、新问题，并结合金山区的实际情况提出对策建议，为领导决策提供参考。

（三）鼓励企业“走出去”开拓国际市场

加强企业“走出去”的政策宣传和指导工作，利用各种展会平台及时引导企业进

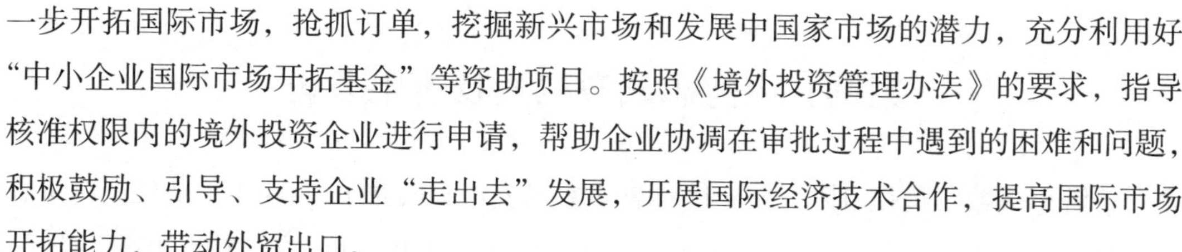

一步开拓国际市场，抢抓订单，挖掘新兴市场和发展中国家市场的潜力，充分利用好“中小企业国际市场开拓基金”等资助项目。按照《境外投资管理办法》的要求，指导核准权限内的境外投资企业进行申请，帮助企业协调在审批过程中遇到的困难和问题，积极鼓励、引导、支持企业“走出去”发展，开展国际经济技术合作，提高国际市场开拓能力，带动外贸出口。

（四）推进服务贸易工作

组织、指导符合条件的企业进行上海市服务外包重点企业的申报、上海市服务贸易发展专项资金的申请等工作。做好金山区服务贸易的前期摸底和规划工作，确定重点服务外包发展领域，打造外贸可持续发展的新增长点。

（五）进一步加强投资促进平台作用

针对金山区各镇、工业区普遍存在招商信息匮乏、储备项目少的问题，进一步搭建投资促进平台，协助各镇、工业区推进招商引资工作。围绕金山区高新技术产业化重点推进领域，加大力度开辟新的项目信息渠道，加强对各镇、工业区招商的分类指导，整理出突出金山相对优势的招商宣传点，为各镇、工业区的招商提供支持。

（六）进一步加强和完善储备项目信息跟踪制度

进一步加强和完善与各镇、工业区联动的项目储备信息跟踪制度。定期或不定期举行镇、工业区基层招商负责人工作例会、信息交流会，交流项目信息，讨论招商引资出现的新情况、遇到的新问题及外资的行业流向和趋势等，及时进行总结和分析，积极推进项目进度。对于已签约项目，继续加大跟踪力度，定期上报进度，协助各镇、工业区推进项目早日落地。

（七）加大对已落户企业的服务力度，努力保持经济平稳增长

继续加大力度服务好已落户的企业，密切关注金山区外资企业的经济运行情况，对有发展潜力的重点企业，鼓励其进行增资扩股；随时掌握企业在经营过程中发生的新问题、新情况、新动态，搭建企业与职能部门的沟通平台，积极协调并帮助企业解决实际困难，努力保持经济平稳增长。

案例：上海忠成数码科技有限公司

上海忠成数码科技有限公司（简称忠成数码公司）成立于2004年，地处上海市金山区北部工业园区，是一家中日合资企业，注册资本120万美元，合同外资108万美元，占地面积130亩，厂房建筑面积26852平方米，是一家集产品开发、设计、生产、销售、服务于一体的生产型企业。公司以电子产品为主导，覆盖家用电器、电子数码产品、电动玩具、便携式DVD、车载电视等领域。

面对席卷全球的金融危机，忠成数码公司认真研判经济形势，寻求生存之道。虽然存在诸多困难，但是风险和利益是共生共存，越是大的危机越有发展和崛起的机遇。传统的危机应对模式和处理办法，已经不能适应当前复杂多变的局面。忠成数码公司立足实际，客观分析自身优势，充分挖掘潜力，迅速扩大主要产品的市场占有率。主要表现在：

（1）受此次金融危机影响最大的是美国和欧洲等国家和地区，而忠成数码公司主要出口目的地是日本，受到的波动和影响不大。

（2）忠成数码公司的产品主要集中在家用视听领域，产品主要定位于普通消费者等一般客户，只有少量产品涉及高端用户，虽然高端产品的销量会受到一定的影响，但是主体市场的需求仍然旺盛。

（3）忠成数码公司已建成比较完整的上下游产业链，拥有产品设计、研发、生产、销售等专业化子公司，产业布局初具规模，综合实力和抗风险能力大为提高。

（4）忠成数码公司聚集了大量的专业化人才，这是忠成数码公司赖以生存和发展的关键因素和不竭源泉，也为进一步加强内部管理、挖潜降耗、节约成本、研发新品、拓展市场提供了有力的智力支持。

基于上述共识，根据产品的特点，充分利用自身的优势，结合市场的需求，公司主要采取以下措施：

（1）进一步扩大市场占有率。在巩固日本市场的同时，注重开发新的潜在国外市场，以迪拜为中心辐射中东地区继而抢滩非洲市场。

（2）注重对国内市场的开发。经过努力，成为2010年上海世博会特许商品供应商。借力上海世博，以此为抓手和撬杆，启动国内市场的销售，壮大销售队伍。

（3）加大新产品的研发力度和投入。不仅对产品的外观设计要有突破和创新，还要加快产品配套软件的研发速度，开发拥有自主知识产权的新产品。

（4）对内部资源进行充分整合。发挥集群优势，分工合作，互补互辅，以团队的

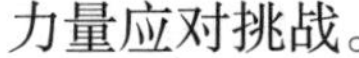

力量应对挑战。

（5）进行产业升级和产品调整。进一步完善产业链和产品线，不局限于现有的产品结构和生产规模，加紧开发和生产大屏幕液晶电视、蓝光 DVD 等新产品。采取不同的产品策略，适当保持对高端产品的关注和投入，维持高端市场。停止生产市场反映冷淡的产品，集中优势资源，扩大市场急需产品的生产。

（6）加强内部管理。通过引进 SMT 等先进生产线和设备，提高生产效率，减少人工支出。加大员工培训力度，培养一支高效、精干的员工队伍，坚持向管理要效益，挖潜降耗，节约增效，同时强化品质管控，确保 ISO9001 和 ISO14001 双体系的健康运行，降低可能的品质损失。

（7）注重企业文化建设，为员工提供一个良好的发展平台，不仅让他们得到技能上的锻炼，更得到管理能力的提升，有更多的机会进步。关心员工生活及福利，落实以待遇留人、以事业留人、以感情留人，稳定员工队伍。

通过上述措施，在此次金融危机中，忠成数码公司不仅没有受到大的影响，相反在国内外市场双获成长，市场份额不断增加，产量稳步提高，从月产 3 万台猛增到近 8 万台，而且还在持续增加，员工也增加到 700 余人，产品订单已经排到 3 个月以后，品质稳定，市场的美誉度和客户的认可度不断提高，忠成数码公司的品牌效应初步显现。

第十五节　松江区

一、2009 年松江区外经贸发展情况

（一）外贸发展情况

尽管受世界金融危机的严重影响，但是在上海市商务委员会的领导下，在松江区委区府及商务委领导的关心支持下，经过全区奋战在外贸战线上的全体同志的共同努力，通过学习实践科学发展观活动，通过国家相关外贸政策的及时贯彻落实，通过加强外贸企业的合作交流、组织引导外贸企业积极参加各类展会寻找新的商机等等一系列积极有效的应对措施，松江区的外贸出口从上半年的降幅 30%逐步回升到目前的下降 14.7%，特别是第四季度更是呈现了恢复性的增长。

2009 年松江区共完成外贸进出口总额 390.67 亿美元，同比下降 15.9%，其中进口

109.73亿美元，同比下降18.7%，出口280.94亿美元，同比下降14.7%。从2009年下半年以来，出口已经出现了回暖的趋势，特别是进入第四季度后，全区的出口出现了恢复性增长，10–12月连续三个月单月出口额超过30亿美元，三个月累计出口达96.3亿美元（2008年四季度出口82.2亿美元），单季度出口创历史第一，同比增长17.2%

1．加工贸易的审批管理

加工贸易是松江区外贸出口的主要贸易方式，为了能在最大限度上使企业的进出口业务通畅无阻，在时间上、成本上都能做到最小化，松江区经委克服困难、积极主动，基本做到合同当天申报，当天审批。

2009年，共审批加工贸易合同批准证12108份（其中变更2915份），涉及合同总金额275亿美元，其中进口料件额95.2亿美元，出口成品额179.8亿美元，另外，共审核加工企业生产能力证明685份。

2．规范快捷地开展验厂工作，为新增的加工贸易企业做好前期开工准备

为了更好地做好新加工贸易企业的验厂工作，松江区从验厂的标准、加工贸易企业书面申请表格的制作，直至赴企业实地验收的具体要求都作了详细的规定，并认真做好申请验厂企业的相关资料的归档工作。禁止三无企业（无厂房、无设备、无员工）开展加工贸易业务，严格把好进出口业务的第一道关。

3．中小企业国际市场开拓资金的申报审核工作

从2002年中小企业国际市场开拓资金实施以来，已经为全区许多中小型外贸企业提供了外贸经营活动的财政扶持。2009年以来，松江区加大了政策的宣传力度。第一阶段的项目计划申报工作完成时，共接受112家（2008年为84家）企业申报，申报559个项目（2008年378个），计划支持资金总额为1014万元（2008年为488万元）。大部分项目扶持资金已在2010年一季度拨付给相关的企业。

4．组织企业参加展览订货洽谈会，拓展外贸市场

2009年松江区组织本区企业参加5月韩国企业采购洽谈会、7月上海市外贸商品内销订货会以及9月的上海跨国采购大会等一系列展览会，积极帮助外贸企业寻找新的市场。2009年9月底，松江区经委与上海百联集团举行了一个“大手牵小手、松江外贸企业与百联集团产销对接洽谈会”，目前有3家外贸企业的产品通过此次洽谈会进入百联集团旗下大型超市进行内销尝试。另外，积极为松江的外贸企业争取广交会以及华交会的摊位，并全程参与4月和10月两届广交会的管理工作。广交会和华交会的参展展位是目前外贸上最为紧俏的有限资源，2009年松江区在这两个展会上的参展企业以及获得的参展展位都是位列上海市郊之首，特别是秋季广交会，松江区参展企业的展位数达到了120多个，参展展位的位置得到了进一步的改善。

表 6-28　松江区外贸出口市场结构

出口地区	绝对值（万美元）	比上年增长（%）
外贸出口产品总额	2809489	-14.7
亚洲	649544	-17.6
欧洲	932098	-10.6
北美洲	1082721	-17.7
拉丁美洲	57270	-17.1
大洋洲	77434	13.7
非洲	10306	4.2

（二）外资发展情况

招商引资力度减弱。2009 年批准外商投资项目 130 个，总投资 10.81 亿美元，比上年下降 22.9%；合同外资 5.21 亿美元，下降 36.4%，其中，第三产业合同外资 1.36 亿美元，占全区合同外资总额的 26.1%。2009 年外商到位资金 5.9 亿美元，比上年下降 33.1%。松江区外商及港澳台投资企业实现税收 86.66 亿元，比上年增长 7.7%。年内在松江投资的新批准、增资国家和地区达 26 个，项目数居前三位的分别为：中国香港特区 35 个、中国台湾地区 28 个和日本 15 个。

二、2010 年松江区外经贸工作展望

（一）明确指导思想

进一步提高服务意识、拓展服务新思路、做好本职工作。一是认真贯彻指示精神，积极做好进出口企业加工贸易合同审批和加工贸易企业生产能力审核工作；二是深刻领会和熟练掌握外经贸工作新的政策法规、实施细则、实行办法等主要精神和内容，确保在实施过程当中准确、完整、不走样；三是加强企业申报材料审核，使报表及时、准确、完整。

（二）完善工作措施

进一步加大政策宣传力度、积极做好开拓资金以及申报工作。2009 年 8 月底举办了申报企业培训班，开展相关的业务培训，切实做好资金拨付的申报工作，争取让申请的企业都能拿到扶持资金。2010 年将在适当的时候再次举办类似的业务培训，使更多的企业得到外贸政策的支持。

（三）提高创新服务服务意识

进一步组织企业参加各类展览订货洽谈会、积极拓展企业外贸商品转内销的领域。面对目前的外贸形势，2010年度松江区将积极组织本区的企业参加各类展览会、订货会、洽谈会以及广交会、华交会，帮助企业积极寻找外贸订单，为松江的外贸企业寻找客户以及市场牵线搭桥。特别是在2009年和上海百联集团合作的基础上，争取更进一步，让更多的外贸产品打开内销市场。

（四）充分发挥桥梁作用

进一步加强横向部门的协调沟通。2010年松江区将继续保持原来对上争取、横向协调的工作方法，针对外贸企业在生产经营中遇到的各种困难，积极与海关、商检、税务等有关部门联系协调，努力解决企业的实际困难。

第十六节　青浦区

一、2009年青浦区外经贸发展情况

（一）外贸发展情况及特点

2009年，青浦区外贸进出口总额为97.2亿美元，同比下降6.2%。其中，外贸出口为55.8亿美元，同比下降9.7%，外贸进口为41.4亿美元，同比下降0.96%。

1．内外资企业出口业务均有下降

2009年全年，青浦区共计有695家外资企业开展进出口业务，同比减少96家，进出口总额为83.12亿美元，同比下降5.83%，占全区进出口额的85.51%；全区共计有461家内资企业开展进出口业务，同比减少31家，进出口总额为14.08亿美元，同比下降8.3%，占全区进出口额的14.49%。

2．贸易方式继续以进料加工贸易为主

2009年全年，青浦区加工贸易进出口企业308家，同比减少66家，进出口总额为58.85亿美元，同比下降0.32%，占全区进出口额的62.03%，其中进料加工进出口为55.88亿美元，同比增长1.59%，占全区进出口额的58.91%，来料加工进出口为2.96亿美元，同比下降26.41%，占全区进出口额的3.31%。一般贸易进出口企业1110家，同比减少

102 家，进出口总额为 36.01 亿美元，同比下降 14.43%，占全区进出口额的 37.97%。

表 6-29 2009 年青浦区进出口分贸易方式及贸易结构变动情况表（单位：万美元）

项 目	出 口			进 口			进出口		
	金额（万美元）	同比（%）	占比（%）	金额（万美元）	同比（%）	占比（%）	金额（万美元）	同比（%）	占比（%）
贸易方式	557797	-9.73	100.00	390821	-0.63	100.00	948618	-6.19	100.00
一般贸易	213642	-20.91	38.30	146505	-2.83	37.49	360147	-14.43	37.97
加工贸易	344155	-1.06	61.70	244316	0.74	62.51	588471	-0.32	62.03
来料加工装配贸易	18304	-28.16	3.28	11360	-23.40	2.91	29664	-26.41	3.13
进料加工贸易	325851	1.09	58.42	232956	2.31	59.61	558807	1.59	58.91

3．机电类产品位列进出口排行第一位

2009 年全年，青浦区主要贸易商品进出口排名前三位的分别为机电、音像设备及其零部件（第十六类），纺织原料及纺织品（第十一类），塑料、橡胶及其制品（第七类），进出口额分别为 56.96 亿美元、9.62 亿美元、6.09 亿美元，同比分别增长 3.37%，下降 7.44%、12.02%。

表 6-30 2009 年青浦区主要贸易产品结构进出口情况表

项 目	出口（万美元）	增幅（%）	进口（万美元）	增幅（%）	进出口（万美元）	增幅（%）
HS 商品	557844	-9.73	414208	-0.96	972051	-6.19
第十六类 机电、音像设备	307789	-0.36	261825	8.12	569615	3.37
第十一类 纺织原料及纺织制品	77173	-4.61	19092	-17.36	96265	-7.44
第七类 塑料及其制品；橡胶	24621	-16.89	36320	-8.37	60941	-12.02
第二十类 杂项制品	54780	-15.22	3469	-19.51	58249	-15.49
第十五类 贱金属及其制品	21556	-37.77	21435	-13.83	42991	-27.76
第十七类 车辆、航空器、船舶	26532	-34.76	14152	-6.44	40684	-27.08
第六类 化学工业及其相关工业	9428	-12.67	19317	-5.06	28744	-7.70
第十八类 光学、医疗等仪器	7579	-4.14	8830	-26.64	16409	-17.72
第十类 木浆等；废纸；纸、纸板	6814	-14.67	8454	-12.66	15267	-13.57
第十二类 鞋帽伞等；羽毛品	4695	-3.59	7453	-38.97	12149	-28.89

4．进出口市场以美国为主，东盟市场份额增长迅速

2009 年全年，青浦区进出口涉及 165 个国家地区，其中出口市场涉及 61 个国家地区，进口市场涉及 98 个国家地区。青浦区主要的进出口市场依次分别为美国、东盟、日本、欧盟。其中，美国市场进出口额为 24.6 亿美元，同比下降 3.28%；东盟市场进出口额为 17.23 亿美元，同比增长 60.32；日本市场进出口额为 15.3 亿美元，同比下降 20.65%；欧盟市场进出口额为 13.25 亿美元，同比下降 18.49%。

表 6-31　2009 年青浦区主要进出口市场情况表

国别 / 地区	出口（万美元）	增幅（%）	进口（万美元）	增幅（%）	进出口（万美元）	增幅（%）
	557481	-9.72	414207	-0.96	971688	-6.18
美国	87808	-23.81	158233	13.72	246041	-3.28
东盟	141426	82.41	30869	3.12	172295	60.32
日本	87274	-17.22	65728	-24.79	153003	-20.65
欧盟	74707	-25.13	57798	-7.94	132506	-18.49
新加坡	64742	111.68	11512	72.07	76254	104.57
中国台湾地区	19373	-4.09	47155	11.04	66528	6.16
马来西亚	46061	148.93	3845	3.84	49906	124.73
中国香港特区	46579	-38.19	1538	12.36	48117	-37.29
德国	13892	-35.16	30803	-7.56	44695	-18.36
韩国	23884	9.39	18660	-3.86	42543	3.15

（二）外资发展情况

1．外资吸收同比下降

2009 年青浦区吸收合同外资 51806.2 万美元，同比下降 3.2%。

其中新批项目 86 个（同比增加 18 个，含 17 个迁入项目），吸收合同外资 25798.4 万美元，同比下降 16.1%；增资项目 76 个（同比增加 17 个，其中吸收合并区外项目 1 个，合同外资 2660.7 万美元），吸收合同外资 26007.8 万美元，同比增加 14.3%。

2．外资工作重点

（1）抓政策学习和宣传

时刻关注国家和本市出台的相关政策，积极寻找对落户青浦区外资企业有利的支持政策。除了学习政策、解读政策、把握政策外，通过各种渠道向投资者宣传政策，

如近一年来集中出台的地区总部政策、服务外包政策等，不仅让符合条件的企业及时得到相关政策的扶持，也增强投资者在青浦区投资的信心，以促进投资者尽快做出投资决定。上海肯耐珂萨人才服务有限公司成为又一家享受服务外包企业政策的企业。

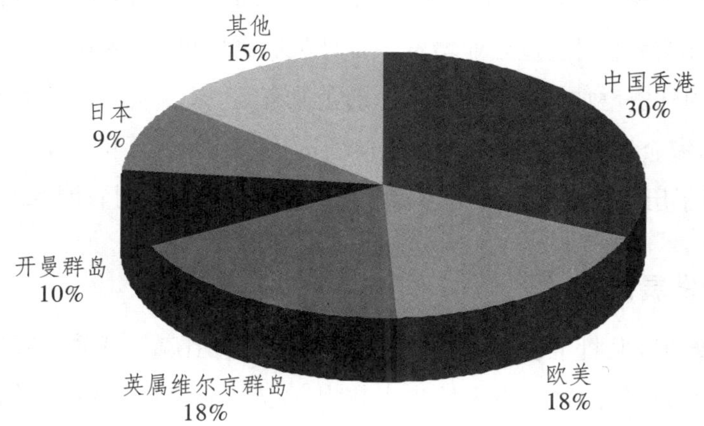

图 6-32 2009 年青浦区外资项目（含增资）来源地结构图

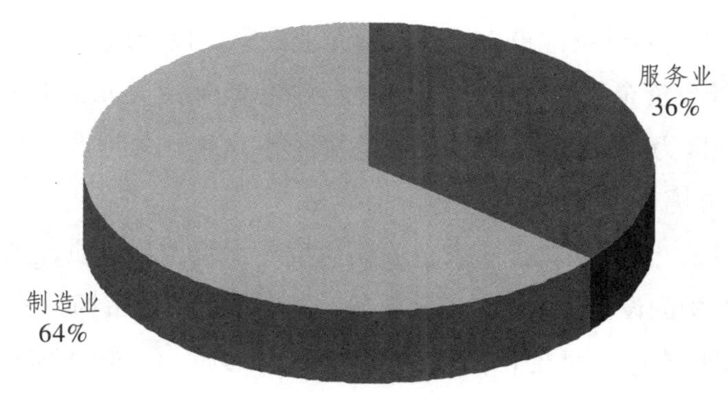

图 6-33 2009 年青浦区外商投资项目行业结构图

（2）抓项目储备

建立各镇、街道、工业园区在谈项目月报制度及存量厂房资源等的动态信息更新和共享机制，积极拓宽项目信息来源，建立储备项目库，摸清家底，为按时间节点完成全年任务和谋划下一年的工作打下基础。

（3）抓项目质量

深入贯彻落实科学发展观，坚持科学选资策略，把好项目准入关，发好“出生证”。通过深入研究、实地走访等形式了解项目背景，对项目进行科学评估，提高引进项目的质量和水平。2009 年引进 1000 万美元以上的大项目 6 个，1 家世界 500 强企业投资新设了 2 家企业，引进 1 家行业龙头企业，还有 1 家 500 强投资的企业进行了跨区整合。

（4）抓企业服务

抓好在谈项目的跟踪服务工作，促使项目尽早落地；加强对落户企业的服务工作，促进资金到位和老企业增资扩股；走访重点企业，为困难企业主动提供服务。2009年共批准增资项目76家，合同外资26007.8万美元，同比增加14.3%，占合同外资总额的50.2%。其中67家是制造业企业增资，合计吸收合同外资24168.8万美元，占比为92.9%。全年合同外资增加500万美元以上的企业有13家，合计增加合同外资17708.5万美元，其中多家企业近年来已多次大规模增资扩股，如海德堡、星科金朋、展华电子等企业，体现了历年引进项目的质量和水平，也体现投资者对青浦区的投资信心。

（三）外经发展情况

2009年，青浦区共批准设立境外投资企业5家，同比减少1家，投资总额合计约942万美元，同比增长126%；劳务输出人数为94人，比2008年劳务输出人数158人同比减少40.5%。

1．境外投资以贸易型投资为主

青浦区2009年度共计批准设立境外投资企业5家，投资总额合计约942万美元，累计批准设立境外投资企业29家，投资总额合计约2560万美元，主要以贸易型投资为主，投资国别地区为美国、日本、中国香港特区等14个国家地区。

2．中东地区为境外工程主要承接地

截至2009年底，青浦区共计3家企业获得境外承包工程资质，主要承接工程涉及玻璃幕墙、钢结构的设计、生产、安装服务，主要承接工程市场为中东地区。目前，青浦区上海美特幕墙有限公司在卡塔尔多哈承接工程一项，合同金额4500万美元。

3．劳务输出人数减少，日本仍为主要市场

2009年，青浦区劳务输出人数为94人，比2008年劳务输出人数158人同比减少40.5%。目前，日本还是主要劳务输出市场，劳务输出人员主要从事缝纫、机械、电子等行业。

二、2010年青浦区外经贸工作展望及重点

（一）外贸形势展望及工作重点

青浦区外贸进出口自2008年6月开始，当月进出口开始出现负增长以来，至2009年8月连续14个月始终处于负增长，直至2009年9月后呈现出恢复的趋势，全区整个进出口已经出现止跌向上的趋势。如果市场不出现大的变化，大型进出口企

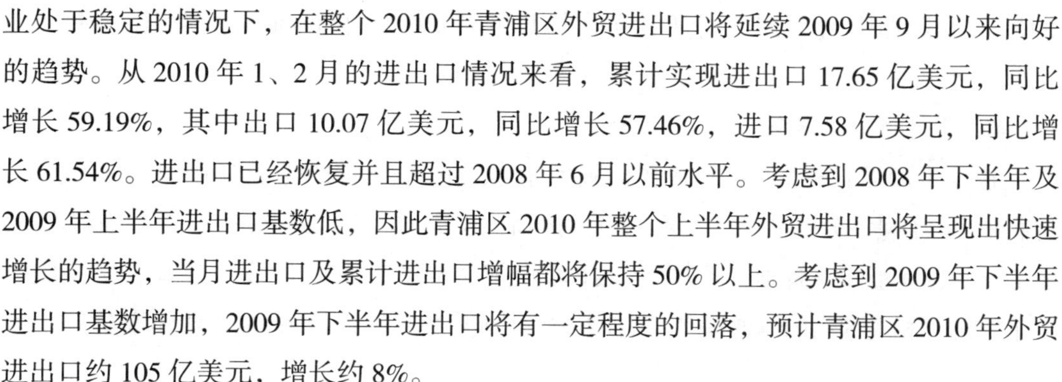

业处于稳定的情况下，在整个2010年青浦区外贸进出口将延续2009年9月以来向好的趋势。从2010年1、2月的进出口情况来看，累计实现进出口17.65亿美元，同比增长59.19%，其中出口10.07亿美元，同比增长57.46%，进口7.58亿美元，同比增长61.54%。进出口已经恢复并且超过2008年6月以前水平。考虑到2008年下半年及2009年上半年进出口基数低，因此青浦区2010年整个上半年外贸进出口将呈现出快速增长的趋势，当月进出口及累计进出口增幅都将保持50%以上。考虑到2009年下半年进出口基数增加，2009年下半年进出口将有一定程度的回落，预计青浦区2010年外贸进出口约105亿美元，增长约8%。

当前，青浦区外贸形势出现了一些积极变化，企稳回升、企稳向好的趋势初步显现，但并不意味着困难时期已经过去，应当清醒地看到，当前外贸发展仍然面临着诸多不利因素和更加激烈的挑战。稳定出口的政策措施成效初显，但世界经济衰退尚未完全好转，外需严重萎缩的局面仍将持续。世界经济的恢复还需要一个较长的过程。总之，既要认识到外贸发展的有利条件和机遇，增强做好外贸工作的信心，保持奋发有为、昂扬向上的气势，又要把困难和问题估计得更充分一些，增强忧患意识和加快外贸发展的紧迫感、责任感，更加扎实、更加深入地做好工作，努力开创青浦区外贸工作的新局面。

1．加强调研分析，强化预测预警

建立健全进出口调研分析和预测预警机制，及时掌握重点进出口企业进展情况，对企业进出口过程中存在的困难和问题，及时协调解决。加强对国际市场的预测分析，帮助企业规避贸易风险，避免不应有的损失。

2．突出重点，扶优扶强

对全区进出口100强企业跟踪联系，加大在产品研发、市场开拓、品牌培育等方面的支持力度。特别关注星科金朋公司，确保其龙头地位不动摇。

3．加强出口品牌建设

集中各种政策资源，确定重点培育对象，大力培植自主出口品牌，引导企业增强综合竞争力。

4．全方位开拓市场

引导出口企业让利不让市场，千方百计保住美欧、日韩等传统市场份额，争取在较短时间内，遏制对美国、日本、欧盟等传统市场的进出口下滑态势，巩固对新加坡市场的增势，大力开拓受金融危机影响较小的新兴市场。充分利用好广交会等国内外知名展会平台，巩固老客户、结交新客户，争取多拿订单，不断扩大贸易渠道。

5．强化政策扶持

帮助企业用足、用好、用活国家、上海鼓励外贸发展的各项优惠政策，发挥政策

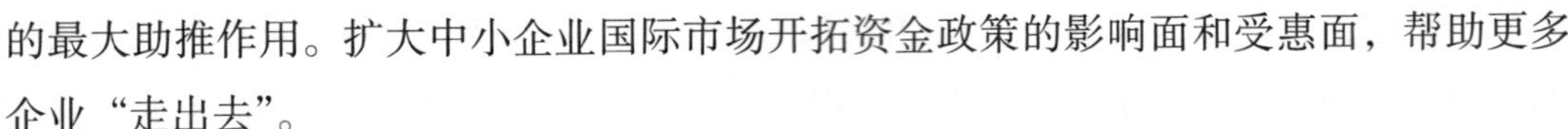

的最大助推作用。扩大中小企业国际市场开拓资金政策的影响面和受惠面，帮助更多企业“走出去”。

6．全力以赴抓服务

进一步加强服务指导，牢固树立服务理念，做到主动服务、优质服务、高效服务。分行业、分企业、分产品、分市场，有针对性地做好工作，关注发展态势，寻找破解之策，真心实意为企业排忧解难，千方百计帮助企业渡过难关。加强与海关、检验检疫、国税、外汇管理等相关部门的沟通联系，齐抓共管，形成合力，为企业创造良好的外贸发展环境。

（二）进一步推进外资工作

1．抢抓机遇，扎实推进招商引资工作

随着青浦区投资环境的日益改善，投资吸引力和竞争力也进一步得到提升，在进一步加快服务业配套设施建设的同时，要主动出击，加强同市政府驻外机构、外国驻沪机构、投资中介机构等机构的长期联络，利用区位优势，加大对青浦区投资环境和投资政策的宣传力度，积极发布投资信息，提升投资者投资信心；同时不断加强对落户企业特别是重点企业的政策宣传力度和全程跟踪服务，帮助企业用足用好各项产业扶持政策，服务好企业，促进以外引外。

2．积极推进产业结构转型升级，推动外资结构优化

依托青浦“大虹桥”地区的特殊区位优势及上海建设“两个中心”和召开世博会的机遇，积极推动外资结构优化。重点建设绿色工业区（青浦工业园区），加强重点产业的产业链和产业集群招商，并按照产业链招商和产业行业目标招商的方法，重点引进能带动和促进制造业水平不断提高的龙头企业和标杆企业，实现经济节约发展、清洁发展和可持续发展。

3．加强政策落实，加快发展现代服务业

通过各种渠道，加强对乡镇、园区招商人员和企业的政策宣传和推介，比如地区总部政策、服务外包政策等，鼓励有条件的企业积极争取。利用调整产业结构的契机，提升服务业吸收合同外资的水平。要抓住机遇，加强研究，适时整合资源、统一规划，探索吸引外资加快发展商贸流通、IT服务外包等服务行业的政策、措施，加快推进商务、商业、创意、研发设计、信息服务、市场营销、咨询服务等行业向青东地区及青浦工业园区集聚，在继续推动产业链从生产领域向产品服务领域延伸、鼓励企业设立地区总部和“三个中心”的同时，积极落实各项政策，发展生产性服务业和IT服务等行业。

4．以切实转变政府职能为抓手，进一步推进行政审批制度改革

随着行政审批制度改革日趋深化，商务部和上海市商务委员会还将逐步下放外资

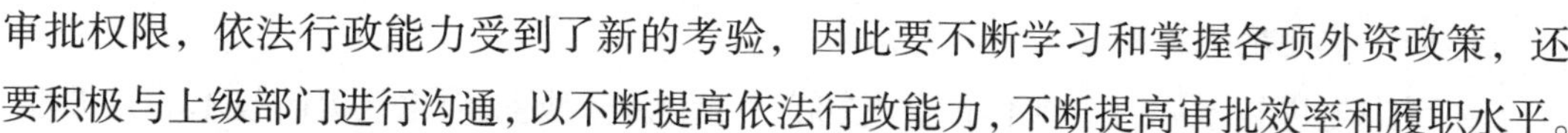

审批权限，依法行政能力受到了新的考验，因此要不断学习和掌握各项外资政策，还要积极与上级部门进行沟通，以不断提高依法行政能力，不断提高审批效率和履职水平。

5．继续加强和各级部门的沟通协调，做好重点项目跟踪服务工作

继续做好重大项目的跟踪服务工作，促使项目早落地。加强对落户的企业的管理和服务工作，挖掘企业的增资潜力。做好部门协调工作，帮助企业解决实际困难，提供有效服务。

案例：日立电梯（上海）有限公司

日立电梯（上海）有限公司（简称日立电梯）是由三方共同出资成立的合资公司，于2006年12月30日经上海市外国投资工作委员会批准设立，2007年5月28日正式在上海市青浦工业园区奠基开工。经营范围主要以电梯的设计、制造、研发为主，厂区规划建设上以环保为第一理念，以服务长三角地区为市场定位，并投资建设电梯研发中心，为企业的持久发展注入新的活力。

日立电梯从建设初期就建立了先进的生产管理、设计管理的计算机系统，内部通信采用了结构布线的先进技术，内部网络主干道全部采用光纤通信。生产管理引入ERP的物流概念，结合生产工艺流程进行动态的定置管理。同时，将日本日立公司的5S（整理、整顿、清洁、清扫、修养）管理融入日立电梯的日常管理工作中，使生产现场、工作环境整洁、有序，为产品质量、工作效率的提高提供了保证。

经过10个月的施工建设，日立电梯（上海）有限公司于2008年3月进行了试生产。在5月28日完成了首台电梯的制造，并举行了首梯的下线仪式。截至2009年11月底已完成电梯生产近4000台，相信随着日立电梯建设的日趋完善，日立电梯产能和效益将会得到不断提升，进一步展现日立电梯的区域价值，达到立足上海青浦工业园区、辐射长三角的产业目标。

目前日立电梯的主要技术来源于日立电梯（中国）有限公司的相关技术。日立电梯（中国）有限公司是广州和日立制作所的合作企业，目前其生产的电梯梯种达到数十种，产品普遍得到国际市场的认可，在产品类型上几乎覆盖了电梯市场的全部需要。日立电梯根据地区的市场定位，接受日立电梯（中国）有限公司的技术支持，全套引进了日立电梯（中国）有限公司四种直梯梯种和两种扶梯梯种的生产技术及相关技术专利，这是日立电梯（中国）有限公司耗费大量人力物力和时间取得的最新先进技术成果，相关电梯技术达到国际领先的标准。依托日立电梯（中国）的技术支持，给日

立电梯提供了充足的发展动力。

在引进先进技术同时，结合日立电梯实际情况进行吸收消化，提高技术的先进性。日立电梯将针对电梯发展的前景和日立电梯的整体规划，逐步健全、完善工艺体系，提高对吸收、消化、应用新工艺、新技术的认识，不断引进先进设备，充分利用公司现有资源，使工艺技术发挥最佳的效果。为适应市场发展的需要，结合电梯结构的特点，将更注重产品工艺的先进性。

由于市场在发展，电梯产品日新月异，日立电梯的电梯制造以节能、环保为前提，不断完善系列和品种，在设备选择上也不断进步，以适应发展需要，在国际同行业处于先进水平。

目前日立电梯的研发中心正在积极建设之中，预计2010年即可建设完成并投入使用。届时强大的研发能力将成为企业发展强大的助推器。在创设研发中心后，日立电梯每年都将投入近百万美元资金，以保持其研发常态，为企业发展提供持久动力。同时企业也在积极申报高新技术企业、知识型密集企业等称号，以此为目标，持续提升企业技术含金量。

日立电梯始终把“以科技为本，全面提升产品技术含量，成为一个具有明显技术优势的电梯生产龙头企业”作为孜孜不倦的追求目标，以电梯制造为核心产业。在今后企业的发展过程中，所有新建、技改项目以及新产品的开发将围绕电梯的新型化和功能化来实施，进一步细分电梯市场，调整经营策略，实现由过去的单一化电梯生产向多功能人性化生产转变，生产符合不同客户需要的不同产品，不断开发出适应各种消费者需求的高附加值、高科技含量、高竞争力的新产品，加快企业做大做强，以保持企业的长期持续的发展。

第十七节　奉贤区

一、2009年奉贤区外经贸发展情况

（一）外贸发展情况

2009年奉贤全区共完成外贸出口35.93亿美元，同比下降13.10%，完成年度目标任务的90%。加工贸易出口20.96亿美元，同比下降8.25%，占出口总额的58.34%，一般贸易出口13.9亿美元，同比下降24.86%。共有1071家外贸企业，其中外商投资企业550家，完成外贸出口27.8亿美元，同比下降12.26%，占出口总额的77.43%。机电、

音像产品出口 15.87 亿美元，同比下降 13.35%，占出口总额的 44.2%。产品主要出口至美国、日本、欧盟等国家和地区。

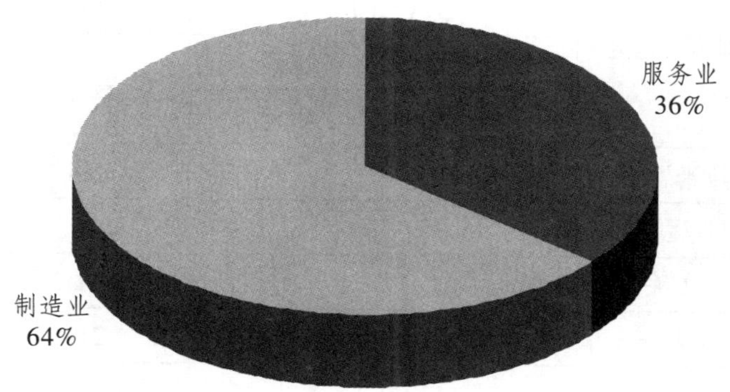

图 6-34 2008-2009 年奉贤区加工贸易结构变动数据图（单位：万美元）

2009 年奉贤区共完成外贸进口 25.62 亿美元，同比下降 9.98%。加工贸易进口 11.05 亿美元，同比下降 14.11%，占进口总额的 43.13%，一般贸易进口 11.93 亿美元，同比下降 11.45%。共有 1071 家外贸企业，其中外商投资企业 550 家，完成外贸进口 21.58 亿美元，同比下降 8.53%，占出口总额的 84.23%。

（二）外资发展情况

1．外资项目审批情况良好

2009 年度奉贤区共审批涉及资金的外商投资企业项目 193 个（其中新批项目 121 个，增资项目 72 个），投资总额 117450.33 万美元，同比增长 11.48%，合同外资 50885.95 万美元，同比下降 7.32%。

表 6-32 2009 年奉贤区外资来源地结构表

序号	国家 / 地区	项目数（个）		投资总额（万美元）	合同外资（万美元）
		新批	增资		
		累计	累计	累计	累计
1	中国香港特区	35	13	68769.3	27522.21
2	中国台湾地区	6	4	552.23	416.31
3	日本	22	18	13396.12	7163.09
4	韩国	6	3	839	754.72
5	新加坡	4	3	2038.72	485.03

（续 表）

序号	国家 / 地区	项目数（个）		投资总额（万美元）	合同外资（万美元）
		新批	增资		
		累计	累计	累计	累计
6	马来西亚	1	2	38.4	27.18
7	印度尼西亚	1		5	5
8	文莱		1	14	10
9	土耳其	1		21	15
10	澳大利亚	2	2	579.01	572.83
11	新西兰	4		770	610
12.	毛里求斯		1	155	150
13	美国	10	5	10915.33	2591.32
14	加拿大	1	1	140.03	37.84
15	墨西哥	2		71	54
16	委内瑞拉		1	0	3
17	德国	6	5	3649.32	2163.2
18	英国	4	1	2406	1769
19	法国	3	1	5933.76	2236.82
20	瑞士	2	2	577.5	377.25
21	瑞典	1	1	274	210
22	意大利	1	2	563.82	311.3
23	荷兰	1	1	126.5	89
24	西班牙	2	1	2495.29	1557.85
25	维尔京群岛	4	4	1620	1004
26	萨摩亚	1		700	350
27	塞舌尔共和国	1		800	400
	合计	121	72	117450.33	50885.95

2. 重点工作

随着全球金融危机影响的延续、内外资企业两税合一的开始、周边国家和地区利用外资竞争引发外资分流的加剧、土地与能源等资源的制约等等，2009 年奉贤区引进

外资遭遇前所未有的困难。面对吸收外资过程中的众多困难，工作条线上的全体人员在区委区府和市商务委的正确领导下，埋头苦干与开拓创新相结合，取得了一定的实效。

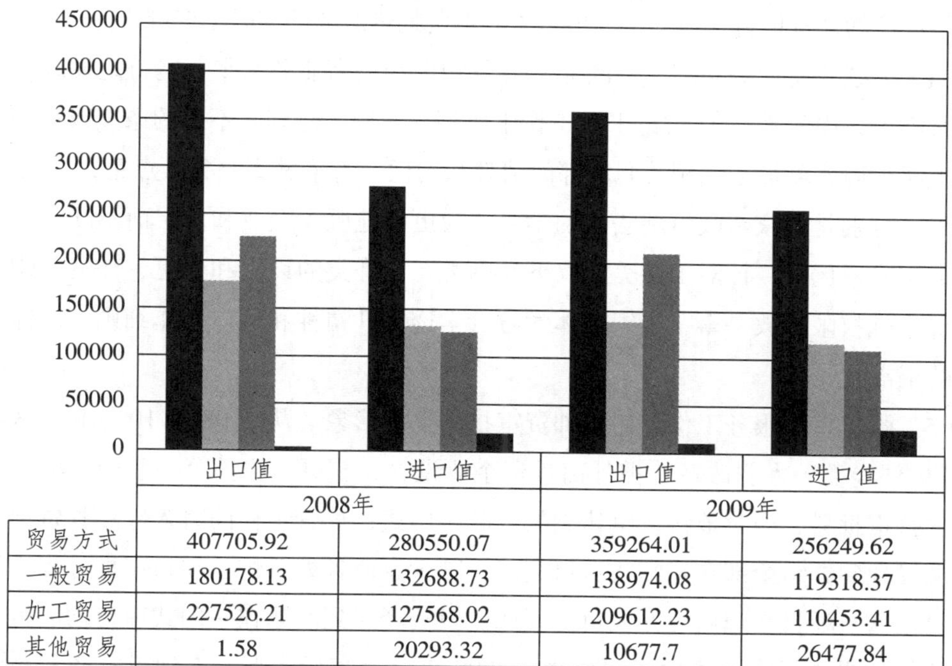

	2008年		2009年	
	出口值	进口值	出口值	进口值
贸易方式	407705.92	280550.07	359264.01	256249.62
一般贸易	180178.13	132688.73	138974.08	119318.37
加工贸易	227526.21	127568.02	209612.23	110453.41
其他贸易	1.58	20293.32	10677.7	26477.84

图 6-35　2008-2009 年奉贤区一般贸易及加工贸易总量及比重（单位：万美元）

（1）经常梳理外资储备项目，做好大项目的跟踪服务。积极与各镇、开发区沟通联系，及时了解掌握区内外资储备项目信息，做好项目落地前的跟踪服务，力促项目早日落户奉贤。如总投资额 7000 万美元、合同外资 3470 万美元的上海江崎格力高南奉食品有限公司增资项目，主动上门服务，对申报资料和程序一口说清，又对其预申报的资料在网上进行了仔细的审阅和修改，使该增资项目在很短的时间内得到了批准。此外，对国誉、格瑞夫等大项目成立地区总部的事项与企业进行了认真的探讨，这两个企业在 2009 年年底都获批了管理性公司。

（2）继续做好外资调研工作，解决企业实际困难。为了全面详细地掌握奉贤区已落户外资企业生产经营情况，不间断地到各镇、开发区进行调研，走访百家企业。认真了解企业在生产经营过程中遇到的各种困难，尽力帮助企业排忧解难，确保企业步入良性经营。同时利用走访百家企业的机会大力宣传政府相关扶持政策，如高新技术企业优惠政策、中小企业开拓国际市场资金补贴、企业技术改造资金补贴等等，鼓励符合条件的外资企业申报多得实惠，同时对有条件的企业鼓励他们增资扩股，在奉贤进一步做大做强。

（3）继续积极与政府职能部门协调，更好地为企业排忧解难。多次会同工商、海关、商检、环保、卫生等政府职能部门召开协调会，力争协调解决外资企业在生产经营中遇到的困难。定期参加投资管理服务中心组织的土地招、拍、挂前的项目征询意见会及租赁厂房的外资项目评估会，为项目入驻奉贤提供服务的同时把好准入关。

（4）继续坚持业务学习，不断完善业务知识和提高业务水平。坚持定期或不定期地进行学习，内容为：① 讨论平时工作中碰到的问题，碰到吃不透的条文或难题，主动向上海市商务委员会或相关职能部门请教和沟通，力争做到业务难点精；② 坚持业务学习，特别是国家新政策新法规的学习，为更好地服务企业和基层而不断提高自己的业务水平。比如，针对1亿美元以下鼓励类、允许类的设立和变更、外资并购境内企业等审批权限下放一事，组织集体学习，学透文件精神和具体操作细则，确保审批工作的正常开展。

（5）强化审改服务工作，树立外资审批的良好形象。从2008年10月起，区经委（当时称外经委）大胆改革，把外商投资企业设立、变更、注销等一系列事项集中到外资项目审批科，同时该科室整建制的入驻一门式，分管主任同时入驻。外资项目的审批从受理到办结全部在一门式窗口完成，减少企业各处奔忙。项目审批过程中严格落实责任人，项目受理后经办人负责到底。投资者遇到问题在一门式窗口均能得到解答，这样的操作极大地方便了投资者。2009年全年实行下来，得到投资者和企业的广泛好评。

3．发展新特点

（1）项目数量与去年同期持平，合同外资总量小幅下降。2009年奉贤区共审批涉及资金的三资项目193家，与去年同期持平；吸收投资总额117450.33万美元，同比增长11.48%；吸收合同外资50885.95万美元，同比下降7.32%，合同外资总量小幅下降；平均单个项目合同外资263.66万美元，同比下降7.8%，项目质量也有所下降。投资总额1000万美元以上的大项目16个，比去年同期减少4个；涉及合同外资33051.78万美元，同比下降18.3%，占同期合同外资的65%。

（2）项目继续向园区集聚，产业符合奉贤区定位。工业综合开发区、化工奉贤分区、现代农业园区、海港开发区等几大经济开发区共吸收合同外资36138.11万美元，占同期合同外资的71.02%。投资总额超过1000万美元（含增资）的16个项目中，有10个项目合同外资总计25677.96万美元进驻上述经济园区，占大项目合同外资总量的77.69%。引进制造业项目主要集中在汽车零配件类、精细化工类、生物医药类、新能源类、信息设备制造类、游艇制造类等产业，基本符合引进先进制造业的产业定位。

（3）增资占比大幅下降，增资潜力已近挖竭。2009年度共审批增资项目72家，涉及投资总额35863.95万美元，同比下降41.91%；涉及合同外资17045.44万美元，同比下降 45.44%，占同期合同外资的 33.5%，同比下降 41.12%，降幅显著。2009 年度利用标准厂房 7.1 万平方米引进项目 35 个，吸收合同外资 3917.49 万美元，仅占同期合同外资的 7.7%。每平方米厂房吸纳合同外资 551.76 美元，同比下降 13.37%，资源利用率与去年同期相比也有降低。

（4）第二产业发展放缓，第三产业较快增长。2009 年共审批 106 个第二产业项目，项目数比去年同期减少 15 个，涉及合同外资 25097.31 万美元，同比下降 33.63%。2009 年共审批 86 个第三产业项目，比去年同期增加了 17 个，引进项目数量增加较快。涉及合同外资 25421.64 万美元，同比增长 49.86%，增幅显著。

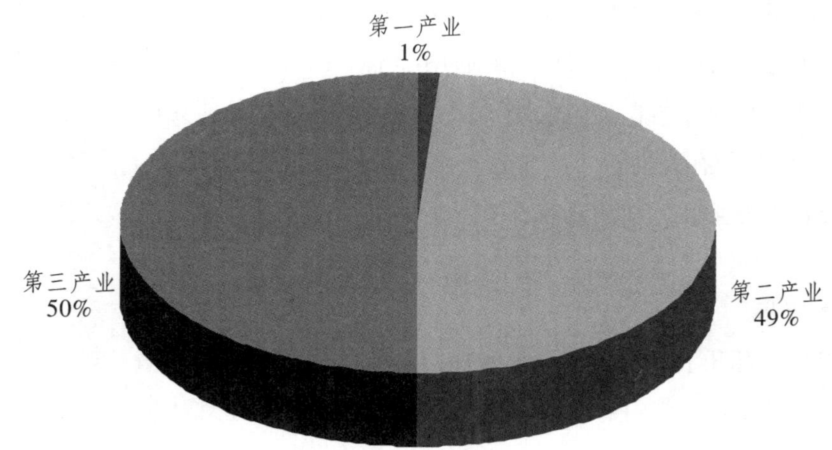

图 6-36 2009 年奉贤区外资投资行业结构图

（5）引进外资区县排位居中，下降幅度相对较小。扣除崇明县和中心城区，2009 年各郊区引进外资的排位中奉贤区以 50885.95 万美元排名第四。闵行、嘉定以 10 亿美元左右处于第一集团；青浦、奉贤、松江以 5 亿美元左右处于第二集团；宝山、金山以 1 亿多美元处于第三集团。从同比下降幅度来讲，青浦与奉贤同比下降在 10% 以内，相对较小；闵行、嘉定和松江同比下降 30% 左右，下降幅度处于中游；宝山和金山同比下降超过 50%，吸收合同外资下降显著。

（三）外经发展情况

1. 单证审批

2009 年，奉贤区共审批加工贸易合同 7276 份，其中新批合同 4703 份，变更合同 2573 份，进料加工 5993 份，来料加工 1283 份。加工贸易生产能力证明共审批 390 份。

2. 政策扶持

奉贤区 2009 年共有 200 多家企业获中小企业国际市场开拓资金贴补，共计金额

800多万元。7家企业获得市保持外贸稳定增长专项资金61.28万元。上海丰科生物科技股份有限公司、大山合集团有限公司、上海高榕农业发展有限公司共3家企业获得农轻纺贸易促进资金补贴285万元。1家服务贸易型企业获得资金扶持。

3．展位申请

奉贤区也积极为区内企业争取参加各种展会的机会。2009年共为区内4家企业，即：艾婴乐、奥林、旺洲、文弘，争取到了5个广交会展位。7月份组织企业参加内销订货会，9月份组织企业参加“跨国采购会”。

4．境外投资

2009年奉贤区共有5家区内企业“走出去”在境外设立公司共7家。上海特设电子有限公司在马来西亚设立1家；上海通用广电工程有限公司在美国设立1家；上海超日太阳能科技有限公司在美国设立1家、德国设立1家、捷克设立1家；上海芯哲微电子科技有限公司在香港特区设立1家；上海浦城矿业投资有限公司在伊朗设立1家。投资总额1515.1万美元，注册资本370万美元，投资涉及行业有电器、变压器、太阳能板等。

5．劳务市场

2009年7月召开了奉贤区清理整顿外派劳务市场专项行动会议，并联合工商奉贤分局、公安奉贤分局等部门对上海鑫浩劳务服务有限公司违规从事外派劳务事宜进行了联合执法。

二、2010年奉贤区外经贸工作展望

（一）以服务为落脚点，多方位联合，促进外贸发展

1．服务中心，加强调研，当好参谋

坚持用科学发展观指导工作实践。以外贸发展中的热点、难点为切入点，有针对性地加强调查研究，做好分析、预警。一是继续完善全区出口在1000万美元以上的重点外贸企业预警、跟踪机制，以加强对外贸形势的研判。二是选择重点出口的机电、高新技术、轻纺、金属等行业和重点企业，进行重点服务，主动服务，上门服务，及时帮助、协调解决企业在进出口中遇到的困难和问题，稳定出口存量。三是对外贸增长、下降幅度大的企业进行有针对性的走访，了解情况，解决问题。

2．加强服务，着眼长远，确保政策落实

一是要进一步加强对工作的责任感和使命感，树立爱岗敬业的理念。保证一周五天每天8小时办公室不断人随时审批，做到在一个工作日内完成加工贸易合同的审批。

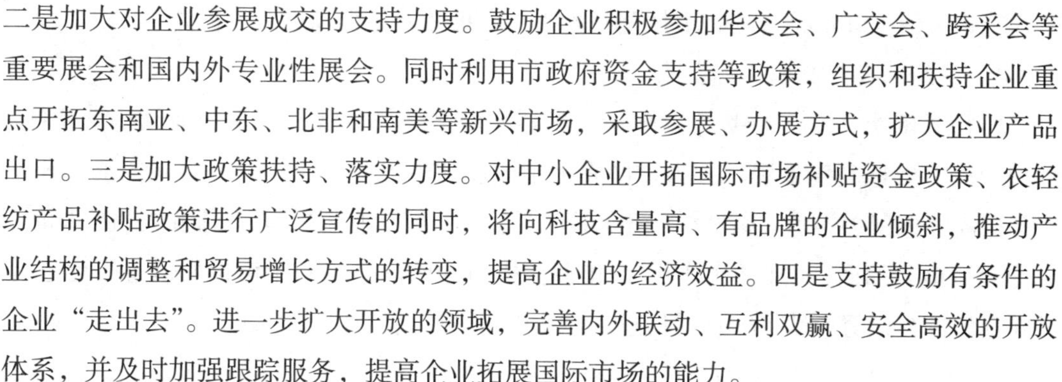

二是加大对企业参展成交的支持力度。鼓励企业积极参加华交会、广交会、跨采会等重要展会和国内外专业性展会。同时利用市政府资金支持等政策，组织和扶持企业重点开拓东南亚、中东、北非和南美等新兴市场，采取参展、办展方式，扩大企业产品出口。三是加大政策扶持、落实力度。对中小企业开拓国际市场补贴资金政策、农轻纺产品补贴政策进行广泛宣传的同时，将向科技含量高、有品牌的企业倾斜，推动产业结构的调整和贸易增长方式的转变，提高企业的经济效益。四是支持鼓励有条件的企业“走出去”。进一步扩大开放的领域，完善内外联动、互利双赢、安全高效的开放体系，并及时加强跟踪服务，提高企业拓展国际市场的能力。

3．沟通协调，形成合力，促进外贸发展

一是加强与上海市商务委员会的联系，及时获取相关政策、信息，争取各类政策的扶持。同时及时将外贸企业统计数据归属到奉贤区，以保证外贸数据的准确与完整，完善外贸数据管理库，为领导决策提供依据。二是加强与海关、商检等部门的沟通，提高工作效率，帮助企业解决进出口贸易中遇到的困难和问题。为大型企业和重大项目提供个性化服务，进一步推广“先期介入，超前服务；一企一策，一厂一策”的做法，提高服务水平，使企业做大做强。

（二）提高专业素质，在吸收外资上开拓新亮点

1．继续抓好政治理论和业务知识学习不松懈

始终坚持学习党的各种优秀政治理论成果，提高外资工作条人员的政治修养；不间断地对国内外经济事件和宏观经济政策进行学习讨论，提高对经济发展的把握判断能力；常抓业务知识学习不松懈，面对外资项目审批权限的进一步下放以及外资网上审批系统的接入，区商务主管部门将承担更多外资审批工作，责任大、任务重，必须把业务知识的学习化成自身强烈要求，努力成为业务行家里手，为投资商和外资企业提供优质高效服务。

2．继续加强专题培训

对外经专管员、外商咨询代理机构工作人员及园区招商工作人员加强专题培训。随着审批权限的下放不断更新和完善其业务知识，进一步提高工作在一线的服务人员为外资企业服务的质量和水平，努力做到“一口说清”，提高整个奉贤的外商投资软环境。

3．继续强化窗口服务，优化投资环境

进一步落实项目审批责任制，明确责任人，做好审批时效记录，年底实行绩效考评。强化一门式窗口受理办事制度。做到三到位，即人员到位、职责到位、工作到位。同时加大政务公开力度，2009 年底外资网上审批系统接入之后，外资项目审批所需材料、

流程、审批依据和审批进程将更加公开透明，审批效率将得到进一步提高。

4．继续加大招商引资的力度

要紧紧围绕“三区一基地”建设，以转变经济增长方式、调整产业结构为主线，继续积极有效地利用外资，大力发展先进制造业和现代服务业。积极会同各镇、开发区和招商办探索多渠道、多方式的招商引资活动。开展专业化招商，产业链招商。同时，注重盘活市内招商资源，加强同上海市商务委员会的联系，利用市招商信息平台进行对外宣传推介，努力获得大项目信息，争取引进一些高质量的大项目。

5．大力开拓吸引外资的新亮点

以引进“地区总部”、“研发中心”和“服务外包”项目成为吸收外资的新亮点。大力宣传国家和上海市的相关扶持政策，走访区内大型企业，鼓励有意向的企业成立“地区总部”和“研发中心”。加强与其他区县的沟通，拓展信息渠道，积极参加各类招商推介活动，力争引进一些“服务外包”项目。

6．继续加大为企业服务的力度

认真落实有关帮扶企业的优惠政策，使现有的符合奉贤区产业优势企业增资扩股，加快产业集群。继续做好跟踪服务工作，完善跟踪服务机制。积极跟踪有增资意向的企业或有存量土地与厂房的企业，鼓励其增资扩股；重点加强对优势企业重点服务，引导劣势企业转变发展观念，加快产业结构调整。

7．继续加强与各部门的沟通与协作

加强与上海市商务委员会外资管理处的沟通，对于大项目和疑难问题争取市里的支持和帮助。继续加强同海关、商检、工商、环保、卫生等部门的沟通和协调，对未落户企业，为其提供足够信息和服务，使其在设立过程中能一路畅通，少走弯路。对已落户企业，有重点地加强对企业的指导工作，并会同相关部门加强对不同行业的培训和个性化的服务。继续加强委内各科室间的交流，在为企业服务的过程中相互协调、相互补位，真正提高办事效率。

8．继续加强与其他兄弟区县的交流学习

面对奉贤区吸引外资在兄弟区县中处于中游偏下的现实情况，积极主动与其他区县交流，学习他们在引进外资和项目审批中的先进经验和特色有效做法，取长补短，争取使工作有新的突破、新的提高。

第十八节 崇明县

一、2009年崇明县外经贸发展情况

(一)外贸发展情况

在国家外贸出口增速持续下降的情况下，崇明县外贸出口呈现逆势增长。2009年完成外贸出口拨交额122.0亿元，比上年增长249.8%。其中以造船为主的工业品出口拨交额121.5亿元，比上年增长250.7%；农副产品出口拨交额0.5亿元，比上年增长127.8%。

1. 工业品出口保持高速增长态势

2009年工业品出口拨交额完成121.5亿元，占全部外贸出口拨交额的99.6%，比去年同期增长250.7%。在全部工业品出口额中，出口占比份额较大的行业为：交通运输设备制造业110.92亿元、金属制品业6.24亿元、纺织业1.43亿元，分别占全部出口额的90.9%、5.1%、1.2%。

2. 农副产品出口实现由降转升趋势

农副产品出口拨交额一举扭转了连续多年下滑态势，实现由降转升的趋势，2009年完成出口拨交额0.52亿元，比上年同期增长127.8%。在全部农副产品出口额中，包括出口速冻蔬菜2170吨、3190万元；盐渍蔬菜1936吨、1245万元；甜酒酿950吨、570万元。

3. 海洋装备产品出口呈现迅猛增长势头

年度统计资料显示，海洋装备产业作为崇明县经济增长的重要亮点，已成为崇明县外贸出口的主导行业。2009年，全县交通运输设备制造业出口拨交额达110.92亿元，占工业品出口拨交额的91.3%，比上年同期的25.71亿元，增长331.4%；而传统的纺织产品制造业下降明显，2009年完成出口拨交额1.43亿元，比上年同期下降34.8%，出口占比份额进一步回落。

4. 内资骨干企业产品出口呈现强劲增长势头

崇明县骨干企业出口呈现强劲增长态势。上海江南长兴造船有限责任公司、江南造船(集团)有限责任公司、中海长兴国际船务工程有限公司等内资骨干企业，2009年度分别完成出口拨交额54.24亿元、36.61亿元、5.35亿元，分别占全部出口拨交额的44.5%、30.0%和4.4%。

表 6-33 2009 年出口交货值前 10 名企业

单位名称	出口交货值（万元）	占比（%）
上海江南长兴造船有限责任公司	542429	44.5
江南造船（集团）有限责任公司	366116	30.0
上海华润大东船务工程有限公司★	147076	12.1
中海长兴国际船务工程有限公司	53500	4.4
上海冠华不锈钢制品股份有限公司★	31142	2.6
上海艺友金属制品有限公司	16880	1.4
上海乾天厨房用具有限公司	8252	0.7
上海纳海针织制衣有限公司	6429	0.5
上海永冠商业设备有限公司★	3655	0.3
上海海岛制衣有限公司	3471	0.3
合计	1178950	96.6

注：★为三资企业

5．各乡镇完成出口额跌多涨少

2009 年，全县 18 个乡镇共完成出口拨交额 120.84 亿元，占全部出口拨交额的 99.0%。实现出口拨交额增长的为长兴镇、庙镇、向化镇、新村乡四个乡镇，同比分别增长 1584.4%、140.6%、36.1%、2.7%；出口额较大的乡镇为长兴镇 96.20 亿元、建设镇 14.97 亿元、新村乡 3.11 亿元，分别占全部出口拨交额的 78.9%、12.3%、2.5%。

2009 年，崇明县外贸出口拨交额增长较快的部分，大多是以生产海洋装备产品为主的内资企业高速发展拉动所取得的。这是由于：一是崇明县新增工业品中出口产品生产企业数量有限，规模不大，存在着出口增长后劲不足的隐患；二是农副产品出口企业仍然以劳动密集型、粗放型加工、低附加值产品为主，缺乏完整的产业链和科技含量，导致几年来出口增长缓慢，需引起有关方面的高度重视。

（二）外资发展情况

2009 年崇明县招商引资由于各种因素起伏较大，引进企业数明显下降，但实现税收保持小幅增长。2009 年，新批准三资企业 33 家，比上年下降 25.0%；项目总投资 1738 万美元，比上年下降 0.9%；合同外资 1225 万美元，比上年下降 13.4%；实际利用外资 2346 万美元，比上年增长 17.7%。

第七章　海关特殊监管区

第一节　综合保税区

一、区域概况

上海综合保税区于2009年11月18日正式揭牌成立，作为市政府的派出机构，统一管理洋山港保税区、外高桥保税区和浦东机场综合保税区，简称“三区”。

按照上海市的部署，“三区”将实现政策、资源、产业和功能的联动、互补，发挥更大的集聚效应，凸显“三区”作为海关特殊监管区域的整体优势，使其成为上海推进“两个中心”建设的重要平台和抓手。

二、2009年综合保税区外经贸发展情况

（一）一般情况

2009年，特别是综合保税区管委会成立以来，“三区”积极应对国际金融危机带来的挑战，采取有力措施，总体保持了区域经济稳定发展的良好局面。

1．洋山保税港区

洋山保税港区承担了探索建设国际航运发展综合试验区的重要使命，目前主体工程建设基本完成，各项业务功能逐步推进。2009年洋山保税港区集装箱吞吐量784.9万标准箱，新引进企业51家，完成固定资产投资22亿元。区内企业实现进出口总额15.6亿美元，同比增长80%，实现税务部门税收收入8090万元，同比增长17%。

2．外高桥保税区

外高桥保税区被上海市商务委员会批准成为“国际贸易示范区”，目前实际运作企业约6000家，世界500强企业有111家在保税区落户，共投资了263个项目。2009年外高桥保税区投资企业实现增加值993亿元，比上年增长4.2%。其中，以国际贸易和现代物流为主体的第三产业实现增加值868亿元，比上年增长5.8%，占87.4%；以出口加工型先进制造业为主体的第二产业实现增加值125亿元，比上年下降6.0%，占

12.6%。全年区内投资企业完成营业（销售）收入6631亿元，比上年增长1.8%，实现利税总额844.43亿元，比上年增长3.2%。投资企业共吸纳从业人员21.59万人，比上年增长10.8%，全员劳动生产率达到46万元/人。

表7-1 2009年外高桥保税区加工贸易进出口额情况表

指标	2009年进出口额（亿美元）	同比（%）	2009年进口额（亿美元）	同比（%）	2009年出口额（亿美元）	同比（%）
保税区合计	551.12	-12.0	422.85	-9.7	128.27	-18.9
加工贸易	70.07	-36.9	30.45	-42.0	39.62	-32.4
其中：进料加工	43.60	-23.3	23.79	-26.5	19.81	-19.1
来料加工	26.47	-51.2	6.66	-67.0	19.81	-41.9

3．浦东机场综合保税区

浦东机场综合保税区于2009年7月3日经国务院批复同意设立，规划面积3.59平方公里，于2010年4月2日完成正式封关验收。

（二）“三区”在招商引资和稳商方面的主要做法

1．加大招商力度，开展外高桥整体招商宣传

树立整体营销理念，举办各类招商主题活动；充分利用中介机构的力量，建立中介机构定期联系制度，促进招商、稳商工作。

2．继续以营运中心培育为抓手，促进招商和稳商工作

一是通过认真梳理备选企业情况，深入宣传营运中心政策，加快了营运中心的认定速度，2009年底已累计完成了139家营运中心的认定，促进重点企业在保税区不断提升功能，整合集团业务，不断做大做强；二是进一步丰富营运中心的内涵，试点生产型、物流型营运中心的培育和认定；三是在营运中心推进过程中进一步了解企业的需求，促进企业追加投资，扩大经营范围，提升在集团中的功能和作用，促进企业进一步成为中国区地区总部。到2009年底保税区地区总部数量已达到13家。

3．推进稳商留商预警机制，主动服务企业

对区内200多家企业建立了分层次走访制度、项目经理跟踪制度以及月度分析制度，及时了解企业经营中存在的共性和个性问题，积极协调有关职能部门予以解决，收到良好效果，促进企业增资，扩大业务规模。

4．进一步改进商务配套条件，打造一流投资环境

针对客户反映集中的交通与餐饮、配套娱乐、便利店、银行分布等问题，外高桥

采取了一系列措施，越来越多的高质量餐饮，健身、美容美发等配套项目落户，为企业提供更好的商务条件；结合轨道交通 6 号线的开通，调整了区内免费班车的路线与班次，更方便企业员工出行。

5．建设外高桥“国际贸易示范区”，积极推进贸易平台建设

在酒类、钟表、设备、文化服务平台等运作良好的基础上，2009 年又建立医疗器械、工程机械等产品大类的交易展示中心，有效聚集企业，聚集贸易，推动贸易便利化。

6．加强保税区贸易产业、外汇创新试点、海关诚信管理等课题研究

不断总结和推出适应跨国公司运作的模式和功能，为跨国公司量身订制更佳的功能和模式，吸引企业落户和在区内进一步发展。

（三）“三区”出口加工业以工业经济为主，实现良好增长

2009 年外高桥保税区积极应对国际金融危机影响，努力提高区域经济综合竞争力，进一步加大对企业扶持力度，精心培育跨国公司营运中心，支持企业加快增长方式转变，促使工业经济实现良好增长。全年保税区完成工业总产值 576.07 亿元，比上年增长 9.5%，工业产品销售率达到 100%。

1．保税区工业企业中外资企业比重大，生产规模大

截至 2009 年底，保税区正式投产加工企业 223 家，其中当年新增投产企业 16 家，筹建及试生产企业 2 家。加工企业厂房占地总面积 159.94 万平方米，厂房建筑总面积 183.15 万平方米。此外，今年新引进加工项目 11 个，加工项目投资总额 1.41 亿美元。

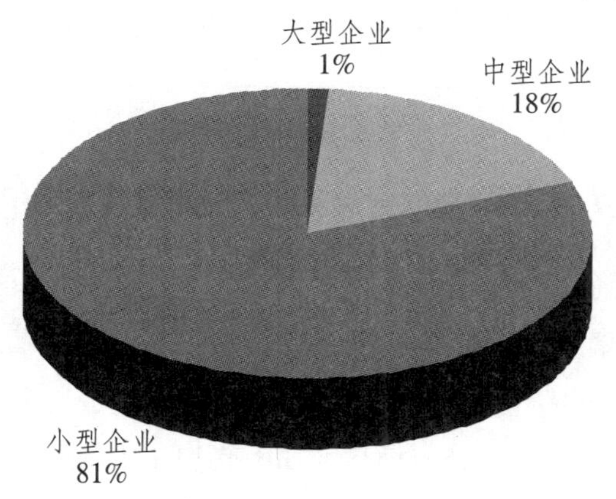

图 7-1 综合保税区加工企业生产规模示意图

（1）从企业经济类型看。保税区加工企业外资比重大。三资企业有 210 家，占 93.8%，其中外商独资企业 160 家、中外合资企业 13 家、港澳台企业 37 家；国有、集体、股份制及其他经济企业 14 家，占 6.2%。

（2）从企业规模标准看。保税区加工企业生产规模普遍较大。产值超过500万元的规模以上企业200家，占89.3%，规模以下企业24家，占10.7%。根据大中小型企业的标准划分，保税区大型企业有2家，中型企业40家，小型企业182家。

2．2009年“三区”工业经济运行特点

（1）工业产值“前低后高”走势明显。从保税区工业产值完成情况看：一季度受到全球经济萎缩影响，生产形势严峻，仅完成产值101.05亿元，绝对值比上年同期下降22.9%；二季度外部环境出现企稳回升迹象，产值降速明显放缓收窄，完成135.27亿元，比上年同期下降4.6%；三季度受益于部分优势企业快速发展，产值逐月持续增长，完成154.9亿元，比上年同期增长2.1%；四季度市场需求旺盛，重点企业产能集中释放，产值增速加快，完成171.09亿元，比上年同期增长36.6%。

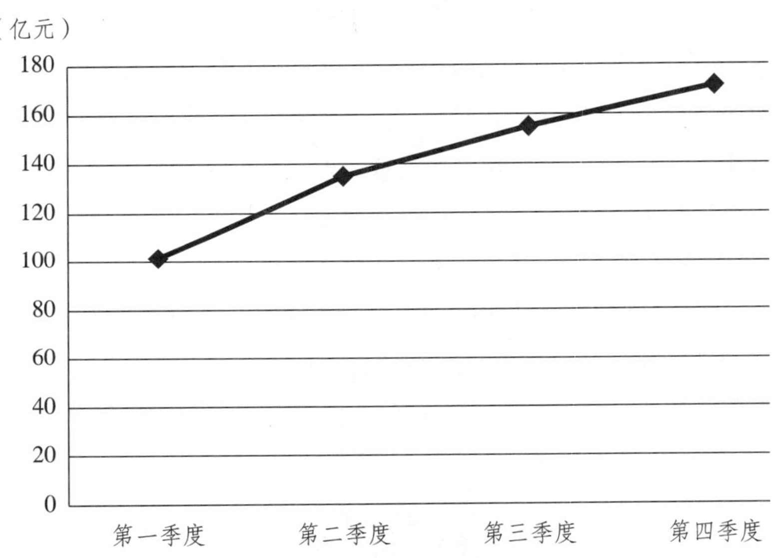

图7-2 2009年综合保税区工业产值完成情况

（2）重点先进制造企业引领作用突出。外高桥保税区通过产业结构的优化调整，重点生产企业的产值集聚度逐年提高，成为推进保税区工业产值增长的主引擎。据统计，2009年保税区产值超亿元的工业企业已有68家，合计完成工业产值530.53亿元，比上年增长12%，占保税区工业产值92.1%。其中联想（上海）电子科技有限公司生产电脑525万台，实现工业产值超过210亿元，占保税区37%，增幅达到57%，是拉动保税区工业产值实现增长的主要力量。

（3）借势国内经济扩大内销成效显著。随着政府各项刺激经济政策效应的释放，带动了国内消费市场复苏和投资需求扩大，为保税区的先进制造企业扩大国内市场销售份额创造了条件。2009年保税区加工企业对国内市场的销售产值完成383亿元，比

上年增长 64%，所占比重从上年的 42%上升到 66.5%。如藤仓电子（上海）有限公司受益于国内“3G”手机的推广，生产的手机零部件供给“苹果”手机使用，产值超过 20 亿元，比上年增长 32%；马瑞利动力系统（上海）有限公司研发的小排量汽车零部件，国内市场需求大，产值增长 57%。

表 7-2　2009 年外高桥保税区加工贸易高新技术产品出口额情况表

指标	2009 年出口额（亿美元）	同比（%）
高新技术产品合计	76.17	-19.7
加工贸易高新技术产品	29.78	-29.2
其中：计算机与通信技术	16.24	-6.3
电子技术	12.10	-46.5
光电技术	0.66	-12.6
材料技术	0.31	-2.5
生命科学技术	0.30	-24.6
计算机集成制造技术	0.16	-75.9
航空航天技术	0.01	63.5

（4）六大重点行业产值贡献突出。2009 年保税区工业行业已有 26 个大类、72 个中类、105 个小类。随着保税区行业结构不断调整优化，以支柱产业为核心的产业集聚效应突出，形成了以电子信息、专用设备制造、汽车零部件制造、通用设备制造、仪器仪表制造、工程塑料制造为主体产业的多元化经济格局。全年保税区计算机及电子通信制造业完成产值 344.75 亿元，比上年增长 29.8%，占 59.8%；专用设备制造业完成产值 40.57 亿元，占 7%；汽车零部件制造完成产值 39.75 亿元，占 6.9%；通用设备制造完成产值 35.21 亿元，占 6.1%；仪器仪表制造完成产值 28.06 亿元，占 4.9%；化学原料及化学制品制造完成产值 23.4 亿元，占 4.1%。这六大行业产值合计占保税区 88.8%。

（四）“三区”外资项目数量减少，投资额增加

2009 年外高桥保税区新批外资项目 90 个，比上年减少 45.8%，占保税区新批项目 35.2%，其中外商独资项目 85 个，比上年减少 46.5%。全年吸引外商投资额 17.43 亿美元，比上年增长 33.3%，占保税区投资额 92.2%，其中外商独资项目 15.79 亿美元，比上年增长 26.8%。合同外资 8.99 亿美元，比上年增长 21.5%；实际利用外资 4.64 亿美元，比上年减少 19.2%。

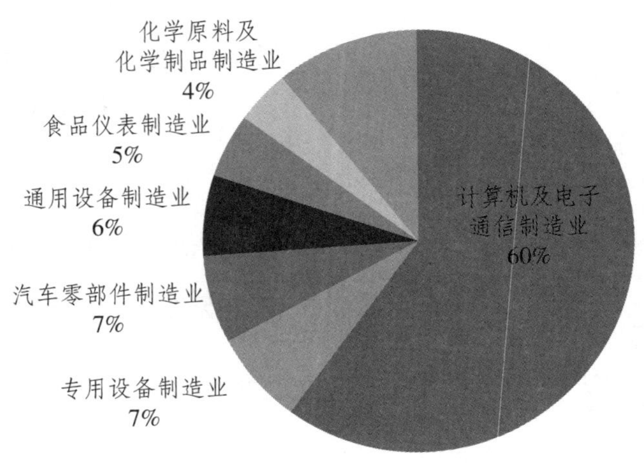

图 7-3　2009 年综合保税区六大重点行业产值比重结构图

2009 年前来保税区投资注册项目的国家和地区有 37 个，与上年持平。① 从项目数量来看：中国香港和日本新批项目超过 10 个，分别为 33 个和 14 个，两者合计占外资项目 50.0%。② 从吸引投资额来看：新加坡 5.82 亿美元（合同外资 2.96 亿美元）、中国香港 4.20 亿美元（合同外资 1.79 亿美元）、日本 2.06 亿美元（合同外资 1.20 亿美元）、美国 1.13 亿美元（合同外资 0.63 亿美元），四者合计投资额 13.21 亿美元，占保税区外商投资额 75.8%。③ 从增资项目来看：中国香港和日本增资项目超过 60 个，分别为 70 个和 65 个，两者合计占外资增资项目 46.9%。

截至 2009 年底，保税区累计批准投资企业项目达到 10497 个，吸引投资总额接近 180 亿美元，达到 179.53 亿美元。

1. 按内外资性质来看

外资企业项目累计达到 7941 个，占投资项目总数 75.7%，吸引投资额达到 150.83 亿美元，占投资总额 84.0%，无论是项目数量还是投资额均占保税区招商引资绝对比重，其中外商独资企业项目达到 7231 个，占投资项目总数 68.9%，吸引投资额 124.65 亿美元，占投资总额 69.4%。内资项目达到 2556 个，占投资项目总数 24.3%，吸引投资额 28.70 亿美元，占投资总额 16.0%。

2. 合同外资和实际利用外资逐步攀升

截至 2009 年底，保税区合同外资达到 83.05 亿美元，占外商投资额 55.1%，实际利用外资已达到 54.95 亿美元，占合同外资 74.6%（以 2009 年外资企业年检外方注册资本为基数）。

3. 按投资国别和地区来看

前来保税区投资注册的国家和地区达到 94 个。按投资项目进行排名，居前五位的

分别是中国香港1953个、日本1562个、美国867个、中国台湾473个、新加坡462个。按投资额进行排名，居前五位的分别是中国香港40.20亿美元、美国23.94亿美元、日本19.42亿美元、新加坡10.76亿美元、荷兰10.55亿美元。

（五）外资企业经营情况良好

2009年外高桥保税区外资企业完成营业（销售）收入6245亿元，比上年增长3.8%，占保税区94.2%；完成进出口贸易额472.36亿美元，比上年减少15.0%，占保税区85.7%；实现利润总额268.3亿元，与上年基本持平，占保税区94.4%；吸引从业人员19.54万人，比上年增长12.2%，占保税区90.5%。

三、2010年综合保税区主要工作思路和重点工作

2010年是上海综合保税区管理委员会全面实质性运作的起步之年，将坚持“边发展、边理顺”的原则，围绕“四个中心”建设的基本目标，按照上海市委市府、新区区委区府关于“三区”联动发展的总体要求，将2010年综合保税区工作重点落实在夯实联动基础和实施重点突破上，为启动实施“十二五”规划做好充分准备。

（一）以国际航运发展综合试验区为核心，全面构建现代航运服务体系

1．推动国际航运发展综合试验区先行先试取得突破

（1）在洋山保税港区和外高桥保税区正式开展期货保税交割业务。推动期货交割业务配套政策细化落地，抓紧完成业务流程设计工作，争取2010年上半年在上海期货交易所推出新上市金属期货交易品种时，在洋山保税港区和外高桥保税区正式试行期货保税交割业务。

（2）在洋山保税港区和机场综合保税区率先开展融资租赁业务试点。会同市、区相关金融部门，结合浦东新区综合配套改革试点，尽快研究形成飞机船舶融资租赁试点配套扶持政策，争取银监会相关管理办法出台后，国内第一批飞机船舶单机单船租赁项目公司（SPV）能在浦东机场综合保税区和洋山保税港区设立运作。

（3）积极拓展洋山保税港区离岸金融业务。协调人民银行、外汇管理局等部门，形成洋山保税港区开展离岸金融业务的基础框架，推动区内企业开设离岸账户操作性政策和措施的落地，为有实际需求的贸易、物流企业境外业务提供资金结算便利，形成发展离岸金融的必要环境，促进特殊监管区域跨国公司总部经济的发展。

（4）拓展保税延展功能。根据国际、国内市场变化，企业迫切需要国内采购的材

料和产品进区进行加工和配送，为此积极协调海关等部门，开展保税延展货物入区整合运作试点方案研究，逐步放开加工和物流企业的保税延展功能。

2．积极培育国际航运中心重要功能

（1）拓展洋山保税港区、机场综合保税区、外高桥保税物流园区出口集拼和中转集拼功能。鼓励面向欧美地区的中转集拼业务主要向洋山保税港区聚集，培育机场综合保税区空运出口集拼功能，做大做强外高桥保税物流园区国际采购分拨中心，理顺贯通出口集拼和中转集拼的业务模式和监管流程，形成低成本、高效率的运作环境，促进国际采购和国际中转业务的开展。

（2）建立洋山保税港区高档进口汽车及零部件展示销售中心。充分发挥洋山保税港“区港一体化”运作和欧美航线挂靠优势，积极引进高档进口汽车品牌，做大做强洋山保税港区进口汽车及零部件展示销售业务

（3）大力发展高端服务业。推动贸易和物流的有机结合，完善现代航运服务功能，逐步形成以航运金融为支撑，以国际采购、国际分拨、国际配送为重点，以航运咨询、法律、会展、研发、维修、测试等为特色的高端服务业。

3．探索洋山保税港区、机场综合保税区配套政策

探索将外高桥保税区的营运中心政策，尤其是物流型营运中心政策，延伸到洋山保税港区和浦东机场综合保税区，在洋山、机场培育若干个物流型跨国公司营运中心。研究落实洋山保税港区营业税免征政策以及船舶特案减免税政策，积极配合研究制定启运港退税制度。

（二）以国际贸易示范区为载体，大力推动国际贸易产业能级提升

1．推动建立离岸贸易区

有针对性学习香港地区、新加坡先进经验，在充分利用现有政策和实现外汇、税收等政策突破的基础上，在综合保税区强化提升离岸贸易功能，探索建立离岸贸易区。同时，推动一批营运中心从主要统筹中国业务向统筹东北亚乃至亚太地区业务提升，使保税区成为跨国公司在东北亚乃至亚太地区的重要贸易节点，从而在离岸贸易中发挥更大作用。

2．夯实国际贸易示范区基础

聚集高能级贸易主体，做大做强医疗器械、工程机械、机电、汽车、钟表、医药分销、酒类、文化设备租赁等外高桥保税区十大专业化贸易平台，构建具有重要影响力的商品进出口集散中心,进一步加大贸易平台在全国和长三角地区的贸易比重。同时，借鉴示范区贸易平台建设经验，筹建适合洋山保税港区特点的大宗商品交易市场。

3．进一步优化贸易便利化环境

主动适应企业现代化经营需求，推动海关、检验检疫、外汇、税务、工商等职能部门的监管模式创新和延伸。进一步推进诚信体系建设和风险管理机制，实施企业分类通关管理模式，深化跨国公司外汇收付汇集中管理等便利化课题研究，并在外高桥保税区海关事务服务中心成功运作的基础上，探索向洋山保税港区和机场综合保税区延伸。进一步降低市场准入门槛，扩大和延伸贸易管理方面的审批事权。

（三）以如期封关运营为目标，推动机场综合保税区基础设施建设和项目引进

1．加快机场综合保税区封关建设

与上海机场集团、现代产业公司紧密配合，加快推进海关隔离设施、巡关道路、监管设施建设，确保 2010 年 3 月份完成封关验收。

2．探索创新机场综合保税区临空物流服务功能

发挥浦东机场亚太航空复合枢纽港优势，发展以航空快件中心、转运分拨、第三方物流、空运保税仓储等为主的航空口岸物流功能，以及检测、维修等物流增值服务功能。抓紧制定出台机场综合保税区管理办法，推动综合试验区的创新政策延伸到浦东机场综合保税区，营造良好的招商和运行环境，确保在机场综合保税区封关验收后，实现项目引进和功能运作双丰收。

（四）以资源优化整合为基础，加快形成三区联动发展整体格局

1．探索创新“三区”业务运作模式

（1）建立上海综合保税区货物调拨体系，实现“三区”间货物流动无缝链接。会同上海海关、洋山、外高桥、机场海关监管部门，在海关无纸通关、分类通关的改革创新基础上，进一步简化通关手续。通过完善、对接外高桥保税区、洋山保税港区和机场综合保税区的海关电子监管系统模块，满足企业运作需求，使货物在“三区”之间的调拨实现无缝链接

（2）搭建“三区”统一的企业经营资质平台。会同市工商、税务、海关、外汇等部门，研究搭建“三区”统一的企业经营资质平台。已在外高桥保税区注册的企业可以直接或以分公司的形式在洋山或空港开展业务，从而鼓励外高桥企业迅速进入洋山、空港，促进两区早出形象和扩大经济规模

（3）继续推进外高桥保税区“空运货物服务中心”项目。将机场货站及监管仓库的相关功能直接延伸至外高桥保税区内，使区内货主直接在外高桥保税区内集中完成抽单、报关报检和提货手续，从而实现外高桥保税区海运、空运的联动运作，大大提

高通关效率。

2．建立管理部门紧密合作的联系机制

综合保税区管委会要和海关、检验检疫、外汇等职能部门建立更加紧密的工作联系机制，抓紧梳理影响综合保税区发展的关键环节和瓶颈因素，主动协调相关职能部门，逐一解决功能政策在操作层面和监管流程方面存在的实际问题，形成可复制的业务模式、典型方案和操作路径，进而快速带动区域相关行业的发展。同时，要积极争取市、新区相关部门的大力支持，落实上海海关支持“三港三区”联动发展的15条措施，推动市检验检疫、外汇等职能部门出台支持综合保税区发展的相关意见，进一步形成帮助企业降低成本、加快发展的服务举措，高效推进“三区”的改革创新和联动发展。

3．推动建立“三区”各开发主体间的战略合作机制

在“三区”统一行政管理体制的基础上，各开发主体之间也需要深度合作、实现共赢。目前外高桥集团与临港集团已签订战略合作框架协议，并启动了仓库租赁合作项目。下一步，管委会将继续推动外高桥集团、港务集团、同盛集团、临港集团、机场集团、现代产业开发公司等几大集团之间进行战略合作，在资金、土地、人力、品牌等方面实现资本、资源的共享和互补，形成合力推进、利益共享机制，促进“三区”的繁荣发展。

（五）进一步营造良好的综合发展环境

1．进一步改善“三区”的配套环境

加大对“三区”及周边区域生活配套设施投资建设力度，完善公共交通、人才公寓（蓝领公寓）、医疗设施、购物餐饮以及日常生活娱乐等必要的配套设施建设，进一步营造良好的综合发展环境。

2．营造良好的投资运营环境

一是积极支持、推动海关、检验检疫等行政职能部门创新监管制度，简化办事手续，优化业务流程，进一步提高货物通关效率，建立快速、高效的企业运营环境，切实减轻企业负担，有效降低企业商务成本。二是初步搭建综合保税区管委会环境管理架构，实现ISO14001环境管理体系对“三区”的全覆盖，打造区域品牌和国际形象，突破绿色壁垒。继续推进外高桥保税区创建国家工业生态示范园区各项工作，为2011年顺利通过国家验收创造条件。三是加强人才开发与服务，把综合保税区人才开发与管理工作纳入市区两级总体框架，启动人力资源专项发展规划调研工作，探索构建紧缺人才和重要岗位关键核心人才发现机制，以工资指导线引导人力资源配置流向，建立规范有序人才市场和劳动力市场。四是加强保税区依法行政和管理，推进区域综合执法体

制建设，强化区域综合执法职能，提高执法水平，落实责任制度，确保区域稳定和平安。

（六）以推动项目落地为重点，不断扩大和加强产业集聚效应

1．积极开展大型招商活动

针对“三区”的功能定位和产业要求，明确招商重点，梳理支持政策，完善激励机制，建立三区招商引资联席会议制度，打造“三区联动”全新品牌。举办大规模招商推介会，并针对贸易、物流以及展示等业务开展专题招商，力争2010年引进20个实体性项目到洋山保税港区进行实质性运作。

2．全力推动重大项目落户

（1）洋山保税港区要利用保税港区营业税免税政策，吸引具有实力的国际航运企业总部入驻，做好上港集团事业部、分公司的注册落户工作，吸引中海集团的油轮项目、中远集团、中外运集团的航运服务项目入区。引入外高桥以出口集拼、出口采购为特点的先锋等项目。

（2）外高桥保税区重点项目包括吸引国药控股公司增资至1亿元设立营运中心，推动美国普华冷链物流服务供应商设立物流中心，引进从事奔驰汽车仓储、展示和销售的“奔驰世界”项目，鼓励亚太区最大的医药与健康产品永裕公司设立大型医药物流中心。

（3）浦东机场综合保税区要结合封关验收及开园运作，积极吸引全球货运、日通、近铁、中外运、嘉里大通、锦海捷亚等一批品牌物流企业落户，初步形成航空物流产业集聚效应。

3．强化企业扶持各项措施

（1）增强财政扶持的导向性。抓紧制定2010年洋山保税港区、机场综合保税区投资企业财政扶持方案，做好与“十二五”财政扶持政策衔接的准备工作。同时根据三区的产业功能定位和发展重点，研究制定综合保税区“十二五”财政扶持政策，并建立与“十一五”相衔接的高效、精简的财政扶持工作运行机制、操作流程和管理制度。

（2）进一步加强企业服务。完善企业服务网络，做好企业走访和调研，会同各行政职能部门建立完善稳商留商协调联动机制，推行企业服务承诺制度，加强企业政策宣传和培训辅导工作，及时解决企业经营中遇到的瓶颈问题，确保企业的稳定发展。

案例：外高桥保税区营运中心

（一）营运中心的概念

营运中心是指在外高桥保税区内以独立法人形式设立的有限责任公司，统一负责公司总部在中国范围或包括中国范围但不仅限于中国范围内的商品分销、进出口以及其他相关服务，整合公司总部原先分散的销售及相关服务业务。营运中心鼓励跨国公司将全国的销售统一放在上海，不仅能完善与加强总部的功能，还能为上海带来税收、就业、物流和资金结算等方面现实的利益。

根据保税区企业运作的实际情况，以书面发文形式（沪外管委 [2006]17 号、沪外管委 [2007]25 号文件）颁布的营运中心基本认定条件是：

① 具有独立法人资格；

② 公司注册资本在 100 万美元或 800 万元人民币以上；

③ 公司总部的资产总额达到 4 亿美元或 32 亿元人民币以上；

④ 公司申请前一年或当年的营业（销售）收入达 15 亿元人民币以上（含 15 亿元人民币），且缴纳工商税收总额 1000 万元人民币以上（含 1000 万人民币）；或公司申请前一年或当年的营业（销售）收入达到 5 亿元人民币以上（含 5 亿人民币），且缴纳工商税收总额 2000 万元人民币以上（含 2000 万人民币）。

⑤ 由公司总部董事会授权该营运中心负责管理中国区域或包括中国区域但不仅限于中国区域的商品分销及相关业务；

⑥ 在保税区注册地实际经营，且在保税区购买或租赁物业建筑面积为 100 平方米以上。

企业认定为营运中心可以享受相应的财政扶持政策，营运中心企业还作为重点服务对象，在海关、外汇、检验检疫、税务、公安、工商等职能部门办事或政策先行先试中享受优先待遇。

截至 2009 年底，139 家营运中心企业数量占保税区 2.5%，完成的营业（销售）收入占保税区 39%，缴纳税务部门税收占保税区 40%，实现利润总额占保税区 44%。

（二）销售情况

2009 年保税区 139 家营运中心企业共完成营业（销售）收入 2550 亿元，比上年增长 2%，占保税区企业营业（销售）收入 39%，成为拉动保税区企业营业（销售）收入走出下降区间、实现增长的中坚力量。在这些营运中心企业中，全年收入实现增长

的企业比例达到55%，超过保税区企业平均水平10余个百分点。其中联想（上海）电子科技有限公司积极调整产品结构，整合国内销售业务，产销扩张继续保持高位运行，完成销售收入比上年增长57.0%，在保税区工业企业中排名第一；明朗国际贸易（上海）有限公司抓住国内消费市场启动的有利时机，进一步拓展销售渠道、扩大市场份额，完成销售收入比上年增长25.9%，成为保税区商品销售额排名第二的贸易企业；此外，营运中心企业上海邦基国际贸易有限公司、西门子国际国贸（上海）有限公司、强生（中国）医疗器材有限公司、沃尔沃汽车销售（上海）有限公司等销售同比增幅也均达到20%以上。

（三）税务部门税收情况

2009年保税区139家营运中心企业共缴纳税务部门税收93.42亿元，比上年增长15.8%，增幅高于保税区企业平均水平8个百分点，占保税区税务部门税收总量40%，保税区税务部门税收增量中有74.5%是营运中心企业贡献的。

（四）利润情况

2009年保税区139家营运中心企业共实现利润总额120亿元，比上年下降3%，降幅低于保税区企业平均水平7个百分点，占保税区企业利润总额44%。在这些营运中心企业中，2009年经营实现盈利的企业比例达到80%，高于保税区企业平均水平20余个百分点。其中，西门子国际贸易（上海）有限公司实现利润5.73亿元，比上年增长63.4%。

营运中心政策顺应了跨国公司内部业务整合和功能提升的要求，跨国公司依托中国市场的发展，利用集团总部的资源和垂直管理体系，以销售为中心汇聚上下游产业，带来人流、物流、资金流的聚集。营运中心已经成为支撑保税区贸易发展的中坚力量，是外高桥“国际贸易示范区”的重要内容。

第二节　金桥出口加工区

一、区域概况

上海市金桥出口加工区是1990年经国务院批准的国家级开发区，位于上海市浦东新区中部，规划面积20平方公里，西连陆家嘴金融贸易区，北接外高桥保税区，南近张江

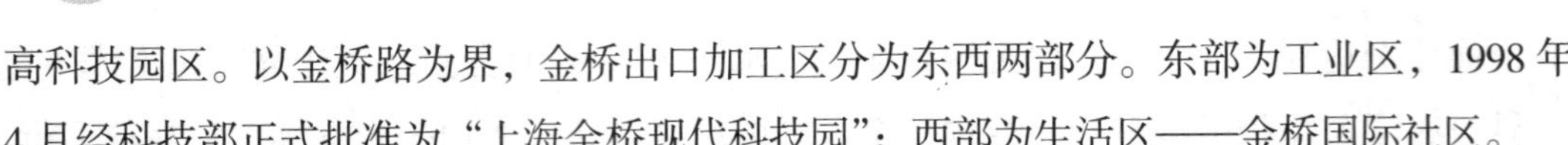

高科技园区。以金桥路为界，金桥出口加工区分为东西两部分。东部为工业区，1998年4月经科技部正式批准为“上海金桥现代科技园”；西部为生活区——金桥国际社区。

金桥出口加工区具备“九通一平”的基础设施配套，其中包括“集中供热”和“卫星通讯”。同时区内的金融、贸易、商检、报关、仓储、运输、科研、咨询、零售、餐饮娱乐、房地产、物业管理等配套服务项目也已基本完善。

二、2009年金桥出口加工区外经贸发展情况

（一）积极贯彻保增长方针，开发区经济增长态势令人欣喜

2009年，金桥开发区工业总产值1672亿元，同比增长12.2%；营业收入2599亿元，同比增长14.6%；上缴税金162.56亿元，同比增长76.44%；开发区工业企业利润163.7亿元，同比增长84.35%，在上海50个国家级和市级开发区中名列榜首。

（二）外贸进出口继续负增长

据海关统计显示，1–12月，金桥开发区的外贸进出口总额完成88.66亿美元，同比下降18.1%。其中，一般贸易下降9.8%，进料加工贸易下降28.5%，来料加工由正转负，较同期下降了6%。

1–12月，金桥出口加工区外贸出口完成386093万美元，同比下降21.4%，其中：一般贸易完成124065万美元，同比下降13.6%，占总量的32.1%；进料加工完成240047万美元，同比下降26.4%，占总量的62.2%；来料加工完成21459万美元，同比由正转负，下降了0.6%，占总量的5.6%。

1–12月，金桥出口加工区外贸进口完成500500万美元，同比下降15.3%，其中：一般贸易完成387771万美元，同比下降8.6%，占总量的77.6%；进料加工完成83681万美元，同比下降34%，占总量的16.7%；来料加工完成10631万美元，同比下降15.4%，占总量的2.1%。

就出口大类产品来讲，主要是占比重较大的机电产品有较大下降。2009年1–12月，机电产品出口358590万美元，占全部出口总量的92.9%，同比下降22.7%。其中，机械产品出口下降16.5%，占总量比重40.5%，电子产品出口下降224%，占总量比重53.6%，运输设备下降了71.8%，仪器仪表下降了38.4%。

（三）招商引资与同期相比有升有降

2009年，金桥出口加工区共完成外资设立和增资项目85个，同比下降20%，利用

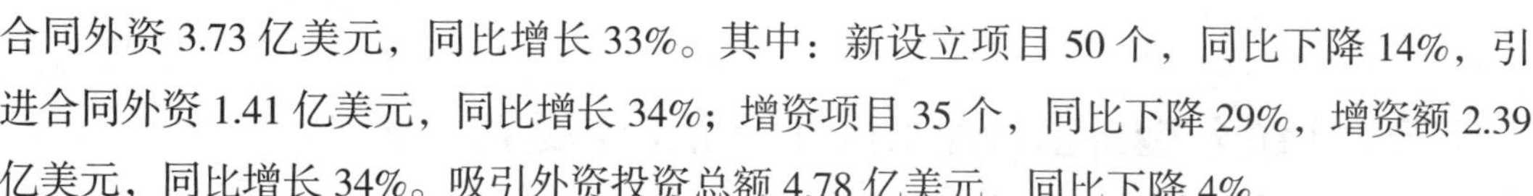

合同外资 3.73 亿美元，同比增长 33%。其中：新设立项目 50 个，同比下降 14%，引进合同外资 1.41 亿美元，同比增长 34%；增资项目 35 个，同比下降 29%，增资额 2.39 亿美元，同比增长 34%。吸引外资投资总额 4.78 亿美元，同比下降 4%。

2009 年招商引资项目中主要呈现以下几个特点：

1. 服务类项目居多

1–12 月，引进和增资服务类项目 65 个，项目数的占比由 2008 年的 64% 上升到 2009 年的 76%；制造业由 36% 下降到 24%。

2. 投资规模依然偏小、减资项目明显增多

引进和增资项目的投资总额超过 1000 万美元的只有 9 个，比 2008 年度下降 25%。减资项目增多，全年减资项目 8 个，减少合同外资 609.58 万美元，同比增长 50%。

3. 独资项目占绝对主导

1–12 月，引进独资项目 43 个，项目数占比由 2008 年的 51% 上升到 86%。

4. 外资来源地

从外资来源地看，以亚洲为主，其次是欧洲、北美洲，分别占引进项目数的 58%、22% 及 14%。

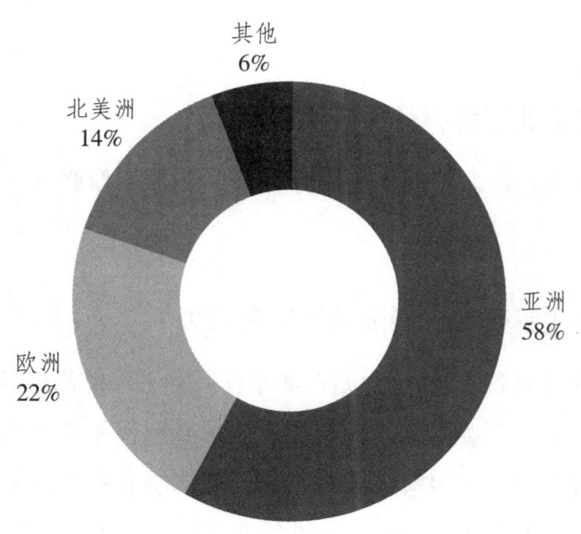

图 7-4 2009 年金桥出口加工区外资来源地示意图

2009 年，金桥开发区在功能性项目上取得突破。大唐产业园、中国移动通讯视频基地、中国电信视讯中心、上海贝尔全球信息技术服务中心、Hengsoft 等一批新的功能性项目相继落户区内，形成了新的特色和亮点，为金桥通信产业从设备设施制造向研发设计、应用服务和视频网络文化延伸发展，为完善产业链和产业集群发展奠定了基础。

三、2010年金桥出口加工区外经贸工作展望

2010年是上海世博会举办年，也是浦东新区开发开放20周年，更是全面推进浦东新区“二次创业”和金桥“二次开发”的关键年。金桥开发区切实把握“两个中心建设”、迪斯尼、大飞机等重大项目落地的历史发展机遇，进一步认清形势，拓展思路，务实创新，全力以赴把区域各项“保增长、促发展、提能级、增后劲”的工作目标落到实处。

（一）加强项目协调服务，提高投资促进成效

坚持以大项目服务推进为龙头，进一步强化招商引资的工作力度，重点协调推进制造业大项目，加快发展生产性现代服务业。

（二）推进产业结构调整，优化经济增长方式

坚持以“巩固强势产业，扶持高端产业，培育新兴产业，淘汰落后产业”为方针，以节约利用资源、提高资源综合利用效率为核心，引导企业提升产业能级，积极推进产业结构调优。

（三）继续加强企业服务，做好亲商稳商工作

树立服务是软环境意识，不断完善服务体系，积极创新服务手段，大力营造良好的投资环境。

（四）加强产业政策研究，增强持续发展动力

综合“新浦东”的格局和体制变化，站在浦东新区和上海的高度，继续积极建言献策。在大力推进先进制造业、高端制造业发展和有效承载现代服务业发展方面，继续积极争取领导重视和部门支持；在国家级开发区的管理体制和服务体系方面，继续积极呼吁进行创新性变革；在扶持企业做强做大和产业集聚效应培育方面，力争出台更有效、更直接、更有吸引力的政策。

案例：上海贝尔股份有限公司

上海贝尔股份有限公司（简称上海贝尔）成立于1984年。1996年，上海贝尔正式

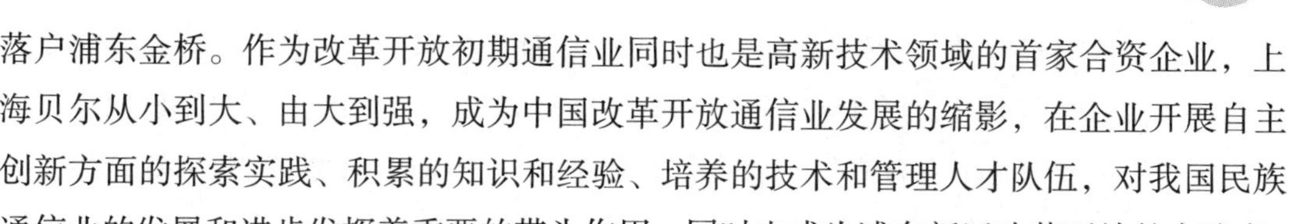

落户浦东金桥。作为改革开放初期通信业同时也是高新技术领域的首家合资企业，上海贝尔从小到大、由大到强，成为中国改革开放通信业发展的缩影，在企业开展自主创新方面的探索实践、积累的知识和经验、培养的技术和管理人才队伍，对我国民族通信业的发展和进步发挥着重要的带头作用，同时也成为浦东新区改革开放的实践者、探索者和受益者。

目前，上海贝尔已被国家认定为国家创新型试点企业和国家级企业技术中心，同时也是阿尔卡特朗讯集团全球三大研发中心之一，可全面进入阿尔卡特朗讯集团（简称阿朗集团）全球技术库。近年来每年研发投入超过 10 亿元，占净销售收入 8%；研发人员超过 4000 余人；每年发明披露超过 600 项，发明专利 100 余项，全部是核心发明专利，三分之一在欧美日注册，还主导或参与国内、国际标准制定近 100 项；与此同时，上海贝尔还设立了承担前瞻性技术开发的研创中心，人均专利数在阿朗集团全球六大研创中心中连续三年排名第一。上海贝尔拥有自主知识产权。上海贝尔目前正积极参与国家重大专项“下一代无线宽带技术”的研发工作。上海贝尔多年来的技术创新实践，为对外合作中实现自主创新和自主发展探索了成功经验。

在过去 20 多年对外合作的成功实践基础上，上海贝尔深刻地体会到，企业开展自主创新，不仅有利于自身核心竞争能力的打造，更将有利于我国综合国力的提升，有利于社会主义和谐社会的建设。特别是当前，历史罕见的国际金融危机正给我国经济带来严重冲击，党中央、国务院把结构调整和自主创新作为保增长的主攻方向，而自主创新正是推动经济在波动中实现稳定增长的强大杠杆，是克服金融危机的根本力量。上海贝尔的实践证明，只有积极开展技术创新，企业才能积极应对危机、实现可持续发展。

在企业实现管理创新的基础上，上海贝尔进一步利用国际资源，加快“引进来、走出去”的步伐，不断提升企业核心竞争能力。在国际金融危机的大环境下，中国通信设备企业在国际市场上已越来越体现出综合竞争优势并已实现快速增长。上海贝尔进一步发挥中国优势，在与全球跨国公司合作共赢基础上，加大对亚太（东盟）、独联体（上海合作组织）、非洲（能源组织）等发展中国家市场开拓力度，加快“走出去”步伐。同时，在全球产业重新整合调整的环境下，上海贝尔发挥自身比较优势，加快“引进来”，在现有制造与产业化中心、研发中心的基础上，进一步完善面向跨国公司全球运营的国际性支持中心，即：技术服务中心、采购物流中心、财务管理中心等。

在技术创新方面：上海贝尔以“打造一个高效、灵敏的研发信息化平台”为目标，不断加强技术能力中心的建设，进一步优化产品开发流程，及时应对多变的市场，缩短产品开发周期，提升研发管理的科学性，降低项目风险，努力成为国家级技术创新基地，以及阿尔卡特朗讯集团颇具实力的研发能力中心。面向技术的研发创新：公司持续加大研发投入，坚持自主创新；加快与全球跨国公司技术的双向流动，有针对性地选择几个关键业务、技术领域作为突破点，如有线宽带接入、光传输、无线宽带接入等，特别是进一步加大对3G产品的研发和产业化力度。国家级技术能力中心建设：进一步优化产品开发流程，及时应对多变的市场，缩短产品开发周期，提升研发管理的科学性，降低项目风险；同时，在全球金融危机的大环境下，公司充分利用自身高效率的比较优势，吸引阿尔卡特朗讯更多全球性研发项目向中国转移。参与国家重大专项的创新：公司进一步推进TD-LTE研发，努力承担更多研发任务，积极争取建设TD-LTD世博会试验网，通过持续不断的自主创新，努力成为具有国际竞争力的研发能力平台。

第三节　漕河泾出口加工区

一、区域概况

上海漕河泾出口加工区是漕河泾开发区浦江高科技园（国家级）的一个重要组成部分，地处上海市闵行区浦江镇，地理位置优越，是距离市中心最近的保税监管区域。漕河泾出口加工区紧邻徐浦大桥（外环线）和卢浦大桥，距离上海市中心——人民广场16公里，距离上海浦东国际机场38公里，距离虹桥机场21公里，距离洋山深水港车程约48公里。轨道交通M8线浦江镇站毗邻上海漕河泾出口加工区。

二、2009年漕河泾出口加工区外经贸发展情况

上海漕河泾出口加工区是实行围网管理的保税监管区域，2009年在原有出口加工区各项保税政策的基础上，进行了保税物流、研发、检测、维修的功能叠加。受出口加工区功能单一、政策优势弱化、成本上升和国际金融危机等因素的综合影响，出口加工区招商形势比较严峻。

2009年漕河泾出口加工区全年进出口总额达到151亿美元，其中出口122.6亿美元（2008年为118.3亿美元），逆势增长3.6%，占整个闵行区出口额的69%；园区创造了约3.7万个就业岗位。

2004-2009年，出口加工区工业总产值从136.11亿元增至937.21亿元，增长6.9倍；

工业增加值从0.99亿元增19.92亿元，增长20.12倍；税收收入从1.16亿元增至17.12亿元，增长14.76倍；出口总额从16.91亿美元增至122.60亿美元，增长7.25倍，经济发展水平位列全国同类园区前列。6年来，漕河泾出口加工区累计出口总额达463.2亿美元。

截至2009年末，上海漕河泾出口加工区共引进各类企业18家，其中外资企业14家。园区投资总额6.90亿美元，吸引合同外资2.52亿美元，实际利用外资2.51亿美元。引进的18家企业中有15家开展进料加工的生产型企业，主要集中在电子信息和医疗器械制造业。

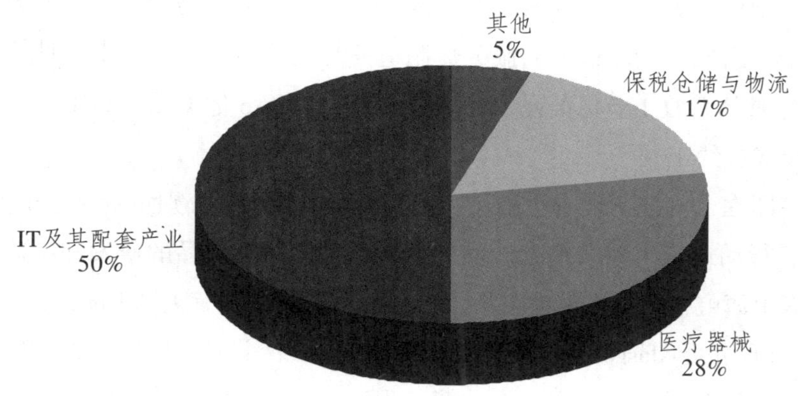

图7-5 2009年漕河泾出口加工区企业产业分布图

三、2010年漕河泾出口加工区外经贸发展展望

2010年上海漕河泾出口加工区将继续稳健发展加工贸易业务，推进出口加工区企业进行保税物流、研发等各项功能拓展，并积极探索保税监管区域政策创新，争取赋予出口加工区更多、更灵活的贸易、服务功能，实现出口加工区政策的全面创新，为上海国际经济、金融、贸易、航运中心建设作贡献。

案例：英业达集团

英业达集团从1991年开始在上海筹备成立公司，2001年英业达（上海）有限公司成立，2002年8月14日，英业达（上海）有限公司建立了全国海关第一本加工贸易联网电子账册，通关时效及账册备案核销速度得到倍速提升，进出口业绩开始了数倍增长。

2003 年上海英业达集团总部成立，并先后在浦江镇漕河泾出口加工区内成立英顺达科技、英业达科技、英源达科技 3 家全资子公司。并于 2005 年获得通过 ISO14001:2004 转版验证；2008 年获得商检分类一等企业；2009 年 6 月获得海关 A 类企业；2009 年 7 月得到中国合格评定国家认可委员会 CNAS 实验室认可证书。2009 年获得美国海关 CTPAT 认证。

英业达集团自 1975 年成立以来，即以“创新、质量、虚心、力行”为经营理念，投入电子产品的生产制造；从计算器筚路蓝缕的时代，经历电话机的全盛时期，现今已迈入行动运算、无线通信、网络应用、数字家庭与应用软件等高科技产品领域。目前每年笔记本型计算机产能配备预计可达 3000 万台、企业服务器可达 300 万台及智能手机 500 万个，已成为全球最大的服务器制造商与全球前五大笔记本型计算机代工厂之一，2008 年整体营收 107 亿美元，2009 年整体营收 126 亿美元，2010 年将会持续增长，较前一年成长约 15%。

英业达集团在台湾地区设有士林厂、北投厂与桃园厂，分别负责笔记本型计算机、消费性电子、行动通信与无线整合产品的研发，与服务器产品的研发和制造，而国内的生产基地有上海虹桥厂、上海浦东厂，国外的生产基地则有美国 Houston 厂、墨西哥 Juarez 厂、英国苏格兰 Glasgow 厂、捷克 Brno 厂。从研发、设计、生产到配送及技术支持，英业达集团均以顾客需求为导向、全球营运为第一考虑，将整个集团及全球布局的力量发挥到极致，这也是英业达集团从软件到硬件、从台湾到全球，提供给客户全方位解决方案的雄厚基础。

未来，英业达集团将会持续秉承好的经营模式，经营理念，不断向上发展，永续经营。

第四节　松江出口加工区

一、区域概况

松江出口加工区，是国务院 2000 年批准的全国首批试点的 15 个出口加工区之一。同年 11 月 9 日起，正式运行。这是继江苏昆山加工区之后，全国第二家正式运行的国家级出口加工区。松江出口加工区是由海关监管的特殊区域，区内实行全封闭管理，落户企业除可以享受国家级工业区的所有优惠政策外，还可以享受出口产品免征增值税，进口原材料、零部件全额保税等优惠政策。松江出口加工区进出口货物部实行保

证金台账实转制度，海关按照直通式或转关运输的办法监管，目前松江出口加工区的通关时间可控制在 6 小时以内。

二、2009 年松江出口加工区外经贸发展情况

（一）物流仓储等业务开展顺利

在经历了 2009 年上半年各项经济指标几乎下降三分之一的困难时期以后，自 2009 年第三季度起，区内企业产能利用率明显提高，尤其是进入四季度后，出口额环比增长更是达到了两位数。据统计，2009 年全年，松江出口加工区完成工业产值 1756.26 亿元，完成进出口总额 330.07 亿美元，其中进口 84.89 亿美元，出口 245.18 亿美元，在全国出口加工区中位列第二。2007 年底开始推行的加工区物流功能拓展现已完全推开，该项业务在松江出口加工区开展顺利，截至 2009 年底，松江出口加工区内批准专业物流企业 13 家，区内专业物流仓储面积已达 14.28 万平方米，全年涉及业务金额逾 194 亿美元; 批准研发功能试点企业 6 家，专业研发人员近 400 人；批准维修业务试点企业 6 家，累计业务金额 32.38 亿元；区内 8 家生产高技术含量高附加值产品的企业获得了检测业务试点许可，累计业务金额达 49.86 亿元; 2009 年全年功能拓展涉及金额达 194 亿美元。

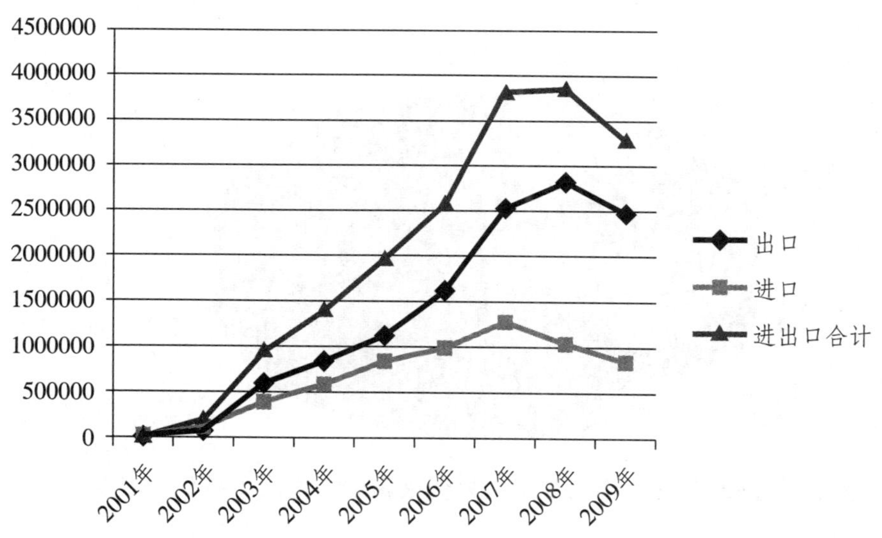

图 7-6 2001-2009 年松江出口加工区加工贸易总金额（单位：万美元）

（二）龙头企业带动工业产值

松江出口加工区内主要以广达集团、国基电子两家企业为龙头企业，区内 70 余家

企业皆为外资企业并从事加工贸易，大多也为广达集团及国基电子的配套企业。

据统计，2009 年全年，出口加工区完成工业产值 1756.26 亿元，同比下降 15.65%，完成进出口总额 330.07 亿美元，其中进口 84.89 亿美元，出口 245.18 亿美元，同比分别下降 14.47%、19.30% 和 12.66%。工商税收得益于区内企业利润及出口转内销的增长，在其他各项指标同比全线下滑的同时依旧保持略有增幅的态势，全年完成 4.74 亿元，同比增长 0.4%，对地方经济带来了一定的促进。

表 7-3　2009 年松江出口加工区各项指标完成情况表

指标名称	累计完成情况	同比增长
工业总产值	1756 亿元	-15.65%
销售收入	1736 亿元	-14.48%
企业利润总额	18.62 亿元	-10.69%
工商税收	4.74 亿元	0.39%
进出口总额	330.07 亿美元	-14.47%
其中：进口	84.89 亿美元	-19.30%
出口	245.18 亿美元	-12.66%

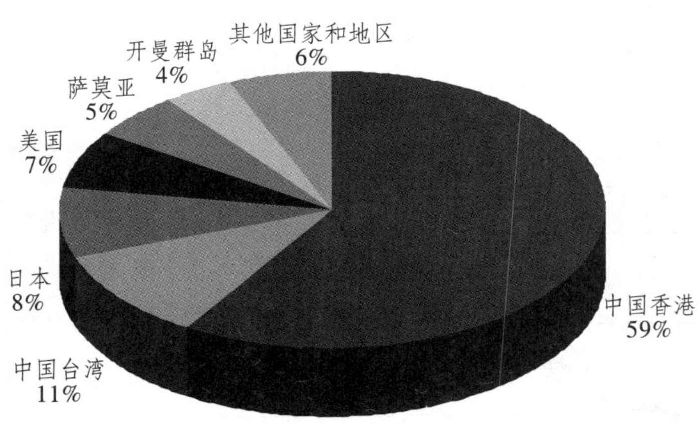

图 7-7　2009 年松江出口加工区外资来源地结构图（单位：万美元）

从上述部分统计数据看，松江出口加工区虽然尚未完全摆脱下降局面，但根据逐月跟踪的数据变化来看，也出现了一些可喜的现象，这些现象主要表现为：部分统计数据 2009 年四季度创出历史新高，如四季度出口额达 86.62 亿美元，创出加工区有史以来的季度出口额新高；区内企业员工人数 12 月底逾 10 万人。企业经济效益明显改善，2009 年四季度区内企业利润总额达 6.88 亿元，同比增幅高达 121%。由此而来的工商

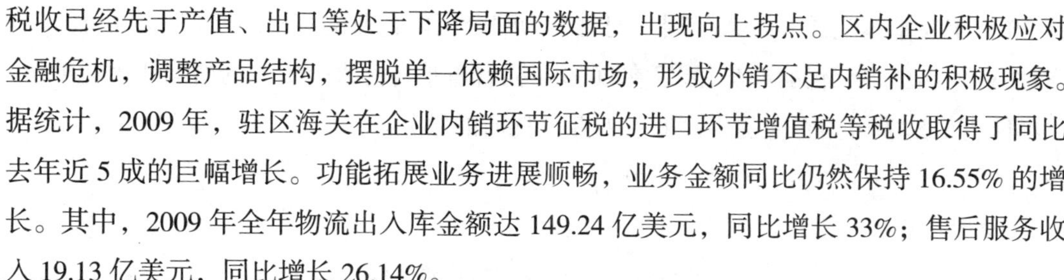

税收已经先于产值、出口等处于下降局面的数据，出现向上拐点。区内企业积极应对金融危机，调整产品结构，摆脱单一依赖国际市场，形成外销不足内销补的积极现象。据统计，2009 年，驻区海关在企业内销环节征税的进口环节增值税等税收取得了同比去年近 5 成的巨幅增长。功能拓展业务进展顺畅，业务金额同比仍然保持 16.55% 的增长。其中，2009 年全年物流出入库金额达 149.24 亿美元，同比增长 33%；售后服务收入 19.13 亿美元，同比增长 26.14%。

（三）配置不足等瓶颈亟待突破

在这一年的发展过程中，一些政策瓶颈亟待突破。如内销维修问题的解决应给出一个明确的时间表、出料加工的审批应有明确的审批程序等等，上述问题不能及时得到解决的话，企业会被迫将生产线一分为二，将内销产品的部分移往区外甚至市外。

其次，松江出口加工区前 6 年的业务发展速度出乎所有监管部门意料，导致的后果就是相关监管部门资源配置与企业需求相比严重不足，当前最突出的矛盾是驻区海关办事处人力资源严重短缺，关员配置是按照每周 5 天每天 8 小时工作时间配置的，而现状是每周 7 天每天 24 小时通关，因此，按简单的数学算法，目前关员人数的配置只是实际需要配置的三分之一不到。这一问题如果不能得到彻底解决，将直接影响企业通关速度，进而挫伤企业扩大经营规模的积极性。

三、2010 年松江出口加工区外经贸工作展望

上海松江出口加工区 2010 年的主要发展目标将把目光向“十二五”看齐，具体为：区内工业总产值年均增长率 10%，至“十二五”末年产值突破 4000 亿元，并带动区外相关服务产业年产值突破 500 亿元；进出口总额同步增长，至“十二五”末突破 600 亿美元，其中出口突破 400 亿美元；区内企业直接提供就业岗位至“十二五”末超过 15 万个，并带动相关服务产业增加就业岗位约 5 万个。

主要依托区内主要骨干企业，充分利用出口加工区功能拓展以后具备的研发、维修等功能，从单一制造环节向上下端延伸，形成高端 IT 产品的设计、生产、销售及售后服务的完整产业链，并不断根据企业发展需要，完善配套服务的硬件和措施，努力将松江出口加工区打造成上海电子产品产业链的集聚地。

为达成上述目标，园区于 2009 年初在区委、区政府的支持下，在区各相关部门的配合下，对 A 区进行了重新规划，拟定了总投资超过 2 亿元的建设项目，包括新建卡口、报关报检综合楼、区内主干道调整、桥梁架设以及查验场地等的新建或扩建，项目预

计2010年底基本完成并投入使用。同时，为配合区内企业的规模不断扩大、品种日益增加、业务不断多元化的趋势，园区在2009年初就着手自身人力资源的增加和培训工作，以期能更好地为区内企业提供高效、专业、优质的服务。

案例：上海广达集团

2008年4季度，源自美国的次贷危机逐渐演变成波及全球的金融危机，导致全球经济增速下滑，衰退迹象明显，使以出口为主的松江出口加工区内企业订单量减质降。而随着全球经济下滑，IT商品的消费也受到了严重打击，电子信息业逐步陷入困境。对在松江出口加工区内占主要地位的电子信息产业来说，产业销售增长的放缓直接影响了企业订单，从而导致了工业总产值增长的放缓。

“我们的设备可以生产出高端的笔记本电脑，这也是我们所希望的，但今年全球销售巨变，高端产品订单骤减，我们必须作出调整。”松江出口加工区龙头企业广达集团负责人在2008年底的产业调研中如是说。2008年以来，全球笔记本电脑销售由原来的高端高价转向了现在的低端低价，笔记本电脑价格大战的打响对于全球知名笔记本电脑品牌代工厂的广达集团来说，由高价笔记本电脑代工转向低价成为无奈却又必须作出的选择。一方面迅速调整生产线以应对全球笔记本电脑销售的快速变化，同时又要不断开发新型产品以保证集团在行业内的优势。企业面临的除了订单量的变动还有生产成本的不断提高。国家统计局数据显示，我国自2008年5月出现“剪刀差”现象之后，连续3个月生产者物价指数同比涨幅高于消费者物价指数，从而缩小了企业的利润空间。原材料、燃料、动力价格上涨，增加了企业的生产成本，对广达集团的利润造成了很大影响。其次，企业劳动力工资成本提高、融资难度增大、节能减排投入增加等因素，企业生产成本不断提高，这也在一定程度上影响了企业的赢利水平。而两税并轨以来，税率的提高又给企业盈利的增长造成了压力。这对于代工利润原本就已微乎其微，有些产品甚至亏损生产的广达集团来说，无疑是给企业的盈利带来了一个又一个困难。与此同时，广达集团本着“福利人群”的宗旨，在众多企业大规模裁员以减少支出的情况下，始终实行温和的管理手段。

至2009年1月，在上述困境和春节长假生产淡季的影响下，广达集团的生产情况跌至谷底，2009年1月产量仅为上年同期63%，产值下跌逾三分之一。直至5月，经济仍不容乐观，工业产值相比2008年同期缩水三分之一，而出口额在2~4月小幅回升后又于5月回落至年初水平，整个上半年的形势可谓一片黯淡。

下半年开始，全球经济逐渐企稳，美国、欧洲、日本等园区出口的主要地区经济环境有所好转，美国经济 3 季度实现由负转正，促使广达集团出口需求扩大。由于广达集团在经济危机中用工比较规范，与外地职校签有长期合同，同时因为并未在危机中大幅裁员，所以在劳务人员中口碑较好，因此当出口需求增大时，能保证充足的劳动力进行生产。与此同时，广达集团下属达利维修业务的开展，使集团的售后服务能力大为提高，并直接提升了产品的市场竞争力，也为集团在订单的争取上取得更为有利的市场地位。也正是由于加工区开展了维修业务使维修效率得到大幅度提高。原来因不能在区内维修，广达集团只能在区外设立维修企业，而维修的产品需要办理繁琐的进出口手续，时间周期较长，客户本来就对需要维修的产品产生了不满情绪，长时间的维修周期更致客户的抱怨；同时，由于缺少工厂拥有的一些昂贵的检修设备，维修的范围也大受限制。达利公司开展维修业务以后，这些问题已经全部解决，需要维修的产品享受到了出口加工区快速通关的便利，制造工厂强大的检测、制造设备使产品的维修能力覆盖了成品的所有部件。

在松江区委、区府及各相关部门的支持下，在集团员工的共同努力下，集团 6~9 月的出口额表现为回暖起稳，连续 4 个月出口额相比年初增长约 5。第四季度开始，集团出口额出现有力回升，四季度单月出口额连创新高，集团单月产值与去年同期比较，也从 2009 年 1 月份的 -40% 逐月上升，到 12 月已为 2008 年同期产值的 77%，至此全面恢复到危机前水平。进入 2010 年，广达集团 1 月、2 月接单分别比去年同期增加 80% 和 48%，企业业绩将有机会大幅成长，其全年目标可能达到营业额 300 亿美元，笔记本电脑出货量亦有望突破 5000 万台，经济效益明显改善。集团将充分利用出口加工区功能拓展以后具备的研发、维修等功能，从单一制造环节向上下端延伸，形成高端 IT 产品的设计、生产、销售及售后服务的完整产业链，努力打造上海电子产品产业链的集聚地。

第五节 青浦出口加工区

一、区域概况

上海青浦出口加工区于 2003 年 3 月经国务院批准设立，是由海关监管的特殊区域，总规划面积 3 平方公里，位于上海市区西部，上海市级工业园——青浦工业园区规划

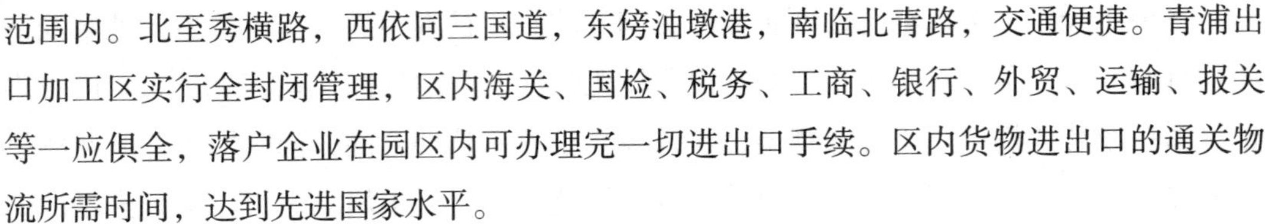

范围内。北至秀横路，西依同三国道，东傍油墩港，南临北青路，交通便捷。青浦出口加工区实行全封闭管理，区内海关、国检、税务、工商、银行、外贸、运输、报关等一应俱全，落户企业在园区内可办理完一切进出口手续。区内货物进出口的通关物流所需时间，达到先进国家水平。

二、2009年青浦出口加工区外经贸发展情况

2009年是青浦出口加工区发展面临压力与挑战的一年，也是促进区域转型升级的实质启动之年。在世界经济的重要转型期，加工园区认真分析形势，立足上海“扩内需、促增长、调结构、上水平”的战略方针，根据区委区政府提出的总体要求，围绕园区下达的全年任务指标，坚定信心，砥砺前行，拓思路，谋对策，把握机遇，突出重点，高标准、高质量、高效率地把各项工作抓紧、抓实、抓成效，实现逆势增长。

（一）主要经济指标完成情况良好

1．进出口情况

2009年完成进口30704.13万美元，年同比增长34.12%，完成出口28489.01万美元，同比增长24.93%；截至2009年底，青浦出口加工区共完成进口85163.7万美元，完成出口76614.45万美元。出口加工区内企业在受到金融危机的短期冲击后，能够较快地调整战略方向，2009年区域经济发展总体呈现出“逐季回暖”态势。斯伦贝谢平稳发展未受危机影响，以及欧菲滤清器快速摆脱产量下滑，年内保持较快增长，对拉动整个区域的产量，实现出口创汇恢复性增长作出了一定贡献。日立海立、晶盟在第二季度逐渐恢复生产水平，逐季回暖并略有增长。

2．吸引投资

2009年完成5285万美元，与2008年同比增长5.07%，完成全年目标（2000万美元）的264.25%。主要是晶盟硅材料增资710万美元，吸引斯伦贝谢组装项目350万美元，斯伦贝谢研发与生产基地项目4000万美元。截至2009年底青浦出口加工区共吸引各类投资约4亿美元，其中合同外资1.8亿美元。在出口加工区17家落户企业中，斯伦贝谢油田设备（上海）有限公司在青浦出口加工区的总投资累计已超过1.7亿美元，新投资的研发与生产基地项目是其全球第52个研发基地、上海欧菲滤清器有限公司充分利用出口加工区加工贸易政策优势，2009单家企业出口约1亿美元，2010年可达1.5亿美元。

3．保税物流

2009年青浦出口加工区功能拓展政策全面放开后，在区内率先拓展了保税物流政

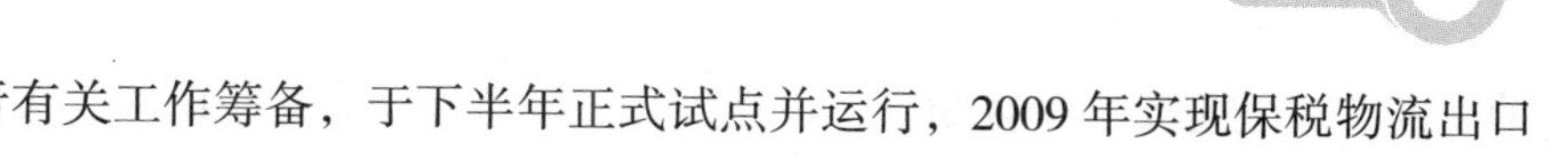

策，上半年进行有关工作筹备，于下半年正式试点并运行，2009 年实现保税物流出口货值 2596.3 万美元，

（二）大力推进功能拓展、辐射、配套、联合等重要工作

1．功能拓展与功能辐射联动推进，扩大发展功效

（1）加强捆绑服务，保税物流拓展有起步。联合海关、检验检疫加强政策研究，建立与落户企业“一对一”的捆绑式研究与服务，探索可拓展的业务类型。现已根据企业申请，批复同意区内欧菲、美晶、巴斯夫、物流公司的保税物流业务，欧菲滤清器、美晶纺织已完成与海关监管系统的联网工作，开展保税物流业务，全年增加保税业务量 2596.3 万美元。

（2）全力推进普惠项目，维修业务试点有落实。积极走访商务部、上海市商务委员会、海关，全力推进普惠业务专报专批工作，在市、区两级职能部门的帮助支持下，最终获得商务部对普惠公司开展国内外飞机发动机维修业务试点的批复。同时，为了更好地利用政策，更快地发挥作用，有效地推进试点工作，已形成加工区管委会与上海市商务委员会、海关开展试点联合审批、单台业务单独审批制度，定期通报制度。该司年内已有 4 台发动机进入维修。

（3）扩大政策宣传，发挥辐射有推动。建立了以区政府牵头，各相关职能部门联合的推广领导小组，奠定政策落实的组织保障。加强内外联动，扩大政策实效，已在区经委、区外商协会的大力协助下，在全区范围内开展加工贸易企业的政策宣讲，挑选出口量大、“外高桥一日游”企业作为重点走访和突破对象。开展网上政策宣传，开展重点企业的走访宣传，把政策精华融入企业实际运作，指导建立符合企业发展业务方案，分别与徐泾的科蓓服装，园区的合岗钢材、科泰电源、博舍工业接洽，其中科蓓服装已进入相关业务模式的探讨。

2．功能规划与环境建设配套推进，加大发展优势

以环境保护优化经济发展，围绕建设“三生”园区的目标，做好一个“加快”、三个“并举”工作，加快建设具有优质发展基础的生态文明区域。

（1）加快三块仓储物流地块的规划与建设，即：监管仓库南侧和标准厂房西侧各 4000 平方米的小型物流仓储，原戎胜地块 400 亩的保税物流基地，为顺利拓展功能提供基础保障。目前，监管仓库南侧仓库已委托高新公司负责建设，已顺利完成招投标工作，进入施工前期准备阶段，可满足区内现有企业需求。

（2）基础完善与体制完善并举。做好基础设施维养工作，完成横一路和西环路的道路修复；进一步加强安全生产队伍建设，组织开展驻区职能部门和加工区全体开展

消防演练；健全安全督查制度，重点监督做好普惠项目建设的验收等收尾工作，尤其抓好施工现场的安全巡查工作，确保项目建设安全、顺利投产。

（3）环境治理与生态保护并举。加强物业环境治理的监督管理，定期进行河道整治、道路清洁等工作，同时加强绿化建设，完成3.5kV变电站的绿化美化工程。

（4）区域大环境与企业小环境并举。注重加工区整体节能减排的生态建设，引导做好在建项目施工单位的节能管理。重视落户企业再建需求，注重企业布局与整体环境的协调统一，改造迪顺空置厂房，满足巴斯夫危险品专业堆放仓库的要求，参与企业设计论证和方案落实。

3．深挖内潜与落实政策结合推进，增强发展能力

在全球经济放缓的背景下，各类投资也大幅缩水，吸引外资压力重重，功能拓展的政策及时雨为加工区发展带来新的机遇。全国出口加工区新项目入区数普遍下降，在严峻的形势面前，牢牢把握政策机遇，注重内部挖潜，想方设法推进招商引资工作。

（1）扩大招商群体。坚持科学选资的同时，拓宽招商种类，坚持招商引资与招商引贸并重。利用功能拓展契机，吸引物流型企业入区。全年新引进物流企业3家，总注册资金1500万元。

（2）强化追踪式服务。对有增资计划的欧菲、晶盟硅材料、斯伦贝谢进行新政策宣传，增强企业发展信心，参与新项目开拓的前期调研、政策分析等工作，协调并获取政府支持。年内已完成斯伦贝谢两个增资项目的签约落户，晶盟硅材料已成功增资并全额到位，欧菲地区总部计划有待与高层接洽进一步推进。

（3）推进产业链建设。东航研发中心的投资意向已确定，将配套服务普惠项目以及东航相关产业；美特尔ATM机项目的合作方德利多富高层已来访考察并进行投资交流，项目初步意向已达成，进入实质性进展阶段。

4．质量管理和亲商服务协调推进，提升发展水平

（1）抓好两项活动契机，提高内部管理质量。以深入学习实践科学发展观活动为契机，结合加工区发展实际，提出“坚持科学发展，促进转型升级，把加工区建设成集加工、研发、检测、维修为一体的现代化综合保税服务区”的实践主题，从加强思想建设、队伍建设、信息化建设、机制创新建设四方面入手，进一步提高内部管理质量。以“百日竞赛”活动为契机，进一步明确科室职能，发挥团队作用，冲刺全年目标。

（2）扩高服务效能，提高企业发展质量。从实体服务转到政策梳理服务，从协助意识转到企业主人翁意识。做好企业来访、服务内容、问题办结等的服务台账工作，加强管委会、驻区海关、检验检疫和企业的四方沟通机制，加强科室服务条线的有效

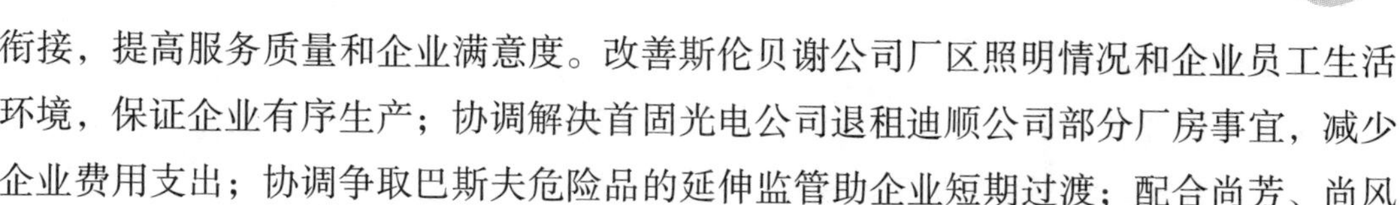

衔接，提高服务质量和企业满意度。改善斯伦贝谢公司厂区照明情况和企业员工生活环境，保证企业有序生产；协调解决首固光电公司退租迪顺公司部分厂房事宜，减少企业费用支出；协调争取巴斯夫危险品的延伸监管助企业短期过渡；配合尚芳、尚风化妆品公司做好公司清退工作。

（3）加强扶持力度，助推企业逆势增长。充分考虑金融危机对企业的影响，给予企业政策扶持，缓解部分企业的短期资金困难，如减免晶盟硅材料部分物业管理费，免去普惠项目建设期间部分厂房租金和斯伦贝谢公司厂房租金等。

二、2010年青浦加工区外经贸工作展望

功能拓展的功效已在全国几家试点出口加工区中逐步凸显，使其无论在业务模式还是业务量、企业利润上都有了前所未有的质与量的飞跃。因此，在加工区经济企稳向好之际，2010年的发展重点要在中央经济工作会议提出的“促转变”上下功夫，加快功能拓展步伐，积极推动出口加工区的转型升级，才是保持未来整体持续性复苏、实现区域经济跨越式发展的重要切入口。

（一）以功能拓展为核心工作

做好一个“确保”，两个“抓好”的推进，全面推进出口加工区功能拓展步伐，快速提高政策实效的作用发挥，切实提高经济发展质量和效益。2010年主要经济目标：出口创汇5亿美元，进出口达10亿美元，比2009年实现翻番；合同外资5000万美元，保税物流出口量1亿美元。

（二）青浦出口加工区已进入区域转型升级的重要阶段

1．确保三个重点推进

一是抓好普惠大修业务试点运行的推进工作，加强有效监管与服务，确保2010年38台大修业务计划；充分利用这次机遇，最大限度地发挥试点实效，体现试点价值，创造试点业绩，及时总结试点经验。二是抓好斯伦贝谢研发和生产基地开工建设，配合做好前期各项准备工作，争取时间，早出成效。三是抓好东航研发中心的签约落户，在土地指标、投资方案上进一步下功夫，争取早日落户，与普惠公司联合形成维修、研发一体的航空产业链。

2．抓好功能辐射推进

一是继续利用网络、中介机构、政府平台等扩大功能拓展的政策宣传，深入政策

引导与企业模式的捆绑探究，争取2010年吸引1~2家区外企业入区。二是加快推进入区物流企业的业务开展，率先开展区内外的保税物流服务，开展区外企业“加工区一日游”贸易方式，同时优化加工区税种，增加收入。

3．抓好政策招商推进

一是做好调研，扩大排摸范围，对已落户江浙开发区并有维修、检测业务需求以及相关配套需求的企业进行大力排摸和调研，坚持科学选资，引进实力型项目入区。二是做好物流招商工作，放眼长远发展，以加快建设现代物流为目标，引进国内外大型现代物流项目入区，为日后开展第三方现代物流作准备。

案例：斯伦贝谢油田设备（上海）有限公司

斯伦贝谢油田设备（上海）有限公司（简称斯伦贝谢（上海））成立于2005年8月。截至2010年6月底投资总额1.676亿美元，注册资本6074万美元（其中最近一次增资于2010年6月完成，此次增资总投资1.2亿美元，注册资本4000万美元），租赁位于青浦出口加工区（北青公路8228号）内的三栋标准厂房共计14000平方米左右，主要生产、加工油田设备及其零部件。

斯伦贝谢（上海）投资者SCHLUMBERGER FAR EAST INC.为美国斯伦贝谢公司（Schlumberger）（简称斯伦贝谢）全资子公司。斯伦贝谢成立于1926年，2008年的营业额为271.63亿美金，在世界500强企业中排名328位。公司业务涉及油田服务、通信、测试与计量技术。

斯伦贝谢在油田设备和服务业内中全球排名第一，以科技领先著称，在2008年，科研开发上的投资约8.18亿美金，全球现有25个研发和技术中心。有来自140多个民族的87000多名员工，在世界的80多个国家开展工作，这也反映出公司的理念，即多样性可以促进创新，强化团队协作，增加对客户需求的理解。员工与客户通力合作，共同致力于提高客户价值。在公司内，所有技术团队和专业部门在不受地域限制的情况下共同协作，分享知识。

斯伦贝谢（上海）成立至今，已连续追加投资2次：2006年7月和2007年4月，投资总额分别增加700万美元、1260万美元；合同外资分别增加350万美元、504万美元。公司2006年4月正式投产以来，效益良好，2006年销售收入2330万元人民币，2007年销售收入10812万元人民币，2008年销售收入29858万元人民币，2009年预计有超过30%的增长。目前，除极少产品内销外，基本远销全球各地。

斯伦贝谢（上海）一期厂房于2006年初完成竣工，2006年4月正式投入生产。二期厂房于2006年9月竣工，2007年1月完成第一个订单。分别生产油田钻井设备以及油田完井设备，现拥有六条生产线。主要产品为：射孔管、井下旋转偏置导向装置、封隔器、安全阀、量规轴、电缆保护器等。

其中油田井下电缆保护器是斯伦贝谢（上海）2009年最新引入的生产线，首批订单已经完成出口，该装置用于保护和支撑井下电缆和控制线的重量，避免在完井操作时对电缆和控制线造成伤害以及避免油井生产管道的振动对电缆和控制线可能产生的伤害，以保证电缆和控制线在油井作业环境中持续正常工作。

第六节　闵行出口加工区

一、区域概况

上海闵行出口加工区位于上海奉贤区内，于2003年11月23日通过海关总署等八部委的联合验收，正式封关运作。加工区总体规划2.7平方公里，一期围网建设1.9平方公里。与上海市工业综合开发区合署办公。

园区现有22家生产型企业，主要从事电子、汽配、机械加工和沙发制造等。经过近6年的努力，上海闵行出口加工区业务量逐年上升，2005年全年出口量仅365万美元，2007年达到10.4亿美元，2009年进出口额21.35亿美元，排名位居全国第11位，上海第三位。2009年，出口加工区保税物流功能正式启动，加工区现有第三方物流企业1家，拓展保税物流业务的生产型企业2家，尚无维修、检测和研发企业。

二、2009年闵行出口加工区外经贸发展情况

（一）基本情况

截至2009年12月份，上海闵行出口加工区累计引进企业共计22家。其中生产实业型企业17家，1家为物流企业，4家为标准厂房建造商。内资企业8家，注册资本为7664.34万元；外资企业14家，总投资额24217.43万美元，总注册资本13066.65万美元，合同外资12226.65万美元。

（二）外贸进出口情况

截至 2009 年 12 月份累计进出口总额（含内销、深加工结转）为 21.35 亿美元，同比增长 1.42 %，其中出口额 11.11 亿美元，同比增长 9.76%，进口额为 10.24 亿万美元，同比下降 6.31%。实际进出境总货物为 14.3 亿美元。其中实际出口额 7.89 亿美元，同比下降 9.96%，实际进口额为 6.41 亿美元，同比下降 11.13%。

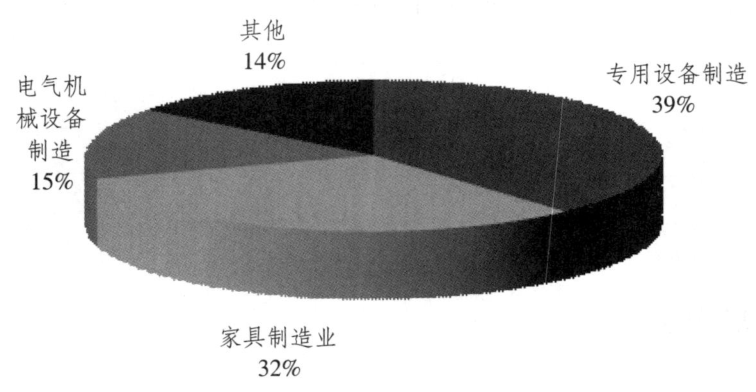

图 7-8 2009 年闵行出口加工区加工贸易进出口额行业比重结构图（单位：万美元）

（三）保税物流业务逐步启动，进展情况良好

保税物流业务从 2009 年 4 月份正式运作以来，到 12 月共实现进出口额 4933.27 万美金，占整个加工区业务量的 2.3% 左右，其中，进口额 2623.07 万美元，出口额 2310.2 万美元。已有 1 家第三方物流公司入驻加工区，3 家区内企业拓展了保税物流功能，但相关业务未正式开展。加工区自建保税仓库项目已于 6 月正式进入施工阶段，该项目占地 92 亩，总建筑面积 29342 平方米。一期启动约 17000 平方米，预计 2010 年 6 月可投入使用。

三、2010 年闵行出口加工区外经贸工作展望

2010 年度，闵行出口加工区将以“坚持科学发展，构建和谐园区”为主线，坚持贯彻开发区“控制进程、夯实基础、蓄势待发”的整体战略部署，充分发挥出口加工区的政策优势，通过全方位的企业服务，逐渐消除全球金融危机带来的不利影响，为开发区在招商引资、产出规模、解决就业等方面作出更大的贡献。

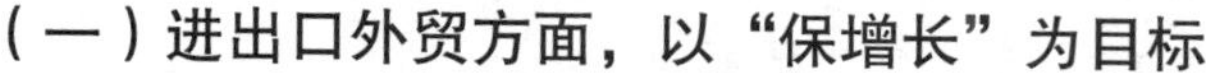

（一）进出口外贸方面，以“保增长”为目标

根据出口加工区的整体发展现状，通过对2009年闵行出口加工区进出口数据以及单个企业生产运行的分析，2010年度，将确保进出口总额在2009年的基础上增加25%，预计达到25亿美元左右，争取达到30亿美元。

（二）招商引资方面，以“拓展部门功能”为导向

组织员工深入系统地学习与招商相关的知识技能，积极探索寻求招商引资的新途径、新方法，以保税物流企业为重点，加大招商引资力度。在公用保税物流仓库尚未完工投入使用的情况下，充分利用区内闲置厂房，积极开展保税物流业务。同时，加大出口加工区功能拓展优势的宣传力度，促使区内企业与区外配套企业形成有机“关联体”，围绕出口加工区，实现由点到面、有先有后、滚动发展的新局面，增强出口加工区在全区范围内的联动效应辐射能力。

（三）企业服务方面，积极与企业进行交流沟通

继续坚持企业随访制度，主动了解企业在应对金融危机时所遇到的困难和问题。以“保姆、管家、顾问、政府”为定位，对国家和地方政府新出台的相关政策，及时跟进、积极争取、逐项落实，为企业送信心、送信息、当“桥梁”、当“公关”，积极向有关部门反映企业在运营过程中遇到的困难，不断增强企业的综合竞争力和应对金融危机的能力。改变以往服务和管理模式，不断创新作为，提升区域功能，促进企业的转型升级，促进出口加工区平稳较好的发展。

总之，在这个全球经济逐渐复苏、世界经济出现复杂多样格局的特殊历史背景下，闵行出口加工区将在新的一年里，坚决贯彻落实科学发展观，牢固树立“为企业服务好”的宗旨，进一步深化企业服务内涵，不断总结发展经验，不断借鉴兄弟出口加工区发展经验，关心企业、安抚企业、帮助企业，带领企业走出困境，促使出口加工型企业快速、健康发展，并积累各种有利条件，为下阶段的进一步提升奠定基础。

案例：创见资讯（上海）有限公司

创见资讯（上海）有限公司（简称创见资讯）成立于1988年，在董事长束崇万先生的领导下，致力于建立自有品牌及通路，经过了草创初期的艰难与考验，终于获致

稳健而飞跃的成长。今天创见资讯已经成为拥有13个国外子公司的跨国性企业，全球员工超过2000多人，并已跻身世界前三大闪存产品领导品牌。

创见资讯认为完善的管理是掌握成功的关键。为了落实在地化经营理念，2005年创见在上海闵行出口加工区投资约10亿人民币，建立了占地面积20万平方米的大规模生产基地，此基地将持续结合台湾地区优势科技产品技术，推出最先进的数码电子产品。

创见资讯拥有完善的进销存与售后服务系统，外销比例占85%以上。总公司位于台北市，子公司则分布于美国、德国、荷兰、日本、韩国等地。另外，创见资讯在北京、上海、深圳及各国主要城市陆续成立营销据点，并与各地的经销伙伴紧密合作建立了紧密的营销网，产品营销全球一百余国。

提供全系列高质量产品是创见对客户一致的承诺。积极创新、优质服务、不断累积品牌价值则是创见多年来不变的坚持。20多年来，创见以自有品牌营销全球，成为世界知名之内存模块与消费性电子产品专业制造商，更连续五年获得“台湾20大国际品牌”殊荣。此外，创见更于竞争激烈的科技产业中脱颖而出，在美国《商业周刊》“2008全球科技100强”排行榜中，勇夺全球科技业第62名及半导体产业第7名。

2009年上海国际经济贸易发展大事记

一月

1月4日 “上海外资网上办事系统”正式开通运行。上海市政府副秘书长、商务委员会主任沙海林，上海市委学习实践活动领导小组第六指导组组长张阿根，上海市纪委常委、市监察局副局长赵增辉出席开通仪式。“上海外资网上办事系统”的开通运行，有利于提高外资行政许可和管理专业化水平，提高外资管理工作透明度，提高政府对外商投资企业的服务和管理能力。

1月16日 上海服务外包工作专题会议召开。上海市政府副秘书长、商务委员会主任沙海林主持，重点研讨苏州技术先进型服务企业试点政策落地，整合上海市政策资源，聚焦服务外包工作。

二月

2月1日 上海“外资统计网上直报系统”正式启用。该系统启用后，形成了覆盖上海外资企业从设立到日常运行的有关统计环节，为政府加强统计监测提供了保证。这是全国首个外资统计网上直报系统。

2月2日 上海入选中国服务外包示范城市。国务院在南京召开全国服务外包工作座谈会，王岐山副总理出席会议并讲话。会上发布了《国务院办公厅关于促进服务外包产业发展问题的复函》（国办函[2009]9号），上海等20个城市入选中国服务外包示范城市。

2月6日 2009年上海商务情况通报会召开。由上海市商务委员会主办，市外商投资企业协会、市投资促进中心和外服公司协办，向外国领馆、外资企业代表、跨国公司地区总部代表、贸易和投资促进机构代表通报了上海经济发展情况和商务运行情况。

2月6日 上海市服务外包工作座谈会召开。会议传达了国务院2月2日召开的全国服务外包工作座谈会精神和王岐山副总理的讲话精神，部署上海市贯彻落实国办9号文相关工作。上海市副市长唐登杰、市政府副秘书长、商务委员会主任沙海林出席会议并讲话。

2月18日　上海首次认定“上海市国际物流（货代）行业重点企业”。中国外运华东有限公司等20家企业被认定，以此推动具有一定经营规模和实力、市场竞争力强的在沪国际物流（货代）企业向规模化、专业化和网络化发展。

2月24日　《上海市鼓励跨国公司地区总部发展专项资金使用和管理试行办法》(简称《试行办法》)发布实施。《试行办法》对跨国公司地区总部给予资助与奖励的申请程序、申请材料、拨付办法等问题进行了明确规定,《试行办法》对跨国公司地区总部将给予新的更多的优惠鼓励政策。

2月25日　2009年上海市商务工作会议召开。市长韩正、副市长唐登杰出席会议并讲话。韩正市长指出,要站在全局的高度思考和谋划上海商务工作,围绕加快建设“四个中心”，在上海加快形成以服务经济为主导的产业结构进程中，充分认识商务工作的重要性，全力提升上海整体竞争力和服务能力。市政府副秘书长、商务委员会主任沙海林在会上作商务工作报告。

2月26-27日　中日反垄断法研讨会在上海召开。商务部反垄断局与日本国际协力机构（JICA）主办，上海市商务委员会协办，研讨会主题是反垄断法的意义以及其对企业活动的影响，这是我国反垄断法生效以来第一次面向中外企业进行的宣传工作。

三月

3月1-5日　第19届中国华东进出口商品交易会（简称华交会）在上海新国际博览中心举行。本届华交会境外客商来自140个国家和地区，达18229人；境外参展企业交易团120家企业，分别来自美国、英国、意大利、日本、韩国等11个国家和地区。本届交易会出口总成交22.4亿美元。

3月6日　上海市服务贸易发展联席会议第二次专题会议召开。会议向22个成员单位通报了2009年工作设想，研究探讨如何加快上海市服务贸易重点领域发展。副市长唐登杰出席会议，市政府副秘书长、商务委员会主任沙海林主持会议。

3月10日　上海贸易便利化联席会议成立。联席会议由上海市商务委员会牵头，由上海海关、上海进出口检验检疫局等10个部门组成，下设工作小组。工作小组牵头起草了全国第一个地方贸易便利化工作的规范性文件《上海市贸易便利化工作规程》、全国第一个衡量贸易便利化工作效率的指标体系《上海市贸易便利化效率指标框架》。

3月16日　上海市商务委员会与工商银行上海分行签署《关于全面支持上海商务事业发展的合作备忘录》。双方将按照“政策性推动，市场化运作”的原则，加强银贸合作,共同推动扩大国内消费、加快商贸业发展、保持出口平稳增长、加快服务贸易发展、提高吸收外资质量和水平、实施“走出去”战略稳定健康发展。

3月20日　上海市政府办公厅印发《关于保持上海对外贸易稳定增长若干意见》(沪府办[2009]29号)。该文件共分八个部分：一是增强为企业服务的意识；二是推进加工贸易转型升级；三是加大金融扶持力度；四是支持企业开拓新兴市场；五是鼓励企业扩大进口贸易；六是提高贸易便利化水平；七是发挥投资与出口的互动作用；八是加大财税支持力度。

3月24日　2009年上海市对外劳务工作研讨会召开。会上对被评为2008年度对外劳务合作企业A级诚信等级的17家企业颁发了证书，并对化解经济危机所引发的突发事件和在危机中积极抓住机遇进行了探讨。

四月

4月8日　上海市政协主席冯国勤一行赴市商务委员会召开"加快国际贸易中心建设，进一步提高对外开放水平"重点提案办理协商会。冯国勤主席一行听取了市政府副秘书长、市商务委员会主任沙海林关于提案办理和上海国际贸易中心建设课题情况汇报，并就全市商务工作进行了座谈交流。

4月14日　自由贸易协定宣讲会在上海召开。商务部、财政部、海关总署及质检总局的资深专家为参会企业详细介绍了我国自由贸易区谈判的情况，以及自由贸易区优惠政策和企业如何利用相关优惠政策方面的内容。

五月

5月8日　举行上海首批境外投资企业及机构颁证仪式。会上为新的《境外投资管理办法》正式实施后的第一批14家境外投资企业及机构颁发了批准证书。同时，上海市商务委员会根据上海市实际情况出台了《关于境外投资核准工作的实施细则(试行)》，大幅精简了企业申请与核准流程。

5月12日　上海联和投资有限公司并购联和国际有限公司项目获商务部批准。这是上海市2009年最大的对外直接投资项目，投资总额约为3.3亿美元。

5月20日　上海市政府印发《关于促进上海服务贸易全面发展的实施意见》(沪府[2009]48号)。意见共有15条，包括加强组织领导、发展服务出口和进口、加大财政支持力度、强化政府服务和服务贸易促进体系、完善服务贸易统计、培育国际品牌和加强人才建设等7个方面。

5月26日　上海市政府办公厅印发《关于促进本市服务外包产业发展的实施意见》(沪府办发[2009]16号)。该文件根据发展高端、承接离岸、完善功能、集聚总部、区域合作的总体思路，制定了财税政策、人力资源与劳动保护、政府其他服务三个方面的实施意见。

5月28日　韩正市长到上海市商务委员会调研指导工作。韩正市长听取上海市商务委员会关于全市商务工作和国际贸易中心课题研究情况，充分肯定商务委员会组建以来的各项工作，指出上海市商务委员会要在促进全市服务业发展中承担主要职责。副市长唐登杰、市政府秘书长姜平参加了调研。

5月30日-6月4日　上海组团参加第42届阿尔及尔国际博览会中国馆活动。上海参展企业累计成交2243万美元，达成合作项目意向6个。

六月

6月4日　上海组团参加在开罗举办的第十四届泛阿拉伯/非洲地区国际汽车及零部件展。唐登杰副市长宣布上海展区启动，并与中国驻埃及大使馆公使衔经商参赞等为上海展区启动剪彩。上海市21家企业共设25个摊位，展会期间接待客商325人，现场成交23万美元，意向成交410万美元。

6月8日　上海组团参加中国（上海）—突尼斯投资贸易洽谈会。洽谈会由上海市政府和突尼斯发展与国际合作部共同主办，副市长唐登杰和突尼斯发展与国际合作部国务秘书出席开幕式并作演讲，中国驻突尼斯大使馆李蓓芬致辞。上海43家企业参加，现场达成贸易意向368万美元，投资意向项目4个，投资额约810万美元。

6月12日　商务部和上海市人民政府签署《商务部和上海市人民政府关于共同推进上海市商务工作全面发展的合作协议》。中共中央政治局委员、上海市委书记俞正声出席签字仪式，商务部部长陈德铭和上海市委副书记、市长韩正签署协议，副市长唐登杰主持签字仪式。合作重点包括共同推动上海市建设国际贸易中心、加快现代流通体系建设、努力搞活流通扩大消费、保持对外贸易稳定增长、提高利用外资质量和水平、支持“走出去”加快发展、大力发展服务贸易、推进电子商务发展、培养高素质商务人才队伍等九个方面。

6月18日　上海市商务委员会与中国电信上海公司签署了《发展电子商务，加快上海“国际贸易中心”建设合作备忘录》。双方本着“政策推动，市场运作”的原则，共同推动上海地区电子商务的应用与发展，营造适合电子商务企业发展的良好环境。

6月24日　上海市服务贸易发展联席会议第三次专题会议召开。市商务委员会汇报了《上海市服务贸易发展中长期规划纲要》，通报了上海本市服务贸易统计等工作情况。唐登杰副市长要求各部门合力推进服务贸易的政策落实、统计和专项资金等工作，推进全市服务贸易健康快速发展。

6月25日　上海市商务委员会和普陀区人民政府签署《关于共同推进普陀区加快

商贸物流建设和商务工作全面发展的合作协议》。根据合作协议，上海市商务委员会和普陀区政府共同建立紧密合作机制，提升普陀区现代服务业发展水平，加快普陀区“商贸物流”功能凸现。

6 月 25 日　上海市商务委员会和浦东新区政府在张江高科技园区签署上海服务外包人才培训中心共建协议。双方共同将商务部、教育部颁发的“服务外包人才培训中心（上海）”铜牌，授予上海服务外包人才培训中心，并为首批“上海市服务外包咨询专家”颁证和首批“上海服务外包人才培训基地”授牌。

6 月 30 日　2009 年上海外商投资企业联合年检工作顺利结束。上海市参检企业 31671 家。年检期间，上海市商务委员会会同工商、财政、税务、市统计局等部门采用一门式办公、网上问答、热线电话和传真服务等多种形式帮助企业顺利通过年检，同时在金融危机的特殊情况下，根据国家的有关规定适当放宽出资期限和开业情况，帮助企业渡难关。

七月

7 月 3 日　上海市政府召开推进现代服务业集聚区建设联席会议专题会议。副市长唐登杰出席会议，要求各部门和各区县高度重视集聚区建设工作，加快推进建设步伐。

7 月 6 日　跨境贸易人民币结算第一单业务顺利落户上海。2009 年 7 月 1 日人民银行等六部委共同公布《跨境贸易人民币结算试点管理办法》以来，人民银行上海总部、上海市商务委员会、市金融办等相关部门积极推进本市跨境贸易人民币结算试点工作，积极协调政策问题，全力推进此项工作的开展。

7 月 8-9 日　第三届中国（香港）国际服务贸易洽谈会在香港会议展览中心举行。上海市商务委员会主办的“沪港中医药服务贸易合作发展论坛”作为洽谈会的组成部分，得到了商务部、国家中医药局与沪港中医药界专家学者的高度重视。

7 月 16-17 日　上海外贸产品内销订货会在上海世贸商城举行。订货会上，超过 170 家外贸企业展示了内销样品，23 家采购企业带来了采购清单，合作意向总金额超过 1.1 亿元。订货会期间还分别举行了“外贸企业进商场合作协议”签约仪式及“外贸产品购销信息网”开通仪式。

7 月 21 日　上海市政府举行第 16 批跨国公司地区总部颁证仪式。副市长唐登杰出席颁证仪式，并为新认定的跨国公司地区总部颁发认定证书。

八月

8 月 1 日　上海市政府下放外资审批权限。将累计投资总额 1 亿美元以下的鼓励类、允许类外资项目的设立和变更事项以及累计投资总额1亿美元以下、不涉及钢铁、贵金属、铁矿石、燃料油、天然橡胶、图书、报纸、期刊、成品油、药品、汽车、农药、农膜、盐、烟草、化肥、粮食、植物油、食糖、棉花、音像制品、原油、氧化铝等23种重要商品，不涉及零售的外资商业企业的设立和变更事项的审批下放到区县人民政府。

8月11日 《上海市技术先进型服务企业认定管理试行办法》发布实施。该试行办法由上海市科委、商务委员会、财政局、税务局、发改委联合制定，并以此作为上海市技术先进型服务企业认定的认定依据。

8月12日 "上海外高桥国际贸易示范区"揭牌。外高桥国际贸易示范区内，将进一步在提升贸易便利化水平、提高市场开放度、拓展国际贸易功能、扩大国际贸易规模、实施纳税人管理制度改革、增强服务辐射功能六个主要方面进行试点和探索工作。

8月15-18日 上海组团参加2009巴西圣保罗国际家庭用品及礼品博览会暨上海商品展。巴西圣保罗国际家庭用品及礼品展览会是南美最大的消费品博览会，每年举办一届。上海参展企业32家，展览面积450平方米，现场成交30万美元，意向成交750万美元。

8月17日 中共上海市委常委会听取了市商务委员会党组关于加快推进上海国际贸易中心课题研究的专题汇报，对加快上海国际贸易中心研究成果给予了充分肯定。

8月19日 《上海市软件出口（创新）园区认定和管理暂行办法》颁布实施。首次认定浦东软件园、徐汇软件基地、陆家嘴软件园、复旦软件园、创智天地园区、天华信息科技园、紫竹科学园区等7家园区为"上海市软件出口（创新）园区"（2009-2010）。

九月

9月2-4日 上海组团参加华交会波兰展。上海等10个省市的131家纺织服装企业参展，展览净面积约1600平方米，主要参展商品为服装、面料及配件，累计成交318.49万欧元，其中，现场成交43.71万欧元，意向成交274.78万欧元。

9月7日 上海市政府印发《上海服务贸易中长期发展规划纲要》（市府发[2009]48号）。该《规划纲要》是上海市2009-2020年上海服务贸易发展的蓝图和行动纲领，也是上海市推进服务贸易工作的重要依据。

9月7日 《上海市服务外包示范区认定管理暂行办法》（沪商促进【2009】567号）颁布实施。上海市服务外包示范区认定小组由上海市商务委员会、发展改革委、经济和信息化委、科委组成，认定办公室设在市商务委员会。

9月11-15日 上海电气（集团）总公司成功收购美国高斯国际公司。作为国内最大的机械装备制造集团之一的上海电气（集团）总公司，共出资1.6亿美元收购该公司，

由此奠定了在国际印刷机械行业的重要地位。

9月14日　上海市政府印发《上海市人民政府办公厅关于建立上海市整顿和规范市场经济秩序联席会议的通知》(沪府办[2009]110号)。联席会议由上海市商务委员会、发展改革委、经济和信息化委、公安局等38个成员单位组成，市政府副秘书长、市商务委员会主任沙海林为召集人，联席会议的日常工作由市商务委员会承担。联席会议负责研究整顿和规范市场经济秩序工作中的重大问题，向市政府提出建议；讨论确定年度工作重点，并督促落实；建立部门配合协作机制，加强行政执法与刑事司法的衔接；指导区县整顿和规范市场经济秩序工作；协调重大案件，办理市政府交办的其他事项。

9月15日　上海市商务委员会与闵行区政府签署依托虹桥综合交通枢纽，服务国际贸易中心建设合作协议。双方在推进上海国际贸易中心重要承载区建设、搞活流通、扩大消费、保持对外贸易稳定发展、发展特色会展经济、加快发展现代物流、推进现代服务业集聚区建设、聚集国际组织和区域总部、推进重点区域和重点项目建设八个方面加大合作力度。

9月20日　《上海商务年鉴》创刊。《上海商务年鉴》是新中国成立后出版的上海首卷商务年鉴。年鉴全面记录上海商务发展轨迹，展示上海商务的崭新风貌和发展历史，为上海市商务改革开放、商务经营发展、商务文化建设等提供多方面服务。

9月21-26日　2009中国(上海)国际跨国采购大会在上海世贸商城举行。市长韩正、副市长唐登杰、商务部副部长易小准出席开幕仪式。来自32个国家和地区的270多家国际采购商、供应商参加展会。大会期间，“上海进口产品展贸中心”和“联合国(上海)采购物流中心”正式揭牌。

9月23日　上海市政府办公厅转发市商务委员会、发展改革委和财政局制定的《上海市服务贸易发展专项资金的使用和管理办法》(沪府办发[2009]36号)。发展资金主要用于上海市服务贸易发展中的重点领域和关键环节，促进上海市服务贸易扩大规模，提升能级。

9月30日　上海清理整顿外派劳务市场秩序专项工作顺利结束。由上海市商务委员会牵头、协同全市各相关委办局自6月18日至9月30日在全市范围内开展清理整顿外派劳务市场秩序专项行动，累计排查各类外派劳务相关企业和机构2384家，依法查处无证无照经营企业12家，清理有经营资格外派企业2家，破获涉及外派劳务诈骗案件4起。

十月

10月9日　上海市商务委员会启动“十二五”规划基本思路的研究工作。按照市

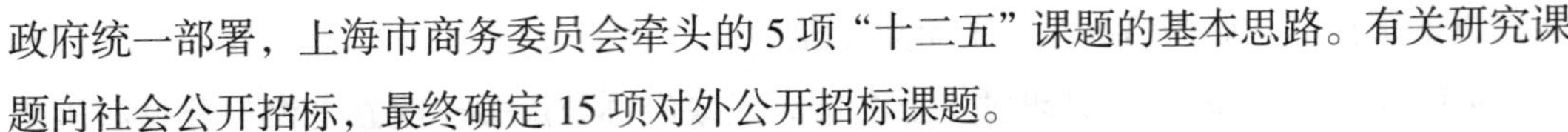

政府统一部署，上海市商务委员会牵头的5项“十二五”课题的基本思路。有关研究课题向社会公开招标，最终确定15项对外公开招标课题。

10月12日 上海《境外投资简明联络手册》和《境外投资实务手册》正式发行。“手册”由上海市商务委员会与上海外经协会共同编制，将为上海市企业开展境外投资提供咨询，以及为上海市企业办理对外投资业务提供全面细致的政策说明和操作办法。

10月15-11月4日 上海组团参加第106届中国进出口商品交易会。上海交易团共3306个展位，794家企业参展，出口成交12.2亿美元。

10月21-22日 2009上海软件外包国际峰会举行。唐登杰副市长出席开幕式并致辞。峰会围绕“信心、责任与合作”主题，探讨我国软件外包发展的应对良策，近1000余人次参加了峰会的4个专题论坛、3个合作交流专场、3场“接发包见面会”和1个专业年会。

10月28日 《上海服务外包人才培训基地认定管理办法（试行）》和《上海服务外包人才实训基地认定管理办法（试行）》（沪商法制【2009】680号）颁布实施。上海服务外包人才培训基地和实训基地由上海市商务委员会委托上海服务外包人才培训中心进行具体认定评估工作。

10月28-29日 第六届中国产业国际竞争力论坛在上海举行。论坛由商务部、工业和信息化部、上海市人民政府联合主办，商务部产业损害调查局、工业和信息化部运行监测协调局、上海市商务委员会、经济和信息化委、发展研究中心共同承办。

十一月

11月2日 上海市人民政府与瑞士诺华公司签署《关于在上海进一步加大研究开发投资战略合作备忘录》。上海市市长韩正，副市长唐登杰，诺华（中国）生物医学院有限公司、诺华生物研究中心董事长兼首席执行官魏思乐博士出席签约仪式。根据合作备忘录，诺华生物将在未来5年内共投资10亿美元在上海建立全球第三大研发中心，针对中国的高发疾病从事新药基础研发。

11月3日 上海市政府办公厅发布《上海市促进服务外包产业发展专项资金使用和管理试行办法》（沪府办发[2009]49号）。服务外包产业发展专项资金主要用于上海市服务外包发展中的重点领域和关键环节，促进上海市服务外包产业健康快速发展，重点支持离岸、高端、总部型服务外包发展。

11月3-7日 2009中国国际工业博览会于在上海新国际博览中心举行。本届“中国工博会”展览面积126,500平方米，参展展位5,302个，共有11.83万观众前来参观洽谈，产品和技术成交17.44亿元。

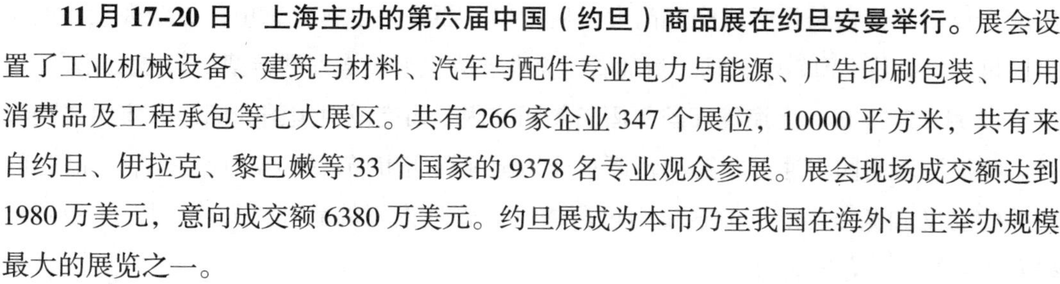

11 月 17-20 日　上海主办的第六届中国（约旦）商品展在约旦安曼举行。展会设置了工业机械设备、建筑与材料、汽车与配件专业电力与能源、广告印刷包装、日用消费品及工程承包等七大展区。共有 266 家企业 347 个展位，10000 平方米，共有来自约旦、伊拉克、黎巴嫩等 33 个国家的 9378 名专业观众参展。展会现场成交额达到 1980 万美元，意向成交额 6380 万美元。约旦展成为本市乃至我国在海外自主举办规模最大的展览之一。

11 月 23 日　上海将开展国际服务外包业务进口货物保税监管试点工作。按照商务部和海关总署发布的《关于开展国际服务外包业务进口货物保税监管试点工作的通知》，上海作为全国 20 个服务外包示范城市之一，将开展国际服务外包业务进口货物保税监管试点工作。

十二月

12 月 1 日　上海进一步下放外资审批权限。将投资总额 1 亿美元以下、单一店铺面积不超过 1000 平方米的商业零售、经营性租赁、职业介绍机构、人才中介公司、会议展览公司和外资并购的审批权下放到黄浦区等 16 个已接入外资网上办事系统的区县。

12 月 4 日　上海服务贸易工作会议召开。会议传达了第二届中国服务贸易大会精神，听取了专家演讲。会议总结了 2009 年以来的主要工作，分析了上海服务贸易的发展环境，提出了上海服务贸易发展的总体思路。

12 月 9-12 日　上海组团参加 2009 东盟中国中小企业商品（越南）博览会。展会在越南胡志明市国际会议展览中心举办，上海、山东两地的服装、面料、辅料、农药、化肥、化工机械等领域的 40 余家企业参展。观众近 10000 人次，其中专业客商 796 人次，实际成交达到 292 万美元，成交意向约 1200 万美元。

12 月 15-16 日　上海商务工作务虚会在松江召开。会议分为“抓世博机遇、建设国际贸易中心、结构调整、完善上海贸易投资环境”四个板块，研究探讨了 2010 年的工作思路、重点以及措施。

12 月 17 日　上海市政府举行第 17 批跨国公司地区总部颁证仪式。上海市副市长唐登杰出席颁证仪式，并为 18 家新认定的跨国公司地区总部颁发了认定证书。

12 月 18-19 日　上海服务外包工作总结会在嘉定召开。会议总结 2009 年上海市服务外包工作，提出 2010 年工作设想，并就专项资金申报、国家服务外包专项资金审计、服务外包业务统计系统，服务外包示范区、专业园区、重点企业认定，以及技术先进型服务企业评审等方面情况分别进行了专题介绍。

12 月 23 日　韩正市长主持召开上海流通领域大集团负责人座谈会。副市长唐登杰出席会议。韩正市长在听取个部门发言后指出，要进一步解放思想，更新观念，抓住世博机遇，抓住上海转型机遇，流通骨干企业要为上海经济发展转型做出更大贡献。

12 月 25-29 日　上海锦江国际酒店集团有限公司完成对美国洲际酒店集团并购项目。锦江酒店集团将通过收购项目逐步开拓国际酒店市场，提升“锦江酒店”品牌的国际知名度和竞争力。同时通过引进国外酒店管理集团的品牌、人才、技术、经验，提升酒店的核心竞争能力。